BARNES WALLIS

A Biography

Books by the same author include:

American Excursion
Charles Lamb and Elia
The Pelican History of the United States (with R. B. Nye)
Venice (with Martin Hürlimann)
The Road to Athens
The Christ's Hospital Book (ed. with Edmund Blunden and
others)

BARNES WALLIS

A Biography
by

J. E. Morpurgo

Longman

LONGMAN GROUP LIMITED LONDON

Associated companies, branches and representatives
throughout the world

© J. E. Morpurgo 1972

First published 1972
Second impression 1972

ISBN 0 582 10360 6

Printed in Great Britain by Butler & Tanner Ltd
Frome and London

Contents

List of Illustrations

List of Illustrations

For Molly, Catherine and Elaine

Acknowledgements

Many have helped in the preparation of this book. Therefore, if some names are omitted from the acknowledgements that follow it is not because their contribution has been small or because I am lacking in gratitude, but only because, were the list complete, it would be almost as long as the book itself.

However, like so many authors, I owe a debt beyond measure to the officials of the British Museum Reading Room, of the Public Records Office, and, in my case, to those who serve in the Brotherton Library at the University of Leeds, in the Library of Sir Barnes Wallis's Research Department at Brooklands, and at the Royal Aeronautical Society.

Among many who have answered my questions, provided assistance or papers are A. E. Allison, R. H. Bridgman, Sir Edward Bullard, Air Chief Marshal the Hon. Sir Ralph Cochrane, Leo d'Erlanger, Herr Euler, David Irving, Percy Giles, Marshal of the Royal Air Force Sir Arthur Harris, H. Hobden, C. W. Hayes, Edward Hyams, W. G. Poskitt, A. W. Robinson, E. H. Rodd, Norbert Rowe, Sir F. Ewart Smith, F.R.S., W. E. Startup, Lt-Col Stewart Chant-Sempill, Air Commodore Whitney Straight, Philip Teed, J. J. R. Trethowan, Mrs Warner, Group Captain F. R. Winterbotham and Miss Jane With.

I am grateful to Jonathan Cape Ltd for permission to quote from *The Mint* by T. E. Lawrence, to William Heinemann Ltd for permission to quote from *Slide Rule* and *No Highway* by Nevil Shute and to Hamish Hamilton Ltd and the Editorial Board for permission to quote from *The Christ's Hospital Book*.

For permission to reproduce the illustrations I record my deep gratitude to the following: Sir Barnes Wallis for Nos 1, 2, 5, 6, 8, 25, 32–34, 36; Lady Wallis for No 7; Vickers Ltd for Nos 10–13,

Acknowledgements

17–22, 24, 29, 30; The Radio Times Hulton Picture Library for Nos 14, 16; Imperial War Museum for Nos 26–28; British Aircraft Corporation Ltd for Nos 31, 37; Royal Aeronautical Society for No 9; Aeromodeller for No 23; Mr Leslie Samson and Mrs Webb for No 15; Christ's Hospital for No 35.

For the most part this biography is based on primary material but several published works have served me well, and are listed in the bibliographical references; it would be churlish if I did not mention especially *The British Rigid Airship* by Robin Higham, *The Dam Busters* by Paul Brickhill, and *The Christ's Hospital Book* edited by Edmund Blunden, Eric Bennett, Philip Youngman Carter and J. E. Morpurgo.

Sir Barnes Wallis's daughter, Mary Stopes-Roe, has been unfailingly helpful, and his secretary, Pat Lucas, has run errands for me as readily—and almost as regularly—as she has done for Sir Barnes himself. For her memory, her care, friendship and support I am enormously grateful.

I owe much to the patience of my personal assistants, Lynda Brown, Shirley Harper, Jane Holford and the late Nansi Pugh, but four people have contributed most to what is good in the book but nothing to its failings.

First, there is my wife. She has seen me through many books, but never before have I asked of her as much as I have in the years that have gone into the writing of this biography.

Elaine Barr has contributed more than careful research. Her confident support at times when I was suffering both physical handicap and totally unexpected set-back made it possible for me to continue, even when I felt tempted to abandon a difficult if enthralling task. She has been an impeccable collaborator, but it is her friendship (and that of her husband, Reggie) that has been most valuable to me.

The unfailing kindliness of Molly Wallis, and above all, her extraordinary generosity in providing me with materials that are both precious and private have given me the chance to write a book that attempts to be more than a mere public account of a great public figure.

Above all, there is Barnes Wallis himself. I have had the

Acknowledgements

privilege of his acquaintance for forty years and of his friendship for almost half of that time, but companionship, however long and warm, could not have led me to demand or expect the courage that he has shown in allowing me to write this book, nor the benevolence that he has proffered to its author.

Because it represents something that is personal between me and Barnes one story must be told here, in the meagre form of an acknowledgement, rather than in the body of the text. When part way through the writing my eyesight began to fail, and without consulting me, Barnes devoted his time and his well-nigh unique ingenuity to designing a magnificent lighted reader, which he then had made as a gift to me, even though he knew that I might use it for discovering a past that, ineffably great though it has been, is not in all respects coincident with the fable.

In the preparation of this book, Barnes has given me free access to his papers—both private and professional—and a great deal of his time. His advice and his didactic skill have been at my entire disposal, but he has never attempted to influence my opinions; instead, he has allowed me entire freedom to write what I believe to be an accurate account. I can but hope that, where I have mislaid the truth, he will not hold it against me.

J. E. M.

Introduction

If achievement and fame were synonymous Barnes Wallis would rank among the best known Englishmen of the twentieth century. His long working life spans virtually the whole of the age of aviation. Time and time again his genius set before his countrymen a precedence in invention which should have put them far in the van of aeronautical developments; indeed, every major advance over fifty years—with the exception of jet-propulsion—owed something to his creative imagination, and many were contributed by him alone.

Nor was his skill limited to aeronautics or aerial warfare. He contributed to the development of radio telescopy and planned nuclear submarines. Himself a man who had learned his craft for the most part 'on the job', he stood nevertheless among the prophets of the new academic technological education. And still he found the time, the intellectual energy and the charity to devote himself to the revivification of a great school.

The technology in which he worked and dreamed—aviation—is that which above all others, at least until the beginning of space travel, belonged to our century, and in our century has seemed most likely to arouse hero-worship.

But achievement and fame are *not* synonymous, and there have been factors—personal, economic and political—which have kept Barnes Wallis, if not obscure then at best well-known to the *cognoscenti*, and to the generality only after much prompting.

Especially in Britain, but to some extent in all countries, there is an interplay between public reputation and public recognition: Tennyson was the best known of all the poets laureate because he was made a lord, and he was made a lord because he was the best known of all the poets laureate. Recognition of this kind was consistently denied to Wallis until his eighty-first year. True, he

xiii

Introduction

was much honoured by his near equals: he was one of the first working engineers to become a Fellow of the Royal Society, and his list of honorary degrees reads like a roll-call of British universities. But, in more public terms, until 1968 a nation that still stands in some awe of titles and decorations allowed one of its greatest inventors nothing more than the award which comes almost automatically to retiring colonels and still-hopeful civil servants.

In a very real sense Wallis's fame has suffered from the very fact of his being English. A creative engineer is subject to the laws of economics: of what merit engineering perfection if the perfected object is too expensive to be useful? And if, like Wallis, he works in a field where the costs of originality and experiment are phenomenal and the rewards often speculative and always long-delayed, it is generally true that the only possible patron is the State. But much of Wallis's achievement belongs to a period when Britain could no longer afford the inevitably vast expense of exploiting his ideas. His work was always set against a background of parsimony; the British aircraft industry had a short, ebullient youth and almost no prosperous middle-age before it settled into impoverished senility and came virtually to death. Above all in the last two decades Britain's economic troubles have woven a shroud for her aircraft industry. New and revolutionary techniques have been developed, vast schemes proposed and sometimes initiated, only to be shelved for lack of funds or set aside by changing political doctrines.

Wallis and many of his fellow-workers in British aeronautical engineering have wrought wonderfully and hoped wildly. But hindsight makes it obvious that the only time in his working career when he could have expected the full thrust of national support behind him was in the unnaturally enlivened war years. Hence the paradox that this essentially gentle man and devout Christian was most supported when he was engaged in the fearsome task of producing weapons of destruction.

Yet Wallis's Englishness has also held him from becoming a brilliant exile, from deserting to the imperial power of our time, the United States, which sensibly has taken over many of his drawing-board dreams and made them into commercial successes. The American public was not told about Wallis, but had it been told it would have greeted with disbelief—and even with patriotic indignation—the information that so many of the most cherished advances of their much cherished aircraft industry came to them by benefit of an Englishman.

At home Wallis's chances of acclaim have also been tempered by circumstances far outside his control. Throughout most of his working life he was the servant of huge corporations. For much of that time the ethos of the industrial giant in Britain was suspect: in the late 'twenties and the 'thirties the particular corporation for which he worked was regarded, without justification but with much fervour, as the principal villain of the popular pacifist nightmare.

Wallis saw creative engineering as an art and himself as a sort of poet, and he accepted without reservation Einstein's observation that 'imagination is more important than knowledge. Knowledge is limited, imagination embraces the world, stimulating progress, giving birth to evolution.' In one of his letters to Leo d'Erlanger he wrote: 'Perhaps I am more of the artist in love with creation than the business man trying to sell his wares.' And, recognising himself as a poet, on occasion Wallis adopted the poet's habitual arrogance, the self-assurance of being one of the 'unacknowledged legislators of mankind'. Acknowledged legislators have usually been most uncomfortable in the company of poets. Worse than this for his chance of reward was his self-damning habit of knowing himself right—and proving it. Nothing makes a man enemies so rapidly as the capacity for being generally right, nothing makes powerful enemies so powerfully as proving oneself right at the expense of men who are in a position to hide their errors of judgement by refusing to admit that they exist. The Establishment has an institutional memory that is longer than the careers of individuals. It does not forget or forgive sins against its predecessors.

In the last resort, however, it would seem that if Barnes Wallis has not had his due share of glory, the explanation must include something more worthy than enmity or chauvinism and less easily identified than historical misfortune. The very length and variety of his achievement makes it almost impossible for the public to grasp that all this came from one man's mind. Already in 1917 he was close to being the senior aircraft designer in Britain; at the age of eighty he could still boast that he had on the drawing-board a revolutionary 'plane that would fly Britain, first among the

Introduction

nations, into the next century. Barnes Wallis's later innovations are so youthful and so progressive that few can comprehend that these are products of the same mind that designed *R.80*, *R.100*, the Wellesley, the Wellington, the bouncing and tallboy bombs. He came close to the point of obliterating his chance of fame by doing too much for too long.

Did Wallis himself care much for fame? Undoubtedly he regretted and even resented the deliberation of the move to oblivion to which others subjected him for so long, for he recognised it as both slur on his work and disadvantage to his future activities.

In his mature years Wallis was not notably shy. True (despite the trumpeting he experienced when the film of *The Dam Busters* was shown) he resisted the easy lure of idolisation, arguing always that he must give his time to the future and had little to spare for reliving the past. But, when it suited his obstinacy, he recognised the value of publicity and could use it most effectively, as at the time when the British Government refused to exploit his revolutionary theories on variable wing-span.

His attitude to the writing of his life becomes then part of his biography. He constantly refused to co-operate with publicists, however skilful, whom he suspected of exploiting him without caring for the things for which he cared. But when finally he agreed to allow a friend of long-standing the exciting privilege of recording one of the most fascinating lives of the century, his own professionalism would not allow him to trespass upon the professionalism of others. In the sense that its author hopes to shift the balance of fame this biography is written in indignation, but the indignation is the author's and not the subject's. And, if this book is written unashamedly in affection, there has certainly been no demand from its subject that it should be written in adulation. No attempt has been made to enlarge the warts so that they hide the face, but where they are thought to exist they have been drawn into the portrait.

1 Childhood

Barnes Wallis's father, Charles, was twenty-two years old and an undergraduate at Merton College, Oxford, when in 1881 he first met Edith Eyre Ashby. The product of an Anglo-Irish family with some aristocratic pretensions but little immediate substance, he had experienced a lonely, gloomy and unsettled childhood. His mother had died a week after his birth, and Charles Wallis's father, a sturdy Evangelical parson, marked down the tiny son as murderer of his young wife, and from that day on took no more notice of Charles than was necessary for the severe consideration of school reports and the prompt payment of school bills.

Edith Ashby was also twenty-two when she met Charles Wallis. There was tragedy, too, in her family background. Her father had been a parson who had turned to schoolmastering, but he died when she was only four years old. The effect on the Ashbys was quite other than that in the Wallis family, for tragedy brought them closer together. After some years spent on a brave and not unsuccessful effort at running her own private school in Hove, the Rev. John Ashby's widow moved herself and her daughter to Woolwich, where a much older daughter, Lily, lived with her doctor husband, Theodore Maxwell, who was both rich and clever.

29 The Common was the setting for a prosperous, generally cheerful and not uncultivated household. There Edith grew up, an intelligent and highly literate girl. From its comforts and suburban security she looked out on the world at large with curious and optimistic glances. In a later generation she might well have established herself successfully in a career. As it was, her mind darted hither and thither into this and that area of intellectual exploration. She tried her hand at poetry, and her

1

achievement was no worse if little better than the poetasting of thousands of other moderately educated and middle-class Victorian young ladies. She dabbled in nature study. She considered the new socialism and found it quite beyond her capacity for sympathy. She went further than convention demanded in her devotion to the Church and committed herself firmly to the High Anglicanism which eventually she was to pass on to her son.

For Edith circumstances were not quite as comfortable as they appeared to outsiders. Her sister, Lily, was gentle to the point where gentleness is infuriating: her cultural interests carried with them not one spark of rebellion. Theodore was hearty, healthy and intelligent only within the bounds prescribed by upper middle-class convention; he, like his wife, never thought to dare outrageous novelty. Edith's mother was a fluent talker who loved to gossip—and generally with charity—about family and friends, but she too shied away from originality or intellectual strain. Thus Edith's intellectual flutterings were stifled so that, against the warnings of some inner compulsion, she came to believe that for her future happiness she must marry a man who could provide for her the same pattern of shining brass fenders, glass-fronted cabinets full of bone china, scurrying maids, afternoon tea with cucumber sandwiches and jolly dinner parties. Perhaps, in addition and if she were very lucky, she might find a provider who shared some of her intellectual enthusiasms.

But Edith was not well-equipped for husband-catching. With acquaintances she was sociable and could be gay, but at the first approach of intimacy, even with another woman, she was apt to scuttle back into self-defending reserve. Further, she was obsessed with her plainness—quite unjustifiably by the evidence of photographs of the time which show a fine-structured face with clear and even mischievous eyes.

When they first met, Charles thought her 'prim, severe, frigid and one who would district-visit'. She, for her part, found him 'compact and rather fast with a face I didn't understand'. But the mutual suspicion soon evaporated and within a few months they were engaged. He had found a companion to take the place of the mother he had never known and the father 'who might just as well have lived in Timbuctoo for all the use he was to his son'. She had the reassurance of a man who thought her

Childhood

beautiful and, at last, the comfort of sharing ideas, enthusiasms
and even doubts.

After Oxford Charles hoped to become a doctor. There would
be no financial help from his father and little from her family,
and so they decided to postpone marriage until he qualified. Both
knew that this was at least four years off, but at first the waiting
time passed happily enough. At weekends they came together
at her home in Woolwich; they visited friends and relations at
Brighton, Eastbourne, Broadstairs, and both took great pleasure
in long walks by the sea; they pressed wild flowers and wrote
verses each into the other's diary. Of an evening they read aloud
from *Villette, Romola* and *Vanity Fair* (a 'horrid, bitter book'
she called it and rejoiced in the fact that she had never met anyone like Becky Sharp and Rawdon Crawley).

On Sundays they shunned profane literature and instead read
aloud from the *Bible*, usually from the *Epistle to the Romans*.

But the strain of waiting began to tell. The pleasant fantasies
with which Edith had enlivened the early days of her engagement
disappeared. The gaieties had vanished, and the frivolities, but
still Edith was heartened by his determination to succeed, and he
was encouraged by her devotion.

As this sense of duty, of dedicating the present entirely to the
service of the future, became the central fact in both lives so was
there awakened in both of them a need to discover some reason
for existence more basic than either had ever known. Had they
been capable of exploring together the religious conscience, had
they been able to establish some mutuality of religious conviction,
all might have been well. But the habit of reticence was in both
of them too strong for any exchange of views on anything so
private as conscience. Tragically, as Charles and Edith separately
fell deeper and deeper into doubt so did each rationalise such
doubts as inability to live up to the sure faith of the other. Even
before they were married communication had almost ceased
between the two on anything more important than practicalities.
Edith's earlier and light-hearted grouse that he rode his intellect
over her opinions gave way to a far more substantial disaffection:
he could not credit that women were entitled to opinions in
matters of the mind. Charles, too, was complaining: Edith, for
all her pretence at interest, was in truth devoid of enthusiasm.
Had they been capable of true intimacy, had they not been

3

reared so firmly in a tradition of reticence—accentuated for him by his childhood loneliness—they might have talked themselves out of the paradoxical suspicions which, in the event, each communicated only to a private diary.

Edith was warmhearted and palpably more sensual than her fiancé, yet she suspected him of loose-living. Charles, for his part, indulged himself in a huge spiritual struggle with his own physical nature, and, because in truth his physical nature was not highly developed, won the battle quite easily. At the same time, he wondered if Edith's patience was not proof of what he had suspected when first they met: that she was somewhat frigid. But obstinately they persisted and in the months after they were finally married the decision seemed utterly right and their patience entirely rewarded. The euphoria of the first months of their engagement had returned and became more intense. 'On me,' wrote Edith, 'has fallen a great happiness, a happiness I have been buying for all these 4½ years.' A year later, just before their first child was born, the ecstatic relationship was still intact.

John Wallis was born on 16 June 1886. Charles had only just qualified and the unearning years had eaten up their small supply of capital. Edith was not yet out of bed after the birth of John when Charles had to come to her with the admission that some of his investments had foundered. For him it was a blow as much to his pride as to his pocket. Edith made no attempt to comfort him or to restore his pride. She blamed Charles as the destroyer of her fantasy, and the shock of financial disaster not only seared itself into her mind and body but also confirmed and strengthened her certainty that in future she must be the hub and guardian of the family.

Meanwhile Charles must have a base for his work and the family a home. In the summer of 1886 a medical practice became available in Ripley, Derbyshire. The Wallises considered their balance sheet and saw this as their last chance. Further, unexpressed but clear in their minds, was the hope that a change of environment would break also the lowering resentment between them. And so it appeared at first. The house which they found at Ripley 'seemed Elysium' and there, on 26 September 1887 in the last moments of something approaching marital happiness for Charles and Edith, a second son was born: Barnes Neville Wallis.

Childhood

But the birth of Barnes was to be the only glory of the Ripley adventure. For the rest the move proved to be yet another disaster. The grim ironworking town was no place for Charles 'with his Oxford ideas' and his reserved and seemingly arrogant manner. The practice had been small before he came and now it dwindled almost to nothingness. Edith, for her part, though she made some brave efforts to participate in church affairs, could not abide Derbyshire or the Ripley people. More and more she came to idealise her home—Lily's home—in Woolwich. Socially, financially, physically and in the perfection of family life *that* was what a home should be.

Then, in December 1889, her mother died. The cornerstone of her idealisation had been removed: 'Woe is me, woe is me, woe is me. And I live. Always that dead face, always.'

There were left to her only the children, John aged three and Barnes aged two. For their sake an effort at recapture had to be made by a return to seemingly perfectible surroundings. Charles, too, suffering as he was from professional disappointment, was ready to try again. A new practice was found in London, and in 1891 the family moved to 241 New Cross Road.

There, on 25 June 1893, Anne Wallis was born, and there on 1 August, two months before Barnes's sixth birthday, came the most brutal blow in a hideous sequence. Charles Wallis returned home from his rounds, took to his bed, and within a day knew that he had contracted poliomyelitis. Both Charles and Edith knew that he would be a cripple for the rest of his days.

Barnes Wallis's first memories are of listening long into the night to his father and mother worrying over money. Money—the absence of money—was to be a central theme in almost every one of the hundreds of letters that his mother wrote to him in the years between his going away to school and her death.

Nevertheless the house in New Cross was large. Appearances had to be maintained. A doctor had to present a brave front if he was to hold the confidence of any patients; especially a crippled doctor who, in those early days, could only visit his patients on an old solid-wheeled tricycle given to him in a rare moment of generosity by the Reverend (George) Winstanley Wallis, on which he pedalled around New Cross, one foot circling uselessly. There was a maid (even if she earned only five pounds a year and her keep), a nanny and an errand boy to deliver the medicines.

5

Barnes Wallis

When the Wallis children roamed New Cross it was a trim well-to-do suburb, full of trim and well-to-do businessmen attracted there for the most part by the ease of access to their offices in the City and the growing commercial area of the West End. Both the District and the Metropolitan railways had stations atNew Cross, and so, after afew minutes of suffering in the smoky tunnels under the river, the top-hatted, frock-coated men of New Cross could reach their offices in the City or in Piccadilly without so much as changing trains.

There were great elm trees lining the New Cross Road, and not far away the open fields of Telegraph Hill. Blackheath was within walking distance, and on the heath golf was still played by enthusiasts wearing red coats so that passers-by could be warned of the lethal sport. The Naval College and the Observatory at Greenwich and the Royal Military Academy at Woolwich were close by, and all added to a sense of spaciousness, even of grandeur. For an adult New Cross was no bad place to live; for a child it was rich with excitement and variety.

Immediately opposite the Wallises' house stood the large Fair-lawn estate: twelve acres around the mansion. The house was deserted. Mrs Wallis bribed the caretakers to allow her children to use house and gardens as their playground. There were glass-houses, a skittle alley, a Paxton conservatory, a lovers' walk and in the house enormous rooms with painted ceilings and intricate high-relief plaster-work, all decaying, overgrown, mysterious and richly romantic to two small boys. Mrs Wallis taught John and Barnes how to build a camp fire and how to roast potatoes in its embers.

From New Cross it was easy to make excursions into London. To the shops, with Edith Wallis, who despite poverty was enormously proud of her appearance and particularly of her tiny feet. (Dainty feet became Barnes's first requirement in a woman.) To great State events: Edith took her sons to the lying-in-state of Gladstone, and it was on that occasion in Westminster Hall that Barnes was first made aware of the wonders of architecture. A total stranger in the crowd tapped the ten-year-old boy on the shoulder and told him to turn his eyes away from the bier, from the pomp and the people, to look up and admire the glory of Richard II's amazing and incomparable roof. ('I have never ceased to revel in its magnificence and genius, and to pass on his advice.')

6

Childhood

But not Fairlawn, not the Metropolis, nor yet his own home, was the true centre of Barnes's childhood. That role was filled, by Edith's insistence and through its own intrinsic energy, by Uncle Theo's house on The Common. Indeed, the contrast between the gloom, introspection and poverty of New Cross Road and the comfort and exuberance of The Common was apparent even to a small boy and often underlined by his mother. The Wallises, as she told him again and again, were the poor relations.

The house in the New Cross Road was full of emotional struggle and the electricity of despair was felt by Barnes from a very early age. There was his father, lonely even with his wife, miserable as only a physican can be who because he cannot cure himself can never find many patients to cure. And there was his mother, proud and energetic, concentrating upon her second son the love, hopes and ambitions that she herself had never fulfilled and that she knew her husband could not satisfy. Over all there hung the despair of a family that lived frugally and yet always beyond its means.

The house on Woolwich Common was something else. Here prosperity was patent and the security of ease and social success. This house, from which Edith Wallis had come and like all the houses of the family except 241 New Cross Road, was the epitome of all that she wanted for her children and of much they could never have in their own home. Very soon it became to them as to her the centre of a second existence, dream-like because it was so substantial, so big, and after the manner of the time, so elegant. The huge ground-floor front room had a fine bow-window facing west over The Common. Above it the drawing-room ran the full length of the house and had a terrace extension, covered by striped awnings. Here among the richly-patterned bowls, the cedar and sandal-wood boxes which Lily and Theo had brought back from a Kashmir adventure, among the glass-fronted cabinets of delicate china, with the fragrance of potpourri hanging on the air, Aunt Lilly held her At Homes.

The house on The Common had a view that was larger than the open space before it, for it looked out into the great military world. Theo could stand at the window of his study—his young nephew by his side—and watch the cadets from The Shop march past, pill-box hats all set at precisely the same angle, tight-waisted tunics, top boots and jingling spurs. Remembering these parades long after, Barnes Wallis wrote, 'They were tremendous fellows. Slightly Prussian? Perhaps, but I don't know, they made splendid officers, of the kind that got themselves killed at the first opportunity as an example to their men.' But the military circle at Woolwich was not all ostentation and snobbery, not all dashing uniforms and the memory and prescience of gallantry. Military visitors to 29 The Common were amply capable of good conversation. Further, because of the military presence and his uncle's favoured position, there was available to his nephew a plethora of fascinating and stimulating sights. The Rotunda, for example, was open to him, a marvellous building 'constructed to hold and preserve for ever'; an immense circular marquee in metal, which housed a museum of artillery and mechanical curiosities 'such as perpetual motion machines, and Gatling guns and cannon from the Crimea'.[1]

It was Edith who taught her children to read, and it would have pleased her to keep their education under her own control for as long as possible. Barnes, in particular, was quick—he could read fluently by the time he was five, could recite his multiplication tables and the dates of the kings and queens of England—but school was inevitable and no less inevitable to Edith was that she must somehow avoid for him the degradation of attending a Board School. At the age of six he was sent to the girls' kindergarten attached to Aske's Haberdasher's at Hatcham and two years later he went to the boys' school.

Little remains in record or memory from those early schooldays except a complete collection of bland termly reports—which show him consistently first in Arithmetic and English but frequently absent through illness—and one very short, short story typed out by him at the time and lovingly treasured among his mother's papers. Written at the age of ten it reveals no great literary promise but psychologists would find it a quarry rich in sinister implications:

Once upon a time there was a little girl, who was very much ill treated by her mother. One night she resolved to run away for she had been beaten that day. So in the middle of the night she ran away. When the wicked mother found that her daughter had run away she was very cross, but being a witch she turned

Childhood

herself into a raven and flew after her and caught her. She then
gave her such a beating that she died.

Determined as she was to secure the future success and future
happiness of her children Edith now began to plague her husband
about their educational future. Only a public school would do,
but for a public school the fees were beyond the Wallises. Charles
aroused himself from his general lethargy and conducted an
extensive investigation of the possibilities. There was, he discovered, but one real chance that his boys could be given a public
school education: Christ's Hospital.

2 Life as a Scrub

The hurdles before entry into Christ's Hospital were many. First the parents had to discover a Governor who was willing to nominate Barnes to take the competitive examination. To him they had to demonstrate need. With a nomination thus secured from one Colonel Newcombe, still Charles and Edith could not by any means be certain that Barnes would follow John who had entered Christ's Hospital in 1899. In 1900, 110 boys sat for only ten places.

Barnes Neville Wallis came seventh in the order of merit, and it seems clear that his place would have been even higher had it not been for his incompetence with Latin verbs. The Headmaster, Richard Lee, decided that Barnes was good enough for immediate entry into the Upper School but on the Modern Side. Charles Wallis's Mertonian pride resented this slur upon his son. He argued with the Headmaster—a rare event this must have been in all Christ's Hospital history for a parent to dare disagreement with God!—and he won. But in the moment of surrender Lee had his revenge. Certainly Barnes could go on the Classical Side but in the Middle School. And at the end of the first term, despite a commendable fifth place in Mathematics and an even more admirable third place in History, the boy who was to have swept straight into the Upper School came out twenty-ninth in a form of twenty-nine boys, and that in the bottom but one form in the Middle School.

And now Barnes rebelled. He would stand for no more Latin. Lee had his revenge twice over for his earlier defeat and could rationalise it by pointing to the fact that the boy's results had not justified the promise of his Entrance Examination. As had originally been intended Barnes could go to the Modern Side but not to the Upper School. He must start again close to the bottom,

10

only one form above the boys whose stupidity was so abysmal that they were destined for superannuation at fifteen.

From now on the academic side of Barnes's schooling went forward with all the appearance of success. Term after term he headed his form in Mathematics. He was never lower than third in Science and usually first or second in English, first or second in French and at least in the first six in German. But his father's interference had cost him a year in the promotion race and the road to ultimate glory among the élite Grecians at the top of the school was irrevocably closed to him by his lack of Latinity.

Nothing could close to him the pervasive influence of the Christ's Hospital tradition. By the standards of the school Wallis's career at Christ's Hospital was short—four years as compared with his brother's six, with the seven of another contemporary, the author John Middleton Murry. But in those four years he came under influences that, perhaps more than any others, were to set the patterns of his thinking and which aroused in him a sense of loyalty and even of obligation. Christ's Hospital became, with his family and his work, the third important strand in his life. For thirty years he served the school and he came eventually to the most important office in the Christ's Hospital hierarchy.

'Christ's Hospital is a thing without parallel in the country and *sui generis.*' The phrase used in the report of the Schools Inquiry Commission of 1867–8 and echoed and re-echoed by Old Blues is as valid today as it was a century ago. In 1811, when the method of entry into Christ's Hospital was under attack, Samuel Taylor Coleridge, the greatest of all her sons, came to her defence (as did his friend and near-equal Charles Lamb). 'We are confident,' wrote Coleridge in *The Courier*, 'that the Lord Chancellor will hesitate long before he attempts to remove a blessing of which there is no parallel in Europe . . . We conclude by declaring solemnly, and on our conscience, that we can hardly imagine a larger sum of goodness and of consolation struck off at once from the ledger of useful benevolence, than would be torn out or vilely scribbled over by the complete success of Robert Waithman's wishes.'

Christ's Hospital is a public school. But in 1900, as today and as it had been from its foundation in 1552, it was much more. Some changes in the social patterns of England—and of Christ's Hospital—had reduced the force of the famous explosion of the school's most explosive and most successful headmaster, James Boyer: 'Boy! The School is your father! Boy! The school is your mother! Boy! The school is your brother! The school is your sister! The school is your first cousin and your second cousin and all the rest of your relations!' But if the universality of the relationship was no longer so entire at the end of the nineteenth century, the School was, and remains, in a sense unknown to other educational institutions, *alma mater*.

This it was to Barnes Wallis from his entry as a 'scrub' into the Newgate Street school; this he proclaimed it to be, explicitly by decades of association as Governor, Almoner and finally as Treasurer and Chairman of the Council, and implicitly in the words that he wrote at the time of the school's quartercentenary:

> Above all other, this Religious, Royal and Ancient Foundation is fitted to be the nursery of those qualities of spirit and mind of which we stand so sorely in need, and to produce . . . leaders who are men of imagination, men capable of bold and original thought, men determined to worship God and in so doing to serve their fellow men.[1]

It is a proclamation of his *credo* but it is more, it is an expression of certainty from whence that *credo* was derived.

Those who find the English public school system distasteful and even socially immoral evade with captious facility the advocate's plea that despite their many faults the public schools appear to have succeeded in livening the sense of individuality necessary to a creator. Faced with portentous lists of leaders of all kinds who have come from the public schools, they put forward their too simple rebuttal: the social atmosphere, they argue, encouraged families of ability and culture to put their sons to public schools. The schools, with such materials at their disposal, could not murder all individuality and intelligence.

Investigation neither proves nor disproves such theories. All that can be done is to open up the narrow window of history to throw some light on the adult mind of such as Barnes Wallis and to attempt an estimate of how much it owes to the circumstances of his education.

It might be argued of some other schools and of their long and successful history as forcing ground for England's great, that they

Life as a Scrub

owe their splendour to the fact that it is the sons of the wealthy, the influential and the cultured who enter the schools; that it is just to assume that it was the family rather than the school which set their feet firmly on the path of leadership. But for Christ's Hospital, and by definition, this cannot be true; almost all the ancient public schools were founded with democratic and charitable intent; Christ's Hospital is unique in that it has remained faithful to the spirit of its charters. Most of the other great schools educate only those who are rich or nearly rich (this at least until the Education Act of 1944 persuaded them to a show of democracy); Christ's Hospital educates only the poor or nearly poor. It has always maintained an upper income bar to admission, and the boys in its care are educated free, housed free, clothed free and, in many cases, sent to University at the Hospital's expense.

The boy-king Edward VI is justly and honourably revered as the school's founder, but the benevolence of the corporate City of London and of individual benefactors removed Christ's Hospital from the money-scratching needs of most charitable foundations. In this security and from the beginning, Christ's Hospital was able to give heed to the quality of its beneficiaries. A munificent institution, it was nevertheless particular and almost miserly in its selection of candidates for its munificence. On the other hand, in 1900 as always, the academic test was not rigorous. Except for certain prescribed places such as those secured by the Wallis boys, the scholar had no particular advantage over the ordinary or even the stupid boy. The one test that remained overriding all others was need.

But in the history of British society need has never been exclusive to one social class. Many of Christ's Hospital's greatest sons came from families that were essentially middle-class; Wallis followed in what was essentially a middle-class tradition. His admission to Christ's Hospital was entirely in the spirit that Coleridge had proclaimed in his *Courier* article: 'To preserve, and not to disturb or destroy, the gradations of society; to catch the falling, and not to lift up the standing from their natural and native rank.'

It was the knowledge of this preservation which later in life was to persuade Wallis to strenuous efforts on behalf of the relaxation of financial exclusiveness which had with time become unrealistic. His devotion to the charitable nature of Christ's Hospital was never dimmed, but he was practical and therefore antipathetic to charity loosely applied.

Wallis was already heir to a tradition before he entered Christ's Hospital. From both parents and from his Uncle Theo he had gleaned a strong sense of continuity. Christ's Hospital strengthened this feeling of continuity that he had from his family. That he was reared in the warmth of history erases one of the apparent paradoxes of his later life: that this man whose career was given to the future should use so often in his writings and conversation the word 'tradition'.

The term 'Public School' is loosely applied to many schools, but when thinking essentially of qualities of personality and leadership it is to the *older* schools that we must look for the product that we need; and though clever scientists can devise means of 'artificial ageing' by which the effects of many years can be brought about in a few days, the quick development of the age-long traditions of a mature Public School lies beyond man's ingenuity and Time alone can give perfection. Thus the number of Schools on which the country can call with certainty for her future leaders is strictly limited, and it becomes the more important that, as their numbers are small, each and every one should be used in this way to its utmost capacity.

If age and tradition be the necessary qualifications of a school for creating leaders, then of them all Christ's Hospital should stand among the best.[2]

This sense of continuity throws some light, too, on his unfailing loyalty to Christ's Hospital and his generosity with time and money in the school's cause. He saw it as part of his responsibility to preserve and improve the standards and the opportunities for competition for those who followed after him.

There are other traits apparent in Wallis throughout his life and not uncommon in those educated in Christ's Hospital which he himself ascribed to his upbringing in the school: self-reliance, independence, pride. If they are the products of a Christ's Hospital schooling, and certainly Wallis, like many others who have written on Christ's Hospital, thought that they were when he recognised them in himself, they can be explained by the combination of inherited tradition and the very lack of useful family influence which is common to all Blues.

There are two other areas in which Christ's Hospital exercised an enormous and lasting influence on Wallis. The first, the circumstance that he was part of the historic migration from London to West Horsham he shared with all his contemporaries. If only because as a boy he knew the profound experience of moving from the constricted area of Newgate Street, with all its compensations of proximity to the greatest city in the world and its constant reminders of tradition, to West Horsham with its red brick novelty and the recompense of spaciousness and surrounding beauty—this move merits some attention here. Wallis and his immediate contemporaries were subjected to the experience of being both the last and the first. For them the effort of adaptation was conscious. It was this early indoctrination which, when eventually he came to be Treasurer of Christ's Hospital, made Wallis so energetic in planning and building. Had his predecessors not gone against most of the advice they received, had they contented themselves with a meagre and suburban site, then, sixty years later, there would have been no possibility of implementing the vast schemes of extension which Wallis started, organised and supervised. But the importance of the move to Wallis's eventual thinking and activities for Christ's Hospital was far more than merely practical. It made his mind receptive to the possibility of change within the framework of tradition, persuaded him (even against his own inherently conservative instincts) that he must listen to the apostles of educational experiment and thus, in the years of his influence, made it possible for him to encourage and even to initiate schemes and discussions which would have been remarkably *avant-garde* in any circumstances but which seem in all other respects out of character in a man whose social thinking was not generally radical.

The second consideration—the benefits that he gleaned from the school's pioneering of science-teaching under the leadership of Armstrong and Browne—leads to an investigation of influences which touched him as one among very few, but which, despite their esoteric nature can be said to have shaped his public career. For Wallis the inventor was, to his own certainty, the product of science teaching as practised at Christ's Hospital in his time, and science at Christ's Hospital was the unique product of the genius of Henry Armstrong and of his disciple, Charles E. Browne.

It is of substantial significance, and not only to the biography of Wallis, that in all the public debate over the reform and migration of Christ's Hospital there was very little discussion of changes in the curriculum. The role of Head Master, the position of Donation Governors, London or the country, traditions ended or traditions extended, all these matters were canvassed in the Press, in domestic and popular meetings, in both Houses of Parliament and before the Privy Council, but even a prophet of glory like G. C. Bell, the Old Blue Master of Marlborough, said little about instruction and nothing, for example, about the introduction of science teaching. Yet, when the new buildings rose at Horsham there was, balancing the Chapel and at right angles to Big School and Dining Hall as the fourth side of the central quadrangle, the Science School: a science school of such dimensions as no other school in the country could boast and of interior design which, by its virtual freedom from conventional class-room patterns, pre-supposed an approach to educational methods challenging to teachers and well-nigh shocking to the generality.

The architects had designed this freak, but they had worked to order, and the voice that shouted the instructions came from Professor Henry Armstrong, F.R.S.

Armstrong was a force in Christ's Hospital for more than forty years and a figure devastatingly familiar both to boys and staff. Few had any understanding of his international reputation as a chemist, and only a small proportion of those who became his guinea pigs were conscious of their privilege. On the days of his visits—as Almoner, Deputy Chairman and eventually Chairman of the Education Committee—his shattering sartorial unorthodoxy stood out like Jacob at a funeral. His wild beard and russet-apple face flaunted excitement to match his startling suits. As late as 1937, the year of his death, the story was still current at West Horsham that he wove, dyed and made up his own clothes. The story was strengthened by the universally held conviction that no professional dyer would have dared such violence—'a colour between that of an orange and a lemon'[3]—no professional weaver could have achieved such gargantuan weightiness and no professional tailor such incomparable shapelessness.

Life as a Scrub

Armstrong had been born at Lewisham in 1848. In 1865 he entered the Royal College of Chemistry where Edward Frankland had just succeeded to Van Hoffman's Chair, and, after eighteen months as a student, became Frankland's assistant in his work on the purification of public water supplies. In 1867 he moved to Leipzig, and there, in the laboratory of Hermann Kölbe, he began his life-long work on orientation in aromatic compounds.

In 1870 Armstrong began to turn some of his enormous energy to the task of pedagogic reform. He had just been appointed lecturer in chemistry for first-year students at St Bartholomew's Hospital. These postulants for a scientific profession he found entirely incapable of scientific thought. They were 'utterly unable to interpret the simplest experimental results, or even to make adequate and correct notes of any chemical change they observed'.[4] Here were post-school students so ill-founded in principles that Armstrong had to start their scientific education afresh with the most elementary practical work.

He turned his attention to the trade schools, to the public schools, to the grammar and elementary schools, and in all he found similar poverty of scientific training and the same deadly lack of enquiring spirit. It became clear to him that there must be instituted two separate but ultimately related reforms: science must be introduced into the schools and such science as was introduced must be taught by entirely new methods.

There was no great originality in Armstrong's demands for more science in the schools. Behind him was a chorus of great distinction: the collective voices of the Royal Society, the Royal Institution, the British Association for the Advancement of Science and the Royal Society of Arts. John Ruskin and Thomas Huxley led the chorus—and Herbert Spencer, whose authority, energy and enthusiasm was such that his four articles on the value of scientific education were re-issued in book form in 1861 under the decently explanatory Victorian title of *Education, Intellectual Moral and Physical* and then translated into thirteen languages, among them, perhaps a little surprisingly, Arabic and Mohawk.

Despite this powerful leadership general enthusiasm was slight —especially in the public schools. There was apathy but there was also downright opposition, and some of it supported by reasoning more substantial than mere obstinate conservatism. Greek and Latin were better as training for the young mind; the schools could not afford the luxury of expensive laboratories, and there was almost no one available to teach science. (Of the 128 schools investigated by the Taunton and Clarendon Commissions only fifteen had set aside some room exclusively devoted to practical work. Christ's Hospital was one of the fifteen.[5] At the time there was also a slur upon scientific education which gave to the predominantly clerical headmasters of the public schools the comfort of defending their cloth and their faith. Thomas Arnold had taught them to see their schools as bastions of sound religion: science was the enemy at the gates.

Against such powerful opposition and the forces of apathy the progress made by Armstrong and his allies was inevitably slow. He helped the cause he favoured by forcing an Education Section upon the British Association. He encouraged the Public Schools' Science Masters' Association (which was to become in time, in the cause of equality between the sexes, the Association for Scientific Education). But the battle for more science went on throughout his lifetime. Meanwhile he worked on the second part of his mission: his novel theories on methods of teaching. Whereas others equalled his energetic sponsorship of the high place of science in the educational process, Armstrong came close to being unique in that he worked out practice to support the theory he expounded. And, if the practice he developed was originally intended exclusively for the teaching of science, it had much in common with other contemporary and more widely-intended developments. Armstrong, in this like his contemporaries, Dewey, Kilpatrick, Montessori and Parkhurst, planned to substitute activity for acquiescence. He proclaimed rebellion against the centuries-old doctrine of learning by rote and example, and set in its place the value and excitement of discovery. His 'heuristic' method was in many ways the most original: the adjective 'heuristic' he lifted from Meiklejohn who had used it as early as 1860, but its derivation from the Greek for 'I have found out' had advantage beyond the descriptive for it touched off appropriately thrilling memories of the one episode in the history of science which was known to classical dons, clerical headmasters—and every schoolboy.

Armstrong put forward his theories for the first time in public at the International Health Exhibition of 1884. By the end of the eighteen-eighties, by reiteration and by using the advantages due to him as a chemist of indisputable eminence, he had won to his side some leading industrialists and even a few educationalists—most of them his old pupils. With their aid, as the century drew to its close, he was granted a prominent position in the development of higher technological and scientific education. But he knew that if his methods were to be tried thoroughly and given the missionary authority of success he must somehow establish a working experiment with younger pupils.

Armstrong's first attempt to set up, within a school, a demonstration of the viability of the heuristic method was characteristically direct. St Dunstan's, Catford, had recently and bravely appointed a scientist headmaster, Charles Stuart. He called on Stuart and persuaded him to organise a small science department on the basis of individual experiment. The innovation was successful, but inconspicuous. This was the moment when the Christ's Hospital removal controversy began to excite the leader-writers. Armstrong saw his opportunity. Here was a famous school —even a curiosity—much loved by the public. Better still for his purposes, here was a rich school with a long tradition of independence, temptingly free from the busybody demands of fee-paying parents, and with a long tradition of devotion to mathematics and to mathematics practically applied to navigation. And in the age-old Drawing and Writing Schools Christ's Hospital had further useful precedents in the 'practical arts'.

The revised Christ's Hospital Scheme of 1891 played into his hands, for now the Royal Society, which had connections with Christ's Hospital dating back to the seventeenth century, was given a place by right on the Council of Almoners. Armstrong had been a Fellow of the Royal Society since 1876. He elbowed his way into the Royal's seat on the Christ's Hospital Council. Once there he was appointed immediately to the Council's Education Committee. The way was open for his greatest experiment. Instead of concentrating upon science teaching he began to devote his energies to the school as a whole. Almost without his knowing it, the heuristic approach to the teaching of science grew into a plan for injecting discovery into every side of school life. At Horsham Christ's Hospital must have an art school, a manual school, a farm where boys could find out by working; these and many other dreams went from his brain to the architect's drawing-board and all in time rose from the mud of the Sussex Weald. Above all he sought out men whose enthusiasm and skill could add term-long and life-long effects to his ideas.

Almost the first that he found was Charles E. Browne, the man who was to carry forward the reform which had started Armstrong upon his services as the second founder of Christ's Hospital.

Chas. E. Browne (the fullness of his Christian name is seldom given to him either in writing or in speech by those who were his boys; to them he is either Uncle Chas., Chas. or, most formally, with the Christian name abbreviated and the middle initial included *à l'Américain*, Chas. E. Browne) had been reared in a North London elementary school and at the age of fifteen had made hs first move as a pupil-teacher in his own school.[6] At twenty-two, still in North London, he was appointed assistant at a small Quaker private school. Even his degree was suspect: from the University of London and by way of evening classes at Birkbeck College! There Armstrong had been his principal examiner. Through him Browne went as Science Instructor to the London Central Technical College, to work under Armstrong himself. He was thirty-three when he came to Newgate Street.

Christ's Hospital, no less than the other public schools, was generally devoted to inbreeding, to staff from public school and Oxford and Cambridge. In some ways Christ's Hospital carried the inbreeding further than most. The majority of masters (and almost all the Upper Grammar or Head Masters) had themselves been Blues. But there had long been a place in the Christ's Hospital teaching staff for a few masters of 'non-academic' subjects (such as handwriting) who did not come from the ancient universities.

Richard Lee appointed Browne and granted him the grand concession of space but he was not prepared to concede to the man he had appointed equality with his colleagues from Oxford and Cambridge. Nor was he willing to give the subject thus admitted to the curriculum equivalent status with classics, mathematics or even modern languages, or to Browne's wild methods the fullness of his trust. He stipulated that throughout Browne's sessions there must be present a master from the mathematical school— according to Lee, to keep an eye on discipline; but, one suspects, to report also on the quality and utility of this strange new subject and the strange new methods by which it was to be taught.

For the methods were strange indeed and not merely to the

classicist Headmaster and his mathematical spy. From an age much given to the pedagogical efficacy of didacticism and rigid discipline, Browne's first notebook stands out like a naughty deed in a depressingly good world: 'The teacher is to afford guidance and suggestions mainly by questions—no telling—I shall adopt the attitude of a co-enquirer, not an authority.'[7] If the boys are to be taught anything it will be in the spirit of curiosity and this they will acquire not by formal lessons but by practical effort, not in the conventional classroom but at a work-bench.

This notebook Browne prefaced with a characteristic acknowledgement:

Genesis—1896, H. E. Armstrong, Governor and Almoner. Heuristic method adapted to C. H. by C. E. B. 1899, Newgate Street.

In a peroration that deserves to be released from the obscurity of a private note-book and blazoned around the walls of every college of education he set himself the task, not of teaching, but of cultivating in his pupils the ability to suspend judgement and to avoid hasty conclusions based upon insufficient evidence.

When, in the 1960s, as Treasurer, he was planning his new reform of Christ's Hospital against a pattern pressed upon the school by the arrival of the Welfare State, Wallis wrote:

It would be a most powerful argument in favour of introducing some measure of reform if we could show that the eight untrammelled years (1900–1908) during which the heuristic method was given full play without the necessity of paying homage to external examinations did, in fact, produce a generation of giants.[8]

Five of Browne's boys were elected Fellows of the Royal Society! Of this very statistic Wallis himself wrote:

This result is in significant agreement with the results available from Eton where out of the six living Fellows who are real scientists (ie. not statesmen) four were trained by a particular science master, Dr Porter. While I admit the danger of arguing a general conclusion from a very limited number of specific instances I feel inclined to agree with Sir Thomas Merton (a Governor of Eton) and one of the four Etonian Fellows, that high scientific achievement is due very largely to the training which a scholar receives when he is young.[9]

The implication of personal debt is there and it is emphasised in many of his writings. In a passage which incidentally removes any sense of surprise that in his last year at school this great engineer won the English Essay Prize, Wallis wrote:

Tall and spare in build, with fair hair and moustache and healthy pallor of complexion, striding swiftly along, his gown billowing out behind him in the wind of his own rapid progress. But, once in his laboratory, all the haste and energy of physical motion were replaced by a serene calm that could only come from the deepest confidence in and love for the thing he had to do. I never heard Uncle Chas. raise his voice; I never knew him give any punishment; I never knew him answer a question save by another; if necessary question after question, each framed with a skill amounting to inspiration, until the laggard brain of his pupil did at last see light. Uncle Chas. (as he came affectionately to be called) did not teach science in the sense usually attached to the word; he used science to teach us to think, to reveal to us the powers we ourselves possessed.

With the persuasive voice of Wallis in his ears—and the supporting chorus of so many of Wallis's school contemporaries who became leaders in the sciences—his biographer must accept the munificence and the significance of the accident that Chas E. Browne was appointed the first senior science master and the heuristic method was introduced at Christ's Hospital just one year before Wallis entered the school.

3 Christ's Hospital, Horsham

Wallis did not come under the influence of Browne immediately on his arrival in Newgate Street but there were others of such quality as was bound to impress a young boy. These were the days when masters were still primarily teachers. They did not live among the boys. Remote, often severe and unsympathetic, there were, nevertheless, many who served themselves up as characters, even as caricatures. Some contrived to reach down into the minds and hearts of their pupils so that their memory lives, fresh and stimulating still in the actions, the correspondence and the conversation of the tiny band of survivors from their regime.

When Wallis first knew them, many were close to the end of their working days, teaching, as it were, with the housebreaker's men looking over their shoulders. There were also a few who must have been facing the future with some fear; men who were destined to make the move to Horsham and who knew that in the course of that process they must change themselves from old-style pedagogues into new-style mentors.

There was, for example, one of the 'degreeless wonders', Henry John Stalley, the Head of the Writing School, who continued with meticulous authority the age-old devotion of Christ's Hospital to fine handwriting. His beard reached almost to his elegant well-corsetted waist; even in the classroom he wore a black frock coat and in its lapel the blue ribbon of the dedicated teetotaller. He seldom smiled and never laughed. The drabness of his history lessons makes all the more surprising the courageous explosiveness with which he was apt to defend even his most unpopular political opinions. A man who, in the very midst of the patriotic effusiveness of the Boer War, could describe that war to classes of boys as 'Mess, Muddle and Make-believe' must have had the makings of a great history teacher.

Barnes Wallis

Stalley has his memorials in the world's museums where the manuscripts of one of his pupils, Edmund Blunden, are treasured for their exquisite penmanship as well as for their beautiful English. He has his memorial, too, in Wallis's unshakable devotion to accuracy and in the enormous body of his notes and correspondence, uniformly written in a clear and firm hand that scarcely changed, no matter what the surrounding conditions or the pressure to which he was being subjected, and that survived even in old age.

There was Henri Bué teaching French at Christ's Hospital and teaching it to the world at large by way of his indefatigable authorship of text-books. He was also the author of one of the most remarkable translations of his day—*Alice au Pays des Merveilles*. Under Bué, Wallis acquired competence as a modern linguist that was not by any means usual in an English public schoolboy.

There was the Reverend D. F. Heywood, who was to become Wallis's housemaster at Horsham, whose self-imposed brand of caricature lay in alternating between colloquialism and pedanticism, between 'Got that solid?' and 'Have you not accepted what is the current coin of the world's intellectual intercourse?'

Above all there was Richard Lee. His portrait shows him, slightly comic to our eyes, mutton-chop whiskers and a round face above the deep clerical collar. He was pedantic in the headmasterly manner of his times and conventional, entirely committed to the Victorian belief that, for boys, the road to Heaven is paved with Latin declensions and lined with Greek verse. From the records of the time and the reminiscences of this last generation of Cockney Blues one draws the feeling that Lee wrapped himself in a cloak of austerity more complete even that that which had been his custom some ten years earlier. The twilight of his reign was also, he he saw it, the end of the great tradition in which he had been reared and which he had served for so long.

Life in Newgate Street was austere to the point of barbarity. The lack of amenities might well have daunted even the prisoners who were among the boys' closest neighbours until the last few years in London. They did not daunt Wallis nor indeed any of his contemporaries who have left a record. In Newgate Street the school was divided into Wards, each of fifty boys, and in the one vast barrack room that was the Ward fifty boys lived the whole of the domestic side of their lives. Here they slept on mattresses laid on plank beds. Here they did their preparation, talked, played and kept such few private possessions as were permitted to them. The discipline and domestic propriety of the Ward was entirely in the hands of a Dame whose quarters occupied one end of the barrack. She had no male assistance, not even from the Grecian 'who occupied a study which was an elevated box, erected in a corner of the Ward, and underneath which he slept on a double mattress screened by curtains from the vulgar . . . far too superior to have dealings with Ward discipline . . . an Olympian God'.[1]

At the end of each Ward there was a ten-foot-square cell containing twelve taps but no basins. Here, in cold water, the boys sought cleanliness for a minute or so a day; far less time than they were forced to devote to godliness.

Meals were taken in the huge Dining Hall. For Sunday breakfast, sausages; Monday, cold spiced beef; Tuesday, Thursday and Saturday, brown bread-roll and butter; Wednesday, ham. For dinner, except on Fridays, fish day, there was pudding followed by meat, the precedence dictated by economy, for if the boys filled their stomachs first with the stodgy and cheap pudding they would not need so much of the expensive meat. For supper there was only bread, butter and milk.[2]

But if the food lacked elegance it was here in the Dining Hall that the continuity of tradition was most palpable. Hanging above the boys were pictures by Lely and others, one of them, by Antonio Verrio, celebrating the foundation of Charles II's Royal Mathematical School with magnificent historical impertinence by making James II the central figure (his brother having died while the picture was being painted).

And here, more significantly than anywhere else in the school, each Thursday in Lent, on the occasion of the Public Suppers in Lent, the boys were reminded of their proud connection with the City of London.

Even in the restricted space of Newgate Street pastimes were many if somewhat violent.

Few boys were given the opportunity to go to the school sports ground at Penge or to join the Boat Club, but there was a good swimming bath, a fives court and on winter mornings rugby football on the bleak asphalt of the Hall was compulsory, 'a good many bruises and, occasionally, a broken limb when the victim was hurled into touch and landed against the granite buttresses of the Hall Cloister'. In the summer cricket, too, was played on the asphalt, eight or nine games in the confined space, and there was a tennis court in the gymnasium in Giltspur Street—but only for Grecians and Deputy Grecians. Some boys took their exercise by running up to the top of St Paul's Cathedral and back. A few, less eager for heart failure and encouraged by Charles E. Browne, took up the new-fangled hobby of photography, a few more the even newer pastime of cycling, but it is claimed that the principal Sunday pastime was betting on the destination of the horse-buses which passed the school gate.

Wallis soon came to participate, with pleasure and ease if with no great distinction, in all that Christ's Hospital had to offer, but not before he had indulged himself in a further rebellion against authority as protest against Lee's injustice in relegating him from what he regarded as his proper place in the school which had built up in the boy a determination to assert himself. In Newgate Street there was little opportunity for what has since come to be called self-expression. Wallis attempted to re-establish pride in himself by minor misbehaviour which placed him in almost continuous dispute with authority as represented by the two junior Ward monitors, F. W. Stewart and Newton Flew. It was a battle of wills in which the armament of age, of position and schoolboy dignity was all on the side of the monitors. But, at least with Stewart, the cunning of the smaller boy found a method of revenge in kind for the considerable pain that his own mischief brought down, quite literally, upon his own head.

The right of corporal punishment in the more usual and more formal manner was reserved to the Warden, who, upon receiving reports from masters, from the Dames, or from the monitors by way of the Dames, instructed one of the Beadles to act on his behalf. But for lesser offences in the Wards the monitors were authorised to administer their own punishment in two kinds: 'fotches' and 'owls'. A 'fotch' was a simple if painful slap on the face; an 'owl' a severe blow given with the knuckles of the clenched fist on the top of the victim's head.

Judicially, as if in preparation for his future as an Indian Civil Servant, Stewart made it his custom to allow his juniors to choose between the forms of punishment. In their many conflicts Wallis chose always to be owled for he knew his skull to be thick and Stewart's knuckles to be tender. Thus, as he reeled away from the uncomfortable meeting he could comfort himself with the sight of authority nursing its bruised knuckles.

But already another disaster had struck Wallis and in a manner far more serious than his battles with monitors and even more malevolent than his failure to hold his place on the Classical Side. One day he stood in his place in the Great Hall waiting for lunch. The babble of seven hundred hungry boys was silenced by the Hall Warden's gavel. All turned towards the Grinling Gibbons pulpit. Wallis watched respectfully as a Grecian mounted the steps.

Wallis heard the first words of the Grace. 'Give us thankful hearts, O Lord God, for the table thou hast spread for us . . .' Then, to his horror, Grecian, pulpit and even the vast Verrio painting disappeared. He saw nothing for the rest of the meal, but he staggered out with the boys of his Ward and managed to get to a geography lesson in the Writing School. Such was the intensity of his headache that the familiar smell of the older part of Christ's Hospital, Newgate Street, which he later knew to be dry rot, on that day went almost unnoticed. Suddenly he could stand it no more. He rushed out and vomited helplessly, until his stomach muscles could no longer stand the pain of bringing up nothing. He was taken across to the Infirmary and allowed to lie down. As for sympathy, there was none. 'You know what's the matter with you, you've eaten too much cake.' Wallis knew that it was not gluttony that had caused his pain. His comparatively short school career was to be interrupted again and again by illnesses, some of them serious—mastoid and scarlet fever—but even at twelve years old this first he recognised as ominous. Like his father and his mother he was a migraine-sufferer.

The British pride themselves upon their public *sang-froid* yet, more than most nations, they revel in an opportunity for mass demonstratoins of sentiment. For all who were closely connected with Christ's Hospital even great national demonstrations were of tiny consequence beside the Exodus. The City of London was the heart of the nation and in some indefinable way Christ's Hospital was the epitome of the City and had been for three hundred and fifty years. It seemed almost as if the City could not continue without Christ's Hospital in its midst;

certainly the reverse appeared as undeniable. Christ's Hospital could never be the same without that intimate relation with the City which the school had enjoyed throughout its previous history.

As Christ's Hospital was so much of the City of London the near-hysterical valedictions were expressed as the City has always expressed its emotions: in public speeches and sermons. The Lord Mayor had his say. The Duke of Cambridge, the arch-opponent of the move to Horsham, said his all over again. The Head Master preached. The Bishop of London preached, at Christ Church, Newgate Street, so that the honour of a St Paul's Cathedral sermon could go to the prince of the Church, Dr Frederick Temple, Archbishop of Canterbury.

There were other less public demonstrations of sentiment. Farewells to each of the many masters and officials who were not going to Horsham. And, on the last night of term the Grecians indulged their heritage for ceremony.

In those days the idea of a Grecian 'degrading himself' to any species of fun or humour seemed too great an impossibility to contemplate; yet on this night a peculiar and unique ceremony was invented, instituted and performed. Forming a long single file, each holding a lighted candle (of four to the lb.), the Grecians 'beat the bounds' of the Hospital, kicking the walls at such well known spots as the 'Gymmer Door', 'Sixes Tubby's Hole', 'The Rid's Staircase', and 'Haggery Stairs'. The round completed, they stretched across the Hall Playground, and having solemnly extinguished their candles (in the best Papal manner) they marched up and down three times, singing lustily 'Auld Lang Syne', when the unexpected appearance of the Warden dispersed them suddenly to their Wards.[3]

Finally Richard Lee, the remote dictator, came down from his podium. At the end of the last Assembly in the Great Hall he spoke once more. His speech was unusually short and hesitant, his great voice dimmed and shaken, the habitual roll of his sentences broken by uncertainty as he commended the boys and their school to the grace and protection of God. Then he marched to the exit and, as the boys filed past him, he shook hands with every one, adding in most cases a few words of encouragement and —most surprisingly of all—the boy's name.

28

Christ's Hospital, Horsham

In May the school reassembled in its new environment. Change was palpable: elaborate grounds, a range of red brick buildings centred on the huge quadrangle and spreading out for several hundred yards in each direction to the Preparatory School in the East, and in the West, to Peele A, the house where the Wallis brothers and the others who had once formed Ward 7 were to make their existence. The green Weald and far horizon in exchange for the claustrophobic settings of Little Britain, Paternoster Square and Ivy Lane. Luxurious playing fields, swimming baths and a gymnasium close to the houses instead of the Hall Play, the long journey to Penge and bathing excursions to the Ditch.

The overweening power of the Dames had been broken. Now, in the conventional public school manner, Matrons supervised health and cleanliness, issued linen, and, unless they were exceptional women, had little influence on the boys' lives. Instead, and again according to the more usual pattern, housemasters and junior housemasters took over discipline and all out-of-school activities: Heywood in Peele A. But the lordliness of the Grecian was still apparent and emphasised by the privacy of study and sleeping cubicle.

Accommodation was far more lavish than in London but, with the exception of the two tiny studies in each dayroom and the equally tiny cubicle in each of the two dormitories of the houses, there was still little privacy for the Blue and none was provided for him until sixty years later when Wallis as Treasurer presided over the building of study-blocks.

Indeed, despite the general lavishness of setting and equipment much of Newgate Street was transplanted to Horsham. There were many public reminders of what had been: a gate, an arch, the whole of a wall reconstituted, statues and memorial tablets. More intimately, there in the airy West Horsham dormitories were the same iron bedsteads with their wooden planks for springs and the same horse-hair mattresses and bolsters. There, next to the beds were the same old wooden settles. Above all, the boys still wore the same unique clothes and still talked their private language.

However, the generation that knew both London and Horsham —Wallis's generation—thought that the metamorphosis was more complete and the break with tradition more drastic than it was in truth. And, despite the comforts of their new environment

29

which all recognised, many in that transitional group, Wallis among them, never quite reconciled themselves to the move. For Wallis more than most, there was a private reason for this preference. Despite the privations of Newgate Street, school life there did not imply a break with home anything like so complete as was now enforced by distance. Passes home had been allowed once a week, and Wallis, deeply devoted to his home, had taken full advantage of them and had also enjoyed in Newgate Street frequent visits from his mother. Now at West Horsham parents were not encouraged to appear on the scene more than once or twice a term, and visits home—other than for family funerals— were strictly forbidden.

Wallis saw little more of the new Headmaster than he had seen of Richard Lee. The opinion of those who knew Upcott— 'The Butcher' or 'Old Guts'—vary from deep affection, through great admiration for his undoubted qualities as an administrator to entire abhorrence of his pious sadism. Unlike his predecessors, Upcott was not a Blue and greater than his concern with transplanting at West Horsham the ancient traditions of Christ's Hospital was his determination to build a great school after the Rugby pattern and to beg or bully his charges into communion with their Maker. But his determination to make the Chapel the centre of school life had an adverse effect upon his boys, for many of them felt that the time that they had spent upon their knees at school was sufficient to last them through life. Not so the Wallis brothers whose piety came more from family than from school traditions.

Many of the best of the London masters had come on to West Horsham, and to their number had been added a new generation of enthusiasts, teachers with the Armstrong spirit, young men who cared about the lives and happiness as well as the classroom education of the boys in their charge. Wallis began to profit from their presence and above all from Charles E. Browne. Further, in the rigid hierarchy of an adolescent society a year can work the miracle of change from oppressed obscurity to dignified seniority. Thus, after the first year in Sussex, Wallis found himself no longer quite insignificant and, although throughout his life he never moved from his remembered preference for Newgate Street, was in consequence comfortably content.

By the beginning of the summer term of 1903 Wallis had

achieved an unsensational academic respectability high up on the Modern Side. In the house he was well-established and could look to being a monitor next year. He was fascinated by Commercial Geography, good at French and German and his English was clear and acceptable to his teachers. He had discovered the knack and pleasure of learning poetry by heart and, if the Mathematics which he was given had not the elegance of that provided higher up in the school to University aspirants by a young Old Blue Wrangler, C. J. A. Trimble (who was later to be one of Eddington's principal collaborators), the neat logic of trigonometry gave him no pains. He was not flashy, but his natural ability was supported by unusual determination to do well; he was coming to accept as a responsibility the need to satisfy his family, and above all his mother, to make up to her for the disasters and sacrifices she had undergone—as she felt, for his sake. His regular letters to his mother contained faithful and detailed reporting on his progress; and the reports were undoubtedly all the easier to write because they were, for the most part, accounts of successes.

Like most youthful victims of educational experiment he was at the time utterly oblivious of his guinea-pig status. He did not know and would have cared little had he been told that few boys anywhere in the country in his generation were subjected to the excitements of experiment and deduction which Browne was able to present to his pupils. Even he was oblivious of the great advance in the status of science at Christ's Hospital represented by the announcement of a new prize; the Willcox. What he did know was that he enjoyed himself in the Science School. He had hopes of the Form Prize for general subjects, and to these hopes he added dreams that he might win the Willcox. He revealed them by the typical schoolboy device of denying them in his letters home. 'Of course I haven't a chance against the fellows in U.F.A.' 'I doubt if I am in the running.' Then carefully qualified hope began to break through his deliberate pessimism. First, 'it would be fun to have a go' and then at greater length after the first hurdle had been passed:

To decide the Willcox Prize (Science) £7 10s we first had a preliminary exam . . . In that I was easily top. The top ten fellows were chosen to compete in the real exam. That lasted all Wed. morning and all Thurs. afternoon. Dr Moody who I imagine is some great man came down on Wed. to inspect the way we put up our apparatus etc . . . I doubt if I shall get it, anyhow I'm not 'on spec.' so please don't you be.

Wouldn't it be a grand thing to have though. A medal costing £1 and £6 10s to be spent on whatever is most useful to you when you leave.

The preliminary examination with its reiteration of observation is typically Browne's—and far in advance of contemporary pedagogy: 'describe what you would expect to observe', 'design a series of experiments', 'how would you investigate'. This was the examination in which Wallis was 'easily top'. There followed the practical examination, even more patently the product of Armstrong's philosophy and Browne's enthusiasm, and on the next Sunday Wallis wrote to his mother a letter even longer than usual and interspersed his account of the examination with drawings copied from his scribblings in the margins of the examination paper.

Wallis won the Willcox Prize and was so excited that he sent off telegrams to his mother and to several aunts and uncles. (He also came top in German and thus won the Form Prize.) But this account of schoolboy triumph is more than a mere excursion into ancient history. It does serve to underline what Wallis had in mind when he wrote sixty-four years later: 'My one asset is that I was taught to *think*—generally quite unsuccessfully—by "Uncle Chas" at C.H.'[4]

Encouraged by his protégé's success, Browne began to dream of using this bright pupil for a further breakthrough on behalf of his precious scientists. He knew that if his work at Christ's Hospital were to achieve maturity—and with it the pioneer concept of science-teaching that he had learned from Armstrong—then he must give it academic and social equivalence with Classics and Mathematics. In the nature of Christ's Hospital this could be done only if he could elevate one of his pupils to be a Grecian and thus proclaim him as destined for Oxford or Cambridge.

It says much for Browne's perspicacity that he chose Wallis as the first of many candidates for whom he was ready to do battle with entrenched tradition, with the demi-gods of Classics and Mathematics, and with their dour commander, Dr Upcott.

For Wallis, he was even prepared to urge a compromise by accepting that if a Science Grecian would be a Christ's Hospital novelty then the novelty could be compounded by sending him on to one of the new-fangled universities: London or Manchester.

Battle with the authorities was never joined. Wallis himself was set against the project; he was restless. Many of his school friends were already flaunting their way round the City, participants in an adult world. He was tired of being taught; now he wanted to do, though quite what it was that he could do he did not as yet know. Above all his sense of family responsibility had matured. It was no longer enough to please his mother; now he felt himself old enough to take away from her some of the strain of riding disaster, of holding the family against failing the standards to which she and her husband were devoted. There were the younger children still to be educated and John was a Classical Grecian. One Wallis at a university was quite enough.

His eagerness to leave school so as to avoid postponement of the time when he could become a breadwinner was to some extent buttressed by the very traditions which stood between Wallis and a university education. Christ's Hospital hagiology is rich with success stories of men who had been thrust out early upon the world and there made fortunes. Not one in the recent procession of Christ's Hospital Lord Mayors had been a graduate. Even there was before him more immediate and more spiritual encouragement for his decision to refuse the chance that Browne proffered. In the course of preparing the boy for confirmation Heywood had added his own question to the Catechism: 'What, boy, is your principal ambition?' With his eyes firmly upon his housemaster's clerical collar Wallis had given the answer that in the circumstances he thought was expected from him. 'To get to Heaven, Sir!' Heywood had rounded upon him in fury. 'No, no, no, boy! To get on, to get on!'

Driven thus by inclination, tradition, family loyalty and his spiritual mentor, Wallis turned his back on academic possibilities. It is inevitable that one should speculate on what would have happened to Wallis had Browne thrust him into a university. The didactic impulse was strong in him and he might well have become a don, or, like his brother John, a schoolmaster. More shattering in the light of hindsight is the knowledge that three of the ten leaving Grecians of 1906 (which would have been his year to take a scholarship) rose to be Permanent Under Secretaries in the Civil Service!

More important than the 'might-have-been' is the further speculation on how much his eventual view of technological education was conditioned by his early tumbling into practical experience. Although he never despised scholastic qualifications, he argued consistently that extended academic indoctrination may be a deterrent to creation. For example, when he was already well-established and on his way to being famous, he wrote of aspirants to his own profession, 'but they have spent so many years of their lives being taught that I find they have been robbed of that most priceless possession—creative originality.'[5] He stood also for the practical:

> I always feel very strongly myself that the development of a first class designer is not merely a matter of cramming with technical knowledge, but depends to a large extent on some mental properties, which are only gained by the attainment of some considerable degree of manual skill in the handling of materials.[6]

Looking back to his own attitude in 1904 and to his rejection of the possibility of a university education it is his desire to be earning his own living which is most significant, but there is another passage in an essay written in 1952 which carries something more than the revolutionary dream of an elderly man who can afford the luxury of both dreams and revolutions. Here, in the words of a highly-sophisticated adult is an undercurrent of regret that he was removed so early from an institution which has his loyalty and affection, and of resentment against the obstacles set before him and his contemporaries by rigid specialisation:

> Has the coming of the Welfare State created the anomaly that life at Christ's Hospital is now extended at the wrong end, and that its inestimable benefits are to a certain extent given to children adequately provided for by the State? The Prep. School is, without exception, recruited from presented boys, and the 2 or 3 years spent therein before promotion to the Senior School would surely be of infinitely more value to boys, School, and

State alike, if these years now spent in the Prep. School were used to extend the School life of a corresponding number of really able boys from 17 or 18 to 20 years of age, the extension being spent in the College of Christ's Hospital at University standard, thus postponing the age at which specialization must begin, and leaving the years of adolescence for the School to mould as only Christ's Hospital can?[7]

In 1904 there could be no speculation and no compromise. Any boy not destined for university must leave school at the end of the term next before his seventeenth birthday. The system was inexorable and accepted without question even by Browne and certainly by Wallis himself. However, despite his usual reticence and his sad experience of attempting to combat Christ's Hospital regulations, Dr Charles Wallis made one more determined effort to mitigate their effect. He could not accept that his son should leave school without some paper qualification. He wrote asking that his son be prepared for London University Matriculation.

Upcott's answer was a flat 'no'!

As he had shown four years earlier Charles Wallis could be pig-headed, though his obstinacy seldom showed in his dealings with the outside world. And he could be bad-tempered. Now he was as much infuriated by Upcott's unreasonable refusal as Upcott had been by his unreasonable request. He enlisted an ally: the boy himself. Barnes bearded Heywood who in addition to being his housemaster was also Head of the Modern Side. The boy's advocacy was forceful and so it is not without piquancy that later in life Wallis was to describe Christ's Hospital surrender to external examinatons as 'a sad step'. Apparently without further consultation with Upcott, Heywood made arrangements for Wallis to abandon all normal class-work so that he could prepare for Matric. The examination was to take place two months after Wallis had left school. He could choose for himself the subjects he would take and work on them in a corner of a form-room without any tuition.

Thus, in an unnatural twilight, Wallis approached the end of his school life. He was one of the majority who had achieved in his schooldays neither of the paradoxical glories that make a boy memorable to his fellows: he was not outstanding and he had never been notorious. As he was not a Grecïan most of the school's social honours were closed to him. He was a monitor—one of six in a house of fifty boys—but he was not and could not be House Captain. He was fond of games but not sufficiently an athlete to achieve distinction on the playing fields. After his early flurry of rebellion he had developed into an undeniably happy boy but serious-minded and conscientious beyond the ordinary. (Almost his last act as a monitor was to send a junior to Heywood for a beating. Not a very unusual occurrence at Christ's Hospital in 1904, but the wrestling with his conscience over this comparatively trivial circumstance is revealing, and even more significant the fact that the debate with himself was all argued out in letters to his mother.) His ability did not go unnoticed by the masters. Only a week or so before the examination for the Rokeby French Prize and in the midst of his term of self-tutoring, Henri Bué suggested that Wallis compete for the Prize, which he won. Most of those who taught him spoke well of him. Browne saw more of him than did the rest of his colleagues, but scientists were still second-class citizens, the Willcox Prize which Wallis had won was a novelty and almost unnoticed, and even Browne seems to have lost some of his enthusiasm when Wallis rejected the sensational opportunity that Browne had opened before him.

His passing from Christ's Hospital was as unnoticed as his passing through the school. But as it approached the boy himself began to have doubts and fears. He had been content; certain in his middle-of-the-way, unsensational position and secure in the protection of order and tradition. He wanted to get on but with what could he get on? 'Everything is the last,' he wrote to his mother, 'everything is ending. Oh! it's awful,' and then with the seemingly certain consequence of an uncertain future looming before him and with quite unconscious prescience, 'Oh! I don't want to be a civil servant.'

Finality was inescapable and the day came when he was shuffled out of Christ's Hospital. But within two months of leaving school, ignominiously he failed London Matriculation.

4 The Thames and Cowes

In a few months Wallis had tumbled from the highest peak of opportunity into the gloomy pit of failure. Christ's Hospital, generally careful of the future of her sons, seems to have forgotten him on the day that he left. An Advancement in Life Fund had existed at Christ's Hospital for almost one hundred years through which the school could help boys in their careers. Wallis was not even told that it existed. He, for his part, had been so bruised in his pride that he would not go back to seek advice or introductions. The comfortable dream of coming soon to the support of his family had turned into the sour reality of being utterly dependent upon them.

Accustomed as they were to far more devastating tragedies and set-backs, now Dr and Mrs Wallis behaved in an exemplary manner. They wanted Barnes to be secure. They needed desperately to remove from themselves the cost of his upkeep, but they would not force upon him a choice of careers; this he must decide for himself.

From the gloom of those 'tinker—tailor—soldier—sailor' weeks came certainty. He wanted to be an engineer.

It would be pleasant to be able to see far-ranging perspicacity in this decision. The truth is more prosaic: he had to have a job. At school in the laboratories he had shown his ability and he had always been fond of doing things with his hands—the Willcox Prize money he had put to buying himself a lathe. But he had been no less successful at languages, he wrote a good hand and was quick at arithmetic. The city was close by and full of Christ's Hospital products who would have been willing to find a counting-house desk for a fellow-Blue.

Nevertheless he would be an engineer.

For weeks Dr Wallis and Barnes stumped New Cross and the neighbouring districts seeking an engineering works that would take on the boy as apprentice. It was a harsh test for family pride and resilience, physically tiring to the crippled father, dispiriting to both father and son. No jobs! Too many apprentices! What qualifications? Finally they discovered the Thames Engineering Works at the foot of Blackheath Hill and there Wallis started his professional career under indentures that were no less rigid than those prescribed in Tudor times. He was to earn four shillings a week.

The Thames Engineering Works made the engines for the ships built a few miles away at Deptford by the Thames Shipbuilding Company. Frequently Wallis was sent with a message to the parent company and in the course of running these errands he fell in love—with ships. It was a romance that would stay with him for life. And for a young man in love with ships the times seemed auspicious. The tiny interlude of euphoria was over which had followed the end of the South African War. Those who could read the signs—and their number was by no means few—saw the implications of the German Navy Acts of 1895 and 1902. Even if Britain could no longer maintain splendid isolation her leaders were determined to hold her superiority at sea. They proposed, although they never succeeded in achieving, a policy of two British keels for every one German. The century of battles had begun; the arms race between Britain and Germany was on and, although horrific in its implications, seemed to carry with it the promise of a magnificent future for a young marine-engineer. But the Thames was not the right place to seize those opportunities. *The Black Prince*, to whose builders Wallis carried his messages from Blackheath, was the last battleship built on the Thames.

So, despite the impending rush into prosperity that spelt out the certainly of forthcoming tragedy, there was at Thames Engineering little work for the young apprentice. The hot weather of 1907 when the temperature in the shops topped 103 degrees set his nerves on edge. His parents were away for a few weeks that summer, and he wrote to his mother 'I am not an energetic individual but it is getting quite unbearable having no real work to do.' Despite his disclaimers he was watching his professional surroundings with mature care.

There was a new manager in full cry when I got back, he being by the way the fourth manager that we are now blessed with, in addition to motor experts *ad libitum*. The firm certainly puzzles me for the average individual it seems strange to crowd on managers in this style when there is no work to be done and none in prospect.[1]

The Thames Engineering Company made several efforts to shed its dependence upon the shipbuilding company, and as a tiny cog in the process of diversification Wallis worked on the first racing-car built in England and on the prototype London taxi cab.

(At the age of seventeen he had made his first acquaintance with the new-fangled automobile. As an act of charity a friend sold to Charles Wallis a tiller-steered, single-cylinder rear-engined Oldsmobile. The car had been shipped by train from the friend's home in Newcastle to King's Cross. There Barnes unloaded the Olds, sat himself in the driving-seat and, never having driven before, began a dashing tour of London including a sprint through the heavy traffic of Park Lane. Each time the cylinder fired the Oldsmobile leapt forward making progress, like a kangaroo, at what seemed a terrifying pace. But the driver's efforts failed to overtake a smart-stepping pair of horses pulling a smart barouche!)

Just at the time when he was casting round for an alternative to Thames, another new engineering industry was in process of foundation.

Flight, the lunatic dream of the centuries, had at last been proved practicable. With the retrospect of his later achievements stretching out behind one and the prospect of certain and sensational developments still to come, it is difficult to accept as undeniable fact that Barnes Wallis was sixteen and in his last year at school when on 17 December 1903 the Wright Brothers dragged an unsuspecting world into the age of aviation. Wallis was as unsuspecting as most and for some years far less interested than many.

On 8 August 1908 the Wright Brothers made their first flight in Europe; on 5 October (a few days after Wallis's twenty-first birthday) at Farnborough, S. F. Cody covered 500 yards at a height of sixty feet in the first official powered flight in England. In the next few years aviation changed from wild dream to industry by way of a period of delirium and substantial bravery, but all this meant nothing to Wallis. In the considerable volume of his correspondence from 1907 to 1912 (the year in which he was suddenly projected into a comparatively leading role in the still tiny British aviation industry) there is only one oblique reference to flight and to the excitements that were filling the newspapers with a new generation of heroes: Edith Wallis called her dog Blériot!

As 1907 turned into 1908 Wallis's restlessness grew and with it his determination to be a marine engineer.

Despite the boredom of life and work at Thames his confidence had returned; enough at least to allow him the luxury of enlisting the little influence he could muster and enough to permit him to face up to the well-nigh inevitable corollary to change: a renewed separation from home. He approached Uncle Tacy, who had made a comfortable career as an electrical engineer. With his aid Wallis transferred his indentures to John Samuel White's shipyard at Cowes on the Isle of Wight.

Edith Wallis was proud but nervous. It had been hard enough to allow Barnes out of her care when he went away to school, but in Newgate Street and at West Horsham she had thought him to be safe in the austere care of distinguished clerics such as Lee, Upcott and Heywood and cossetted by dames and matrons. Now loneliness and temptation threatened her twenty-one-year-old son. Good church-woman as she was she addressed herself to the Vicar of Cowes. The Reverend Mr Barclay recognised his responsibilities to the pious mother of a pious son: Barnes must go into sanctified lodgings in the house of his verger, Cox. With meals Mrs Cox would charge her boarder thirty shillings a week. Barnes's wage-packet from White's contained seven. Mrs Wallis decided that she must find the rent and an additional five shillings a week for her son.

Barnes was miserable with a sense of guilt at thus once more burdening his mother. He was miserable too with Mrs Cox who grumbled about the oil which his boots transferred from the shipyard to her holy carpet. When she demanded that he strip in the scullery and scrub himself before entering the house Wallis gave notice on the spot. By this time he had one close friend in the works, Jack Darnell, a fitter just out of indentures. He put his predicament to Darnell who suggested that Wallis should move to a poorer quarter of Cowes and share his lodgings and indeed his bed. For this, for miserable meals and the fleas which devoured Barnes but spared Darnell, the rent was to be thirteen shillings a week. Still more than he was earning but a step towards fulfilling his ambition of aiding his family.

White's was a lively firm eager to find and to encourage ability in its young men, and Wallis was soon moved into the drawing office at the huge salary of twenty-five shillings a week. There he could use the magnificent set of drawing instruments given him for his twenty-first birthday by the whole family clubbing together. And Cowes was a good place to live. There were clubs for every conceivable sport, and despite his typically youthful complaint that he had 'barely time to write one letter home per week' Wallis took part enthusiastically in most of them. He played croquet, went riding, joined the shooting and rowing clubs. He bought himself a pair of second-hand fencing foils, deserted the Christ's Hospital rugby football tradition to play soccer for the works, went on long cross-country runs and took up boxing.

In the evenings he played chess, bridge, took dancing lessons and attended evening classes under one of the draughtsmen. He also resat his Matriculation examination, and this time passed. He began to take an interest in music, thought of learning the piano but contented himself with musical soirées at the house of an East Cowes doctor. For a while he was so excited by music that he would include quotations in his regular letters home, as for example:

It starts with three notes in the bass which go down something like this only of course the intervals are not right [there follows an indecipherable musical quotation] and then it goes up in the treble then those notes come down again. Do you know it? . . . Everything was so glorious that he played from eight till twelve and then I lost the last ferry and had to get a boat to row me across.

If his religion was as yet untouched by any profound feeling he remained a regular churchgoer, and made some timid investigation of forms of Christian expression other than the respectable High Anglicanism in which his mother had reared him, paying inquisitive visits to churches of other denominations and with no great difficulty removing each of them from his list of possibilities.

Barnes Wallis

On one Sunday two were discarded, the first, the Salvation Army, having come to him while he was at breakfast 'full band of about twelve, a speaker, a banner, a sweet Salvation lassie and a big drum all complete. May I never hear another!' That same morning he sampled the United Methodists,

And came away marvelling that anyone could stop a nonconformist, at least if they have ever entered an Anglican Church.[2]

Although he was suitably sociable at the tennis club or at dancing classes there is no evidence in his letters or in his memory that he ever sought the company of a girl. Not until the First World War (when he was close to thirty) did he take a girl to a theatre—and then only a cousin. Not until the same time was he kissed by a girl and not until he was in his mid-thirties did he kiss a girl: his fiancée. As he grew older he developed a charm, an old-fashioned courteousness towards women which has roused in them admiration, affection—even adoration—but he never attempted the offhandedness, the easy assumption of equality which is the hall-mark of the man who is comfortable and successful in the company of women. Psychologists could draw grim conclusions from this absence of natural eagerness for female companionship on the part of a clearly masculine being. Certainly the pattern was already set in his childhood, but it was reinforced at Cowes in those early days of separation when all the pressures seemed to come together to make his mother not merely the central personality in his life but in a very real sense the unique focus of his existence.

Now Edith Wallis was seriously ill. The asthma to which she had been subject for many years had reached the state where constant nursing was necessary—an additional harsh burden upon a family budget which had never stretched far enough. Even a medical family could not find good nurses if it could not afford good wages. The comings and more particularly the goings of nurses added another gloomy note to the regular correspondence that passed between mother and son. Barnes could not hide from himself increasing consciousness of his mother's loneliness. He was miserably aware that her illness was desperate and that financial difficulties were becoming ever more intense. She left him in no doubt about her conviction that he was the true centre of her existence. She suspected all other women of designs upon her son; he, on his side, demonstrated more than ordinary dutifulness.

Barnes wrote that he was learning to dance. Edith replied: 'Be careful about the dancing! So afraid of this mixed company.'

His brother, John, married the local vicar's daughter and Edith wrote to Barnes:

> John calls the Vicar and Mrs Statham 'Dad' and 'Mum'—I feel I have lost something, dearest Barnes, before I have gained it . . . He is now beyond my influence altogether,—he belongs to someone else, so I turn more than ever to you, dear son, and much as I desire your happiness, I do hope that it will not just take the form of an engagement.[3]

She dreamt about Barnes and wrote to him of her dreams; prayed for him and told him of her prayers. This obsessive concern could have caused resentment. Instead it aroused a response that was to continue long after his mother's death and even into old age. For the moment it brought about a renewal of his determination to make practical provision for his mother in return for her care for him. Many, indeed most, young men would regard constant overseeing by a demanding mother as an obstacle to social and even to professional progress. Barnes welcomed each step that he made in his career as a step nearer to the day when he could set up house for all the family—by which, it seems, he really meant his mother. When in a letter he told his mother of this ambition she replied in a sentence that can be interpreted in more than one way:

> You dear blessed thing, planning for 'our all living together'— But it would be such heavenly bliss to me, that I refuse absolutely to think of it,—the disappointment if you went abroad,— would be so awful.

Any closely-knit family that cannot match its pride with the weight of its purse knows something like the borrowings, lendings, givings and sellings that went on among the Wallises

towards the end of the first decade of the century. Fortunately
Uncle Theo was generous—especially to young Barnes. Uncle
Tacy would lend on occasion even if his wife resented his action.
Barnes received five shillings a week regularly from his mother
and sometimes an extra shilling. Mrs Wallis sold a silver tea-pot,
some rings and two antique plaques in order to pay some bills
and the nurse's wages. Barnes sold his bicycle—and then the
beloved lathe which he had bought with the Willcox Prize money
—the lathe which had stood for so long at the foot of his bed—
so that his mother and father could have a holiday; and received
a letter that, in its detailed accounting, reveals all the desperate
impossibility of the situation:

... Father and I (as John has nothing in prospect, and may be
home in the Autumn) feel we really ought *not* to spend to go
away,—not even your loving present, which is really needed to
help in the necessities. Father is getting no bills paid to him,—
and we have exhausted our credit overdraft,—so that what we
are going on now, is his salary paid last June, and £20 Auntie
has advanced for the trap. I have to meet Father's insurance,
(£7.12s.), Charlie's school fees (£7), the servants' wages, and our
keep, and all incidental, small expenses,—as well as eventually
to pay the trap in Sept. but then I shall have £16.13s.4 from
Ben towards it that month. That is why we can use the £20
Auntie advanced. This says nothing about Father's drug bills.
Of course, if we could depend on the money coming in, that is
due to him, it would be different. For instance, Mr Adams owes
him £17, *three alone* make £28.10s.—but there it is, the money
does not come in to him and we must face the fact that we may
have John at home for some time. It is a year now since he took
his degree (July 29th) and during that time till now he has been
principally not merely at home but, poor darling, quite dependent on us for pocket money, minor clothes (such as shirts,
collars, repairs etc.—I paid 30/- for this the 1st week in June
even and he may be again). Not for anything would I have him
think we grudged it, *because we don't*, nor should I even talk
to him as I am doing to you, but I think I owe it to you, to tell
you freely else you might think I ought to use your gift otherwise. Annie's travelling to the Sch. of Art come to 2/6 a week,
and I have just had to pay £3 fees for her, (last week) and last

week to £4.4s. for rates. So much did I hate giving poor dear John money, for *his* sake, that I used,—but you must not breathe a word, please,—I used to hide a little here, and there, in his things—just a little now and again beside what we gave him regularly, and as he never said a word to me, I firmly believe he thought what I meant him to think, that he had overlooked it. Well, I shall have tired you . . .[4]

The deterioration in his mother's health was regular but at each stage so slight as to be scarcely perceptible. Her family had lived with her illness for so long that it came to be part of the inescapable background to their lives, so that they almost convinced themselves that it had no term. Then, on 29 August 1911, the never-ending came to an end, the inevitable happened that all had refused to foresee. At 1.45 in the morning, with no more immediate warning than a decade of illness, Edith Wallis died. She was fifty-two years old. Her husband was by her side—but no other member of the family. Barnes was in Cowes.

When, next day, the news reached him it was as if he himself had been condemned to a lifetime of solitary confinement. Disasters he had already known and many more were to come his way. Adversity he was accustomed to and would never escape entirely. He was to achieve happiness in marraige and to experience public bitterness. He was to enjoy fame and to suffer rejection. He would come to be a spectator to the death of friends and colleagues, to be forced to stand by while young men destroyed themselves in pursuit of the fulfilment of his ideas. And he was never to achieve the dispassion which tradition (but not, perhaps, reality) demands of the scientist, never to develop an armour against tragedy. Yet as nothing in all his life (except, perhaps, his marriage) contented him quite so profoundly as his relationship with his mother, so was there nothing, either before or after the event, that affected him so deeply and permanently as her death.

He had just bought a sailing-dinghy but had not yet given it a name. It remained nameless for all the years he owned it because in his own words 'it is customary to call a boat by a girl's name, any other girl's name but Edith would be unthinkable' and he could not bring himself to rub at his sadness by giving the boat the only name that the boat could have.

45

Barnes Wallis

His affection for his brother John had been much strained because he accepted without many reservations his mother's view that John had deserted her when he married; his sister he had seldom regarded with more than dutiful filial care; he was fond of his younger brother but Charles was too much his junior to become his confidant. There remained within the immediate family only his father, himself desperately lonely, bewildered by the loss of his wife, shy even with his son, and, because of his own sickness, never notably competent in the conduct of worldly affairs. In time Barnes transferred his duty to his father, but the immediacy of sympathy was never there on either side of the relationship.

Outside the family Wallis had few close friends. It is not uncommon that young men, struck for the first time by tragedy, turn for comfort to young women. Whilst his mother was alive he had felt her defending eye always upon him; now that she was dead her presence seemed even more real than it had been in her lifetime. He would have seen himself a traitor had he placed any other woman on the pedestal he had for so long preserved for his mother. Indeed, for the rest of his life he was apt to judge all women by the standard of his mother as he remembered her. Other women must have her charm, her intelligence, her capacity for devotion, her notable courage—and her small feet—or else be found insufficient.

It may be impertinent to conjecture about the true consequence of his mother's death. But facts are inescapable: hitherto he had not shown himself a young man far out of the ordinary; within two years he was to start upon a heterodox and mercurial career. Before 1911 Barnes Wallis was little different from a thousand other conventional, impoverished and rather earnest young men from good homes and good schools. The one touch that is unusual is the intensity and exclusive nature of the relationship with his mother. Certainly there is as yet no demonstration of genius nor foretaste of a career that is to slip the bonds of customary progress. He began to work for an engineering quali-fication, the A.M.I.C.E. He ended his apprenticeship, was duly appointed to the firm's ocean-going trials staff and began to run trials on 40 knot destroyers. Extend the graph of professional progress in the direction that is indicated when Wallis was twenty-four years old and one places him ten years later as a senior in the drawing-office and twenty years later as a manager. At fifty or thereabouts he joins the board of a middle-sized engineering firm and at sixty-five he retires with a decent pension, a large bungalow, and a small sailing-boat. For such men there are no biographies.

But after the death of his mother the placid direction of this line of progress was broken and it went soaring upwards towards unique achievement. The violent change came so soon as to force speculation that here, in part at least, was cause and effect. He had not fulfilled his ambition to support his mother, and his failure made him all the more determined to prove to himself that had she but lived he would have done for her what he had set himself to do. Now his father needed his help and he knew that his mother would have wished him to do for her husband what he could no longer do for her. By tragedy his ambition was strengthened.

White's had taken enthusiastically to the Diesel engine. Wallis wrote to his superior suggesting that he be trained as one of their specialists on Diesels. Many years later he was to remember this letter as much more than it really was and to describe it in terms that would seem to indicate that already in 1912 he saw and was attempting to follow his own star. The letter itself is far more modest and by no means prescient. It refers to his good time-keeping record, to his knowledge of French and German and to his earlier experience of engine erecting and driving gained with Thames Engineering. Above all it emphasises his willingness to work hard:

> I should be willing, while learning the running of our engines, to work in the shops at the usual men's hours—i.e. start at 6 a.m.—and to work at the test bench as a fitter; if necessary and after training would enter into agreement to remain with the firm for any period you might consider necessary.[5]

The job was his at thirty-five shillings a week but fortunately without a contractual term.

This promotion gave him more immediate association with ships than ever before. Now, on frequent occasions, he left the drawing-shop to sail on trial-runs and, despite the gloom that was on him because of his mother's death, he could not resist

47

pleasure whenever he was at sea. Ships were his true consolation, even, one can say, his true love. Later in life he was to claim that, however successful his career as an aircraft-designer, he never lost a sense of regret at leaving ships. One of the most moving and certainly the most sensitive passages in his note-books, written when he was in the midst of the exhilarations and frustrations of the Wild Goose tests—the first practical demonstrations of his variable geometry theory—goes back in memory even beyond the days at Cowes to his first contact with ships in his apprenticeship. He writes how, one evening in 1950, he was wandering around the Vickers-Armstrong Establishment at Thurleigh. It was, for him, a comparatively idle excursion and he looked at the machinery he had devised in a rarely detached manner. He watched the three electronics specialists at work correcting some faulty gear. Then the sight of stokers at work on the coke stoves–a simple chore when compared with all the superlative technology around them—suddenly jerked at his mind and took him back over the years to

a lonely slipway on Thames-side holding the half-wrought hull of a destroyer. Night-time, and the occasional flicker of a light as some riveter's mate blows the bellows of his little forge; the clouds scudding across the moon, and the lap of the water as the tide come in; and the spirit of the ship speaks to my spirit.

He never felt this same romantic awe for aeroplanes or even for airships that had once been his when he worked with ships, but built upon his earliest experiences as an apprentice engineer was a dramatic structure of emotional commitment to 'these things, my children, my babies, the only things that *I* can do', so that he could write in 1950 what he felt but could not yet describe in 1904:

I am intensely sensitive to the atmosphere that all these things combine to create; things of beauty, things of power, things that seem able to conjure up in my spirit the very spirit of romance until I seem faint with the wonder of it all.

But memory, like experience, could not stay for long in this euphoric condition; the brutality of the world was inescapable,

Edith Ashby Wallis,
mother of Barnes Wallis

Dr Charles Wallis, father of Barnes Wallis

Professor Henry Armstrong F.R.S.

'Uncle Chas.' E. Browne, Senior Science
Master at Christ's Hospital

Barnes Wallis in Christ's
Hospital uniform, aged 13

Wallis at Mrs Bloomfield's, Cowes, Isle
Wight, 1908, aged 21

Sub-Lieutenant B. N. Wallis,
1915, aged 27

Molly Bloxam Wallis, 1925, aged 22

and into his recollection of that moment of high delight by the Thames there entered the inescapable memory of its miserable conclusion. When at Thurleigh he found himself reliving the happenings on Thames-side, age had not made him more worldly. And into his somewhat naïve revulsion others may build a parable that can stand for so many creators and, at the same time, for much of Wallis's life: beauty, simplicity and genius cannot resist the unconcern and harshness of the ordinary. The spirit of the ship spoke to his spirit:

until the cold grim dawn begins to break and the thrill of it all is shattered and one boy's spirit is made sick as a party of water-side ghouls go down the slippery slopes to their boat to look for the body of a woman who has been drowned; with foul words and filthy jests that thank God I do not half understand.[6]

At Cowes, in these last days with ships, delight was frequent and the 'cold grim dawn' never came. But these were his last days with ships.

5 Mr Mountain's

The preface to Wallis's entry into airship designing goes back to 1884, three years before he was born, to the moment when two French Army officers built a non-rigid airship, *La France*. In it they equalled the speed of a fast-running man and achieved a height of 1,000 feet; above all, they had achieved powered flight.

Fourteen years later, Count von Zeppelin formed a company to construct rigid airships at Friedrichshafen on the German side of Lake Constance. Zeppelin's first successful ship flew on 2 July 1900 at just about the time that Wallis entered Christ's Hospital; his third stayed in the air for eight hours and in one flight covered 211 miles; his fourth crossed the Alps to Lucerne and flew back again to Friedrichshafen.

Britain made a short, abortive and not untypical début in the early history of airship construction. In 1902, Colonel J. L. B. Templer, after a quarter of a century as the Army's first and only 'Instructor to the Corps of Royal Engineers in the art of ballooning', persuaded the War Office to sponsor the building of a non-rigid. He had made from gold-beater's skin two 50,000 cubic feet envelopes, then ran out of money and the Government's blessing.

In 1905 the firm owned by E. T. Willows of Cardiff began building a series of small non-rigids notable for the introduction of swivelling propellers as a control system. Two years later, Colonel J. E. Capper (like Templer one of those pioneers who survive and rise above the pressures of service orthodoxy) revived Templer's scheme, took over his envelopes, brought in the American, Cody, as a collaborator, and created a semi-rigid, *Nulli Secundus I*. Three hundred feet long and twenty-nine feet in diameter she was driven by a 50 horse-power Antoinette engine at 16 miles per hour. Her first flight, on 5 October 1907, took her from Farnborough to London, a distance of thirty-two miles. She circled St Paul's Cathedral, hovered over Buckingham Palace, and making no impression against headwinds came down on the Crystal Palace cycle-track; she had been airborne for three and a half hours. Rebuilt, as *Nulli Secundus II*, she added only thirty-eight minutes to her log before she was scrapped.

The stumbling adventures at home were scarcely noticed by those in authority. British statesmen did their best to avoid accepting hard facts, and the Tory Administration in company with most diplomatic commentators persisted in ignoring the threat represented by Count von Zeppelin.

Now there was in Britain a new monarch whose antipathy to his German Imperial nephew was almost as obvious as his delight in all things French; and in France an anglophil Foreign Minister, Delcassé, who, rare among his country's statesmen, held office for seven years. France and Britain came closer together than they had ever been since the days when they had been one nation. As relations improved between France and Britain so did it become possible for Britain to think of allowing the Royal Navy some respite from the strains of world-wide vigilance for this role could now be shared with the French Navy. But as relations improved between France and Britain so did relations deteriorate between Britain and Germany. British and international efforts to limit naval armaments by conference had all failed. Even with the relieving support of the French, the Royal Navy—and therefore Britain—faced disaster if it could not keep up with the power of the Kaiser.

In 1907 the publication of Bülow's vast expansion programme made it imperative that Britain too must enlarge her navy. There were a few—a very few—in high places and a few more close enough to the heights to practise persuasion upon their superiors who realised that expansion no longer meant just more destroyers, more cruisers and more battleships. Two dimensions had been added to the exercise of sea-power: under-the-water and in the skies. Germany was ahead in both these new elements, and it is not without interest or significance that among those in Britain who nagged for advances to counter German pioneering there were several who were missionaries alike for submarines and for aircraft. But, the enthusiasts who battered at the heavy doors of

Whitehall demanding that Britain make some effort to provide her Armed Forces with eyes in the sky were divided among themselves as to whether the future lay with aeroplanes or with airships.

There is a second theme in the preface to Wallis's entry into airship designing. The Admiralty and the War Office planned, politicians proclaimed and connived, but somewhere active in the scenario of almost every British military development in the last decade of the nineteenth century and the first of the twentieth there was another power: Messrs Vickers.

The rise of this long-established Sheffield steel firm to substantial national and international influence was comparatively recent and had been comparatively sudden. Much of it was based upon the business daring of Albert Vickers, one of the family that at the turn of the century still controlled the firm's policies. It was Albert Vickers, with his brother Tom as technical adviser, who began that complex of overlapping direction, mutual shareholdings, interlocking licences and sales agreements that made Vickers' directors as influential as Foreign Ministers and better connected than kings. There was in the world scarcely a major producer of weapons with which Vickers did not have some more or less intimate business connection. By the turn of the century almost all British naval fire-power, except that provided by small arms, depended upon Vickers manufacture or Vickers licence. When in 1901 the firm completed H.M.S. *Vengeance, The Times* reported that 'it was the only ship in the British Navy which had been built, engined, armoured and supplied with heavy gun mountings by one firm'.

So it was that when Fisher pressed upon the Committee of Imperial Defence the need to enter at last into the airship race—in which, thanks especially to Count Zeppelin, the Germans were already laps ahead—it was to Vickers at Barrow that they turned for design and construction of the prototype rigid. Naval Estimates for 1909 included a sum of £35,000 for His Majesty's Airship *Number 1* (which came to be known disparagingly as 'Mayfly').

The Admiralty, Vickers and indeed all Britain were entirely lacking in airship theory and no one was available with any knowledge of airship construction. Those who were given the task indulged in hasty exercises in amateur espionage at Lake Constance; they dredged theory and practice from their recent and comparatively untested experience in building submarines; for the rest they worked pragmatically, and in such terms their courage was considerable and their achievement by no means despicable. 'Mayfly' was 510 feet long, 48 feet in diameter with a capacity of 600,000 cubic feet. As was only proper in a naval vessel, she was constructed over water. Her two engines were 200 horse-power Wolseleys. Such was British inexperience in airship-matters, that many of the parts for this, the British ship which was to challenge German hegemony in the air, were perforce made in Germany.

Nevertheless, there were many novel features in 'Mayfly'. And it is some compensation for national pride that 'Mayfly' was the first airship to be built basically from the new material, duralumin, for try though they did, the Germans never became proficient in the use of this light alloy.

However, 'Mayfly' never flew. Moored to her mast she could withstand winds of up to 45 m.p.h., no inconsiderable performance, but she was too heavy to lift. After being considerably modified she was eased from her shed and promptly broke her back. Two years of effort had ended in fiasco. The President of the Court of Inquiry, Rear-Admiral Sturdee (later the victor of the Battle of the Falkland Islands) called 'Mayfly' 'the work of an idiot'. His view was substantially held in Whitehall and the naval rigid-airship programme was virtually abandoned.

One junior draughtsman at Barrow came out of the disaster with some reputation. H. B. Pratt was not even part of the 'Mayfly' team but he had watched carefully and had attempted to transpose what he saw of the design-process into theoretical calculations. He announced to all who would listen, first that 'Mayfly' was too heavy for her lifting power and secondly, that, even if this incapacity could be set right, she would break her back at the first squall of wind. So it had happened, but Pratt's perspicacity did not endear him to his superiors. In 1912, with the threat of war and the promise of war-production upon them once more, Vickers turned to all their submarine-technologists for a five-year personal commitment. Pratt refused and was released without regret and without any reference to his demonstration of wisdom and theoretical ability in the new field of airship design.

Out of work, he answered the first advertisement he saw and

was accepted as a draughtsman by the firm of John Samuel White. At Cowes at the next drawing-board to H. B. Pratt was B. N. Wallis.

The two young men became close friends, in part because both were ambitious and vocal about their ambitions but more particularly because both were keep-fit enthusiasts. Without benefit of club or competition on two or three evenings a week together they would set off by train to destinations in the remoter parts of the Isle of Wight and return to Cowes running across country. On the way out and on occasional week-end trips in Wallis's still unnamed sailing-dinghy the talk was of ships, engines and, frequently, of airships.

Early in 1913 the German Government placed an order for ten new Zeppelins. The news startled the British Board of Admiralty and the Board's lone airship enthusiast, Admiral Jellicoe, was able to press upon his opponents the need for a public demonstration of active competition. Winston Churchill, the First Lord, though he would not shift from his general antipathy to lighter-than-air craft, saw that it was politically expedient to do something and placed an order for one rigid for the Royal Navy. Inevitably, but as usual reluctantly, the Admiralty turned to Vickers: underwater, on the water and on the land Britain prepared for war with the aid of Vickers and, ever-watchful, the board of Vickers looked up at the new element of warfare and spent time and money on pioneer work in non-rigids and fighter aeroplanes. But there was not available within the firm nor indeed within the whole country a sufficiency of men qualified to design and supervise the construction of such new-fangled machines as submarines, aeroplanes and rigid airships. If he was to fulfil his orders Sir Trevor Dawson, the Managing Director, must use beyond his conventional seniority every man who had shown competence or expert knowledge; overnight his subalterns must be promoted to be generals. Dawson remembered the young man who had understood so well the technical propensities of airships that he had forecast the disaster to Vickers' first essay into the construction of rigids. He was horrified to discover that Pratt had been permitted to leave Vickers; those who had committed this solecism were ordered to correct it; Pratt was discovered, and summoned back to Vickers as Chief Draughtsman—Airships. It was a magnificent opportunity for a man still in his twenties.

As Wallis bade good-bye to Pratt an impulse as much personal as professional forced him to ask Pratt to keep him in mind for a job on rigids. The impulse brought practical results more speedily than Wallis could have dreamed possible. On 1 August at 5.30 in the morning as he was leaving his lodgings to go for a long day's sailing he met the postman carrying a letter from Pratt.[1] There was a job waiting for Wallis as Chief Assistant on the designing of the 'Zeppelin larger than any yet made'. The Admiralty, said Pratt, had also ordered from Vickers three non-rigids and had promised orders for a large number of 'Zeppelins as soon as we produce the goods'. Pratt made it clear that he had a free hand to appoint his own staff, and promised Wallis 'a good salary and prospects'. Immediately, Wallis telegraphed inviting Pratt to share a week-end's sailing. Pratt came the next week-end and out in the Solent the two young men settled Wallis's future and the future of Vickers Airship Department. Wallis confessed that he scarce knew a rigid's stem from her stern and Pratt promised to pass on all his own knowledge. Would they be free of busybodies in Whitehall and at Barrow? Pratt reassured him. Dawson had made the contract conditional upon non-interference from Whitehall and, even better, he had given to Pratt an undertaking that he need be responsible only to the Managing Director. If Barrow so much as raised its head Pratt could use the bark and bite of the great Sir Trevor himself.

Pratt went back to London and within a week all was settled in a brief, formal and entirely inauspicious letter from Vickers House:

> As arranged with you verbally by our representative, we shall be glad if you will start your duties in our Airship Drawing Office on September 1 next at a salary of £3.5s.0d. per week.[2]

Wallis gave a week's notice to White's, packed up his few belongings and moved back to New Cross. On 1 September 1913 he began a frantic but happy existence. Each morning including Saturday he was up at six o'clock and at work soon after seven. A sandwich at the desk for lunch and then work again until eight at night. On Sundays he took Communion and then left for London, but on Sundays work ended at four o'clock and then

Pratt and Wallis treated themselves to high tea and the string orchestra at Lyons' new Corner House.

This was the heyday of William le Queux. German spies were suspected behind every lamp-post, and consequently that part of Britain's airship-programme for which Vickers was responsible was cobwebbed with security arrangements. Two tiny offices close to the Vickers building in Victoria Street were rented in the name of Mountain and their windows veiled with green blinds so that no spy might glimpse what was going on. Wallis could not accustom himself to the demands of secrecy, and when left in charge of the office he would greet any caller who asked for Mr Mountain with an unhesitating denial which had to be corrected in embarrassment after a noticeable pause for thought.

But there was as yet little that the Germans could learn from Pratt or Wallis and much that the Pratt team could gather from their country's seemingly inevitable enemy. Happily for them, some information on Zeppelin design came their way during the winter of 1913 by courtesy of the French. In April of that year the German Army's latest airship had made a forced-landing on a French Army parade-ground, whilst still on her trials with the Zeppelin Company. Her crew was courteously and lavishly entertained and, as the champagne was passed and the toasts were exchanged, the French rushed in their few airship experts and with them photographers, artists and even the Assistant Naval and Military Attachés from the British Embassy in Paris. The dossier of *LZ.216* reached Victoria Street in November.

Much information came more openly. Indeed, Winston Churchill had ordered non-rigids from the Parseval Company in Berlin and, right up to the outbreak of war in August 1914, such advances in construction as were transferable from non-rigids to rigids were freely passed to Pratt by his German Parseval colleagues. In the first week of May 1914, for example, Pratt was in Germany with Commander E. A. D. Masterman and Colonel E. M. Maitland (the holder of the world record for ballooning, a man who had ascended to 18,000 feet and survived a parachute descent from 2,000 feet), to discuss various technical problems with Parseval officials in Berlin and to examine, in some detail and with the entire co-operation of the Germans, the newly-built car of the latest Parseval. This was three months before the outbreak of the First World War!

Meanwhile, the group at Mr Mountain's was expanding and Wallis was finding it by no means easy to maintain unchallenged his dignity as second-in-command. Already he knew that he was the best designer in the team—better even than Pratt—but of the seven men working under him one was a graduate, one a Whitworth Scholar, and all the rest came from engineering colleges.

You can imagine the type of man who knows everything that is to be known about musical theory and simply thinks in counterpoint and harmony and so on, and yet cannot compose a line that is not branded with the stiffness and want of inspiration of any amateur.[3]

Nevertheless, he envied them because 'most of them are fearful bloods at mathematics'. At school, he had learnt trigonometry; now in 1913 and 1914, he tried to learn calculus. He bought Sylvanus Thompson's book and studied it on the train journeys to and from New Cross. The motto on the title-page delighted him: 'What one fool can do, another can.'

The conversation at Victoria Street was all of struts and spans, of cabins and motors. Airships had become a mania with these young men. Fortunately, they did not know that in the exercise of this enthusiasm they were almost alone. The Army, having decided to back aeroplanes, had shuffled off the airship arm onto the Navy and at the Admiralty Winston Churchill was more concerned with political bravura than with the realities of the airship programme. Early in 1914 Churchill assured the House of Commons that by the end of that year there would be fifteen airships in service.[4] Only three of the vaunted list were rigids— a fact that he did not mention—and of these three, two were never more than drawings and the third, the *No.9*, the Pratt–Wallis ship, was not operational until 1917. At the outbreak of the war Britain had five tiny blimps and two foreign-built non-rigids—a Parseval from Germany flying as *H.M.A.4* and an Astra-Torres from France. Given Churchill's often expressed view that airships were too vulnerable and too clumsy to be decisive and given the utter blindness to the advantages of airships as a reconnaissance arm shown by most senior naval officers, it was unlikely that the work in Victoria Street would receive much encouragement.

Although this was not as yet obvious to Pratt's team, what was at once obvious and sinister was the jealousy of Barrow. Despite all Dawson's promises everything that was done in Victoria Street was altered or questioned at Barrow.

> Their object [wrote Wallis] is entirely a political one (in the little Vickers world) for they bitterly resent the design work being done in London, so they do their best to prove that the system is unworkable.[5]

The division of responsibility between designing and building was impracticable, but when Pratt complained to Sir Trevor Dawson he 'only smiled and said that if we gave them enough rope they would hang themselves in time'. Wallis, commenting upon this in 1914, added a note of exasperation which was to recur over and over again in his conversation and correspondence: 'it's a most extraordinary firm'.[6]

But for Wallis, as for the five hundred thousand young men who volunteered in the first four weeks, the declaration of war on 4 August 1914 solved all problems. He rushed off to the nearest recruiting office, boasted his experience on destroyer trials and was mustered into the Royal Navy as an Engine Room Artificer.

Pride in his new status was short-lived. When he returned with the King's shilling to Victoria Street Pratt was quite properly incensed. He stormed at Wallis and then went to see Sir Trevor Dawson. Immediately, a message passed from Dawson to the Marquis of Milford Haven and within twenty-four hours Wallis was out of the Navy, his only achievement: probably the shortest naval career in history.

This was ignominy—and worse. There was then as always in Wallis a sturdy, straightforward patriotism which, coupled with his shy eagerness for the company of men less complicated than himself, in 1914 as sometimes before and often later, made life in the Forces especially attractive to him. Now he felt as if he had been denied his native right to be with his contemporaries who were about to fulfil their responsibility to their country. Pratt understood something of all this for, although he took seriously his responsibilities to the airship programme, he too was subject to the great wave of sentiment that swept through the youth of England in that August of 1914 and he too was attempting to silence the voice of conscience that kept insisting that designing airships was no job for a man whose country was at war. At first he revealed nothing of his sympathy to Wallis; instead he took refuge in the age-old panacea of employers: he gave Wallis a week's holiday.

Wallis had come to believe that his father depended considerably upon his company. He would not go away for the vacation unless he had made suitable arrangements for Dr Wallis. Hastily Barnes assessed the possibilities: it was essential that they should find somewhere which could be reached by an excursion train. He decided for Weymouth.

Once arrived, immediately it became apparent to Wallis that, in his mood of frustrated military enthusiasm, the decision had been disastrous. He had expected a quiet watering-place. Instead he found 'a mixture of naval port and garrison town'. The journey to Weymouth had exhausted Charles Wallis, and whilst he was resting Barnes went out in search of sun and 'some peace of mind'. He climbed up from the shore to a ledge half-way up the cliff.

> Some territorials coming along the top must have spotted me, evidently a coward and a shirker, and amused themselves and showed their patriotism by heaving a few clods of earth over the edge at me. None hit me and perhaps were not meant to; no doubt the intention was just to give a reminder that my fellow countrymen etc. etc. à la white feather brigade. It was impossible to come up with them, and even if they had obligingly waited while I climbed the cliff I could never have identified who of the party threw, and should have looked a bigger fool than ever, speechless and out of breath. So I stopped where I was and slunk back to the town later on. I never stirred out during the whole afternoon and it had been a beautifully sunny day, but I felt I would rather stew in a musty sitting-room than face a repetition of such an incident.[7]

Wallis was not serving as he would have wished to serve, nor could he explain himself to those who were. His holiday was ruined. He would have gone straight back to London had he not felt that in London, even at Victoria Street, there was nothing for him that could compensate for the frustration of his patriotism, and had he not known that he was committed to give his father a rest—'tied by the leg . . . I must not leave him so there is the end . . .'

At the end of the week Wallis went back to London, to Mr Mountain's, and threw himself into his work even more energetically than before, but still he could not believe in the integrity of what he was doing and still he envied the men who were even then preparing to follow the B.E.F. to France or patrolling the narrow seas. However his new excess of energy seemed to spur his skill, and it was in these months that Pratt realised for the first time that in Wallis he had an assistant who as designer and man of ideas had already outstripped him. With entire generosity he admitted the fact to Wallis and with entire sense from now on left much of the creative work to his junior whilst more and more he himself took on the role of organiser, entrepreneur and liaison officer with Barrow and with the high officialdom of Vickers.

The planning of $N.9$ stumbled forward, bedevilled by lack of enthusiasm at the Admiralty and by lack of cohesion in Vickers. Still Pratt had the ear of Sir Trevor Dawson, but the rest of the Vickers hierarchy was coming to resent not only Pratt but all his team, and not least his Chief Assistant who was developing a reputation for single-mindedness and lack of that respect which those above him thought their due.

At Barrow and along the road from Mr Mountain's at the Vickers headquarters in Victoria Street they knew, too, that there were more certain profits in shipbuilding and gunmaking than could ever come from airships and, unlike the designers, were aware how little chance there was that $N.9$ would ever be completed. The First Lord, Winston Churchill, continued to be strangely blind to the possibilities of airships. Before the war he had urged his objections on the grounds of economy. Now— and with a little more perspicacity—he favoured aeroplanes. Admiral Sir John Jellicoe had succumbed to Churchill's persuasiveness, and now that he was in command of the Grand Fleet he dedicated himself to a defensive strategy without ever appreciating the potentiality of airships as eyes of a navy which from bases at Scapa Flow, Harwich and Dover was guarding Britain's waters. The admirals imagined themselves—and the British public saw them—as fit successors to Nelson's Band of Brothers, but they were emotionally incapable of accepting innovation. Submarines they had been forced to tolerate, but the addition of a third dimension, the air, to the intellectualism of naval strategy was quite beyond their capacity. Most of them shared the low opinion of the airship arm so often expressed by one of their number, Sir Doveton Sturdee. The sole courageous innovator high in the Royal Navy, Admiral of the Fleet Sir John Fisher, had lost much of his authority in the four years immediately before the war when he was away from the Admiralty and his 'fishpond' of young, energetic and technological enthusiasts discredited. At one time Fisher had been Churchill's naval tutor. When, in 1914, Fisher came back as First Sea Lord his former pupil was relishing the adventure of being First Lord of the Admiralty. The combination which should have been so successful and so original failed to work. Churchill had his own ideas; one of them was entire opposition to airships.

Still high above Pratt and Wallis but of profound significance to their future careers there was yet another quarrel in progress. The Board of Admiralty had long resented its dependence upon Messrs Vickers for so many items of naval armaments. Most recently and most important for those working on *No.9*, the Admiralty, its senior officials and senior officers had found Sir Trevor Dawson's dealings with the Parseval Company distasteful; and his insistence on a virtual monopoly in airship construction, though in business terms comprehensible to an office-boy, was to them yet another example of Vickers' high-handedness. With the country at war the Admiralty saw its opportunity of re-instating itself as superior to a mere armaments firm and renewed over *No.9* the campaign of complaint, change-of-mind and uninformed supervision which had ruined the Mayfly project. Wallis had gathered to himself in all innocence a bevy of enemies who as yet did not so much as know his name but who, even if they were agreed on little else, were of one opinion about men who dedicated themselves to airships. He was marked down for distaste by the Civil Service, by Winston Churchill and by the senior officials of his own firm.

In December 1914 a Minute started its rounds of the Admiralty recommending the abandonment of *No. 9*. It did not reach Fisher, the First Sea Lord, who was already quarrelling with his political overlord over the merits of their different conceptions of grand strategy. In February 1915 at the very moment when the Fourth Sea Lord was writing on the Minute 'I am not in favour of spending more money on airships', the First Sea Lord was in all ignorance ordering more non-rigids. The Minute was also kept away from the Fifth Sea Lord although ostensibly he was the admiral responsible for all naval matters. On 13 March 1915 the matter was closed; the First Lord of the Admiralty added to the Fourth Sea Lord's note: 'Nor I—W.S.C.'

The immediate effect upon Pratt and his team was unemployment. For his part, Wallis was back where he had been seven months earlier and this time not only was he free to join the Services but now he knew that Pratt would not interfere. Indeed Pratt was even quicker to the recruiting station than Wallis: he joined the Artists Rifles on 14 March 1915.

Wallis was more ambitious. On 17 March, from his brother John's home at West Horsham he wrote to the War Office outlining his qualifications. Three days later, which says much for the expedition of the War Office but little for its perspicacity, he received a duplicate reply informing him that 'no vacancy exists for a temporary commission in the Royal Engineers to which with your qualifications you could be appointed.'

Dejected but still determined Wallis returned to London and took his place in the queue outside the first recruiting office he came to; he was in the mood to join any unit in any capacity so long as it would get him away and into the war. At these anonymous recruiting centres early in 1915 the investigation and inspection of recruits was by no means rigorous. Even so Wallis was summarily rejected by the Army Medical Corps sergeant responsible for testing eyes. He was too short-sighted to be killed behind a rifle. This new blow to his pride and set-back to his ambition knocked into him both sense and cunning. Pratt was in the Artists Rifles, an officer-producing unit. With his professional-family and public-school background there was little doubt that Wallis too would be accepted by the Artists provided he could hide his myopia. He made his application, was accepted provisionally and when he came to the medical tests was passed as a perfect specimen, sound of limb, mind—and eye. In the bustling medical centre where twenty or more men at a time were undressing, undergoing tests and dressing again, Wallis had stripped in a position as close as he could come to the sight-testing card and had learnt by rote the letters that would pass him into the Army.

Wallis escaped the shock that in two wars so many men have

felt when they have been tumbled from the comforts and the individualism of civilian life into the herd-anonymity and rawness of army life. Indeed he seems to have retained throughout his short military career a euphoric approval of the Army. Admittedly the Artists was atypical. The regiment still held to a valid connection with its title, and there were among the recruits many with no small reputation in the creative arts (for example, the singer Harry Plunket Greene and Emile Cammaerts, the Belgian poet who had settled in England). There were also many, like Pratt and Wallis himself, who came close to the right to call themselves artists, and at this stage of the war almost all Artists were well-educated. There was undoubtedly a certain element of cocooning in a unit of this kind, and Wallis was then and was always to remain so much of his class and time and in this sense entirely the son of his parents—that he was convinced that a good education and gentility are synonymous. More still, he enjoyed in the Artists, as he had enjoyed at Christ's Hospital, the sense of being part of a formal entity and, as at Christ's Hospital and whenever the opportunity came his way throughout his life, the masculinity of the society delighted him. More subtly, he positively relished being under orders. The paradox, if paradox it be, is by no means uncommon; there is in life in the Army, and particularly in life in the ranks, a possibility of relaxation, or irresponsibility that many men who in their private lives are much given to questing and questioning find comfortable. The Army was to Barnes Wallis akin to what the Roman Catholic Church has been to so many creators: his escape from the pressure of decision.

The new Artists drilled in Russell Square; then those of them who were destined for commissions and overseas service—Wallis among them—were sent to a training centre at High Beach in Epping Forest.

By this time Wallis's professional experience had been recognised. He was promoted to the rank of Pioneer Corporal. The centre at High Beach was based upon an hotel and because the only existing drainage was a cess-pool the camp-site soon developed a most unpleasant and potentially dangerous saturation. There followed for Wallis an episode which varied, and turned almost inside out, the Army's oldest and still current joke.

He was summoned by the Adjutant.

' You're an engineer, corporal.'

'Yes, Sir.'

'Then go off and design a sanitary system.'

Wallis spent three days in the Reading Room of the British Museum and then designed and built with their aid a vast system suitable for a thousand men. Of all his engineering feats it remained among those of which he was most proud.

It is ironical that Wallis's pleasant life in the Artists was brought to an end because Winston Churchill lost his job. The formation of a Coalition Government was announced to the House of Commons on Wednesday 19 May 1915. Churchill had fought for his position 'as though the salvation of England depended on it'.[8] On 21 May he wrote to Bonar Law and demanded that he be judged 'justly, deliberately and with knowledge' and claimed, 'I do not ask for anything else.' He was asking to stay at the Admiralty; instead he was shuffled off to the Duchy of Lancaster and, because the Liberals had to pay the price of coalition with some senior offices, his place at the Admiralty went to the one-time Conservative Prime Minister, A. J. Balfour. Admiral Sir Henry Jackson became First Sea Lord in the place vacated by Fisher who was given as a sop, but a sop of some immediate importance to the airship programme, the Presidency of the Admiralty Board of Inventions.

The new administration looked with distaste upon the policies of its predecessor. On 19 June, three weeks after taking up office as First Lord (and two weeks after Flight Sub-Lieutenant R. A. J. Warneford, RN had become the first man to shoot down an airship, *LZ.37*), Balfour called a meeting to discuss a renewal of airship construction. T. R. Cave-Browne-Cave, in charge of non-rigids, was given orders to put through a programme of rapid expansion. As for rigids, there was only one that could be seen as a real possibility for service: *No.9*. Commander E. A. D. Masterman, an officer who had already some experience of airships, who had been Pratt's companion on those pre-war visits to Germany, was given responsibility at the Admiralty. But the materials that had once been intended for *No.9* were rotting in the yards at Barrow; the Vickers construction crew had gone back to more lucrative work on submarines and ship repairing; even the sheds at Walney Island had been handed over to the Royal

Naval Air Service for aeroplanes. The Chief Designer, H. B. Pratt, and his senior assistant, B. N. Wallis, had disappeared.

The Admiralty worked quickly; it persuaded the War Office to be rid of Corporals Pratt and Wallis; and translated them into Sub-Lieutenant B. N. Wallis RNVR, posted to the Royal Naval Air Service at Walney Island, and Sub-Lieutenant H. B. Pratt, posted to the Royal Naval Air Station at Kingsnorth in Kent, the headquarters of the Navy's activities with non-rigids. In theory Pratt was to control the new *No.9* programme under the general supervision of Masterman and also to act as liaison officer with Cave-Brown-Cave while Wallis supervised the actual construction at Barrow. In truth neither man achieved much except a feeling of frustration with the Admiralty, with the Royal Navy and with Vickers. At Kingsnorth Pratt found twenty-five RNAS officers killing time; at Barrow Willis had no executive power and, although there was ample cause, he was not as yet equipped to accept Pratt's advice to 'fight with Vickers people as much as possible over any alterations in design'. Instead he spent most of his days preparing a handbook for *No.9* and writing letters to Pratt.

To anyone who experienced military security in a later war the exchange of letters at this time between the two friends is amazing. Written in longhand on official notepaper they are a compound of technical detail, abuse of their superiors and attacks on government airship policy. Wallis in particular, but sometimes Pratt too, succumbed to depression. Twice, Wallis had to argue Pratt out of his intention of throwing in his hand and applying for a commission in the Army; and for a few days in September 1915 when it seemed to both of them (and, though they did not know it, to Masterman himself) that Masterman was not likely to break down the obstacles raised against *No.9* by both Admiralty and Vickers, they formed a mutual conspiracy to join the Balloon Section under Colonel Maitland at Roehampton.

> All the officers in that section are R.N.V.R. who take the balloon with their winches and a section of 30 men per balloon over to Flanders and to the Dardanelles and get a sufficiency of excitement . . .[9]

Again to anyone who served in a later war there is in these 1915 letters between two very junior officers a quite remarkable air of still being masters of their own fate. They jibbed at authority —in that there is nothing unusual—but what seems incredible is that they were also convinced that they could circumvent authority. The haste with which Masterman and Dawson acted to placate him when Pratt did eventually hold over his superiors— naval and civil—an offer he had received of a Gunner commission seems to demonstrate that their conviction of freedom was justi- fied. Less surprising is their mutually-held belief that in time of war only active service could satisfy their manhood. For so many of their contemporaries—even for those who survived the horrors of Flanders, Gallipoli or Mesopotamia—the aftermath of 'excite- ment', the consequence of the 'real stuff' which Pratt and Wallis craved, was disillusion and disgust. There seems little doubt that in the life of Wallis his escape—which certainly at the time and probably forever he regarded as a deprivation—had a profound effect on his emotional make-up. It could be said of him that he never moved from Rupert Brooke romanticism to Siegfried Sassoon scepticism, that his simple patriotism was never rocked. Somehow, too, he avoided that sense, so common in men who came through the First World War, of being a rare survivor from a lost generation. It was at Walney that he made most of the few friend- ships that were to last him a lifetime. Among their number were several who between the Wars and in the Second World War were to achieve great distinction in the Royal Air Force, among them Ralph Cochrane who was to make frequent and seminal appear- ances in Wallis's professional life-story, notably when as Chief of the Royal New Zealand Air Staff he backed the Wellington and later when as commanding officer of No. 5 (Bomber) Group he had overall charge of the raids on the Dams.

For the moment Wallis relished the companionship at Walney but it was hardly experience of war. With the brutal realities of what was going on in Europe he had very little contact.

Life at the Mess [he wrote long afterwards] was very comfort- able—almost a family affair. We had formed the habit of regu- larly gathering there as soon as the sun was over the yard-arm for a cherry brandy or an egg flip made with rum . . . Indeed as far as we were concerned, apart from the excitements and transient dangers inseparable from the trial flights of airships, there might as well have been no war.[10]

There was, however, one moment in the autumn of 1915 when Wallis nearly added his name to the list of war casualties. There were stationed at Walney Island a few small blimps, 30 m.p.h. *Betas* taken over from the Army in 1912. These were used to patrol the west coast of Scotland searching out U-Boats and enemy raiders. Wallis was heartily sick of inaction and preparing a handbook for an airship that he was convinced would never fly and so he accepted with enthusiasm an invitation to go out in a *Beta* commanded by George Scott. They ran into heavy sea-mist, groped their way down the coastline and staggered southwards through the night. By morning the mist had turned to fog. Scott took the ship up and Wallis saw a peak which he recognised from his rock-climbing excursions as the 2,000 foot Black Combe. Pointing the bow of the ship in what they felt to be the right direction they set off once more only to prove their navigation dangerously accurate. The ship was flying low again, too low, and there immediately below them were the spark-spitting chimneys of Barrow Steelworks. Scott pointed his ship downwards and westwards towards Walney Island and suddenly not a hundred feet below them was the entrance to the airship shed and, blazing brightly in front of it, a huge bonfire which had been built by the Station staff to guide home their missing ship! The *Beta* was a small ship—only 35,000 cubic feet—but even had she been one-tenth of the size and had her gas ignited there would have been no hope for her crew. Helplessly the captain hauled on the rudder; the blimp hit the top of a shed and shot upwards. An eternity of a few seconds later she came to a halt and those aboard felt her being hauled downwards. The impact with the shed had uncoiled one of her furled mooring-lines and a spectator on the ground had had the presence of mind to seize hold of it.

6 The First World War

By the autumn of 1915 Pratt had become the negotiator, the counsellor, the team-manager. Wallis at Barrow was the airshipman and, being closer to the ship that seemed not to progress, his were the greater frustrations. He was a Sub-Lieutenant RNVR with no hope of battle, a designer with no authority, a Vickers man who had never before worked at Barrow and who now that he did came dressed as a naval officer—to the palpable disgust of the other Vickers men. His frustrations were enlarged by the conflicting news that came with such rapidity and regularity from Pratt in the South. 'Sir Trevor Dawson has all arranged', then, a day later, 'Masterman is fed up and is going back to sea.' Another day, and Wallis learnt that they would have to work under officers of the Royal Corps of Naval Constructors who knew nothing of airship design. Four days later, on 29 September 1915, he heard that the Third Lord had 'definitely quashed the idea of construction by the Admiralty direct as it was considered that the work could be done more expeditiously by efficient manufacturers.'[1]

At the beginning of October the Third Lord's decision was ratified. Vickers were to be generally responsible for all rigids, and Pratt was to be 'head man' and answerable not to the Admiralty but immediately to the directors of the Company. Wallis was to be his second-in-command and Chief Draughtsman to the project. Vickers were particularly requested to put to Wallis that if he decided to accept this suggestion 'he cannot be permitted to retain his uniform'.[2]

Now, it would have seemed, all that remained was for Pratt and Wallis to resign their commissions, surrender the uniforms of which they were so proud and get back to work on *No.9*. But the Royal Corps of Naval Constructors made one more attempt to get a hand on the airship programme. It was suggested that, instead of going back to Vickers as ordinary employees, Pratt and Wallis should be transferred to the Corps and seconded to Vickers. Even the Third Lord could not easily resist this proposal but the Air Department was adamant. As Pratt wrote to Wallis on 22 October:

> The RNAS people would much prefer us to return to Vickers rather than take our knowledge and experience to the DNC to whom they bear no goodwill.[3]

To this letter Pratt added a postscript:

> I think that we have a good chance of coming off on top yet if we hold out long enough. Remember that the fact of your being kept loafing about is all part of the game—a sort of psychological pressure to get us in a state of such 'fed-up-ness' that we will take anything that offers. For any sake don't chuck up and join the Army or anything of the sort—you couldn't do better to suit the enemies' point of view.

The enemies, it is clear, were not the Germans but the conspirators at the Admiralty. To their number Pratt soon added his one-time colleagues in Vickers and a week after he had bidden Wallis not to give up he himself succumbed—if temporarily—to Vickers animosity and consequently once more decided to apply for a commission in the Royal Artillery. Certain junior directors and other Vickers personnel, he told Wallis, 'have formed a league of self defence . . . such as to make my position quite impossible . . . I would merely be nominal chief to satisfy and bluff Sir Trevor and the Admiralty.' Then, changing his tune, Pratt went on to beg of Wallis:

> Don't be down-hearted old chap we may get a chance yet. Our education in the diplomacy of business is proceeding at any rate. One does not need to go to the trenches for a fight.[4]

Fortunately for Pratt and Wallis there were men at the Admiralty, notably Craven and Masterman, who were disinclined to sacrifice to petty jealousy the only team in Britain that might conceivably put Britain back into the airship race. Fortunately, too, Sir Trevor Dawson was not easily bluffed. Pratt was encouraged to withdraw his application for a Gunner commission. The more junior of the recalcitrant from Barrow were summoned into the not unterrifying presence of Sir Trevor and informed that they could choose between losing their jobs and working under Pratt and with Wallis.

Victory won, but there were still details to be arranged. Should Pratt and Wallis revert entirely to their pre-war status as Vickers' employees? Or should they be allowed to remain as RNVR officers?

With Sir Trevor Dawson entirely behind him, the promise of a free hand in the selection of staff, and the comforting knowledge that Commander Craven, who had once been Dawson's assistant at Vickers, was to be given the role of Admiralty liaison officer with their project, Pratt recommended that both men resign from the service.

> As everything is now quite satisfactory I take it that you will come as chief draughtsman. I am going to ask £400 per annum for you . . . Armstrong and Beardsmore are to build to our designs so we shall practically run the entire Rigid Airship industry.[5]

The possibility was irresistible. On 28 November 1915 Sub-Lieutenant B. N. Wallis RNVR submitted his resignation to the Director of Air Services. Next day he was at work, still in Barrow but out of uniform.

Undoubtedly the malice and mischief that he and Pratt had experienced in the summer and autumn of 1915 seared deep into Wallis's mind. He could not understand how in a time of national crisis, men in positions of authority or creative possibility were ready to sacrifice the national interest for their own. Pratt had suggested that in this miserable process the two of them had learnt diplomacy. In truth what Wallis had learnt was contempt for what was to come to be called the Establishment, suspicion of those who had influence without the professional knowledge to use it sensibly, and lack of patience for those who put position before creation.

But the future now seemed certain. *No.9* was the pivot of the nation's rigid airship programme and *No.9* was their responsibility.

Soon they were also given charge of *No.23* which the Admiralty had ordered in October 1915 and which was also to be built by Vickers, and thus indirectly for the sister-ships *No.24* and *No.25* which were ordered at the same time to be built respectively by Beardmore's and Armstrong Whitworth's but to Vickers' designs. In January 1916 a fifth ship was commissioned from Vickers, *R.26* (the first with the *R* prefix).

At the outset they were deluded into thinking that their control was real, that everywhere their allies were in charge. The naval supervisor at Barrow, Commander F. L. M. Boothby, was intelligent and friendly, and, if the Royal Corps of Naval Constructors had managed to have posted to Barrow one of its own technical officers. He and the Corps' principal adviser on rigids, Constructor-Commander C. I. R. Campbell, had soon shown themselves capable of comprehending airship problems and of being as ruthless as Dawson and Masterman in their attacks upon 'the enemies'.

However, the chain of command was so complicated that administrative malfunction was inevitable. Each party to the processes of decision had the right to put forward his own ideas and modifications; all had to be considered and most used by the designers. Worse still the whole machinery of control was susceptible to pressure on its parts and the consequent instability was felt ultimately and most unhappily by those who were doing the real work: Pratt and Wallis. Each of the so-called co-ordinators had to guard his own future. Even Dawson was not entire in his support because for him the airship department was but a tiny part of the Vickers empire and Vickers were becoming increasingly involved with heavier-than-air machines and many of the younger men in the firm were urging upon Dawson that this way lay the future and this way lay the route by which Vickers could shake off the overweening power of Government departments. (Already in 1916 they were building—if in small numbers—five different aeroplanes. Early in 1916 the Government decided that Vickers at Weybridge should concentrate on the Farnborough-designed SE5a fighter scout. The first was delivered to the Royal Flying Corps in June 1917 and by the end of the war Vickers had built more than one thousand—a greater production than any other aeroplane factory.)

There was, too, implicit within the reconstruction of Vickers Airship Department the seed of conflict and disaster. J. E. Temple, for example, had been junior to Wallis in the 1914 Drawing Office but when Churchill halted the airship programme early in 1915 Temple had gone to the Admiralty as a Lieutenant RNVR. To persuade him to return to Vickers at the end of the year Pratt had offered him the title of Chief Calculator and had set him down in the hierarchy as directly responsible to Pratt himself and therefore the equal to Wallis as Chief Designer and to the Works Manager. Such calculations as were too intricate to be carried out in the Drawing Office were undertaken by Temple on Pratt's instructions and passed on to Wallis—as results —either by Pratt or more often, because of Pratt's frequent absences, by Temple himself. Yet at these very moments of Pratt's absence Wallis, in his other capacity as Assistant General Manager, became automatically Temple's senior and was therefore in the ambiguous position of receiving what amounted to instructions from his junior. Whenever Wallis sat in on a conference between Temple and Pratt he found Temple's explanations lucid and exhaustive, but when Pratt was away and Wallis asked for the same courtesy he was answered with a quick-fire lecture which was at once unintelligible and beyond exegesis. So, when he could, Wallis took to reworking for himself Temple's calculations— which hardly improved efficiency and undoubtedly damned personal relations.

At all levels there was bickering and conniving, thrusting and malice. Even the two air-services—the Royal Flying Corps and the Royal Naval Air Service—were in direct competition for essential aeronautical materials, notably engines, and there were within the RNAS itself two factions debating and sometimes conspiring against each other.

Such elation as was caused among the airshipmen by the Admiralty decision to increase the number of airships might have evaporated had they remembered that there were in the whole of Britain only two sheds—at Barrow and at Kingsnorth—capable of housing ships of the 23 and 23X class and one more—also at Kingsnorth—which could house *No.9* but not the larger ships. It took longer to build a shed than to build a Zeppelin.

Once under way the airship programme was set back by events far outside the control of such as Pratt, Wallis or even Craven, Masterman and Dawson: by demarcation strikes and by the Easter Rebellion in Ireland which held up the supply of flax for gasbagnets.

The work for which Pratt and Wallis thought themselves uniquely responsible stuttered forward. Their 23 Class was the *No.9* but slightly longer and fuller at bow and stem. The limits of the extra length were dictated by the dimensions of the shed at Barrow.

Meanwhile by 1916 German airships were capable of cruising at 55 m.p.h., could patrol at a height of 15,000 feet and had a disposable lift of six or seven times that theoretically—and still only theoretically—available to *No.9* (which was, at all events, in many respects a Zeppelin of the 1913 vintage), four or five times that which might be available to the 23 Class. Zeppelins were already proving their worth as eyes to the High Seas Fleet. At the end of May 1916 *L.11* and *L.24* were responsible for the greatest contribution that was ever made to modern warfare by rigid airships when they sighted Jellicoe's ships and enabled Admiral Scheer to slip the noose that had been prepared for him. Zeppelins were already pioneering long-range attack on civilian populations. The value of the moat which since 1066 had defended Britain against her continental enemies was at last thrown into question. And the Germans were completing one Zeppelin every ten weeks.

The incompetent administration of the British airship programme, the eternal wrangling and frequent changes of mind and policy remain humiliating. It is well-nigh incomprehensible that during the four years it took to put *No.9* into the air the Germans built almost one hundred Zeppelins—and a devastating comment upon British Service procedures at the time that the number of flying hours she logged in all her service was only twice the ninety-five hours achieved by one Zeppelin, *L.59*, on one non-stop flight.*

Considered, however, for what this period provided to the small group of professional airship designers and some eventual compensation becomes apparent. Notably for Wallis as so often

* At that time no British ship, rigid or non-rigid, had logged a non-stop flight of more than fifty hours.

the man on the spot who had to deal with modifications, correct failures and improvise alterations, it was from these experiences that he learnt the versatility and ubiquity to which he was to remain devoted. He it was who had to produce new forward buffer wheels when the originals broke off as *No.9* left her shed for the first time on 16 November 1916. When after her maiden flight on 27 November 1916—the first by a British naval rigid— the Admiralty refused to accept the ship because she could not lift her contract weight of 3·1 tons, it was he who supervised the removal of both rear engines and their replacement by one Maybach salvaged from *L.33*—a Zeppelin which had come down in September at Mersea on the Essex coat. It was he who organised her refitting with lighter gasbags; he was actually aboard *No.9* on her speed-trials on 13 December 1916, and it was at his suggestion that her auxiliary rudders were removed. During the lunch-break he supervised their removal and the amendment much improved her hitherto erratic steering. On *No.9* and her successor *No.23* the training in empiricism that he had received from Chas. E. Browne was refined into practicality.

Whatever difficulties Pratt, Wallis and their superiors were called upon to face, two important technical developments seemed to heighten the promise of the British airship: the growth of sources of hydrogen supply and the approach to feasibility of airship mooring-masts.

At the outbreak of the war there had been but two tiny hydrogen plants in Britain. As airship stations were established each was equipped with a small portable plant capable of producing hydrogen at 2,500 cubic feet per hour. After the revivification of the rigid programme and the decision to build ships with a capacity of one to two million cubic feet it became clear that these arrangements for hydrogen supply were both inadequate and inordinately expensive. The Admiralty Hydrogen Section provided an answer, and early in 1917 a plant was opened at Howden using the Water Gas Contact Process and capable of producing 7,000 cubic feet of gas per hour. The capacity of the Howden plant was soon doubled and meanwhile two giant plants were established at Kingsnorth and Barrow each capable of producing 60,000 cubic feet per hour.

The inefficiency of existing methods of mooring and handling was palpable to all the warring nations: here was the great vehicle of the future, capable of shrinking oceans and yet, once on the ground, she was ponderously supine and could be manœuvred only by a battalion of infantry hauling upon ropes to the direction of bugle-calls. Already before the war 'Mayfly' had been ruined on the ground, and there had been several further disasters of the same kind.

Orders were given to intensify experiments in mechanical handling but, even as they came closer to feasibility, it was still obvious that an airship on the ground was excessively vulnerable to accident.

The notion of mooring airships in the open without the protection of sheds or screens had occupied the attention of airshipmen for some years. By the beginning of 1916 it was clear that the programme of building sheds was falling behind the rate of construction of non-rigids and far behind the tactical needs of the Services. In so many airship developments Britain had groped forward by imitating the Germans (and the Americans by imitating the British). In this business of mooring, however, the Germans had made no progress whatsoever and indeed intelligence reports indicated that they had abandoned all ideas of mast-mooring. In Britain, late in 1916, Commander Masterman produced a mooring-mast for non-rigids which proved extremely successful. When the rigid production-programme was intensified the problem of mooring became even more pressing. At first independently and then in collaboration, Masterman and Wallis began to work towards a mast-system.

Masterman had in mind certain propositions about a good mooring-system: the ship must be able to fly to her mooring without preliminary landing, with a minimum of outside assistance, a high safety factor and in all weathers; once moored she must be free to ride head to wind; the operations of gassing and fuelling must be rapid and practicable. Finally she must be able to fly off direct from her moorings. Once the collaboration between Masterman and Wallis was complete and Masterman's ideas were incorporated in the Vickers scheme a successful mooring-mast system was available to Britain. Wallis was adding his part to Masterman's success throughout 1917 and on into 1918. Although it was substantial, his contribution, which consisted mostly of providing Masterman with the design-theory, the completed calculations and his own experienced observations of all the trials, it was being made at a time when he was hard at work on his own prime tasks, at first of designing and testing *R.23* and later of designing *R.80*. But he was becoming ever more certain of his own role in the story of airships and ever more certain that he must accustom himself to undertaking any task that the role demanded.

There had been no actual estrangement from Pratt, but the rapid divergence of their interests and activities had left Wallis without any professional confidant whom he could also regard as a personal friend; now in this association with Masterman he found some compensation. Masterman was a sterling representative of the finer type of senior serving officer: intelligent, energetic, well-connected and socially competent, a type which Wallis admired and to a degree envied. He could match the intelligence and energy but not, as yet, the social competence or the connections in high places. He took comfort from the mutuality of trust and was not without understandable pleasure in Masterman's frequent hints that he shared the suspicion of Vickers common to serving officers but had infinite confidence in one man at Barrow: B. N. Wallis.[6]

Coincidentally it had been Masterman who had pressed upon their Lordships the need for a new conception in airship design. His arguments, contained in a paper which began to go the rounds of Whitehall in September 1917, were for the most part strategic: the Navy must throw off its obsession with North Sea action and look to the need for operating over the Atlantic in the defence of convoys; but the technical consequence would be a ship smaller, stronger, faster and more readily manœuvrable than any that had been produced hitherto. In the face of his arguments and with the guilt of Jutland and of their own miserable record of achievement upon them, the Admiralty could not sustain their distaste for Vickers. An airship to the Masterman pattern must be built and probably only Vickers could build it. Years of muddle, delay and interference were cancelled by a rush of enthusiasm; the order for *R.80* was given without so much as the proviso that Vickers should first produce satisfactory designs. Wallis must add this new burden to the many he carried.

Wallis, for his part, did not regard it as a burden. This was to be his own ship, and as he moved happily into a new and successful professional relationship with Masterman he was able to indulge himself in the pleasures of personal creation secure in the knowledge that he had been promised independence of the Admiralty and Royal Corps of Naval Constructors.

In this atmosphere of freed activity Wallis prepared specifications for *R.80* in less than two months, and her specifications were put to the Admiralty on 22 November 1917. More important, something was released in him. He felt himself to be no longer inhibited by supervision nor hindered by the irrelevant grammar of submarine construction which had hitherto bedevilled the thinking of British airship designers. To the experience and ability which he had gathered in his years on airships he now added individuality, the touch of an artist's enthusiasm. He brought feeling—aesthetic delight—to the service of technical efficiency and set his technical competence to the task of creating something that, because it was beautiful as well as functional, would be better than anything that had gone before. When it was completed, *R.80* was the artist's airship, among Wallis's works the prelude to *Swallow* rather than to *R.100*. In the turmoils and triumphs of this creation he began to look outward from the narrow environs of engineering, out towards those areas of endeavour where techniques become crafts, notably towards architecture. And, in his newly-discovered enthusiasm for architecture and his simultaneous excitement in personal creativity he began to experience a fellow-feeling—still humble and scarcely expressed even to himself—for those scientist-craftsmen of the past who had gone beyond the apparent limitations of their medium and made an art out of science and craft. His *R.80* was to be a ship of only 1,200,000 cubic feet that would give a performance in speed and endurance superior to anything in existence; superior even to ships of twice the size. Her operating costs would be a trifle less than 75 per cent of those of any other ship, and because so many parts were standardised (a notion that Wallis was to develop to the ultimate in *R.100*) the time spent in building, and therefore the cost, would be far less than for the hitherto conventional ships. Everything that was now known to aerodynamic theory was to be applied to *R.80*; gondolas as well as hull were to be streamlined, and he was able to promise that by using new methods of construction he would reduce by up to 50 per cent the weight of the cars as compared even to the latest Zeppelins. *R.80* would be driven by four 230 h.p. Wolseley-Maybach engines, could make 60 m.p.h. and maintain an average speed of 50 m.p.h. for almost 4,000 miles. In a mass of detail—all of it worked out by Wallis—there were features never before introduced into an airship, such as the balancing of port-side water containers by starboard-side petrol tanks. He even included in his specifications colour coding of all control wires, electric cables and pipes.[7] Within a week of Wallis's plans reaching Whitehall Vickers received approval for building a prototype. Four months later, the Admiralty (but not yet the ultimate authority, the Cabinet) agreed to the construction of a second and similar ship, *R.81*.

But unknown to Wallis the old jealous faction at the Admiralty was aroused by this too-easy acceptance of his work and by the dangers of surrender to the Vickers hegemony. In the spring of 1918 a secret paper was circulated among Admiralty officials and forwarded to the Cabinet casting doubts upon the potential of *R.80* and contrasting her unfavourably with two captured German ships, *L.45* and *L.49*. There was some justification in these criticisms: *R.80* had a ceiling of little more than 12,000 feet compared to *L.49*'s 20,000 feet, and her top speed was slightly lower, but to dramatise their opposition to Vickers and to Wallis's designs the authors of the secret paper exaggerated the Zeppelins' efficiency and underestimated the performance of *R.80*. Even without this animus it was inconceivable that Admiralty complacency and non-interference would continue.

Wallis had designed a beautiful and original ship and it had been accepted for construction by his own firm and by the Government. He had arrived at the head of his profession. Add to this his enthusiastic participation in pioneering the mooring-mast experiments and his new-found and easy relationship with Masterman, and these years could have been a time of delight for him.

Yet it was not so. Despite the comfort of overwork he could not reconcile himself to what, even now, he regarded as his non-participation in the war. He was still accepted as a member of the Walney Mess, but even at Barrow there were frequent reminders of deprivation, such as in visitations from Commander Craven, magnificently gold-ringed and gold-peaked although he too was now working for Vickers. Once away from Barrow, Wallis was still horribly aware of uniforms, of the sneers of the 'white-feather brigade' and the disdain of waitresses and bus-conductors. His brother, Charles, was in France flying as an observer with the Royal Flying Corps, and Wallis's new friend, Masterman, was still very much a serving officer. There was in truth nobody to whom Wallis could unburden himself. The long experience of loneliness and frustration combined with the stresses of over-work to bring about a general deterioration in his health, which he refused to recognise, through migraines of ever-increasing severity occurred more and more frequently.

If the last months of the Great War seem to be in Wallis's life a strange mixture of achievement and deprivation, of exultation and misery, there is another sense in which they must be seen as the years when he missed a turning which other and lesser men close to him took eagerly, a turning which he did not find for another decade. One can be speculate with sorrow upon what he might have achieved had he realised in 1918 or 1919 that the future lay with heavier-than-air machines. Wallis's rare competence in the use of light alloys could have shortened by many years the development history of British metal aircraft construction, and for him personally might have obviated the many set-backs and miseries which he was to suffer in the 'twenties.

From August 1918 to July 1919 Wallis, with his colleagues at Barrow, was working on experiments for the Air Board designed to demonstrate the potential of duralumin for the structural members of the wings of aeroplanes. Supplies of Grade A spruce, such as early in the war had generally been specified for wing-construction, had become exhausted. Experiments had also been undertaken with steel, but in war-time high tensile steel was as rare as spruce; steel, like wood, was subject to climatic change and particularly difficult to work. All this and much more Wallis and his team reported with obvious and well-argued partiality for their own duralumin, and their persuasiveness was successful. In February 1919 an order was placed with Vickers for three 50-ton Vigilant Flying Boats, the largest ever constructed (length 115 feet; height 42 feet; span 220 feet) powered by eight Condor Rolls-Royce engines totalling 5,200 h.p. These were to be constructed throughout in light alloy, even the hull would be built up of duralumin with a wood covering. As Wallis wrote in a document dated February 1919:

> Large machines such as this would be impossible if one were dependent on wood . . . with the wooden type of construction the economical limit of size from the point of view of performance appears to be about 10 tons; in the case of duralumin construction the limit has not been reached even in the cost of the 50-ton machine now under construction.[8]

Yet he missed the logic of his own arguments as they might have been applied to his own career.

There were other and substantial signposts, but all of them he failed to read: by 1918 aeroplanes were achieving speeds of 150 m.p.h. and could climb to 24,000 feet. At the end of the war bombers such as Germany's Gotha could carry a load of sixteen 112 lb. bombs and sustain 80 m.p.h. for eight hours. There were in Britain over 3,000 first-line planes in service and 350,000 men and women employed in the aircraft industry.[9] In comparison with this vast development and substantial improvement the British programme of rigid airship construction had proved ineffectual.

Why did Wallis fail to take note of what was even then obvious to so many others? The answer is difficult to substantiate and is almost without documentation, but undoubtedly his preoccupation with R.80 blinded him to the need to think out his own future and the future of aviation. Even the frustrations and disappointments which airshipmen had suffered in the war years contributed now to a sense of complacency, for in R.80 he was certain that the lessons of past failures were all put to good use and that now there could only be success. Similarly, the perspicacity that might otherwise have been his was blunted by moving so much among naval officers who had dedicated their careers to the airship arm. Towards the end of the war there were some real achievements to the credit of British naval airships. From June 1917, when the convoy system was initiated, Royal Naval airships had escorted 2,216 convoys without so much as permitting an attack on one surface ship. Nevertheless the real inspiration to naval airshipmen was the record of the Zeppelins; in all their vicissitudes they continued to take heart from the persistence and success of the enemy. Further, though the progress of heavier-

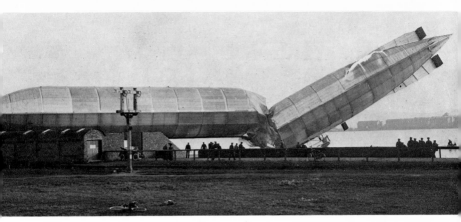

Rigid *No 1*, 'Mayfly', breaks on launching, 24 September 1911

R.80 on her maiden flight

than-air machines was apparent to many, the military significance of that progress was most obvious to those who knew the battle-fields of Flanders. The aeroplane was still essentially a tactical weapon and even to those who had time for thought of the future it seemed just as unlikely that aeroplanes could be used for civilian purposes as that the even more new-fangled tank might be used in the place of omnibuses or charabancs.

> The outstanding and peculiar advantage of the Airship for Air Transport is its capacity for making non-stop Voyages of long duration; whereas from inherent limitations, the Aero-plane will probably never—unless some radically new principle of design is discovered—be capable of carrying a Passenger Load for greater non-stop distances than 2,000 miles, and for economical operation, will probably never be used for non-stop flights of more than 1,000 miles; whereas, on the other hand, the only limit to the non-stop length of flight that can be made by an Airship is determined by the size of ship, and 10,000 miles is quite practicable.[10]

Thus a Vickers report drafted in the last months of the war, and the view expressed was supported not only by reference to long-distance flights achieved by Zeppelins during the war but with an account of the almost-forgotten success of the pleasure-flight company, Die Deutsche Luftfahrt Aktien Gesellschaft which with four ships between 1910 and 1912 had flown without mishap 17,221 passengers on 826 flights, lasting 1,833 hours and covering 102,675 miles—and had made a profit.

> These Airships had spacious passenger cabins, holding thirty passengers, fitted up in a most luxurious style, with inlaid mahogany panelling, carpeted floors, and comfortable arm-chairs; in general shape and style similar to a Pullman Car, with large windows from which the passengers could look at the everchanging scenery, and were served with lunch or tea as required from a buffet . . . at the rate of 100 Marks (or £5) including lunch . . . the attraction was so great that places had to be booked ahead.[11]

With such sybaritic persuasiveness the airshipmen—Wallis among them—argued themselves into a shaky confidence in the future. The aeroplane would be at most the railway-train of the 'twenties—good for short express hauls—the airship would be the passenger-liner, the ocean cargo-boat.

The eyes of the airshipmen were somehow hypnotised by the Atlantic crossing but, in the same series of persuasive papers produced in the autumn of 1918 at the instigation of Vickers, even they had been forced to admit that it 'must be recognised that safe direct Trans-Oceanic commercial flying between points more than 2,000 miles apart is an impossibility'. There were two feasible alternatives: the route London–Ireland–Newfoundland– New York or the route London–Azores–Newfoundland–New York. The Ireland route they accepted as a possibility for either aeroplanes or airships but they proved to their own entire satis- factions that to transport each way across the Atlantic thirty tons of passengers and mail a week would need twenty-four planes in regular service as against only four airships. The total capital required for an aeroplane service they set at almost £4 million as against a little over £2½ million for the airship service. And, they insisted, the most stalwart argument in favour of airships was their much higher safety factor.

An aeroplane is entirely dependent on the proper working of the Engines for its sustenation in the air, and should any of the engines break down, the result would be a forced landing on the water with the consequent possibility of total loss on a rough sea.

In the case of an Airship, the only result of the breaking down of any of the motors is the reduction in the speed, and as a speed of ·8 full speed can still be maintained with even half the motors out of action, there is no possibility of the Airship being lost owing to the possible failure of the engines alone. The only result would be that the arrival of the Airship would be somewhat delayed owing to the reduction in speed.

These complacent words, written in 1918, rang out for almost two decades. Disaster after disaster—to *Shenandoah*, *Akron* and *Macon*, to *R.34* and *R.101* and finally and irrevocably*

---

* 'Irrevocably' in world terms, but *Graf Zeppelins I* and *II* were not dis- mantled until 1 March 1940.

for rigid airships to the *Hindenburg*—made tragedy out of optimism.

Meanwhile, in June 1919, within months of the writing of the Vickers report, two Royal Air Force officers, John Alcock and Arthur Whitten-Brown, flew a converted Vimy bomber non-stop from Newfoundland to Ireland. The flight took just under 16 hours and the Vimy maintained an average speed of 120 m.p.h. A few weeks later *R.34* went out from Scotland to Long Island— almost twice the distance of the Alcock and Brown flight—in 108 hours, and after a rest of three days flew back again, making the trip, with the aid of following winds, in 75 hours. Even the statistics of the airshipmen were now questionable. (*R.34* was not, in design principles, a British ship, but an exact copy of the *L.33* which had crashed in Essex in 1916.)

Nevertheless Wallis and his colleagues, bewitched by *R.80,* turned obstinately away from doubt.

7 *R.80*

For many men of his generation, 11 November 1918 was a day of liberation. In this, unlike most of his contemporaries, for Wallis the excitement and significance of Armistice Day were almost non-existent. His brother was now safe and that was the sum of his immediate personal involvement. He had worked for victory harder than most men, had suffered disappointment and frustration, but he had not shared in the seismic knowledge of his time. If he was to remain obstinately Victorian perhaps the cause was here: he had not suffered the great communal experience which for most Englishmen snapped off the last remnants of Victorianism.

If in these more human terms the Armistice meant little to Wallis neither he nor any of his airship colleagues could hide from themselves the implications for their own careers of the war's end. Two days before the Armistice Masterman had written to Wallis:

> I console myself with the following reflection, viz: that if airships are superior to aeroplanes as the size of both increases, nothing can stop the eventual development of airships, since the world always progresses in the end whatever checks and setbacks there may be to development. You and I are like Moses. We have led the children of Israel so far along the road, but may possibly not see them right into the Promised Land.[1]

But much of this argumentation in which they indulged over the comparative merits of airships and aeroplanes was whistling in the dark; they were to a large extent the helpless victims of national and international policy.

First, it was made abundantly clear that, even were airships to be permitted a future, the virtual monopoly enjoyed by Vickers would be broken. Secondly, if airships were to have any future at all that future would be bedevilled by the rivalry between the Admiralty and the Air Ministry. Within months of the end of the war, airships suffered from this rivalry in an odd manner, for in the struggle for power they were thrown in by both parties, seemingly as a concession but actually as a means of clearing the decks for more vital disputes. It was agreed that the Admiralty was still to be responsible for the design and for the employment and housing of airship personnel but the size of the airship establishment was to be fixed by the Air Council after receiving recommendations from the Admiralty. The training, discipline and welfare of airshipmen was to be in the hands of the Royal Air Force. Although it was accepted that those who flew and maintained airships were Royal Naval personnel, once they were qualified for promotion above that appropriate to the airship establishment they were then to be transferred to the Royal Air Force and thus inevitably to aeroplanes. The origins of this confused and ludicrous situation ante-dated the Armistice. For example, it had been decided that 'no Court of Inquiry could be convened until its findings were known because whose responsibility it was to convene one was determined by the findings'. Immediately after the end of the war confusion was confounded and the ludicrous made farcical when the Air Council accepted the responsibility for civil airships but simultaneously refused to promote maintenance ratings unless they passed RAF examinations which included questions about aeroplane engines and Air Force store-keeping methods; and the Admiralty countered with a demand for the return of all airship personnel, but not the ships, to naval control.

Moreover, the British Government, as indeed all Allied Governments, had a vast and justified respect for German rigids, which were to be handed over intact to the Allies. If Britain got her fair share the demands for home-built ships would fall accordingly and for home-designed ships might vanish altogether because it would be much easier and much cheaper to copy and improve upon Zeppelin models.

Nor was this all; within months of the Armistice, the Germans were getting ready to evade the Article forbidding them to construct Zeppelins of more than one million cubic feet. Their new-style *Bodensee* would break no agreements. On the other hand it was bound to prove a substantial threat to British sales in world markets and especially to its British equivalent, *R.80*.

At home several companies, including the Cunard Line, put proposals to the Government for commercial airship-lines. Vickers were well aware that if their ships were to be used they could not wait upon the results of such negotiations but must themselves form part of a commercial consortium, but they were by no means convinced that the vast expenditure could be justified.

If they were to survive against all these odds British airshipmen had to persuade their masters that airships were the civil aircraft of the future, and the Vickers team must prove that Vickers ships would be the best and most profitable of all. So it was that from the Armistice on through 1919 and into 1920 Barrow mounted a frenetic campaign of persuasion in which Wallis was inevitably involved as technical adviser. Plans poured from Barrow: for a South African Service, for a service to Canada, for ships that might be sold to the Swedes or the Americans, for ships that could carry on a regular service between London, Paris and Rome.

The prognosis of the Rome service is particularly interesting both because in it is demonstrated the faith and care of the airshipmen, and because in it, but with convenient hindsight, one can see underlined many of the disadvantages of airships. The plan[2] presumed the use of only one airship making two return flights each week to a time-table after this fashion:

Leave London 7 p.m.	Monday and Thursday
Leave Paris Midnight	Monday and Thursday
Arrive Rome 12.30 p.m.	Tuesday and Friday
Leave Rome 9 p.m.	Tuesday and Friday
Leave Paris 10.30 a.m.	Wednesday and Saturday
Arrive London 2.30 p.m.	Wednesday and Saturday

To work this service two full crews would be necessary, each making one round trip a week. It was, of course, sensible to allow eighty-one hours a week at the mast in London—the home station —as this would give ample time for current repairs, but there was another reason for reducing to two periods of eight and a half hours the time spent at the mooring-mast in Rome for the planners knew that the deterioration of fabric was rapid under the impact of brilliant sunshine. But the most important influence upon the schedule was the problem of super-heating. Superheat is the amount by which the temperature of the gas inside the envelope exceeds the temperature of the air outside. Airships, in a manner not unlike glass-houses in summer, stored up heat in the interior of the chamber and the effect was to give the ship false lift which would be lost on the removal of the external source of heat. It followed that although it was possible to ballast a ship in such a manner that she would stay in a condition of equilibrium so long as she remained exposed to bright sunlight, at the moment of entering a cloud, or at the moment of turning so that only a small portion of the external surface was exposed to the sun's rays, she would immediately lose lift.

To combat this the ship for Rome was scheduled to leave London in the cool of the evening and to arrive in Rome at an hour when conditions due to superheat had settled to their probable maximum for the day. Because Rome's average temperatures are so much higher than those of London the departure from Rome was fixed so as to give more time for the dissolution of the effects of superheat.

The route envisaged for the proposed service was by no means direct. By allowing additional stops at Lyons, Marseilles, Toulon and Nice, it avoided the crossing of the Alps—an important consideration not so much for safety but because the route chosen had no obstacles higher than the 2,000 feet foothills of the Cevennes; a height that could be surmounted without the expenditure of additional ballast and consequently without loss of cargo-carrying capacity.

The hopeful proposals for the Rome Service were, of course, never implemented. Although the possibilities were real and the economics not by any means gloomy the investment costs were considerable and already heavier-than-air machines were proving their superiority for short-haul services. A regular London–Paris passenger service by plane had been instituted by Air Transport and Travel Limited as soon as the war ended (three years before the first regular commercial service in America). By the middle of 1919 there were two British companies and one French operating regular services linking other main centres in Europe, and although fares proposed for the *R.80* were minimally lower per mile than those for the equivalent and existing heavier-than-air service, civil planes were already averaging 100 m.p.h., almost twice as fast as *R.80*.

Elegant but small, *R.80* was in direct competition with aeroplanes for short or medium hauls and of no possible use for longer distances. The one hope left for her was that she would please the United States Navy.

Wallis, like his colleagues, was not modest in his sales efforts. His ship was better than any Zeppelin. She had a gross lift of 36·5 tons and a useful load of 15 tons. Her top speed was 60 m.p.h., her ceiling 16,000 feet and her range 4,000 miles. He had bettered the Germans in the use of duralumin. He had reduced the large fineness ratio from the Zeppelin's 10:1 to *R.80*'s 7·3:1, and thus had gained aerodynamic advantage.

The American airshipmen had no domestic capacity for building airships, so that, if their service were to continue, it would have to be with ships purchased abroad. But the philosophers of America's airship programme were determined upon a ship of at least 3,000,000 cubic feet with a useful lift of 40 tons, endurance of 200 hours and a normal speed of at least 70 m.p.h. The much smaller *R.80* did not come close to any of the American *desiderata*. Consequently the career of *R.80* was almost ended before she had flown her trials.

The realisation of impending failure was not yet upon Wallis. For most of 1919 he worked frantically on *R.80*, on plans for the future use of airships and on perfecting the Masterman–Wallis mooring gear. Masterman was in Germany with the Allied Control Commission, and his absence placed upon Wallis yet one more responsibility, for it was left to him to arrange patent protection for their joint invention. To this end he called on the services of the firm of Abel and Imray, Patent Agents and its Managing Director, Arthur Bloxam.

This was a family choice as Bloxam's sister, Fanny, had been a close friend of Edith Wallis and in 1916 had married Edith's widower, Barnes's father. There was also another point of contact between the designer and his agent: Bloxam had been a distinguished and original teacher of chemistry at the Goldsmith's Institute. He had many contacts with and much admiration for Henry Armstrong and Chas. E. Browne. He was also a man after the Wallis family heart, austere with all except his children, a voracious reader especially of Victorian novels and a keen walker. The only mark against him (from the Wallis point of view) was his stern dedication to the Evangelical wing of the Church of England. Bloxam had a son and five daughters and before very long this fact was to become for Wallis far more important than dealings with Abel and Imray over patents.

Indeed, out of a sense of obligation to Vickers, but against Masterman's wishes, Wallis soon surrendered most of his rights in mooring gear patents. His total profit from his part in the invention was one handsome Swiss clock—the gift of Masterman.

Nevertheless, because of Masterman's absence, and though with *R.80* building in 1919 he had less and less spare time, what little time was his he gave to mooring-mast experiments. And this obsession helped to round off his knowledge of the detail of airship construction and performance and incised into his experience a myriad of tiny facts and into his character as an engineer a power of decision and adaptability.

The reaction of Wallis during the mooring-mast tests on 1 September 1919 can stand as exemplar to the rest. For these trials *R.24* was used under the command of Wallis's favourite captain, Major Hartford. Colonel Boothby was in charge of the mooring party and Wallis had overall supervision of the trial.

The airship came very near to being wrecked because Hartford, using engines in reverse to co-operate with the winch and handling parties, found that they could not be driven in this manner for more than five minutes without boiling dry. Wallis, on the ground, did not know this: twice the ship rushed and hurdled the mast, almost out of control. Eventually Hartford saved her by valving gas. Eventually and by degrees *R.24* was worked down.

The ship had suffered no harm but Wallis greeted the captain as if he was eager to do him much damage. Hastily Hartford explained himself. Wallis calmed down and listened carefully to the explanation. With Hartford he went over the ship and the obvious that he had never before considered broke in on him. In ships of the *R.23* class the radiator was placed abaft the propeller so that when running astern on the swivelling propellers no cooling air stream passed through the radiator. He ordered a comparatively simple adjustment and at the same time designed a guard to prevent the rope from fouling the coupling.

In September much happened to dash his hopes: first, and without reference to the designers, all the engineering staff were given a month's leave. Next, Wallis was told that he must economise on gas, and late in September he was shattered by news of a kind which inventors (like authors) suffer only too often: some-one else—in this case Siemens–Schuckert in Germany—was at work producing a mooring-mast on the same lines as he and Masterman. (Eventually the similarity proved slight.) In October came what seemed at the time the harshest blow of all: Hartford was demobilised; for any future experiments they would have to break in a new captain.

Disappointment and insecurity were the very stuff of existence for airshipmen, but as for Wallis, it seemed that his enthusiasm blossomed out of the difficulties with which he was forever faced. There was in Wallis's family background so much experience of disaster and frustration as to make him in his professional life notably resilient to setback. Thus, in the winter of 1919 when the faint-hearted were beginning to despair of airships Wallis appeared notably cheerful, even for him more than ordinarily energetic and rich with ideas for *R.80*, and for the future of commercial lighter-than-air aviation.

Then suddenly, in December, the mask cracked under the years of strain. The devastating migraines which he had suffered since his schooldays, and more than ever before in the last months of war and the first of peace, increased in regularity and intensity. He was close to complete physical and mental breakdown. Specialists were consulted; it was two months before he was allowed to receive mail or visitors, four months before he left the nursing home near Hyde Park and almost six months before he was back at work in Barrow. But the role of quiescent invalid was beyond his competence. Whenever he came close to recovery he bustled himself into a relapse. Having held himself over the years from warm personal relationships, he could neither understand nor relax in the rush of affection with which he was surrounded. Pratt was among his first visitors. Determined upon helping Wallis to recovery by indulging in cheerful bedside gossip Pratt was treated instead to cross-questioning about *R.80* and then, having admitted in all innocence that there must soon be some reorganisation of the Design Branch at Vickers, found himself subjected to a bombardment of long, acrimonious and sternly argued letters from Wallis.

Another colleague from Barrow, Victor Goddard, dared a hearty letter to Wallis, now convalescent, which began 'My dear old Wally' and gave what to most men would have been the flattering and comforting news that 'many people here inquire after you and look upon me as somewhat sanctified because I saw poor old Wally when I was in town'.[3] In reply he received a somewhat frigid lecture on life and its meaning which did not so much as refer to the twinkling suggestion 'Have you found the girl at last? That seems more likely . . .' Even the Directors of Vickers did their best to urge Wallis out of his depression. He was given indefinite leave and an increase of £50 a year to his salary.

But neither Wallis nor his friends could hide from themselves the validity of some at least of the causes of his depression.

The letter[4] in which finally Wallis put to Pratt from his sick-bed notions as to how Vickers should reorganise is remarkable in many respects: for its length (almost 3,000 words), for its lucidity, for its detail (even the size and location of each office was included), for its well-nigh brutal demonstration of the changed relationship between the two men which settled Wallis as the innovator and Pratt as the administrator. It is all the more extraordinary that this letter should have come from a man who, according to his doctors, was not yet recovered from a breakdown.

But when, late in May 1920, Wallis went back to work it was clear to the Vickers Board that the airship construction programme was floundering. *R.38* was to go to America, *R.33*, *R.80* and the uncompleted *R.36* and *R.37* to a non-existent civil aviation service. As the only ships operational with the Air Force were *R.32* and *R.34*, and the Air Ministry wanted no more lighter-than-air machines it had become virtually impossible to train crews even for civil aviation or for the Americans, who had no training facilities of their own.

The acceptance of Wallis's scheme for reorganisation was implicit but by now of little value to him or to Vickers. There was, however, still so much excitement over *R.80* that Wallis, once recovered from his breakdown, could again close his mind to the future and concentrate on his very own ship.

Barnes Wallis

When the time came for trials Wallis's hopes and expectations were justified. *R.80* proved herself faster than he had expected, and her gross lift some two tons better than he had estimated; she would be the perfect airship.

His certainty was not shared by the Chief of Air Staff who, in January 1921, calmly and cruelly announced that *R.80* was of no further use to the nation. There followed a short reprieve while the Americans used her for training crews, but on 20 September 1921, what was perhaps the most beautiful and efficient airship ever designed flew on her last flight, from Howden to Pulham, with on board all the commanding officer's livestock. She had logged seventy-three hours in all.

Months before this ignominious end to his masterpiece but long after most of his colleagues in airships had accepted the inevitable, Wallis came at last to the realisation that he must no longer hide from himself the possibility that his future had become all past, that he was close to another of those devastating blows which fate seemed to him to reserve for the Wallis family. He was thirty-three years old, approaching the age at which for most men the signs are set clear and inescapable: this was the narrow path to success, the other the wider road into the dull but large fields where congregate the many who for the rest of their lives must serve as supporters to the brilliant few. For him there was no signpost; if airships failed as they seemed bound to fail he could not expect even the miserable comforts of unenterprising security. Instead, he would be a man without a profession and even if he tried to shift ground, tainted with his undisputed eminence in the hierarchy of an industry that had been at best a freak, a sport in aeronautical development, at worst an unmitigated disaster. But, out of desperation or obstinacy, still Wallis refused to admit to himself that he must leave airships. The Americans had refused his *R.80*; now he would offer them the man who had designed her. To arrive at the point where he so much as considered quitting England demonstrates the measure of his hopelessness. He was still bitterly aware of his responsibility to his father and in wider but scarcely abstract terms he had never learnt to love foreigners, not even (perhaps least of all) Americans. Against this, already in the years immediately after the First World War the United States seemed the Nirvana of technologists; and, perhaps too, in his decision to approach the Americans, there was a touch of satisfying superiority; Wallis was not free of the conviction that he was proposing to confer a privilege upon his employers. In this case the confidence was not unjustified, for Wallis, if not as yet many others, was well aware that his *R.80* was Britain's greatest achievement in airship construction. Although the U.S. Government would have none of her, Wallis knew that some American airship experts were aware of the qualities of *R.80* and a few of them far more enthusiastic on her behalf than even the most enthusiastic of their British counterparts.[5] Among these few was Commander J. C. Hunaker, U.S.N., since 1917 the American most in the confidence of British airshipmen, and a man Wallis knew well from his frequent visits to Walney Island. Hunaker was now flying a desk in the Bureau of Construction and Repair in Washington. To him there was no need for Wallis to rehearse his qualifications, and Wallis's letter on 22 January 1922 came straight to the point. After nine years of designing and supervising construction he could not face 'the prospect of remaining relatively inactive on research.' He wanted 'a real job' in America.

The reply came back all too quickly in a letter which was courteous but offered no encouragement. Indeed, for the most part it was a rehearsal of Hunaker's own discouraged and discouraging view of the future of airships in America. True, the United States Navy had plans for enlarging its airship arm and already the Navy Department had negotiated the purchase of *R.38* from Britain and of *LZ.126* from Germany. True, the United States Government was talking of building for itself similar ships and was in fact well advanced in preparations for constructing a 3,000,000 cubic foot ship after the pattern of the late Zeppelins. True, a vast new shed was almost completed at Lakehurst, New Jersey. But Hunaker feared that most of this was little more than paper-planning. The spirit of the nation was against energetic development of the airship arm.

There is great political agitation directed against the expenditure of money on naval expansion and, while the argument is going on heavily, the matter of funds is held in abeyance. As things stand now it appears to be unlikely that authority can be obtained to build or acquire any additional rigid airships.[6]

As if to emphasise the likeness of their plights, Hunaker then gave back to him almost exactly the words that Wallis had used in his letter of self-invitation:

> . . . for the next year or two I am quite certain that we will have to sit back and amuse ourselves with experiment and research until the general financial condition is improved.

Wallis was learning; learning to consider a relationship between politics—national and international—and the development of his own technology, between the future of airships and his own career. He, who hitherto had seen himself always as a brilliant worker, who nevertheless understood little and cared less for the great world outside his work, in despair had begun to appreciate that if the scientist works in a vacuum he may suffer the destruction of the vacuum at other hands and with it the destruction of his own work. In these months he began to realise that he must learn to influence the thinking that would influence his thought. He began to develop the approach to problems which was to lead eventually to the sensational paper on the economic importance of the Ruhr dams produced early in the Second World War (and therefore to the dam-busting bombs), and also to the thinking about Commonwealth security and communications which inspired the pleas he was to make in his seventies and eighties for long-range cargo submarines and very long-range, very high-speed planes.

The shutting of the American door shut the door also on an impulse which was out of character. Wallis, who even then could be adventurous with ideas, never acquired that impulse to roam which makes of some men travellers and, when it is most advanced, emigrants of a few. He had no real wish to become an American and, despite the bleak prospect which he faced, he was in truth relieved that equivalent bleakness on the other side of the Atlantic lifted from him that sense of responsibility to his work which might otherwise have led him to accept Americanisation for the sake of airships. Wallis erased the untypical episode from his mind and later in life, although his memory was acute and his delight in reminiscence active, denied fiercely that it had ever taken place until faced with inescapable documentary evidence.

But in 1921 if not America what then? Britain was floundering in political and economic crisis. The replacement boom which had followed immediately upon the Armistice could not last; by the summer of 1920 prices were falling and unemployment rising. A year later there were two million unemployed in Britain. The war had solved few international problems and the weary Coalition Government found itself an unwilling participant in military epilogues to victory, in Russia, Asia Minor and Ireland. These adventures were not on a scale that could keep Vickers prosperous and the economic chaos was of a kind that spelt the end of pioneering industries. The curtain came down quickly upon an unfinished play; in an effort to economise and, one suspects, with some sense of relief that now the fruitless and expensive optimism of the airshipmen would be silenced, Vickers closed its Airship Department.

Some employees were shuffled off to other branches and a few were given a year's severance pay. With their customary genius for hedging bets the Directors offered to Wallis a retainer of £250 a year so that he could continue to toy with airship ideas against the day when airships might come back to favour. They added to the offer one substantial condition: that he must not work for any other aircraft firm.

This, seemingly the end of all his practical dreaming of airships —and of his cherished financial security—coming as it did less than a year after he had suffered a serious breakdown might well have broken Wallis's heart and with it his mind. Perversely, he took this latest and most vicious buffet from fate as encouragement towards the fulfilment of a long-held ambition. Back even in his days at Cowes he had it in mind to make up to himself for his refusal to accept Chas. E. Browne's suggestion that he go to a university, and over the years he had often felt the wish to remove the sense of inferiority that then and still in 1921 he suffered from time to time in the presence of men with academic qualifications. Now Vickers had given him his chance: he would use his enforced leisure and his retainer to take a degree.

At the first opportunity he rushed from Barrow up to London to discover the regulations, bought the necessary books in the Charing Cross Road and on the short train journey to his father's home was already at work studying for his Inter B.Sc. Few men knew as much as Wallis about the principles of engineering as they applied to airships; he had active memories of marine engineering, and, from those days in the Artists Rifles at High Beach, a lunatic recollection of sanitary engineering, but London University External examinations were not set to suit the designer of *R.80*, nor even the one-time draughtsman at Cowes or the one-time corporal in the Artists. Certain advantages were permitted Wallis because of his ex-Service status, but still, for the most part, he must cross the same barriers as boys half his age if he was to achieve the distinction of a B.Sc. It was in truth an uninspired and uninspiring process but Wallis was so set upon this course that he devoted to it all his seriousness of purpose and ingenuity of mind. At the earliest opportunity—five weeks from the day when he had decided to take a degree—he sat the first examination for Inter B.Sc. and, without even waiting for the results, began work at once on work for his Finals.

This new task so filled his thoughts and absorbed his energies that even the arrival of the first instalment of his retainer he did not see as the end of a chapter, a full-stop written to his association with airships, but as the optimistic motto at the head of a new story. For, on the very day when his first tiny cheque arrived he received also the news that he had passed Inter.

Since he had left the Artists Rifles he had been well but not lavishly paid. He had spent little on himself, but the deeply ingrained habit of family loyalty had persuaded him out of some of his savings in support of his father and his sister, and here, at least, there was some cause for optimism. Charles Wallis seemed in better health than for years past and under the cheerful care of his second wife was discovering the energy to enlarge his practice. Barnes's sister, Annie, to whose support he had contributed since well before the First World War, had left Art School, found herself a post as nannie to an English family in India and on the boat out had found herself also a husband. Now she was off his hands. (This particular optimism was ill-founded. Within a year, Annie, her husband and a new-born child were back in England and Barnes had accepted as an inescapable duty the bolstering of their shaky finances—a duty that he continued to fulfil for another forty years.) But, for the moment, he felt that he could survive, even on little more than twenty pounds a month. He pawned some of his belongings, moved back as a lodger to his father's house at New Cross and settled to the elementary but mostly unfamiliar problems of civil and mechanical engineering.

Wallis set his sights on the first examination of 1922, but before he came to the test he was dealt yet one more blow. Early in December 1921 he received an unofficial letter from Craven. Vickers' last hope of selling airships had rested upon a prospective deal with Japan which had now fallen through. It seemed likely that the firm would soon be forced to stop even the retainer they were paying Wallis. Craven insisted that he was not yet sure whether or when the formal quittance would come but two days later it was written:

Owing to the present state of the Airship Industry, we regret that it is necessary for us to give you notice that we shall be unable to continue paying you the retaining fee of £250 per Annum, after the end of the present month . . . We take this opportunity of thanking you for your loyal and efficient service to the Company.[7]

At that moment Wallis had received half the promised retainer but he had also forfeited his right to severance pay and so the great firm of Vickers could congratulate itself on saving something of the order of £500. Others would have seen this as sharp practice and patent ingratitude to a distinguished servant. Had he not been so passionate in his pursuit of a degree, for all his loyalty to the firm even Wallis himself must have tried to fight the decision. Instead, as if disinterested, he hurried through a hollow exchange of letters with Craven and accepted as final the usual empty formality from a senior to a junior he has treated with less than due loyalty: 'If at any time, or in any place, I can be of help to you, please be sure to let me know.' Craven filed the letter and forgot the whole affair as he prepared for his impending promotion to the post of Managing Director. Wallis, though left without funds or prospects, also forgot it. He pawned a few more possessions and settled back to his studies.

He had been planning to take Honours but a recurrence of migraine prevented him from sitting two of the required papers. However, just five months after passing Inter., Wallis achieved the academic respectability he had so often envied in others.

8 Chillon and Courtship

One day in the early summer of
1922 Wallis, now acknowledged by his few sophisticated contemporaries as Britain's outstanding airship designer, called upon the
scholastic agents, Messrs Gabbitas–Thring, and applied for a
post teaching Mathematics to School Certificate level at Chillon
College, an English-type public school in Switzerland. Chillon
were glad to have a mature master with a London degree at a
salary of £220—out of which Wallis had to pay the agents' commission. Wallis went off to Switzerland, his foot on the first rung
of a new professional ladder which he knew even then that he
could never hope to climb to the top. He comforted himself with
the thought that his move was only temporary; he was in Switzerland not to teach but to learn. At school he had shown himself a
better than average linguist. With practice he felt that he could
bring his French to a level which would make him once more
useful to the aircraft industry or (even more likely) to Vickers,
not as a designer but as a salesman, the more stable and more
lucrative side of the business. He thought he had always envied
the salesmen their freedom from the nagging uncertainties of
design, from the impossible pressures of completion dates and
from the *prima donna* rivalries of the creative departments. Now,
after some months at Chillon, he could come back to Vickers as
one of the bustling, untroubled businessmen and better equipped
than his new rivals because his French would be somewhat better
than theirs and his technical knowledge infinitely greater.

His true motives for change were more complex than these
bravura interpretations which he presented to his family and
with which he half-deluded himself. He was uncertain that there
would ever be a future for him in Vickers or indeed in engineering; yet, and paradoxically, he could not bring himself to believe

that airships were finished and would never again need the designer of *R.80*. With this more hopeful part of his mind he looked upon Chillon as nothing more than a pause for breath. As he expressed it in a letter to a new and hugely important correspondent, Molly Bloxam, in a phrase which demonstrated if nothing else the magic that she was already exercising upon his hitherto dour personality, the Swiss adventure gave him a chance to amuse himself even if he had to do it by 'working like a slave and living principally on bread and butter'.

Professionally there was again some basis for his otherwise frivolous optimism, for he had come to know the entrepreneur who was already making plans to begin the tale all over again.

Commander Dennistoun Burney was a man of vast energy and considerable ingenuity. During the war he had invented the paravane, a device for cutting mines adrift from their moorings which had undoubtedly contributed much to the safety of Allied merchant shipping. By the time the war ended Burney had amassed not inconsiderable royalties and—equally important for his future status as a consultant to Vickers—already he had an office in the London headquarters. Then it was that he turned his mind to the needs of Imperial communications, and, though at the time he had never so much as flown in an airship, convinced himself that airships provided the best solution to the problems of transporting people and goods to India, Australia and New Zealand.

Burney began to walk the corridors of the Vickers building seeking allies and recruits. He went outside Vickers for advice: to Dr Hugo Eckener in Germany, the successor to Graf von Zeppelin. Dr Eckener was hard at work on *LZ.126* but he gave Burney much advice and reinforced his optimism about the future of airships.

Back in England, Burney looked for financial supporters. Vickers were not enthusiastic. But, unsure of the future profitability of wars, the Vickers Board decided upon a policy of diversification: into locomotive manufacturing (a decision which eventually came to nothing because Barrow's high standards led to them being out-tendered) and into electrical equipment (a decision which led to the acquisition of an interest in and ultimately to the control of British Westinghouse).[1] And the Vickers Policy Committee had agreed to some investigation at Barrow of the commercial possibilities for airships, and prepared and issued proposals for a Trans-Oceanic Airship Liner—a bold scheme which depended for its success upon Government support; but this, as ever, was not forthcoming.

Thus, when Burney sought the aid of his own Board for his new airship schemes, they had many reasons for refusing him. Even the successful transatlantic round-trip of *R.34* in the summer of 1919 had not impressed them; certainly not half as much as the much more recent disaster to *R.38* (another ship destined for America) which, on 21 August 1921, on her fourth testing flight and in full view of the people of Hull had broken her back. Even more persuasive upon the Vickers Board was the fact that their own team was not so much as invited to the Court of Inquiry which followed the disaster. True *R.38* was not one of their ships, but Pratt, Wallis and Temple were experts almost unique in Britain and, if in adversity the Government would not call for their advice, there could be little hope for future co-operation.[2]

Nevertheless, as Vickers had always based its fortunes upon a judicious mixture of pioneering and exploiting traditional success, so even now despite the record of disillusion with airships the Board gave Burney limited support. He could continue to preach his missionary sermons from a Vickers pulpit and if only the Government would play its financial part Vickers might be persuaded to change the direction of decision. Burney was not put off, and even the Vickers Board must have wondered if their runner was coming into the betting when their equally hard-headed colleagues at Shell Petroleum agreed to financial participation in the Burney Scheme.

Therefore, though he knew little of the scurrying after support, of the high finance and high politics upon which his future depended, nevertheless, Wallis had some reason for his faith in Burney. Less than four months after Wallis had been dismissed by Vickers Burney succeeded in having his scheme placed before the Air Council.

Meanwhile at Chillon, and despite all his disappointments, Wallis's enthusiasm for airships was not dimmed. He was asked to give a lecture to boys and staff on the principles of lighter-than-air machines. For weeks he prepared models and lantern-slides and when the occasion arrived he made the most of it; either life

Chillon and Courtship

at Chillon was so drab that any diversion was a relief or else on this, a very early exercise as a lecturer, Wallis demonstrated well nigh fully-fledged that genius as a public expositor which, with the aid of radio and television, was to make him so notable in the days of his fame. At all events the boys offered to take up a collection so that the lantern could be hired again and the lecture repeated. The headmaster's wife commented graciously upon the beauty of his voice and the headmaster enviously upon the ingenuity of his models. Enviously and also slyly, for the next lecture in the series was to be on astronomy and would be given by the headmaster. Dutifully Wallis accepted the broad hint as an order and, although he knew nothing of the stars, proceeded to build with great care a demonstration planetarium 'cutting out every star and in its proper magnitude'.

The boys at Chillon were quick to exploit his mechanical virtuosity. For the end-of-term entertainment they asked his help with the stage effects. Night after night when his duties were over he set about building a device for producing a sunset:

> . . . a beauty, it lasted about 10 minutes—then there was an interval of 2 or 3 seconds complete darkness, and then I did a moonrise and lit a hanging charcoal fire—all electric of course. . . . I simply loved it standing behind the scenes with a stop watch, working the resistance and listening for the cues. . . . Now that we have the apparatus every play they do will have to have a sunset in it somehow.[3]

When he could close his mind to the realisation that his true career was over, these days at Chillon were wonderfully contented. The shedding of immediate liability for the livelihood and even the lives of colleagues, and release from the need to serve as a leading propagandist for the future of airships gave him a chance to revert to the cheerful irresponsibility of his days at Cowes. He learnt to ski and tried to learn to skate. After the years of comparative isolation he enjoyed this sudden return to living as part of a community and even allowed himself some social life outside the school group.

He liked the boys, enjoyed teaching and was more than ordinarily delighted to find that as a teacher he was an undoubted success. His methodology he took from Armstrong and Browne, but he had behind him what his mentors had not: a great store of practical experience, and those who studied under him at Chillon not only learnt to find out for themselves but also revelled in his frequent breaks from precept and exercise into reminiscence and anecdote. Years later one of them wrote to him of his Chillon days: 'The approach to engineering which I learned from you there has been a major influence in my life, and has been an immense help in all sorts of problems.'[4]

For all this, Wallis could not bring himself to accept that this period of eased tensions was the reality of his life. When the headmaster offered him a permanent appointment he took the invitation as a compliment—and turned it down. Griselda-like he waited patiently for his recall to Vickers. 'All my heart is in Airships and I *have* worked so hard.'

The patience and indeed the buoyancy with which he faced life in and around Chillon had a new and all-important support: Molly Bloxam. Wallis was thirty-five years old, but his inexperience in matters of this kind was so complete that as yet he could not bring himself to admit what many a boy half his age would have known and relished at once. He had fallen in love.

Molly Bloxam was then seventeen years old. She had first heard of the Wallis family when her aunt married Dr Charles Wallis as his second wife.[5] At that time she was only ten and her interest in the marriage centred upon the possibility that at last she and her brothers and sisters would have some first cousins (a remote possibility: Fanny Bloxam was fifty-three when she married!). The substitute cousins who were eventually introduced into the Bloxam household were no compensation. One, John, was himself married and had children. Another, Charles, was a soldier. As for Cousin Barnes, he had grey hair, talked to her father about his patents and occasionally teased her or gave her sweets. In the years between her tenth and sixteenth birthdays she heard little and thought less of the Wallises. Then came a family party and a visit to Southwark Cathedral for the Shakespeare Birthday Service and a fragment of conversation which utterly changed the relationship between the two. First, somebody asked Molly the question with which patronising adults so often shatter the young: 'What are you going to be when you leave school?' At that time Molly had no doubts about the future. She was going to be a doctor and she said so without hesitation only to be

crushed by Dr Charles Wallis's Victorian sneer, 'A lady doctor!'
Everybody laughed; everybody except Barnes, who turned angrily
on his father and spat out: 'She could hardly become a gentleman
doctor.' Molly looked at him gratefully and, for the first time,
found grey hair enormously attractive. Now she listened carefully
to everything he said and, like the headmaster's wife at Chillon,
listened above all to that beautiful voice, and she became increasingly aware that Barnes was looking at her more often than
he looked at anyone else, that he was forever manœuvring to
sit next to her, that his conversation was directed at her.

These were the days of flapper emancipation. But it had not
reached the Bloxam home at 27 Kidderpore Avenue, Hampstead,
where Arthur Bloxam, all unmindful of the paradox that he
included Robert Browning among his favourite poets, attempted
to maintain in Hampstead the spirit of Wimpole Street, to hold
the worldly safety and secure the eventual heavenly salvation
of his daughters and four sisters. There was little chance for
Molly to encourage a courtship and such chance as there was was
further debilitated by the lack of privacy inevitable in a large
family. For Molly the situation was almost impossible even had
she been free from these parental and family obstacles. She was
very young, entirely without experience and she could hardly
credit that her elderly and distinguished step-cousin had fallen
in love with a mere schoolgirl. Worse still, this same step-cousin
was himself utterly incompetent and, like her without experience
in the handling of such matters, could not even bring himself to
talk to her about the possibility that they might conspire to
circumvent parental supervision. In the months before Wallis
left for Chillon he had called occasionally at the house in Hampstead. They played cards together and Molly noticed that he
could not see the cards. (He should have worn spectacles but was
trying to hide the need from Molly.) He gave her a record of his
favourite guitar music. She dared not play it in front of her family
and so made an extraordinary number of visits to the bathroom
carrying with her a portable gramophone and drowned the sound
of the music with the noise of taps, cisterns and flushing water.
He took her—and her sister—to the theatre. But still there was
little advance in the relationship and it might well have ended
from lack of confidence on one side and lack of drive on the other
had it not been for the coincidence that both were in the process

of taking examinations, Wallis his finals for his degree, Molly her
Matriculation. He gave her a good-luck charm to take into the
examination room. She, greatly daring, wrote to congratulate him
on passing his B.Sc. And then he discovered that she was terrified
of the mathematics which she would now have to face for Inter.
At last he had found a subject on which he could converse and
write without inhibition, a language and occasion for courtship
to which even Arthur Bloxam could not object. He left for Chillon
cheerful in the knowledge that he and Molly could 'get to know
each other by letter'.

Wallis wrote about everything and anything: ten, eleven or
twelve pages every other day on his life at Chillon, his ambitions—
even, in great detail and complete with diagrams, how to play
Rugby Fives. He had given up smoking. Did she approve? (Like
Mark Twain he gave up smoking with some regularity.) Occasionally he played bridge for money. Did she mind? He told her anecdotes against himself such as he had never told before to anyone
except his mother. In the very same letter in which he began the
lessons in mathematics—'Now here begins lecture one, from me,
Barnes, to you, Molly, on the very delightful subject of the
Calculus,' he admitted 'I don't *talk* like this to people.' By the
beginning of December 1922 if still only by implication he was
even prepared to proclaim a special relationship—'I've never had
a girl-friend before' but still he wrote of that relationship as
'one between good friends'.

For her part Molly could hold off family curiosity and paternal
suspicion by insisting that Barnes was giving her a correspondence
course in mathematics. And though social and personal inter-
polations into the correspondence began to grow in number,
length and frequency the course was a reality and most thorough.

That 'lecture one' began with philosophy and went on to
history. It is worthy of some quotation because it shows Wallis
as an apt teacher—if stumbling lover.

The calculus is a very beautiful and simple means of perform-
ing calculations which either cannot be done at all in any other
way, or else can only be performed by very clumsy, roundabout
and approximate methods. No one would suggest that you must
be able personally to manufacture a needle before you are
allowed to tell the time—these things are tools, or instruments,

put at our disposal by the accumulated experience of our fore-
fathers and we are quite justified in making such use of them
as our skill and ingenuity can contrive. So with the Calculus—
it is a mental tool, left at your disposal by the great mathematicians of the past. It was first discovered—perhaps formulated would be a juster term—by Newton in 1697, I think.
Simultaneously, by Leibnitz in Germany. On looking up my
notes here, I see that Leibnitz published his first statement in
1684 while Newton had the idea long before that. Each accused
the other of plagiarism, but historians now think that there is
little doubt they may be regarded as simultaneous discoverers.
Simultaneous discoveries in science are not rare things—they
are usually the result of accumulation of (perhaps) hundreds of
years of thought and two great investigators arrive at the same
result at the same time.[6]

So, as many a younger man has argued his suit by showing off
before his girl his prowess as a swimmer or his ability to drive
cars at breakneck speeds, the unsure lover played the confident
tutor. The teacher progressed but the suitor became more aware
of what he was about and, being aware, adult and yet so incredibly
timorous in this unfamiliar situation, began to have doubts about
the propriety of a man courting a girl half his age.

He wrote back home for reassurance, not to Molly herself,
but to his step-mother, Molly's aunt, Fanny Wallis. That he
should have chosen her as his confidante shows some development
of sophistication; Fanny was one of the few in either family who
had escaped the prudishness of the older Bloxams without taking
on the severity of the older Wallises. She replied immediately
that she could see nothing wrong in a man of thirty-five proposing
to a girl of seventeen—something much stronger than anything
that he had dared suggest even to her. She wished him luck.

So it was that when the Christmas vacation came Wallis used
his tiny store of money to return from Switzerland to London.
He rushed to Hampstead, and after an afternoon of somewhat
grim and forced sociability managed to separate Molly from the
family guardians for the time that it took her to walk him to
Hampstead Heath Station. It was a miserable December evening
with icy rain bucketing down in a manner that seems peculiar
to these parts of North West London. Still for this ordinary

middle-class couple of extraordinary incongruity standing together outside Hampstead Heath Station the situation was set for high romance. Here was Molly, pretty but only just adult, her mind full of a confusing mixture of scarcely understood new ideas of emancipation and themes from severe Victorian novels, and here was Barnes, a man close to middle-age, whose professional experience was so vast and so distinguished that its recent end was true tragedy, a man who had touched the hems of fame and then collapsed into obscurity and insecurity, but also a man who had never kissed a girl. The romantic moment could have brought high poetry or dark disaster; instead this scene of avowal was turned by North London's foul weather into knockabout farce. Declarations of high-principled love had measured the distance to the station. Now, in grand summary, Wallis halted in his stride, bent low over Molly (he was almost six feet, she five foot five), and the rain that had gathered in the brim of his bowler-hat cascaded into her face and down her neck.

In the years to come Molly would demonstrate over and over again her complete imperturbability. She is a woman who has the gift of placidity without the dullness which so often goes with it, the genius to be a man's equal without ever taking from him the support of feeling her dependence upon him. Never again was she to need her gifts quite so much as in this moment when she was hit simultaneously by a proposal and a flood of water. Perhaps the situation was made easier because, in a manner that was already outmoded and with inelegant circumlocution so unlike his habitual clarity, Wallis merely asked if he could ask her father if he could ask her to be his dearest girl. Years later Molly admitted that her first reaction was to accept immediately a proposal that was not yet absolute.[7] Some innate sophistication held her from easy acceptance, but it was agreed between them that Wallis should talk to Bloxam, to seek from him permission to take her out free from the chaperonage of her sister. They did not so much as kiss.

Having maintained her calmness in the face of a near-proposal and a cold bath Molly ran home and immediately and excitedly announced to her assembled family that Barnes was in love with her. There was an aeon of silence and then Mr Bloxam rose to his feet and moved towards his daughter: 'You poor child!'

Molly, who knew her own thoughts and knew too her father's

inflexibility was at once miserably disappointed for the present and terrified for the future. Her disappointment strengthened her determination and her terror was fully justified when the Wallis family came to Kidderpore Avenue for Christmas Day lunch.

That Christmas Day of 1922 Arthur Bloxam found it easy to exclude Barnes Wallis from the benefits of the Christmas spirit. No sooner was lunch over than he summoned Wallis to his study and there treated him to a diatribe against men who robbed cradles. Offering no concession of kindliness or comprehension he refused to countenance any further association between his daughter 'and a man old enough to be her father'. Ordinarily hot-tempered and entirely capable of frenetic rows with men, equals or superiors, who questioned, undermined or otherwise endangered his professional achievements, in these entirely unfamiliar circumstances Wallis found himself dumb, incapable even of sensible thought.

He stumbled out of the house, struggled back to New Cross and went to bed suffering one of the worst migraines of his life. Adding to his misery was a rare lack of confidence. Perhaps his love for Molly was in some way disgusting. Perhaps to love at all was to be tainted? Throughout his youth on the rare occasions when Barnes had dared approach his father with any of the problems which are natural to boyhood he had been held off, usually with pious evasions, but on occasion with some harsh Biblical reference which, whilst it emphasised his father's crushing sense of sin, also drilled into the boy a feeling that normality was vice. Barnes had learnt nothing in the monkish years of his young adulthood, and struggling now under the indignity of disappointment and unanswered rebuke he came close to accepting the dreary philosophy in which he had been reared. Love was sin, a shameful weakness of body and mind. He took the way back to rectitude that Victorian muscular Christians would have recommended: he went off on a walking-tour, exhausting himself out of the delirium of love by adding an occasional afternoon round of golf to a morning of hard and lonely walking.

It almost worked, but when in mid-January 1923 he heard from Craven that Burney's schemes were about to be accepted by the Vickers Board and that Wallis could again serve, at first as a member of the Contract Department, but soon with airships again, he could not hold himself from breaking the news at once to Molly. Nevertheless he signed himself unromantically 'Ever your affectionate cousin, Barnes'.

With Molly's blessing and with the excitement of airships once more in the forefront of his mind he went back to Chillon, resigned, and returned to London to be a paying guest in his own home. Molly made his happiness almost complete by insisting that she still needed to pass her examinations and that this was only possible if Barnes continued providing his correspondence course in mathematics. As some men carry forward their courting with imperfect poetry so Wallis conducted his most comfortably with the perfection of sine and cosine.

Craven's recall of Wallis had been a little premature. Burney's scheme for the foundation of the Airship Guarantee Company had not yet been ratified by the Government, but Amery was known to favour the scheme, and when the Conservatives came to power in October 1922 he had been elevated to First Lord of the Admiralty. Still he and the new Secretary of State for Air, Sir Samuel Hoare, shelved a decision on the scheme until July 1923 and even then hedged around their agreement with provisos about Treasury approval and Parliamentary supervision.[8]

Meanwhile Wallis had to be content with his appointment in the Contracts Department. There he was treated as if he were a promising recruit; and with some justice because from 1913 until 1921 he had been so involved with the particular that there had been no time for him to discover the general. It was his enthusiasm for learning everything that he could about Vickers' operations as much as his overriding loyalty to the firm that made these neophyte exercises acceptable to him. With increased experience, more and more varied responsibilities were thrust upon him. In some months of work as a salesman he brought to Vickers £29 worth of orders. For the rest, with a salary of £1,500 (though not paid until 1924), he began to enjoy himself, to be content with the variety of problems that he was called upon to settle and to be flattered by what he now came to regard as recognition by his masters of his undoubted versatility. That it was percipience on their part is probable, for it was to Barnes Wallis that Vickers turned for a verdict upon the practicality of a scheme for building all-metal flying-boats. He set to the task—his first substantial contact with the problems of designing aeroplanes

—with enthusiasm and reported with conviction that flying-boats of this kind were a promising commercial possibility yet—he could but add with a wistful glance towards the boardroom—not as economic as his beloved airships.

And the spring of 1923 was made cheerful by growing optimism about the great love in his private life.

Molly's persistence—and the mathematics coaching—began first to circumvent and then to erode her father's obduracy. Letters between Barnes and Molly became more frequent (although his were still signed 'your affectionate cousin') and by June they were even seeing each other. Bloxam had relented sufficiently to allow Barnes to take his daughter to a theatre—providing always that he took her sister as well. With the consciousness that, whatever and whoever attempted intervention, she was going to marry him and in so doing would be taking on the responsibility for a man she already knew to be a genius, Molly grew rapidly more mature. And Barnes seemed to grow younger. Against the day when they might go to a dance together he again took dancing lessons. He began going to theatres. He admitted, with sorrow, that he had never heard a Gilbert and Sullivan opera, had only once been to Kew Gardens, and was only now becoming interested in the names of poets. Under the effects of her teasing he began to realise his almost entire lack of humour, and with the same deliberation that he gave to engineering started to teach himself the art of the throwaway line. Greatest achievement of all: he taught himself to laugh at himself.

Suddenly, the call came for which he had been waiting—and the manner of its coming was a shock. His confidence in Burney had been evaporating since his return from Switzerland. Now it was drained by the extraordinary substance of Burney's proposals for their partnership in the airship which Burney at last had authority to produce. This airship, said Burney, was to be designed under his chairmanship. As his assistant Burney would have an engineer called Isherwood, but the operative members of the committee would be a strange quintet: Scott, Colmore, Richmond, Nixon—and Wallis who would be Secretary to the Committee. Of course, Burney added, the Secretary of any committee is really the most powerful member because he is 'in a position to manipulate the minutes thereof in any way that he, the Secretary, wishes.'[9]

Barnes Wallis

Wallis was shaken by the casuistry but even more by the unprofessional notion of designing by committee. He asked for time to think over the plan. In a night passed sleeplessly shock grew to despair. He considered each of his potential colleagues. He had nothing against Isherwood. Wallis knew him to have done a competent job on designing direction-finding gear for naval guns. For the others: Nixon was a pre-war stockbroker; Richmond a chemist whose sole acquaintance with airships was doping the envelopes of small non-rigids; Colmore and Scott, old comrades from Walney, Wallis recognised as brave men, but bravery was no qualification for building an airship, and they were typical young Service officers, gay, casual, a sight too ready to abandon serious pursuits in favour of girls or drink.

Next morning, uncompromisingly and without further explanation he refused any part in the scheme. He would join Burney only if he were granted sole charge of the design, though if that were given him he would do his best to wean H. B. Pratt from a secure post at Barrow and would be willing to see Pratt made General Manager.

Burney temporised; now it was he who must have time to think.

Nevertheless, 'partly I suppose to justify my contention, partly perhaps to demonstrate my own skill',[10] Wallis went ahead with work for which he had no authority. Much of the time that he should have given to the Contracts Department, Wallis spent on privily designing an airship which would meet the Government's requirements. Early in 1923 he took his drawings and his calculations to Isherwood and then to Burney. Isherwood had no doubt that Wallis was their man but Isherwood was close to resigning his post with Burney. Burney temporised a little longer and then, having received no evidence that the others could offer him an alternative, on 15 May 1923, formally offered Wallis the post of Chief Designer to the Airship Guarantee Company. Colmore, Scott, Richmond and Nixon would not be joining.

Wallis was delighted, but his pleasure was short-lived. Now he had the right and the time to scrutinise Burney's schemes in depth. He persuaded Pratt to join the team (but only temporarily), and when together the two old colleagues studied the estimates for passenger airship-services that had finally persuaded the Government into grudging acquiescence to the Burney Scheme hey found them ridiculously optimistic. Wallis, with the comparatively recent disaster to *R.38* in mind, was worried, too, that but of a natural desire to get something going, Burney and his supporters would abbreviate the experimental period. Although Wallis could not hide from himself or from Molly his excitement at once more working openly on an airship-programme, at the same time he tried to argue himself out of enthusiasm. If the suggestion of marriage was seldom if ever voiced between them the possibility had become a probability as Bloxam's resistance weakened, and Wallis was miserably aware that, with marriage, he must add responsibility for the comfort of wife and perhaps children to the responsibility which he already accepted for his own family. Further, he knew that Bloxam was himself sufficiently involved in the commercial and technological world to appreciate to the full the risk that his putative son-in-law would be taking with his own career and therefore with Bloxam's daughter's comfort if he were to accept Burney's offer, and so Wallis was afraid that the decision he wanted to take would shatter Bloxam's growing complacency and turn him once more to implacable objection.

Characteristically, in this moment of crisis he found himself thinking about his mother more often than usual. Attempting to confide in Molly his perplexity over the Burney offer instead he raised the wraith of his mother's memory as a substantial barrier between them. This was something he could not share with Molly.

You may think it silly for a man, but although it's nearly twelve years since she died I simply can't talk about it without making an idiot of myself. She was absolutely everything in the world to me. Everything, in a way I suppose you would hardly understand.[11]

For a while it seemed that the decision over the post with the Airship Guarantee Company was to be taken out of his control, for again there was havering, this time by Vickers. Now that Wallis had been back with them for a few months they had come to realise his value as a general engineering consultant. The hint came down to him that, instead of going to Burney, he might be appointed General Manager of one of the Vickers depots in the Midlands.

This comfortable way was open for a few days only, but while it lasted Wallis saw it as the perfect solution. Others had decided for him that he must go the route of security rather than the road of adventure and risk. What is more it absolved him of another burden that he felt would have been close to his conscience were he to have leapt at Burney's offer. Surely, he argued (first to himself and then to his superiors) the post of Chief Designer was properly not his but Pratt's.

Then two things happened which settled his future in entirely the opposite manner to that which in a few days he had taught himself to accept. Pratt decided to refuse a post with Burney (though he did agree to attempt one last exercise in airship design) and Vickers appointed as one of their nominees on Burney's board the director for whom Wallis worked and he asked immediately that the Midlands offer should be rescinded and that instead, for a few months, at least, Wallis should remain a member of his staff but attached to Burney.

Under the pressure of compulsion every uncertainty was quickly eroded.

There is now, in my mind, not the least doubt that in 2 or 3 years from now, we shall have the most wonderful series of our liners running from England to India, twice every week and back, in $2\frac{1}{2}$ days! Carrying 200 passengers each, and mails and parcels. I don't care if I die after that. It will only be the start of course and the line will subsequently be extended to Australia and New Zealand, and then there will be other lines.[12]

But Wallis's own fears about the practicality of building a safe airship speedily in Britain carried immediate weight with Vickers and with Burney. There was only one possible alternative if a passenger line were to become immediately feasible: Britain must turn to the Zeppelin Company.

At this time most of the Americans and French and some in less affluent nations were separately but scarcely secretly attempting to manipulate the rules that they themselves had made, each seeking to find commercial advantage by circumventing the prohibition against the Germans building large airships by constructing ships in their own countries but under licence from the Zeppelin Company. Britain went further than her rivals: in the

British plan, the Germans were to undertake not only all designing but would also make all the component parts of a ship which
could then be constructed in England. By this means, not only
would the prohibition be evaded but also the British could have
at short notice a 5,000,000 cubic feet ship built upon principles
well-tested by long and successful experience and this, because of
low wages in Germany, at a cost almost one third lower than the
theoretical cost of building the same ship at home. Burney went
to Germany to negotiate and took Wallis with him.

This was Wallis's second venture outside Britain. An older
Wallis once confessed himself heartsick for the beauties of
Switzerland but even when he could well afford it he made no
effort to return. Generally he found his intellectual travels with
the printed word sufficient. For him the rainbow ended in
Trafalgar Square or up on the hills of the Lake District.

> I don't think exciting things are the most interesting . . . lots
> of things about work, swimming, cricket and tennis . . . and the
> rustling of the trees are much more interesting to me than
> journeys to the continent which anyone can make who buys a
> Cook's ticket.[13]

Nevertheless, Wallis seems to have enjoyed himself in Germany
and not merely because he was deeply and powerfully engaged in
important airship matters. He thought Friedrichshafen and Lake
Constance beautiful and, despite his protestations of puritanical
disapproval of his own behaviour, he relished the new experience
of staying in a luxury hotel; obsequious waiters served him the
best food he had ever eaten. 'Generally I don't care a hoot
what I eat . . . but here one actually thinks what new delicacy
they are going to spring.' Justifying the relapse by his exhaustion,
he took to smoking once more, 'ventured on a huge German cigar
and found it very good.' His German had evaporated since his
schooldays but had it been fluent he would still have found some
difficulty in explaining to the room-maid that, amidst all this
luxury, he really wanted a cold bath each morning.

Neither sybaritism nor its antidote in cold baths equalled for
him the pleasure of his dealings with the Zeppelin Company.
They showed him their Airship Museum ('Count Zeppelin was a
very wonderful old man') and gave him a history of the firm—

which he offered to lend to Molly. Conferences went on sometimes
for six hours at a time and, when Burney had to leave to attend
a Cabinet Committee in London, Wallis stayed on in sole charge
of the British end of discussions which could eventually involve
expenditure of eight million pounds.

He was elated, entirely confident, and eventually travelled
back to London certain that he had done a good job. Soon the
Zeppelin scheme was abandoned, and it was to be more than six
years before Britain had a new airship, but the collapse of the
dealings with Zeppelins was no fault of the novice negotiator.

For the moment all seemed to be going well for Wallis. He
was once more entirely certain that Burney was a man with whom
he could work. Wallis was beginning to allow his mind to wander
more freely than had ever before been possible to him as a
practising and practical engineer. He claimed that he never
dreamed but twice during that summer of 1923 he reported to
Molly that he had woken up in the morning with the ghost of a
new idea lingering in his brain. With great care he explained
to her that 'inventions' were not born fully-developed and that
even ideas had to be checked by weeks of patiently-wrought
paper-work. For this 'invention' that was in his mind, and so that
he might be more capable of doing his own stability calculations
he began private lessons in rigid dynamics—'the most appalling
stuff'. No less patiently he set about presenting to Molly the
problem that was behind his new idea: just as bridge-builders
had been forced to 'invent' new techniques when they came to
designing bridges with spans of one hundred feet or more, so as
airships grew bigger the airship designer could not 'simply take
existing forms and methods and multiply them by two'. He was
close to a solution to the problem of size, and in that solution
was the germ of the idea of geodetic construction.

As his work progressed so did his private life. Although as
yet they had not so much as kissed each other and although
marriage was never mentioned in their letters there was between
him and Molly Bloxam an implication of certainty that some
day not so very far away they would be husband and wife. Insinua-
tions began to appear more frequently in their correspondence.
Did he like children? Had she noticed how coincident were their
tastes? She loved walking, the countryside, flowers, games. (The
last was not true but because he was fond of games she let him

believe that it was.) He for his part quoted poetry—above all Tennyson—because poetry and love seemed to be consistent, and because he knew that she liked Jane Austen he read *Emma*. When, with all the pleasures of a man who was skilful with his hands but now had few opportunities of practising a craft, he built himself a crystal set and tuned it more and more often to concerts of classical music.

Like many a shy man he was finding that he could communicate more easily on paper. His letters, written almost daily to Molly even at times when they were meeting with some regularity, are for the most part prosaic, full of gossip about work, friends, personal activities. They remained, for the most part, as respectable and formal as the hat, gloves and stick which—most surprisingly to those who knew him twenty or more years later—he always carried. But there is a subtle change in the tone of the mathematics lessons which seems to indicate that these were the real love-letters. Whether he knew it or not, his aim was no longer teaching Molly mathematics so that she would pass examinations. Now he was attempting to bring her alongside so that she could go with him on the intellectual soarings for which he was now flexing his mind. There is, too, in the growing use of airship examples, a further clue to the ardour that is but half hidden by the careful tutoring, and far more significant than the mathematics is a phrase thrice repeated over three months: 'I would like to write you a book about airships.'

In the more mundane parts of his letters reminiscence became more frequent, as if he were deliberately filling her in on that part of his life which she had not known. Still, with the one exception which has already been quoted, he kept even Molly away from that mined plot in which he guarded his memories of his mother and, for quite different reasons, he seldom mentioned his brothers or his sister, but there was much that he told her about his life at Cowes, his time in the services and his early work on ships and airships. With increasing frequency his letters touched upon his schooldays. On almost the first occasion when he mentioned Christ's Hospital in a letter to Molly it was with unabashed sentiment such as, even to her, he had seldom revealed on any other subject except airships (and, of course, in that one solitary reference to his mother.) 'It's the most wonderful school in the world,' he wrote, 'I love it and so does everyone who went there.'[14]

Barnes Wallis

As Molly was determined to share his enthusiasm for airships so, sensing his feeling, was she keen to know more of Christ's Hospital. She asked him questions about his own life at school, about the history, customs and *mores* of the institution. He answered them with delight, sent an edition of Lamb's essays containing the two seemingly contradictory ventures into reminiscence, *Recollections of Christ's Hospital* and *Christ's Hospital Five and Thirty Years Ago*, supported it with a drawing of his own Ward in Newgate Street with on it—marked with a cross—the window under which he had slept for two years. Then, as if to refill the springs of recollection, he went back to West Horsham. It was early in the school summer vacation. There were, consequently, no boys about and few members of the staff, but when Sergeant Fuggles told him that Chas. E. Browne had not yet left for his holiday, Wallis presented himself at the door of his old tutor. It was a wonderful reunion. Browne showed him over the new laboratories and the Engineering School that had been built soon after Wallis left school. They discussed educational theory. Browne was delighted to hear that, after all, Wallis had taken a degree. Thereafter, Wallis's visits became frequent and he was asking Molly to go down with him.

However, this first return to Christ's Hospital added a strain of tragedy to his generally happy habit in reminiscence. Sergeant Fuggles had lent him the key to the school swimming baths, and swimming there alone he was miserably reminded of stilled voices. Eight of the Peele A boys of his short school generation had been killed in the war. Two more would never leave hospital and one was blind. History was irrevocable, and all that he could muster at that time was a sense of sadness, but, he wrote to Molly, in what now seems the incongruous slang of the time 'it would be ripping if one could help'.

So it is no exaggeration to claim that the germ for two of his greatest ideas, geodetic construction and the Royal Air Force Foundation, were both glimpsed by him for the first time in that summer of 1923.

In so many ways that was among the happiest periods of his life. His future in airships was at last certain. He was earning good money. He was sure of Molly. He was bubbling with new ideas. He was working hard but still he had ample opportunity for exercise and for the hobbies which he so much enjoyed. (Once he had built his own crystal set he built others for his relations and friends.) By joining the Territorials, he had revived his old flirtation with the Forces. Vickers had established their own anti-aircraft battery, and Wallis joined as a gunner. His rationalisation of his motives was convincing enough. The best way to learn how to make airships invulnerable was to learn all that one could about the methods available for shooting them down. But there was also in him some need to compensate for never having seen action in the war. Next time, he was convinced, the war would begin with a huge air-attack and the anti-aircraft gunners would be the first into active service—and he had no doubt that the next time was coming soon.

No less real and certainly more revealing of something permanent in his character was his almost sensual pleasure in antisybaritism. Early in *Seven Pillars of Wisdom* there is a passage which, taken out of context, seems fit description of this element in Wallis's nature:

> The body [writes Lawrence] was too coarse to feel the utmost of our sorrows and of our joys. Therefore we abandoned it as rubbish: we left it below us to march forward a breathing simulacrum, on its own unaided level, subject to influences from which in normal times our instincts would have shrunk.

Lawrence continues the passage into a justification of homosexual practices for which Wallis could not in any circumstances find excuse—to which in fact he was to become in time more than ordinarily censorious—and yet there is an affinity between the two men, between the intellectual turned man of action and the practical man who as yet had been deprived of action, which goes far beyond this physical self-driving. By 1923 Wallis, revelling in the hardness of camp life, his pride in his own resistance to exhaustion, his enthusiasm for testing himself against foul weather, even the joy he found in the roughness of his Territorial uniform and the tightness of his puttees, had reached a level which some would call masochism. Undoubtedly Wallis was then, and was to remain for some years, close to the boundary-line where deliberately invoked discipline becomes aberration, so that from time to time aftersight catches in his correspondence glimpses of a hideous possibility; had it not been for the entirely sane influence of Molly this masochism could have taken over and might have become for Wallis what Lawrence's homosexuality was for him. Unlike Lawrence he had never experienced the ultimate release of adventure and danger (and undoubtedly resented this *lacuna* in his own experience). Instead, and surprisingly in a man who had but recently and for the first time fallen in love and no less surprisingly in an essentially shy man, he found his moments of greatest content when in the company of men indulging in those activities which—good Victorian that he was—he dared to call 'doing manly things'. The embryo of this trait had been with him since his school-days; the trait was to remain with him throughout his life. Again like Lawrence he found some comfort in the congenial irresponsibility of the ranks.

1923 was his year of miracles. He had found love; he had broken out of the silence that had been on him since his mother's death; he had again someone with whom he could communicate about his ambitions and his ideas; he was involved in pastimes which gave him profound pleasure; he was feeling the stirrings of originality; innovation was in his mind and shattering possibilities that owed nothing to precedent provided by others.

He could not know that there was a storm on the horizon which threatened the perfectibility at least of his professional life. It would have taken a soothsayer to recognise a speech made at Plymouth on 25 October by Prime Minister Baldwin as a prelude to renewed and eventually final disaster for the airship.

The Conservatives had reached office by pledging themselves not to introduce Protection; now Baldwin admitted that he saw no way of stemming unemployment without accepting the remedy which his party had rejected at its election. This made the dissolution of Parliament inevitable and now, at last, with a new election pending, Wallis saw the danger-signs.

> This wretched election is upsetting all Airship plans [he wrote] because the Bill authorising the subsidy from the Government was to have been passed this session and now of course, it can scarcely go thro' the new Parliament until say March. And if the Liberals come back that awful man Winston Churchill is a bitter opponent of Rigid Airships and very likely he may try to stop it altogeher.[15]

Chillon and Courtship

The Liberals did not come back. But the General Election of 1923 brought the Labour Party to power for the first time. When on 23 January 1924 Ramsay MacDonald took the oath as the first Labour Prime Minister, even the most rabid Socialist must have seen that such was the tenuous nature of his strength in the House and of his agreement with dissident Liberals that it was hardly worth his moving to 10 Downing Street. However, there were enshrined in the principles of his party two doctrines, pacifism and state control of industry, which were bound to force them to look hard, early and antipathetically at the great industrial empires, and first of all at the great armaments empire of Vickers. Ramsay MacDonald's Cabinet was a distinguished team. But for Wallis, Burney and the airship industry as a whole there was one truly sinister appointment which would most immediately affect their future: the Air Ministry.

Brigadier-General Christopher Birdwood Thomson had given up his commission—originally held in the Royal Engineers—to run as a Socialist candidate in 1919. He was defeated, lost again in 1922 and even in the Labour year, 1923, could not find a seat. In order to bring him into the government MacDonald gave him a peerage. The future blared out in his choice of title. Brigadier-General Lord Thomson of Cardington had only to pronounce his style to bring uneasiness to all who hoped for independence and fruitfulness in the airship programme. The Conservative member for Bedford (the constituency which contained the airship station at Cardington) read the implications and in a debate on 21 March 1924 begged of the Government that it should not attempt to build its own ships.[16] Burney and Wallis worried over the appointment. Wallis was prepared to continue designing against the day when national sanity would prevail but Burney was not content to found his future upon optimism alone. Whatever he was not, he was without doubt an outstanding member of an as yet unfounded profession: public relations. He took every opportunity offered and created opportunities for himself and for his colleagues to explain and recommend his schemes to a public beyond Westminster. Wallis soon became embroiled in the process. His readiness, unusual among scientists of all kinds, to present his professional ideas to an amateur audience dates from this period and with it

119

some of his unpopularity in certain quarters which resented both his eagerness for public support and the skill with which he sought it.

The first occasion when he deputised for Burney as a public speaker (a lecture to the Royal Colonial Institute at Bristol) he found himself speaking at very short notice on a subject to which hitherto he had paid very little attention. On that morning in March 1924 Wallis was summoned to Burney's office. Burney had a cold and would have to cry off the Bristol engagement but thought it best for Wallis to take his place. He had forgotten the exact title of his promised lecture and could not find the relevant correspondence. He thrust at Wallis a box of slides and a paper he had presented two weeks earlier to the Cambridge Aeronautical Society—a paper which Wallis had not read. There was just enough time for Wallis to catch the 1.10 from Paddington and in the train he made a list of the slides. Once arrived at the Institute in Bristol Wallis asked the Organising Secretary what it was he was to talk about. 'The Political and Economic Effect of the Development of the Commercial Airship on the Empire'! There was an hour left for him to collect the thoughts he did not know he had. Somehow he struggled through the lecture and the struggle was successfully hidden from the audience.

> Do you know [he wrote to Molly] I shall never be so frightened again for I have discovered a most marvellous thing. You just give up control of your brain *entirely*, and speak automatically. *It's perfectly extraordinary*, for in some most wonderful way, the jolly old brain carries on by itself. Effortless, rapid, sensible, out pours an even flow of words.[17]

Standing, as it were, in his own audience, he was even able to recognise his faults as a speaker. From now on he diligently set himself to correct these failings so that, with time and practice, he was to become one of the best and most sought after of all lecturers. But, far more important, in that hastily contrived Bristol lecture he discovered the subject-matter which would serve him with appropriate adaptation for the rest of his life. For airships he would substitute aircraft of whatever kind were his current interest—or even submarines. Others turned the Empire into the Commonwealth but forever the substance of most of his talks was the role of the airship, the plane or the submarine in securing and improving the economic and political future of Britain as the focus of the Empire.

On 14 May 1924 Ramsay MacDonald announced his Government's decision about airship policy.[18] His distaste—and that of his colleagues—for the proposed Burney–Vickers monopoly had been foreseeable.

However, disastrous though it was to prove to those whose responsibility it was and debilitating to Burney and his followers, MacDonald's policy did not shut the door on private enterprise. The Burney Scheme was rejected; no Labour Government could accept a Vickers monopoly; but airship development was to be continued and indeed intensified. The Air Ministry was authorised to undertake at Cardington an extensive research programme. Civil Service designers were authorised to plan and Government workshops to build a 5,000,000 cubic feet ship. Funds were set aside for the building of a terminus and for an intermediate base for an airship service to India. As a sop the Airship Company was to be offered first refusal of a contract to build a second ship.

From the moment when the Prime Minister announced the Government's eagerness to build its own ship and at the same time conceded grudgingly its acceptance of Burney's alternative proposals the Press seized upon the intriguing possibilities of this competition, a symbolic testing of opposing political creeds. In *R.100* and *R.101* the doctrines of free enterprise and of socialism were set for the first time to public trial. The competition and the debate went on for six years under floodlights provided by the newspapers. But the error, if error it was on the part of the Government, was not so much in setting up a race; the mistakes the Cabinet made were, first that the attempt to build two ships was made when Britain had available scarcely enough expertise to build one successfully and, secondly, that having at the nation's disposal so very few men who knew anything much about designing airships it handed the responsibility for its own ship to men whose knowledge and skill were insufficient for the task.

When, in July 1924, Wallis was confirmed as Chief Designer to the Airship Guarantee Company he had no time to realise that he was the one man committed to either project who had ever taken a major role in building an airship. Of the one-time designers several had gone over to aeroplanes, some back to submarines and ships, and some of the rest, including Campbell, her chief designer, had died in the crash of *R.38*. Vickers, the only private concern still in airships, had lost H. B. Pratt, and J. E. Temple was about to go. His place as Calculator had already been filled by an ex-Woolwich cadet who, having just missed the war, had then gone up to Oxford and taken a Third in Engineering. His limited post-university experience as a stress and performance calculator at De Havillands had been considerably interrupted by his enthusiasm for flying planes and for writing novels. Nevil Shute Norway was twenty-four years old when he joined Wallis.

If Wallis was unique it scarcely worried him but—and in this Burney agreed with him—he found it sardonic that the team chosen to design the Government ship was formed of the members of Burney's discarded Committee: Richmond, Scott, Colmore and Nixon, with the addition of another ex-naval officer, now Director of Airship Development at the Air Ministry, Group Captain P. M. Fellowes. Those who so recently had been discarded by Burney almost immediately demonstrated their new-found prestige in a needless explosion of tactlessness. The powers had decided to give the Airship Guarantee ship the number *R.100*, to their own ship the number *R.101*. Scott explained the decision to Wallis:

> We have given your ship the number *R.100*, as showing that it will be no more than a rehash of the German methods and therefore the last of an outdated form of construction; whereas, as our ship will be of entirely novel design, embodying the latest and most up-to-date materials and engineering methods, and we regard it as the first of an entirely new series, and have therefore decided to give us the number *R.101*, that is the first of the new series.[19]

It is no longer possible to discover if this was the real reason for the numbering. Equally it may have been some fiction invented by Scott either out of arrogance or (and it is not inconceivable) as a sophisticated leg-pull. Whatever Scott's intention it was inevitable, and he should have seen it as inevitable, that

Chillon and Courtship

Wallis would resent both the information and the manner of its telling, and that the insult to his professional activities and his colleagues would fester.

For the moment, however, and though there was much worse to come, Wallis had no energy to spare for jealousy. Experience had taught him that the airship programme was susceptible to public whim and practical disaster but, with his mind churning at technical possibilities, Wallis allowed himself to see only opportunity. He closed his mind to doubts, and this buttressing of his professional certainty gave him also new confidence to attack the problem of his personal future.

Molly's father had grudgingly agreed that if, despite separation, Molly decided to reject his advice and disdain his wishes and if Barnes continued in his selfish and malevolent courtship of a girl young enough to be his daughter, then Bloxam would accept a provisional engagement. Molly was, by her own evidence, certain that she was in love but she was not yet so certain of her own ability to face up to her father to be able to admit to herself, and certainly not to Barnes, that they could consider themselves engaged. Barnes was supported in abstinence by family tradition: by the long period of engagement endured by his own parents and by his father's frequently reiterated statement of admiration for his father-in-law. Barnes's grandfather, who had never kissed his wife-to-be before their marriage and even after the ceremony lay with her only to produce children. But after two years in limbo Barnes was finding that the delights of nobility were wearing very thin. Early in 1924, probably hoping that relaxation of regulation would prove to both of them the inappropriateness of their relationship, Bloxam conceded that they could meet without chaperonage and could correspond freely. When Barnes, with a rush of courage caused by the new security in his professional life, taxed Bloxam with the impossibility of contrived postponement, Bloxam moved to his penultimate line of defence. Molly was to go abroad for three months. If, at the end of that time the two of them were still determined upon folly he would agree to an engagement. Molly herself, by no means free of pleasure at being the cause of wrangling between the two men she most respected, with scant grace and without telling Barnes what it was that she had decided, went off to Switzerland for the summer.

Barnes wrote to her daily and in almost every letter, by protesting his readiness to await her return before seeking a decision, pressed decision upon her. In almost every letter, too, he denied plaintiveness—and was urgent in the plaintive cry that she must arrive at her own conclusion. A new thought struck him and began to worry its way through his letters. Perhaps she would not accept him because his profession made his life a poor risk. If she wished it he would turn to some other and less dangerous branch of engineering. Molly was far too well-balanced and by now far too determined upon marriage to accept an offer that she knew would have been fatal to their chance of happiness; an offer that she was well-aware was not intended to be accepted.

In September 1924 Molly returned from Switzerland. Barnes was at Kidderpore Avenue on her first evening back. He had worried himself into the conviction that he really did not know which way her decision would go. As if they had not been courting for more than two years he announced undying love and, with full Victorian drama, proposed marriage. Molly, the child of her generation as he of his, answered with an unequivocal yes, hurried out to break the news to her father and with it a no less unequivocal refusal to return to her medical studies. Bloxam recognised defeat, but there was still one more line of resistance open to him. He suggested the necessity for a long engagement. After all Molly knew nothing of housewifery and she needed time to learn. Barnes and Molly rode hard over this obstacle. Six months was quite long enough for a course in cookery and domestic science. They would marry on the anniversary of their first real meeting. Bloxam capitulated and all concerned prepared for a wedding on St George's Day, 1925.

Meanwhile, and against the tenor of his intentions, Wallis had accepted a commission as Second Lieutenant in the Vickers Royal Artillery Battery. His delight at having 'this very considerable honour' thrust upon him is almost unbelievably naïve in a man of thirty-eight years. As always ambivalent about accepting responsibility, that side of his nature which held him from pleasure in being set above his fellows was demonstrated in terms no less naïve:

I'm never so happy holding a commission, you have to be dignified and dour to get such a jolly time because there's a good deal of ceremonial connected with the mess and so on. Still one is very comfortable in camp, has a servant, later dinner and so on.[20]

A fiancée—soon to be a wife—a Gunner commission and an airship; for the first time in his career he was the undisputed master of a vast and original project. Burney could handle politics and finance. Wallis was delighted to have Professors Bairstow and Pippard as consultants and eager to gather round him a team of young and efficient subordinates, but *R.100* was his and his mental skills expanded to meet the challenge of solo creation.

9 *R.100*

In the last months of 1924 with very few excursions to the drawing-board and none to the laboratory or testing-chamber, Wallis dreamed up an entire airship, complete in detail and rich in original features. By the end of 1924 he set on paper the basic outline of her design, many of the novel *minutiae* of construction, and the complicated programme of theory and experiment which must serve as prelude to her building.

The ambitious hopes for *R.100* and the multiplicity of service which she was called upon to fulfil set before her designer problems of enormous complexity. The ship must be so built as to weather not only normal but also occasional catastrophic conditions—she must be able to ride through disturbances even more onerous than those which had destroyed *Shenandoah*. In time of war she must serve as what he insisted on describing as 'a naval *recognisance* vessel', and even the worst buffetings of nature could not match the possibilities that would come with battle. In peacetime conditions his ship would carry, at 90 m.p.h., 140 passengers, 7 tons of luggage and another 7 tons of mail 3,761 miles. From Capetown she could reach non-stop Freetown, Rio de Janeiro or Dongola. Flying at 72 m.p.h. and with the same load she could fly 6,017 miles so that the outer limits of her non-stop flight would be Trinidad, Calcutta and the Eyre Peninsula in South Australia. As a vessel of war loaded with 20 tons of bombs she could fly at 90 m.p.h. and achieve a length of flight of 4,473 miles, enough to get her non-stop to a destination in Senegal, to Aswan or to Buenos Aires. Finally and triumphantly, he announced that as a naval scout flying without offensive load at 56·7 m.p.h. his ship could fly 17,890 miles non-stop and reach any place in the world.

Seen from an age that has known the feats of the astronauts

these boasts seem puny, but in 1925 the non-stop record of aeroplanes stood at 2,734 miles. Even today, almost half a century later, no commercial airlines fly as much as 17,890 miles without a stop for refuelling.

Endurance was not the only advantage claimed for the putative *R.100*. Regardless of weather conditions, she could start and end her voyage on a mast 170 feet high.

The possibilities which Wallis forecast demanded a vessel of strength such as had no precedent in previous designs: under normal flying conditions a safety factor of three and under 'catastrophic conditions' a safety factor of two. These considerations and the fact that the ship was to be twice as large as anything built hitherto anywhere in the world added to the conclusion that if the designer followed earlier exemplars her total weight would have held her earth-bound to eternity. But Wallis was set upon building a ship from first principles, guided only by theory, experiment and calculation; never again would an airship be put into the air, as *R.38* had been, without any consideration of the aerodynamic forces that she must meet. His planning was meticulous and he placed innumerable theoretical problems before his two distinguished consultants, Professors Bairstow and Pippard.

First must come the preliminary calculations which would enable the structure of the ship to be set out, the overall dimensions to be fixed, the weights of the structure to be estimated and the position fixed of power units and passenger quarters. The second stage would involve laying out the plan for the mesh wiring throughout the ship, the tensions on the various parts of the mesh would be dependent on the internal gas pressure. Conversely, he argued, since the precise design of the mesh wiring would affect to a considerable extent the loads in both transverse frames and longitudinals, the mesh wiring pattern must first be established and the resultant reactions discovered in transverse frames and longitudinals under various degrees of inflation. As a preliminary to the design of the girders of the hull and before any other work could be done, Wallis claimed that it was necessary to consider the compressive strength as struts of built-up girders of the type decided upon for the construction of the ship. Next, and before the design of the frames could be settled, it would be necessary to discover the longitudinal shear forces and bending moments that would come from the differing distribution of lifting force and fixed weights. It would also be vital to establish the longitudinal shear force and bending moments due to dynamic considerations.

This done he would be ready to consider the transverse frames. Since the reaction due to the sum of all the external forces is exactly balanced by the difference in reaction of the longitudinal shearwiring on either side of the frame, it would now be possible to determine the forces in the various members of the transverse frame both under normal flight conditions and also in the special circumstances prevailing when an adjacent gas-bag was deflated. The sizes of the members and also the distortion of each frame under the worst conditions of loading could be fixed theoretically. Penultimately, his team should come to calculating the design of the longitudinal girders, shearwiring and external frames. Finally, in so far as structural design was involved, it would be necessary to consider purely local loading such as fins, rudders, power-units and bow-mooring gear.

Such theorising was novel not only in Britain—where it was not attempted on anything like the same scale by the team working on the rival state-sponsored ship—but even in Germany. It showed Wallis in a new light: his thinking was entire and at the same time wonderfully detailed. He was demonstrating his ability to settle into his mind all the complexities of design, the interaction of one part upon another, and to use both imagination and logic to build by thought alone a complete airship that was nevertheless the sum of all practical parts.

Even so, this competence was not invention and it is remarkable that, coincidental with his acceptance of this new responsibility for total planning, he should have suddenly discovered in himself a genius for finding novel answers to questions which had exercised the minds of airship engineers since Zeppelin's first endeavours early in the century. In 1924 and 1925 there were registered in the names of Wallis and the Airship Guarantee Company (sometimes with Burney's name added) more than twenty patents under the general heading 'Improvements in or relating to Airships'.

In the light of subsequent events far and away the most interesting series of patents related to the 'skeleton'. They poured out: new schemes for mesh wiring, for riveting members, for building girders out of duralumin tubes from sheet-metal rolled up spirally and riveted with a helical gear for maintaining the front portion of the ship free from efficiency-sapping external protuberances such as cars, struts, and wiring. All tended to make possible a new concept in aerostat construction: a method of organising the design so that all stresses, loads and reactions remained constantly in balance, all horizontal and vertical forces in every member equating to zero, all deflections in correspondence with the forces elongating the members. This, the 'dream-idea' of which he had written to Molly in the summer of 1923, was to take years to reach maturity. Nevil Shute, who was himself partly responsible for much of this work on *R.100* writes in his autobiography *Slide Rule* of the frustration and 'satisfaction almost amounting to a religious experience'. The system that Wallis proposed and the essential calculations he describes thus:

... each transverse frame consisted of a girder in the form of a stiff, sixteen-sided polygon with the flats at top and bottom; this girder was twenty-seven inches deep and up to a hundred and thirty feet in diameter. Sixteen steel cables ran from the centre of the polygon, the axis of the ship, to the corner points, bracing the polygonal girder against deflections. All loads whether of gas lift, weights carried on the frame or shearwire reactions, were applied to the corner points of the polygon, and except in the case of the ship turning these loads were symmetrical port and starboard. One half of the transverse frame, therefore, divided by a vertical plane passing through the axis of the ship, consisted of an *encastré* arched rib with ends free to slide towards each other, and this arched rib was braced by eight radial wires, some of which would go slack through the deflection of the arched rib under the applied loads. Normally four or five wires would remain in tension, and for the first approximation the slack wires would be guessed. The forces and bending moments in the members could then be calculated by the solution of a lengthy simultaneous equation containing up to seven unknown quantities; this work usually occupied two calculators about a week. In the solution it was usual to find a compression force in one or two of the radial wires; the whole process then had to be begun again using a different selection of wires.

Barnes Wallis

When a likely-looking solution had at last been obtained, deflection diagrams were set out for the movements of the various corners of the polygon under the bending moments and loads found in the various portions of the arched rib, and these yielded the extension of the radial wires under load, which was compared with the calculated loads found in the wires. It was usual to find a discrepancy, perhaps due to an arithmetical mistake by a tired calculator ten days before, and the calculations had to be repeated till this check was satisfied. When the deflections and calculated loads agreed, it was not uncommon to discover that one of the wires thought to be slack was, in fact, in tension as revealed by the deflection diagrams, which meant that the two calculators had to moisten the lips and start again at the very beginning.

. . . After literally months of labour, having filled perhaps fifty foolscap sheets with closely pencilled figures, after many disappointments and heartaches, the truth stood revealed, real, and perfect, and unquestionable; the very truth. It did one good; one was better for the experience. It struck me at the time that those who built the great arches of the English cathedrals in mediaeval times must have known something of our mathematics and perhaps passed through the same experience, and I have wondered if Freemasonry had anything to do with this.[1]

Originality is seldom as original or invention as spontaneous as the myth-makers would have us believe. The achievements of others are always present, both in the conscious and the subconscious mind of an intelligent human being; the bell that arouses him to the creation of novelty may have been ringing through his thoughts for decades before its significance occurs to him. Archimedes floods the bathroom; the apple falls on Newton's head; Benjamin Franklin flies his kite; Fleming sees the mould on the culture; all these are events in the middle of a story, they are not the opening lines. Thus, too, with Wallis and geodetic construction one cannot say that 'here, at this moment, Wallis invented geodetic construction'. Indeed the history of geodetic construction was long, and not all of it uniquely connected with Wallis. It underlines the semantic difficulty which one has in attempting to classify many of Wallis's activities. To describe him as inventor or discoverer is to misrepresent for it presses emphasis away from his continuous and frequently routine application to his work as an engineer and highlights instead, and falsely, a spasmodic inspiration. Yet if he is listed merely as a designer the description is unwarrantably pallid for a designer may be no more than a competent draughtsman who derives originality out of generally accepted principles. Better to place Wallis in all categories: inventor, innovator, designer, artist-engineer, sometimes all at the same time and always some.

This complexity of function adds to the difficulty of marshalling the account of any one of his major achievements according to an orderly sequence. If men of his profession are, just as other creators, influenced by their fellows and by their own memories, they are, nevertheless, far more than most creators, in a position to experiment with ideas even before those ideas are fully formulated. The engineering-designer's creative work—and above all such an innovation as Wallis's use of geodetic construction—is a complex of novelties and long-established and sometimes ordinary-seeming principles. Some of it he borrows from the work of other engineers and some from his own earlier achievements. The beginning is all history and the end gradual obsolescence. In between there are forays, essays that tend towards a conclusion which even the creator himself does not recognise, experiments which even he does not see as foreshadowing a conclusion—and a great many starts, some of them false and most of them considered by him only as ends in themselves.

Thus geodetic construction was a discovery and an innovation which came from the work of many engineers and which, even in Wallis's mind, had its origins back in 1923. It was worked out in the years of design, amendment, addition and construction that went into *R.100*. It was to come to fruition in the magnificent stability of the Wellesley and was to have its apotheosis in the war years when Wellington after Wellington was battered in the skies over Occupied Europe but still flew back to its base in Britain. Dream, drawing-board, essay, experiment, trial—and a good many errors—went into the effort. The viability of the theory was established, first to his own satisfaction theoretically and then practically, but once fully proved there was a great deal of tinkering, changing, improving, doubling-back upon the proven theory in order to fill in gaps revealed by practice. There are in Wallis's name, well over one hundred patents that may be said to relate

—overtly or indirectly—to his intention of building a 'plane on geodetic principles.

The term 'geodetic' needs a line of explanation: as Wallis and his fellow practitioners use it it has only an evocative connection with its etymological origins. The definition is constant as stated by the mathematicians Thomson and Tait in 1879 and quoted in the *Oxford English Dictionary*:

> If the shortest possible line be drawn from one point of a surface to another, its plane of curvature is everywhere perpendicular to the surface. Such a curve is called a Geodetic Line.

The first full step towards the use of goedetic construction was that designed by Wallis for the gas-bag wiring of *R.100*. In technique and methodology he had already made a giant leap forward in designing *R.80*, but in one respect—the system of netting to retain the gas-bags—like every other airship under construction *R.80* slavishly followed German examples. All rigid airship designers everywhere and throughout the history of lighter-than-air craft knew full well that this was in truth the crucial problem before them: how, having regard to the varying outward pressure of the gas-bag could it be constructed to lie within the internal diameter of the regular polygonal form of an exceedingly light but very large and relatively flexible structure? The German solution was comparatively simple, a system of wiring to longitudinal girders, coupled with bracing wires for transverse frames. When this method was used the variation in pressure which came with height caused the tension set up in the wire mesh to increase from the bottom to the top of the gas-bag and the consequence was a relatively heavy side-load on every longitudinal girder; no serious matter for those girders in tension but for those in compression having the effect of augmenting the natural tendency of a strut to bow sideways and thus reducing the buckling strength and hence the Factor of Safety. The Germans, like their imitators, did not know how to calculate these factors. Unlike their imitators, however, the Germans had behind them the vast empiricism of a successful airship industry and instinctively they learnt to make adequate allowance for lateral loads.

That both *R.100* and *R.101* dispensed with the German method came indirectly from a ruling of the Airworthiness of Airships

Panel which decreed that on future airships the longitudinal girders must not be subjected to any side-load from the differential tensions in the gas-bag wiring. In effect this ruling eliminated all possibility of attaching the wires to the longitudinal girders and at first and even second glance seemed to eliminate airships, for at the time there appeared to be no other way than the German of transmitting lift to the rigid framework.

At third or fourth glance the *R.101* team came up with a solution that eventually was to prove no solution at all: a system of parachute harness through which the lift was taken by the wires right down to the bottom of each transverse frame. As a laterally loaded wire must assume a curved form and in order to prevent the top of these curved wires from allowing the gas-bag fabric to rub against the longitudinal girders, the designers of *R.101* were compelled to leave large gaps between the gas-bags and the girders. In the eventual struggle to reduce overweight and improve the performance of *R.101* the gas-bags were let out with, as we shall see, disastrous consequences.

A solution similar to parachute wiring was considered by Wallis and quickly dismissed. Instead, he hit upon the notion of geodetic construction. As yet, of course, his ideas were vague and certainly his mathematical expertise was too unsophisticated for him so much as to apply the term 'geodetics' to what he had in mind, let alone to indulge in the highly complicated and esoteric calculations that are involved in transferring geodetic theory to the purposes of practical construction. What he did know was known to every engineer: that a wire held at the ends and loaded radially and uniformly throughout its length must deform into the arc of a circle. This elementary and universally-held knowledge he extended into a hypothesis that at once seemed to bring him near to a possible answer to the unanswerable problem set by the Airworthiness of Airships regulations. He would have attained his object if he could so splay out the wires that restrained the gas-bags that whatever the gas pressure the load per foot run remained constant. Now Wallis's nights teaching himself advanced mathematics began to pay dividends. He knew that he was involving himself with the properties of a helix; that in a parallel or right cylindrical bay every one of the diagonals is a helix and that for such a parallel it would be possible to establish the arrangement of helices so that the loading per unit

length of each helix would remain constant and the whole system
of wiring meet the obvious requirement that it lie within the
circular cross-section of the hull of the airship. He could design
his mesh-wiring to this regimen of helices, attaching each wire
to circumferential and longitudinal jack-stays which in turn
would be attached to the hull framework at the centroid of each
joint. But now theory and Wallis's mathematical agility foundered. All that he had worked out was for a parallel bag but
no gas-bag on *R.100* or any other ship was a parallel cylinder.
Intuitively he felt that the theory still held for a non-parallel
bag but he knew of no way of calculating the design nor even of
any way of demonstrating its validity. Temple, Burney's mathematical adviser, insisted that the system would not work, but,
just as Wallis could not prove his theory, so also Temple could
not disprove it by calculation. Wallis sought out A. E. Webb, one
of his former assistants at Barrow and now a Lecturer at University College, London, and through him was able to put his theory
to L. N. G. Filon, F.R.S., the Professor of Engineering at University College. Filon was intrigued. Within weeks he provided a
written report confirming Wallis's theory, adding that the wires
in the non-parallel hull would be *geodesics* (and thus, for the first
time, introducing the word to the vocabulary of aeronautical
engineering) and adding all the mathematical formulae necessary to enable Wallis to work out the pattern of wiring.

For his airship plans Wallis had several assistants, among them
not only Nevil Shute Norway but also a colleague from the war
years, a chemist of distinction, Philip Teed, who had done much
important work on airship fuels and who was even now at work
producing a synthetic substitute for the goldbeater's skin that
had hitherto been used for lining gas-bags. The atmosphere in
the design-team was enthusiastic and cordial, but despite the
pleasure that he took from all-male company, Wallis had not then
—and never developed—any great capacity for establishing close
friendships with other men.

Meanwhile his wedding day was upon him. The ceremony took
place at St Luke's Church, Hampstead. It was a correct assembly:
the middle-class men in their best morning coats and their
middle-class wives wearing, most of them, the frocks that they
kept for great occasions. But a few of the younger women had
bought, especially for this wedding, frocks in the new and sensa-

tional style. This was the year when, for the first time in modern history, the hem-line was at the knee. Wallis was encased in his morning coat, uncomfortable and restricted.

Molly Bloxam was not yet twenty-one when she became Molly Wallis. Her husband was sixteen years older. If there is no such thing as a typical marriage then still, and from the very beginning, this marriage must be regarded as rare and the role of Molly Wallis in the creation and sustenance of genius can scarcely be overestimated. The parts that she had to play were many and she played them without submerging her own entirely individual personality. Here she was, at the beginning of married life, a pretty, intelligent and essentially sociable girl, the product of a warm, close-knit and sociable family with a better than average education, married to a man almost twice her age, who had no knowledge of women, whose entire emotional involvement had hitherto been centred upon the memory of a mother who had herself found only unhappiness in marriage. Barnes was at that time almost entirely lacking in sociability except in so far as it was to be found in all-male and generally impersonal entities like the Services. He was completely involved with work that she could only dimly understand. All in all, Molly had to be for him wife and friends, audience and—the one role she could not take on (and would never take on) with full success—substitute mother. In due course, as the children were born, so to some degree she had to play as well the role of father to them, for though Barnes was a dutiful parent, and would claim that he was a good father, the existence of children could never be allowed to interfere with his work nor, more subtly, could he accept easily the change in relationship between husband and wife which comes inevitably with the intervention of a new generation. Yet, against all these difficulties, Molly remained sensible, constantly interested both in what was going on close to her: in Barnes, the family and Barnes's work; and also in the world outside the home. She was—and is—no saint. She could be sharp, no more patient with fools than Barnes himself, comfortably certain of the rightness of her own views and, though unshakably loyal, never blinded by the brilliance that was so close to her. She was the one person who saw the chink in the armour of genius and who was not afraid to stick her knitting needle through the hole.

Not that life was notably difficult for her in those early days of their marriage. Young though she was and, according to the genteel euphemism of the times, innocent, her short experience as a medical student had given her sufficient realism about the functions of the body to allow her to approach sex with mature sanity and a sense of pleasure—pleasure which happily she shared with a husband who had been so unnaturally long a celibate. She enjoyed, too, the effort of creating a home, and in this was rarely fortunate in that his perennial pleasure and skill in doing things with his hands made him far more than ordinarily useful and content 'doing things around the house'.

Their first home was in Woolwich, a flat in a recently converted house that had once belonged to General Wolfe. The change in spirit wrought in him by Molly and by marriage was pleasantly demonstrated by his delight in this remote association with Wolfe. The ghosts of other generals—John Nicholson and George Gordon—had marched occasionally through the suburbs of his childhood experience. Now he expelled the two severe Victorians from his enthusiasm and set up in their place the romantic hero-victim of Quebec.

Wallis's pleasure in the reading of poetry increased and was enhanced by the knowledge that in this he was following his great predecessor in the house, but for Gray's *Elegy* he substituted the poetry of Tennyson (an old favourite), Browning and Kipling, and in truth his enthusiasm (like Molly's) did not spring either from association or from literacy sophistication. Instead, it was an indirect product of their self-sufficiency, of their comparative freedom from the conventional need for entertainment. Reading aloud to each other was a relaxation that satisfied them both. (Later they were to add singing in choirs and some interest in music, but the fact that Vaughan Williams' *Sinfonia Antarctica* was one of his favourite compositions had less to do with musical appreciation than with Wallis's great admiration for Scott of the Antarctic and, also, with his enjoyment of Tennyson whose *Ulysses* stands as preface to the Vaughan Williams work).

The flat was very elegant and became still more so under Wallis's skilful ministrations. He even turned the soaring height of the rooms to his own advantage, building himself a tall ladder-seat on which he could perch with his drawing-board and there continue his work out of earshot of the chattering of Molly's sisters when they came to visit.

Wallis, although for the most part a considerate and courteous companion, at times when his work became more than ordinarily difficult became also more than ordinarily inconsiderate. Sometimes he would disappear across London and spend the day with some unnamed expert, returning late at night or even early next morning, seemingly all unconscious of the fact that Molly had passed her time hovering tearfully near the telephone uncertain whether or not she should report his disappearance to the police. Often the dinner which she had prepared for him so carefully after the pattern learned at the cookery school would shrivel and dry in the oven while he worked at some near-intractable detail in the design of *R.100*. But for Molly these were the penalties of being married to a man of distinction—a man of whose genius she was now certain—and the compensation was in his entire readiness to explain and his great ability as a teacher. Molly was part of his work.

Soon too a child was on the way. Barnes was full of good intentions and rushed to buy appropriate reading matter. A new children's classic had just appeared; Barnes read it aloud to Molly and following Pooh's example she 'knitted a little vest for our first-born'. Barnes Junior was born on 1 February 1926 and, almost immediately, after the Christ's Hospital fashion, came to be known as 'Littley'. Barnes Senior was so delighted that he gave up smoking—not for the first time, nor yet for the last—and invested in an education policy.

Hanging as a cloud over the gratifications of home and the excitements of work was the increasing pressure of Governmental distaste for the Airship Guarantee Company and its experts. The tone had been set from the beginning and not merely by political considerations. The Civil Service was in entire agreement with its temporary political masters and determined to continue antipathy to private enterprise even when those political masters had been replaced.

It is in every way preferable that the Government should undertake this work because it can be done carefully and thoroughly, military considerations can be kept in view from the onset, and at the end of the development stage the Government will still be free to subsidize a commercial airship service.

Thus a note produced in Whitehall as early as February 1924.[2]

There was constant prying by officials into the affairs of the Airship Guarantee Company and with it occasional efforts to lure over members of his own staff on to the other side. By the middle of 1925 the antagonism between those who supported *R.100* and the *R.101* group was in the open; the unlikelihood of co-operation between them obvious even to the moderates in Whitehall, and the strain of conscience had begun to bear down upon the already overburdened Chief Designer of *R.100*.

Air Vice Marshal Sir Geoffrey Salmond was one of those who still hoped for collaboration between the two teams. After a meeting in August 1925 he wrote to the Secretary of State for Air a letter reporting a conversation from which it is clear that Wallis himself did not believe in the possibility of co-operation: Salmond wanted co-operation between the design staffs through a Co-ordinating Committee but saw that it was impossible since, as Wallis pointed out to him, this would mean Wallis handing over the results of years of work which belonged properly to Vickers. He was, however, ready to give Salmond himself the solutions he had reached. This confidence Salmond felt bound to refuse, for he could not be sure that he would not inadvertently give away Wallis's 'secrets' to the government designers.[3]

Salmond was not the only exponent of co-operation on the Government side. Colmore was always openly friendly and even in the secrecy of Government papers there is evidence that his eagerness for sensible liaison was more advanced than Wallis believed and more genuine than in later years Wallis would admit. Scott, a simpler man than the others and capable of both courage and insensitiveness, never understood that cheery demonstrations of knowledgeability about wines was scarcely the way to Wallis's heart or mind. It is significant that no effort was made to bring Wallis together with his real opposite number, V. C. Richmond, although Richmond was the one senior member of the *R.101* team he did not know at all. Despite this, it must be admitted that Richmond was from time to time ready to pass on to Howden the results of Cardington experiments.

Generally, the failure to co-operate was the fault of organisation and, if one must also put into the scales the arrogance and tactlessness of the Cardington team, it would be unfair to ignore on the other side the weight of Wallis's fierce professional pride.

Throughout the years of uneasy association he continued to despise the technical qualifications of the men responsible for *R.101*. He never changed his view that *R.101* had been misconceived and as time passed after the eventual tragedy eroded the need for conventional respect for the recently dead, his opinion of individuals became more openly scathing.

In a detailed criticism of *R.101* he explained severely how J. D. North, the Boulton and Paul designer employed by Richmond, evolved a system of transverse frames triangular in section, in order to avoid the necessity for transverse bulkhead wiring, thus losing 500,000 cubic feet that might otherwise have been available for gas. Further, according to Wallis, North, relying presumably on the clearance between gas-bags and structure, so designed his girders that bolts, nuts and even the points of taper-pins protruded into this space, with the consequence that if any movement of the gas-bags brought them into contact with the structure, small holes would soon be made by their chafing.

It is the crudest piece of design which I have ever seen. It is, in fact, inferior to the framework of the Naval Ship No. 1, the girders of which were designed by the *Works Manager* who was not a technologist in any sense of the word.[4]

Of F. M. Rope, whom others have described as 'close to genius' and whose parachute wiring innovation was at the time highly regarded by the experts as 'one of the most brilliant and progressive features of the design of *R.101*',[5] Wallis complained later that his enormous harnessing system, although intended to strengthen the gas-bags against any unexpected internal pressures and also to communicate the gas lift in the gas-bags to the framework, resulted instead in a large loss of internal space 'which since nature abhors a vacuum, was filled with air'. Wallis did not specify the criticism but it is also clear from the patents that for Rope's system there was a third claim: that it held the bags away 'from touching the longitudinal girders' and any other sharp projections, so that if Wallis was right here was a case of two designers on one ship cancelling each other: of Rope cancelling North.

Much of this criticism came only after forty and more years of recollection. It is scarcely worth speculating whether the devastating condemnation was clear in his mind even at the time when the competition was in spate and, if so, whether with his indubitably greater experience and wisdom he could (or should) have issued some thunderous warning about the quality of engineering in *R.101*. Certainly, even then he had the competence to judge *R.101*, and it is likely that had he been presented with all the facts about the airship in its design period he would have commented adversely exactly as he did forty years later. But even had he issued his warning it is unlikely that anyone would have regarded his comments as anything but the product of pique.

Once, indeed, he was consulted about *R.101* when, at Colmore's request, Richmond passed on to Wallis some highly confidential information about the manœuvring valve which had been developed for the ship. Wallis thanked him, congratulated him somewhat icily on the ingenuity of the design and then, in an outburst of gratuitous sincerity, confessed that 'until it has been shown unsatisfactory I prefer the arrangement we have worked out for *R.100*.'[6] More brutal still: with the somewhat specious excuse that he had no place at Howden in which to keep secret papers, he returned all the specifications and drawings, having held them for only three days, thus demonstrating to Richmond that there was nothing in his designs worthy of consideration or emulation. His motives were honest but his methods were hardly likely to encourage further exchanges of confidences.

There was an irreconcilable incompatibility between Cardington and Howden and its cause was as much methodology as politics or personality. The team at Cardington may not have been quite so incompetent as Wallis came to think. Harold Roxbe Cox, who was responsible for the shape of *R.101*, proved by his subsequent career that he was no mean authority. J. F. Baker, A. G. Pugsley and J. D. S. Collins, who, with Cox, were in charge of stress-work, all moved on to demonstrate their skills. Many, but never Wallis, were prepared to recognise the genius of Rope (who like Richmond died in the crash of *R.101*). Of Richmond himself it is true that even some of his own team wondered how he had achieved his position; nevertheless he was a fantastically hard worker and, if no genius, he was undeniably an able organiser.

In the contrast between Richmond and Wallis lies the real difference between the two ships. Wallis came close to grasping it himself. When he boasted, 'I designed every part in that ship myself,' he made the corollary clear: the designer of *R.101* was not by his definition an engineer and was utterly incapable of designing anything for himself. But behind the despising was something more profound. In the 'twenties Wallis was already sensing in himself a difference from the generality in his approach to design problems, a difference that was eventually to distinguish him from most of the engineers of his age. Already Wallis saw himself as a creator, an original solving all problems 'on my own drawing-board'. Richmond was a manager. So, beyond the competition between capitalism and socialism there can be read into the rivalry between the two great airships another symbolism: the team against the individual. If the older and outmoded method produced the more modern ship and the new co-operative system only tragedy, nothing is proven; except perhaps that Wallis was right in thinking that the *R.101* team was made up of incompetents and that we are right in thinking that Wallis was a genius.

Salmond continued to try hard. When there was a proposal for a test flight with a non-rigid he wrote to Group Captain P. F. M. Fellowes, the Director of Airship Development now stationed at Cardington, that he would like Burney and three of his colleagues to be included among the passengers:

> I want them to have every opportunity of discussing the recent aerodynamic trials with your people. I do not want anything held back . . . I do not agree that there can be a loss of dignity in doing this; on the contrary, I think a large-minded outlook —knowing our strength—is the correct line to take. I feel this very strongly.[7]

To some extent Wallis agreed with Salmond whom he liked and respected. But he was by now so confident in his own powers as a designer, and so sure of the lead that *R.100* had taken over its rival, that he could show no great interest—only a mild curiosity —in the work of the Cardington team.

Salmond wrote again to Fellowes:

> Mr Wallis asked what exactly we were testing out as regards the ring . . . he stated that he did not wish, in any way, to crib any design work, but he was extremely interested to see how the test worked out. Would D.A.D. report on this?[8]

D.A.D. would not. Instead he splattered his contempt and dislike for Burney and his men through minutes and letters. For example, in a letter to Salmond:

> It seems to me that we are allowing Burney because of his political influence to cause us to spend an enormous amount of time and effort to placate him and to prevent his forcing his ideas on us. We know well that he has no practical knowledge whatever of airships or their possibilities . . . I still believe that he was only a contractor and he was to fulfil his contract only if he would come to heel. Fancy if Handley Page, Sopwith and all these people behaved like Burney, no progress at all could be made.[9]

Fellowes's antagonism and obstructionism had powerful support. A Cabinet paper sent to one of his colleagues as early as 1924 set the pattern for the attitude that Government employees should take with regard to their free-enterprise rivals: an attitude for all the world like a senior schoolboy hunched over his examination papers lest his answers be cribbed by a junior who is taking the same tests:

> Many thanks for sending me a copy of your excellent Notes of the Conference at the Air Ministry on 28 April with Sir Trevor Dawson and Cdr. Burney. I agree that it is not necessary to let Dawson and Burney have copies. We often have outside people sitting on Committees here from whom we should not withhold Notes of a meeting at which they were present, but generally in very different circumstances from Burney's attendance at your Conference. I mean they come for us to pick their brains and not for the purpose of picking our pockets![10]

There is in that letter a slip of the pen which may well be significant: the omission from the penultimate sentence of Dawson's name with the seemingly deliberate corollary that it is Burney who sticks in the Whitehall gizzard. For all the bitterness spewed out by Fellowes, his colleagues and their political superiors, despite all the distaste urged from the other side by Nevil Shute Norway and without in any denying that the conflict between concepts was real, that it led to stupidities (especially on

the Government side) and ultimately to disaster, there was
another factor which exacerbated relations between the supporters of the two ships: the character of Burney.

From six years of minutes, letters and records of meetings, it
is only too clear that those on the Government—the *R.101* and
Cardington—side were forever being upset by Burney's personality.

> Nothing could be more out of place than stunts and the sort
> of extravagant atmosphere which Burney never fails to excite.

So runs an incomplete, undated and unsigned draft in the Air
Ministry files. Or again:

> One recognises, of course, his enterprise and fertile imagina-
> tion, but where concrete facts of business are concerned it
> cannot be said that the Air Ministry (or presumably Vickers)
> have any reason to be particularly impressed with his ability.[11]

Earlier an official of the Air Ministry had written of Burney's
plans for development:

> I am, however, very loth to recommend this course in view
> of the grave doubts I feel as to the adequacy of the precautions
> Cdr. Burney is likely to take . . . and I do feel that with our
> past experience of Cdr. Burney's rather unbalanced optimism,
> we should be taking a very serious risk.[12]

By the spring of 1926—when he and Molly moved to Howden
so that he could take over day-to-day control of the building of
what he had come to regard as *his* ship—Wallis's loyalty to his
chief was under considerable strain; indeed he had come to agree
privately with the view of Burney held by the Cardington team
and the Civil Service.

Open reproach came first from Burney. Wallis, he complained,
was too engrossed with detail. That detail did concern Wallis
is undeniable and demonstrable, but Wallis maintained that
devotion to *minutiae* is a prime function of the designer. More
seriously, Burney began to question the utility of Wallis's development of mooring masts and put forward various proposals of

his own, culminating in 'some very far-fetched suggestions for a water-landing airship.'

Later Wallis was to set down 'the reversal of our previous friendly relationship' to the account of his refusal to follow Burney 'in this impracticable proposal', but far more devastatingly he came to claim that 'for me the whole atmosphere at Howden was spoilt by the personality of the Managing Director'[13] and the distaste that he felt for Burney was not by any means entirely the product of professional despising. As Wallis had come to resent and suspect the social behaviour of many of his old R.N.A.S. comrades, notably Scott, so now, but in an even more advanced manner, his innate puritanism aroused in him repugnance for Burney's worldliness, for his drinking, gambling and gallivanting. Molly, by nature less severe than her husband, nevertheless took on much of his censoriousness, and disapproved of Burney's heavy drinking and all-night gambling sessions at Le Touquet. But more profound as a cause of dissension was Burney's assumption that he owned the brains, the professional effort and even the private lives of his subordinates, and this arrogance became more obvious and more intrusive after the Wallises moved to Howden, in the midst of Burney's personal empire.

Sorry though they had been to leave behind the elegant ghost of General Wolfe, both Barnes and Molly had been at first delighted with Howden. The privacy of their little white bungalow was precious to them and so too was its proximity to the evidence of Barnes's creation. They found nothing incongruous but rather something satisfactorily appropriate in the conjunction of bucolic peace, 'rabbits running about in the grass and cows poking their heads in our bedroom windows, the larks singing all day long', and the 'unimaginably huge thing' (the airship shed) 'St Paul's would look silly inside it, only the dome would stick out.'[14] Their pleasure found expression in outbursts of spontaneous and childlike gaiety. Molly was again pregnant when first Barnes showed her the shed and he wheeled her round on a trolley left by some workmen:

We went careering over the concrete floor at a tremendous rate . . . When Barnes shouted there were 15 echoes and more 'cause you couldn't count after that; they ran into each other.[15]

But soon their privacy and their happiness were disrupted by

Above: R.100 in flight, jettisoning water-ballast. *Below:* The lounge
on *R.100.* On the landing, the late Nevil Shute Norway

Above: R.101 crashed in a wood near Beauvais on her maiden flight, 5 October, 1930.
Left: H. B. Pratt

Burney and they were reduced to indulging in all kinds of protective measures to keep him out of their house. Sometimes they would turn off the lights, disconnect the bell and lock the front door. On one occasion Scott called and he, Molly and Barnes were sitting after dinner 'talking none too tenderly or quietly about Burney . . . and lo there he was oozing into the drawing-room.'[16]

Nor was Mrs Burney more sensitive than her husband. Uninvited, she would settle herself on Molly for hours on end and spend most of the time 'telling me how to bring up my children'.

Last Sunday [Molly wrote to a friend] we entertained high life. Mrs Burney, her sister, an American friend (female) and ditto (male) spent the night here (not at this house) en route for the Lakes. They were to spend a week motoring there, then drive over to France . . . Poor things—what a summer holiday. And just imagine touring the Lakes in a car, and a *closed* one.[17]

The Government, the Cardington team, and his own subordinates, all came to dislike Burney but could not find alliance even in their commonly-held opinion of his malevolence. Temple wrote to Wallis:

I have seen nothing of your friend C.D.B. during the last month or so. The last occasion was when 'stick-in-the-mud' read his paper attacking Airships. I had a scare letter, followed by wire and sundry telephone messages, imploring me to write him an outline to base his reply on. I spent all the Sunday obliging him and had a letter of thanks in due course. I don't suppose he'll acknowledge the assistance however.*[18]

In 1929 Burney published his book, *The World, The Air and the Future* with its seemingly sensational but, as history would soon reveal, not exaggerated view of aerial warfare, and one does not have to be hypersensitive on Wallis's behalf to regard

* Temple's letter is undated but it was probably written in 1927 and 'stick-in-the-mud' is almost certainly E. F. Spanner, whose opposition to airships was continuous, frenetic and—if by accident—almost entirely justified by events.

as somewhat grudging the acknowledgement of the 'able assistance of Mr B. N. Wallis who was responsible for the mechanical design and who for the latter period as chief engineer was in charge of the construction at Howden.'[19] Burney's view of their relationship was at odds not only with the facts but also with Wallis's view of the facts. Already early in 1926 a sense of unique and helpless responsibility was beginning to oppress Wallis. His appearance became suddenly more haggard, migraines struck him frequently and he was guilty of sudden explosions of anger. After one such episode he wrote a note of apology to Molly and in it the revealing phrase:

> When you feel that the whole organisation from Burney down is practically marking time until you produce an idea it is very trying. Like as if you were an oracle that wouldn't work.[20]

To Burney, the oracle working or not working was '*my* chief designer', *his* man just as *R.100* was *his* ship; he was the entrepreneur, the presiding genius and the patron. He could afford to be gracious—according to his own lights and when he remembered. And he remembered but seldom.

However it was not only migraines that Burney brought on in Wallis. Somehow Burney's arrogance uncovered in Wallis a steeliness, an equivalent and uncompromising arrogance which seldom showed him at his best. It is most clearly revealed in a long and seemingly unimportant correspondence which passed between them in 1926 and 1927 about an article which Burney had been asked to produce on Airships for Arthur Mee's *Children's Encyclopaedia*. The implication from the correspondence is clear. According to Wallis, Burney knew little about the history of airships, had not the power to establish general principles and had no knowledge of technical details. What was more, he did not even understand the purpose of an encyclopaedia!

Egocentricity, lack of generosity and even over-confidence, with an effort could be forgiven in Burney, but he was guilty of more heinous failings which helped to bedevil the already tense situation between the *R.100* and *R.101* teams. On more than one occasion he issued instructions to Wallis at Howden which implied the previous agreement of Cardington and then bustled off to America or to the continent leaving Wallis to face from Cardington a bland refusal damaging to his dignity. Strike at Wallis's dignity and immediately out came the sword of his disdain.

In the tiny airship industry not all was gloom or bile. If progress was slow it was none the less technically resplendent (and most of it struck off by Wallis's originality). There was a sense of dedication and purpose among the industry's workers. Richmond, for example, said of his work that it made of him 'one of the most fortunate of men, for I can earn my livelihood doing what I love most in the world', and, lower in the hierarchy when, in the spring of 1926, most of their fellows went on strike, the hands at Howden stayed at their benches. But by the end of 1926, behind the skill and the enthusiasm, and out of sight of the proud and optimistic gaze of the British people the web was already constructed of jealousy, obstructionism and inefficiency which three years later was to destroy the *R.101*, bring to a shocking death so many of the protagonists and write *finis* to the history of British airships. The rivalry between *R.100* and *R.101* was genuine, but it served as an excuse for secretiveness and for machinations that were caused by incompatibility, by pique, pride, arrogance and bitterness. Even these personal conflicts cannot be seen in clear terms of the Blues against the Reds. If Wallis turned up his puritanical nose at the social behaviour of Scott and his other one-time colleagues in the RNAS, so also on the Government side Fellowes came to distrust Salmond whom he thought a weakling ready to make easy-going concessions to Howden conceit. Colmore won no respect by his pacific efforts, either from his colleagues or from the leaders of the *R.100* faction, for both sides took his striving after conciliation for the easy way out of a lazy and indecisive nature. The three Armed Services were each anxiously pursuing their wish for supremacy over the other two, and the Navy and the Army joined together in malicious alliance only when they saw an opportunity to frustrate the ambitions of the upstart Royal Air Force. Lord Thomson blinded himself with the bright vision of his own political future, and Barnes Wallis soured his humanity with the acid that came from his certainty that alone among men he had the skill to build a good airship. Vickers had long since dissipated its lukewarm enthusiasm for airships, replaced it with excitement over the bright future of heavier-than-air machines and in consequence was unwilling to stake much of money, space or time on *R.100*. Further, as we have seen, the Board, no less than the Government, the Civil Service and the Cardigan team, had tired of Burney and was at one with its rivals in hoping that he would tie his own noose. Burney rushed hither and thither, waving the wand of his arrogance over all, including his own staff, so that his enemies became ever more virulent and his subordinates ever more insubordinate. On all sides men of ability, foresight, determination and unquestioned courage behaved like jealous schoolboys.

Wallis, certainly, had neither the position nor the inclination to bring about a change of heart. At very best he shuttered his mind against the 'political' environment, immersed himself in the immediate, in thinking about the ship that was growing to the direction of his imagination and skill. His home life, now as never before secure and peaceful, coupled with his white-hot excitement over the development of *R.100*, encouraged in him this comparative freedom from involvement with the struggle and erased even from his conscience any wish to use his knowledge to prevent disaster. Malice and tragedy were entirely foreign to the ethos of the small brick bungalow at Howden where Molly, remarkably cheerful in her second pregnancy, still contrived a growing interest in his other and (let it be admitted) to him his more exciting child, *R.100*. Day after day she would take her knitting, climb up into the girders of the airship and sit there quietly watching the growth around her. Evening after evening she would listen, and with developing understanding, as he talked of new plans, new inventions, new dreams for airships.

However, the surrounding atmosphere was inescapable even to Barnes at his drawing-board, and during 1927, almost without his becoming aware of the reason or the consequence—and certainly without his ever revealing his awareness to Molly—he began to shed some of his certainty about airships. Now, for the first time, his actions show what his statements ignored, that he was searching for some other possibility. He knew that *R.100* would be a success and a unique success at that. But, still dimly, he was coming to read the signs and coming also to seek ways of escaping from the chains which bound him to the eventual failure of the notion of lighter-than-air machines.

Significant for the future was the opening of a lengthy correspondence with technicians of the Blackburn Aeroplane Company. At first Wallis's letters seemed to him—and presumably to his correspondents—no more than a sequence of questions seeking information that could be applied to the development of airships, but fairly rapidly, though still subconsciously, his interest in aeroplanes grew and became more intimate and more self-interested.

By now troubles with Burney were more frequent, more acrimonious and more debilitating to the progress of *R.100*. The letters, memoranda and minutes that passed between the two men in the last months of 1926, throughout 1927 and on into 1928 demonstrate an entire tumbling out of sympathy. Burney was justifiably impatient to see *R.100* in the air but unjustifiably convinced that he was better equipped than Wallis to discover engineering short cuts. Wallis was certain—perhaps beyond reason—that the only proper way for an aircraft designer was the way of total involvement in every detail. Burney's eagerness lured him into issuing orders that implied some more and some less radical changes to Wallis's designs and, because he knew enough to know that he could not justify his decisions on any grounds out expedience, he reverted to a quarter-deck manner.

For example, Wallis had invented an ingenious machine for riveting the tubular parts which formed the skeleton of the ship. In similar structures it was usual to insert rivets from the outside and as the shank of the rivet was inside the tube it became well-nigh impossible to determine with any accuracy whether it was properly shaped. With Wallis's machine the rivet-head was *inside* the tube and the shank protruded so that it could be shaped exactly to the requirements of a counter rivet-head.[21]

To Burney the time this took to develop seemed potentially disastrous to his plans. Suddenly he lost patience and issued his *diktat*. He had, he said, discussed the matter with the Air Ministry and had official agreement to putting the rivet-head on the outside of the tube. Wallis gave no immediate reply to Burney. Instead he wrote off to the Air Ministry. Was it true that they had agreed to a change of this kind 'without reference to the questions of design and production which are necessarily involved'?[22] From the Ministry he received only a cold and evasive reply, but despite the 'Strictly Private and Confidential' heading of the letter its substance was reported to Burney—and did nothing to improve relations between the two men.

Worse was to come. In April 1927 a meeting took place in London between Wallis and Air Ministry representatives at which plans were discussed for the control cabin of *R.100*. The decisions arrived at were confirmed with Burney who proposed one comparatively unimportant amendment. Early in 1928 Wallis produced his guidance drawings. They did not include Burney's alterations. Each man now proceeded to amend the other's orders without informing the other. Burney issued his instructions direct to the Drawing Office at Howden. When the work was completed Wallis realised what had happened and immediately put in hand alterations. Wallis argued that he was only trying to follow Burney's wishes; Burney claimed that, although he had not approved of Wallis's plans, he had decided to accept them in their entirety rather than face further delays. Wallis, said Burney, was a cheat: he had deliberately given a false impression to the Air Ministry and had left with officials there the conviction that the Company's design had been altered, whereas in truth he had ignored the Ministry's request for alteration because he thought it unnecessary and unjustified. What is more Wallis was secretive: he had not reported to his chief his discussions with the Director of Airship Development. Wallis spat back that Burney didn't understand the engineering issues and did not listen when they were explained to him. He was interfering and either inefficient or idle. If Wallis would accept discipline, replied Burney (with some justification), collaboration between them would become more likely. If Burney would recognise his Chief Engineer's superior knowledge, complained Wallis (with equal justification) Wallis would be able to accept Burney's authority in matters organisational. For the moment Burney had the last word and accompanied it with reproof and instruction:

> I have frequently expressed my opinion that you do not go round the Drawing Office at frequent enough intervals with the result that not only is there a considerable waste of Drawing Office time, but also, as in the present instance, there is waste in the shops.
>
> I should be glad if you would make it a constant rule to go round the Drawing Office at a fixed time every day, so as to prevent a recurrence of instances of this character.[23]

And Burney's revenge was even more devastating than mere quarter-deck disciplining. His American contacts were flirting with the idea of ordering from the Airship Guarantee Company a nine million cubic feet ship. *Los Angeles* (formerly an Eckener Zeppelin) under the command of Commander Charles E. Rosendahl, U.S.N., was demonstrating magnificent potential from her base at Lakehurst, New Jersey. In January 1927 *Los Angeles* made a successful landing on the aircraft carrier *Saratoga*. Fourteen months later she flew from Lakehurst to Panama and, after a day there, back to Lakehurst, 2,250 miles in less than forty hours' flying time. The American press was enthusiastic about the future of airships but the Americans had still no real capacity to build for themselves. Burney spent more and more time at the Madison Hotel on New York's 58th Street, at the Galleon in Washington, D.C., or in conference with American bankers and politicians. If the Americans were to provide the money then they must also have considerable say in the shaping of the ship. Burney's letters to Wallis from the other side of the Atlantic became more and more technical, as if there were some expert sitting by his elbow as he wrote, and his detailed instructions for future improvements of the *R.100* design were by implication criticisms of Wallis's designing. The tail portion should be 'fattened' with a steep curvature into the point of the tail. He was convinced that this would not add appreciatively to the loss of efficiency through windresistance. Tail engines, he thought, could be mounted entirely within the framework of the ship and cooled by fans and ventilators. If it could be made feasible to use kerosene with gas fuel in Bristol Jupiter engines then the new ship could be run by nine engines, four in the fins and five on the tail.

In these instructions and many more there was nothing to which Wallis could take legitimate exception. Burney was his chief and Burney was the money-raiser. But he had come to suspect that Burney enjoyed making his subordinate dance to his tunes, that even when the suggestions were not his own Burney took some delight in passing them on as orders to his Chief Engineer. Wallis was not built to be a puppet and his recent experience on *R.100* had confirmed in him his instinctive preference for playing first violin and wherever possible solo.

To Wallis the aeroplane industry became ever more inviting. There he would be free of Burney and free to design. Burney, all unwittingly, pushed Wallis closer to the act of desertion to another camp when he began to insinuate that unless Wallis could get *R.100* flying—and soon—then Burney must leave him to grapple with the problems that seemed to beset this prototype ship while others, even some junior to Wallis such as Teed and Norway, dealt with the post-*R.100* developments. Burney's manner was by no means impeccable but he had reason on his side. Far more than Wallis he was susceptible to political and financial pressures. He was ready to ride the criticisms of those of his fellow Members of Parliament like Frank Rose who, on seeing the first picture of Wallis's girder construction, asked the Secretary of State, 'Has the Hon. Gentleman assured himself that these photographs are not enlargements of some schoolboy's essay with a No. 3 Meccano set?'[24] What Burney could not face was the seeming eternity of delay and, believing that much of it was caused by Wallis's determination to design every detail for himself, he believed Wallis incapable of handling both the immediate and the future. The most ardent supporter of Wallis's methods must admit that his perfectionism, even his individual genius, did not make for rapid development, but many of the delays to *R.100* were far outside his control. After the General Strike labour conditions at Howden deteriorated; in 1927 and again in 1928 and 1929 the fitters went out on strike. There was a shortage of money for research, and confusion about sources of instruction.

The difficulties faced by the *R.100* men were not all created by the conflicts of interest or personality. Early in the programme (although the fact was not revealed to the public until 1927) it was discovered that in Britain there were no adequate facilities for making gas-bags on the scale required and the contract had to be farmed out to a German firm, B.G. Textilwerke G.M.B.H. of Berlin. In 1927, after suitable experiment, Wallis decided that the proposed power-unit of paraffin–hydrogen engines was inadequate and reverted to Rolls-Royce Condor engines. There was no suitable mooring-mast at Howden. *R.100* was designed to the limits of the existing shed, and this was inadequate for *R.101*, and so the Air Ministry insisted that when the time came for flying trials on the two ships they must be undertaken from Cardington.

10 The End of Airships

For year after year, through 1926, 1927, 1928, and on into 1929 Wallis grappled with every detail in the building of *R.100*. Both the general public and his fellow-professionals were coming to recognise Wallis as a celebrity. When he gave a lecture at Howden the crowd queued for hours. He was invited to speak to the Cambridge University Air Squadron, and then, in September 1928, he won recognition from his peers. For his 'distinguished work on airships' he was awarded the Silver Medal of the Royal Aeronautical Society.

In the midst of his professional preoccupations still he found time to teach Molly to skate and to play golf; still on occasion he joined her at tennis and coached her overarm service; still he brought into their joint lives touches of boyish romanticism:

> He was just going for a brief walk when he poked his head in at the sitting-room door and beckoned to me. I went out and he made me shut my eyes and open them outside the front door where I saw a little gold new moon lying on her back. We bowed to her 7 times. We always do the first time we see the new moon.[1]

And with this romanticism more than a touch of his persistent anti-sybaritism. They called on 'neighbours', walking eight miles each way, five 'lazily' by road and three to the inflexible direction of a compass-bearing, through bogs and hedges, over swollen streams and under barbed wire. In January and in Yorkshire the four-months-old Mary was given her first cold bath, and the moment that Wallis imagined some improvement in the weather the whole family slept out of doors in a tent of Wallis's creation, two sides and a roof, just enough to maintain an impression of privacy but not so much as to destroy the desirable illusion—if illusion it was and if desirable then only to Wallis—of being exposed to the elements.

As *R.100* grew so did the number of visitors. They swarmed to Howden: officials, Members of Parliament, distinguished foreigners, spies from Cardington, engineers and hosts of tourists. Official visitors and sightseers took up Wallis's time and exhausted his patience. The official visitors also exhausted his even more limited supply of drink so that Molly complained (without hope) that they should receive an entertainment allowance.

The contours of Wallis's existence seemed set. Despite disappointments, postponements, tension between Howden and Cardington, dissensions within the Airship Guarantee Company and despite his feud with Burney, still it seemed that at last he had arrived in the middle of great events. But over a decade Wallis's self-knowledge had developed phenomenally so that by the end of 1927 he knew that he could no longer be satisfied with the task of perfecting and polishing a creation that was already substantially complete. He knew that he was an original. He knew, too, that his situation would become worse once *R.100* was ready for her trials and much worse when she proved herself in commercial flight, for it was obvious that if *R.100* was the success he expected then she would serve as a prototype for many ships. Burney was negotiating with the United States Government for *R.100*-class ships to take over a mail run to New York. But technical triumph, commercial success or commercial failure: all would leave Wallis, at best, no more than a supervisor and, at worst, unemployed.

As so often in his life, Wallis's uncertainty first broke surface as worry about money. For a middle-aged married man with total responsibility for a wife and two children and some share in the care of a father, a sister and brother-in-law, there could now be no easy escape to some new Chillon. And, again, as so often in his life, pessimism and overwork combined to bring about in Wallis two seemingly contradictory compensations— his health broke and he recognised and followed the beckonings of his new professional interest.

The association of physical with mental strain is now commonly accepted and there can be few better textbook demonstrations of the relationship than Wallis's medical history during the last years of the *R.100* programme. Insomnia, frequent migraines, a nervous breakdown and a bout of blood-spitting which was thought (mistakenly) to be tuberculosis and which led to him giving up smoking—this time irrevocably, although for ever after he romanticised the cause—gave him frequent contact with doctors in 1927 and 1928. His medical advisers recommended a holiday in the sun, and for once Wallis took their advice although it meant missing the dinner of the Royal Aeronautical Society at which he was to receive his Medal. Elaborate precautions were taken to prevent Burney from stealing the show and the Medal. Masterman was briefed as proxy so that Burney could not usurp that delectable role and Barnes and Molly went off to Menton.

They spent the time lying in the sun and swimming in the warm sea. The limit of their return ticket was forty-five days and on the forty-fifth day Wallis returned to England in full trim. Perhaps France had worked her miracle; more likely idleness had proved a greater enemy than sickness, the sun-soaked beach at Menton could no longer compete with the responsibilities for *R.100* nor with his still private excitement over designing aeroplanes.

This belated desertion to the cause of aeroplanes of Britain's leading airship designer was no sudden resolve. Even while he was pressing the cause of airships in well-documented paper and fluent lecture, he was beginning to regard with increasing curiosity the development of heavier-than-air machines. The process was hastened by a geographical accident. Close to Howden is Brough and there Jack Rennie was designing for the Blackburn Aeroplane Company the largest all-metal hull seaplane in the world. Wallis's correspondence with Blackburn over technical details useful to *R.100* had led to an invitation from Rennie, and soon Wallis was a frequent and insatiably curious visitor. Still Wallis would not admit to Rennie, to Molly or even to himself that seaplanes had potential far superior to airships, but soon, as he studied Rennie's *Iris*, he came to be obsessed by the crudeness that hampered aeroplane design. Rennie he liked but his work he despised. He decided on an essay in designing a seaplane wing. He could bring to it his unique experience in the use of light alloys, and this, at first, was the sum of his novel contribution to aeroplane construction. Indeed, as late as August

1931 when he had already transferred his entire loyalty to heavier-than-air craft, he was commenting still after reading an American report on duralumin:

> I have so long felt like a Prophet crying in the wilderness, that it is encouraging to see someone else actually coming to the same conclusions . . . And I am quite convinced that the most important work which we can undertake is not the development of stainless steel, but the investigation of reliable means of rendering light alloys free from corrosion.[2]

It was to be an important contribution and it did strengthen his conviction that he could change the aeroplane industry. It was not, as so many authorities have suggested, geodetic construction.

Of less importance to Wallis but none the less adding strength to the pull towards aeroplanes was his disdain for the backwardness of the heavier-than-air men in using the latest advances in engine design and fuel tank construction. In such matters, he was sure, his *R.100* team were far ahead of the aeroplane builders. 'It is a little surprising to me,' he wrote in a letter to the Master of Sempill (in his first draft the phrase was much stronger, 'I am considerably shocked'), 'in view of the tremendous success we are having with the tanks . . . that aeroplane designers are so little interested. I have seen some of the tank work for large "all metal" flying-boats and am very much surprised' (in the first draft 'astounded') 'at the tremendous complexity and expensive construction which is [unnecessarily] adopted.'[3]

But in the late spring of 1928 the rigid airship programme, and especially *R.100*, came under particularly heavy fire from its old enemy, E. F. Spanner. Wallis's pride and his sense of loyalty were aroused; he could not admit (and even decades later would not accept) that any of Spanner's criticisms were valid and, an even more powerful factor in holding him from moving, as Spanner's attacks became even more virulent so did Wallis's determination increase that he would stay with *R.100* until she had soared magnificently into success and so proved the folly of her critics.

Much of the substance of Spanner's attack was based upon a purely instinctive feeling that Wallis's constructional theories were pipe-dreams. Wallis could evade this mode of attack by dis-

missing it or by calling Spanner a 'mugwump'. It was more difficult for him to ignore Spanner's secondary criticism. Was it not
true, said Spanner, that originally Burney had promised a pay-
load of 20 per cent of the total lift, a radius of 3,750 miles and an
average speed of 80 m.p.h., whereas now in lecture after lecture
and paper after paper Wallis was suggesting a pay-load of no
more than 14 per cent of the total lift, a radius of only 2,600 miles
and an average speed five miles an hour less than Burney had
offered four years earlier? If so (and undeniably it was so) 'was
the game worth the candle?'[4]

Spanner's vitriol poured out into the Press, into pamphlets
and into private letters to men of influence. The airship programme, he urged, was a waste of public money; worse still, it was
a potential killer; the lives of the British public were at risk;
Burney, Wallis and all who supported them were both profligate
and dangerous. Finally, and for Wallis most devastatingly,
Spanner turned his attention to the Royal Aeronautical Society
and read that most distinguished body a pious sermon on its
duties. The Society, he said, was 'the guardian of Britain's air
prestige and the premier aeronautical authority in the world.'

> Sir Alan Anderson urged the policy of safety before everything
> . . . To admit that the Royal Aeronautical Society is either
> unable or unwilling . . . to subject to criticism a technical
> design of such importance as the one put forward by Mr Wallis,
> seems to me to place the Society in an extremely weak position
> —a hopelessly weak position if anything goes wrong subse-
> quently.[5]

It must stand to the glory of the Royal Aeronautical Society
that in 1928 its Council, many of whom admitted that they did
not fully understand Wallis's theories, were nevertheless sufficiently courageous and so much convinced of Wallis's technical
skill and integrity that they flouted Spanner, continued to give
their professional encouragement to Wallis and demonstrated
their faith in his genius by proffering to him not one but several
invitations to read papers at both London and provincial meetings.
Even if there had been no Spanner, Wallis's dream of transferring his attentions to aeroplanes might have been inhibited
by his heavy and virtually total responsibility for *R.100*, had

not accident, once more, played its part and given him his chance. Among the visitors who flocked to see the curiosity at Howden was Sir Robert McLean, Chairman of Vickers Aviation and Chairman also of the Supermarine Company which Vickers had just acquired. McLean was a man of inspired vision, entire integrity and, according to Wallis, supreme genius in handling men—a manner of praise which can with justice be interpreted as rare genius in handling Wallis! Already McLean had behind him the not inconsiderable achievement of reorganising the Indian Railways. A pale, ascetic-looking man with a great, hooked nose, he had in his make-up much of Wallis's own puritanism. At their very first meeting Wallis recognised McLean as the antithesis of Burney. The genuine grace with which McLean acknowledged the superior technical skills of the men he was gathering around him, coupled with the knowledgeable zest with which he commented upon their work, met with an immediate response from Wallis. McLean, for his part, reacted promptly and favourably to Wallis; within hours of their first meeting he was casting about for a way of bringing to his side the originality and zeal which he recognised in the airship designer. It was not easy. First, McLean knew the size of Vickers' commitment to *R.100* and Wallis's vital role in making that commitment secure. Secondly, and perhaps of even greater importance to McLean, he knew that his newly amalgamated companies were already overloaded with *prime donne* and his experience as a leader of men had long since taught him that two geniuses in one team spells no work and much trouble. At Weybridge the Chief Designer for Vickers Aviation was R. K. Pierson, long a leader in the industry, one of the great pioneers, whose Vimy bombers had been an outstanding success in the First World War. (It was an adapted Vimy, with Alcock and Whitten-Brown as co-pilots, which in 1919 had made the first non-stop crossing of the Atlantic.) The length of Pierson's career had not drained him of ideas— for some years he had been concentrating his skills upon the possibilities of streamlining aeroplanes—but his usefulness to Vickers lay as much in the respect and affection with which he was regarded by senior Royal Air Force officers. Many of them had known him when they were young fighter-pilots in the Great War, a time when designers, if they had merit, served virtually as simultaneous translators turning tactical notions into immediate

design practice. As the one-time battle-pilots added rings to
their uniform sleeves and became ever more powerful as decision
makers for the growing junior service, so was Pierson's position
strengthened, until by 1928, when Vickers Aviation acquired the
Supermarine Company, Pierson was uniquely regarded as the Air
Force's own designer, almost as an RAF officer himself.

With Supermarine there had come into the Vickers camp
another outstanding designer, less clubbable than Pierson but
no less original: R. J. Mitchell. A poet among engineers, a strange
combination of soaring vision and down-to-earth practicality,
he had already shown himself to be both a fine inventor and
a superb organiser, and those who worked with him thought
none the worse of him for his occasional outbursts of fiery
temperament.

There was a third member of the team scarcely less important
than the others but far less likely to resent the addition of Wallis.
Captain 'Mutt' Summers was Chief Test Pilot to the amalgamated
companies and considered by many to be the finest test pilot in
England and perhaps in the world. Summers had many rare
capacities apart from courage and a delicate touch on the controls
of a 'plane. He spoke fluent German, had made himself entirely
acceptable to the leaders of the German aircraft industry so that
he was allowed a view of many of Germany's new 'planes, and he
had an almost photographic memory for the external details
of aeroplane design and intuitive ability for interpreting the
implications of what he saw. He was, in truth, a superb intelligence agent both for Vickers and for Britain.

It was not until their second meeting, a few weeks after the
first, that Wallis told McLean of his experiments with a seaplane
wing, but already McLean's mind was made up. Providing always
that Pierson, as the senior man, would accept another colleague,
like Mitchell only slightly less senior than himself, he would face
the inevitable and not inconsiderable wrath of Burney and move
Wallis to Vickers Aviation. So as an experiment to discover how
the two men would react the one to the other, McLean blandly
suggested to Pierson that he should take his small son to Howden
to see the wonders of *R.100*. The visit was an entire success. All
Wallis's charm and didactic skills were exercised on the boy and,
for his part, Pierson's quick and generous mind responded immediately to the ideas that Wallis put before him, for he knew that

if Wallis was right in his design notions then, despite his entire and confessed ignorance of aeroplanes, this man had hit upon the best answer so far devised for the much-desired change from wood to metal construction. On his side, Wallis was stimulated by Pierson's patient and perspicacious questioning and delighted with the boy's excitement. When Pierson returned to London he reported to McLean his admiration for the airship designer and the pleasure that he found in his company.

With Pierson's support assured McLean saw no reason for further hesitation. Early in November 1928 Wallis was summoned to Weybridge, shown around by McLean and Pierson, offered a post as Chief Designer to the consortium—Pierson and Mitchell were also Chief Designers—and Wallis accepted. The one concession made to the needs of *R.100* was that Wallis should not leave Howden until after the ship was inflated in March or April 1929 and that thereafter he should remain at the disposal of Airship Guarantee to handle any major problems. McLean, for all his integrity, had been a successful administrator for many years and he knew that kid gloves are of little value when cutting barbed wire. The decision was communicated to Burney with an arrogance to match Burney's own and accepted with surprisingly good grace.

There was still some hope that *R.100* (and indeed *R.101*) would fly late in 1928 and promising negotiations with the United States and Canadian Governments, as also (much more difficult) with the British Post Office, seemed to predict a sound commercial future for the ship and her sister-rival. Burney prepared for that happy possibility by announcing that he did not intend to stand again for Parliament; a decision that may have been hastened by the imminence of a General Election and the strong possibility that he would not be returned. The Labour Party began to look optimistically across the floor of the House of Commons at the comforts of the Government benches and thinking now that, once in power, it might take credit from the near-certain glory of two major maiden flights, tuned down the volume of opposition even to the Capitalist ship.

There was, too, proof being written in the skies of the true potential of airships. In October 1928 the *Graf Zeppelin* made her maiden transatlantic flight. Carrying five tons of mail and twenty passengers she covered 6,168 miles between her home base at Friedrichshafen and Lakehurst, New Jersey, in 111 hours 44 minutes.

R.100 and *R.101* were still not airborne and as 1928 turned to 1929 it was clear, at least to those with some knowledge of the technical problems yet to be faced and of the slow machinery of the Airworthiness Board that would have to provide a certificate before either ship could fly, that a more realistic prognosis would give for the maiden flights a date some time late in 1929. However, the spur provided by *Graf Zeppelin* did create a rare moment of understanding between Howden and Cardington. Now, when it was virtually too late, information began to flow between the two teams.

For Wallis the belated sense of urgency aroused in Britain by *Graf Zeppelin* and the many demands now being put to Howden by Professors Bairstow and Pippard as assessors of airworthiness, seemed to represent only a further disappointing delay to his move from Howden to Weybridge, from airships to aeroplanes, but his mind, and indeed he himself, was only half in Yorkshire. When necessary he would still wrench himself away from the, for him, novel fascination of aeroplane designing and return his entire attention to *R.100*. Yet even the backs of the letters that he wrote to Molly during his frequent absences at Weybridge are covered with rough pencilled calculations, most of them relating to the use of light alloys in heavier-than-air machines.

As for the British public: it had almost forgotten the rivalry and the race between *R.100* and *R.101*. Now in a late upsurge of pride and perhaps as some relief from economic crisis and unemployment, the British took both ships to their hearts and warmed the national spirit with the knowledge that at last Britain would have a commercial airship fleet double the size of Germany's! Public hopes were much increased by customary easy acceptance of platitudes mouthed in Parliament and by frequent reminders in Press and Parliament of spiritual associations between the impending and great future of the British airship and the nation's great and ancient traditions wrought upon the seas.

Evocative notions of this kind called out hope even to Wallis who had never lost his romantic feeling for the sea and ships, and tended to revive even his jaded enthusiasm for airships. For

the ordinary newspaper reader who had no cause to be dispirited
about airships but much else around him to arouse depression,
the effect was sensational, and thus it was that in 1929 public
optimism about the future of British airships produced a typically British exercise in public sentiment. It was begun in Parliament on 29 April when that arch-beginner Sir Harry Brittain
asked the Conservative Secretary of State for Air to follow nautical
examples by giving the two airships names more romantic than
mere numerals. *Graf Zeppelin* had a personality; *LZ.127* like
R.100 or *R.101* was a number on a specification sheet. Reinforced
by the attention paid to the German airship Sir Harry Brittain's
suggestion spilled over into the public annexe to the chamber
of the House of Commons—the correspondence columns of *The
Times*—and there another arch-beginner had his say. A. P.
Herbert's list of possibilities was long and, as was to be expected,
included some irreverent or frivolous suggestions with some that
were dutiful and some poetical.[6] *Queen of England* might have
upset Celtic susceptibilities, but *Flying Briton* was for all in these
islands and more respectable than *Daddy Longlegs* or *British
Matron*. Herbert's allusive suggestions were set down without
exegesis, and it is only sad and sour after-knowledge which can
write in after his proposal *The Great White Whale* the line from
Moby Dick: 'He sank without a ripple of renown', and that can
add to Herbert's *Fairy Queen*:

> Through thicke and thin, both over banke and bush
> In hope her to attaine by hooke or crooke.

Looking back upon the letter from Herbert's successor in the
correspondence columns such elaboration is well-nigh inescapable: 'What is wanted is not a single name ... Shakespeare gives
us a pair of arch and airy names ... *Oberon* and *Titania*'.[7] *Ariel*
and *Caliban* would have been more appropriate.

In the 1929 General Election Labour became the largest party
in the House of Commons although its chance of exercising effectively the role of government depended once more on an uneasy
alliance with the Liberals. Ramsay MacDonald was back as Prime
Minister and, as his Secretary of State for Air, MacDonald called
again upon the one man who would not let die the ancient hatreds
between the supporters of *R.100* and his own faction, the mentors of

the Socialist ship, *R.101*. In a speech marking the opening of an infirmary at Dewsbury, and in an entirely gratuitous aside, Lord Thomson put an end to the romantic notion of naming the ships:

> People are always asking me to give a name to *R.101*. I hope it will make its reputation with *that* name. If I know anything about the crew who man it, it is that they would like to stick to *R.101*.[8]

His conclusion was possibly correct but his pointed exclusion from consideration of *R.100* could but serve to reopen old wounds.

Meantime at Howden it seemed that there would never be an end to the new set of delays caused by the need to satisfy the airworthiness experts. At one stage, and with entire justification, Professor Bairstow insisted that a girder be removed from the ship itself so that it could be subjected to laboratory inspection at Birmingham University.

R.101 was in far worse plight than her rival. Both ships had already cost considerably more than their respective sponsors had hoped, both had prospective performance rates below their original specifications, but whereas the modifications that Wallis had made to his first *R.100* designs had been successfully carried out and although the more obvious detail of *R.101*—her exterior profile, passenger quarters, control car and chartroom—were all superlative, it had long been clear to the experts that there was nothing superlative about her technical qualities. She had but 35 tons disposable weight as compared to *R.100*'s 54 tons. Her engines were heavy and inefficient and her fuel tanks insufficient for the planned long voyage. At this late date (1928 and early 1929), with *Graf Zeppelin* triumphantly riding the skies of the world and, for all that Cardington knew, *R.100* almost ready, the only solution for the ailments of *R.101* was most drastic surgery. Half the elegant promenade deck was sacrificed, so too were the crew's quarters (the crew were moved into some of the valuable passenger accommodation) and washing facilities were reduced for both passengers and crew. Most severe of all, it was decided to remove one of two reefing booms between each longitudinal. Her very shape had been altered.[9]

Worse was to come. When *R.101* was subjected to shed tests in the summer of 1929 it was discovered that her diesels could not run at the contracted speed without causing devastating vibration; that as her proposed variable-pitch propellers were not yet ready, the forward port engine would have to be used exclusively for reversing. It then transpired that *R.101*, intended as she was for long-distance and tropical flying, had been designed to fly at altitudes not greater than 2,000 feet and in an English climate.

In September *R.101* came to her lift and trim trials and Colmore reported that as atmospheric conditions in Asia would cause the loss of eleven tons of disposable weight, *R.101*'s chances of operating the Indian route were nil. He proposed further surgery and suggested that if a number of reefing girders were removed *R.101* might be able to make Cairo non-stop—but only in the climatically favourable months from November to March. The dream of a flight to India could not become a reality unless all the original engines were used for forward flight and a Condor added for reversing power. But a Condor could not be added unless more lift was provided. Thus, at the end of November 1929 (six weeks after *R.100* had made her maiden flight), the penultimate indignity was prepared for *R.101* when the Secretary of State announced surgery such as no British airship had suffered since 'Mayfly'. Nobody rose in anger to point out that after five years of design and construction and seven of discussion the total profile and potential behaviour of *R.101* was to be altered in a manner so profound and in such haste that it was impossible to forecast the consequences. *R.101* was to be sliced in two, a new section added and the whole patched together again; on the operating table a man of five foot six tall was to be made to stand six foot high.

All these troubles for *R.101* would not have greatly perturbed the Howden team and its leader had it not been for one insuperable inconvenience to them that followed inevitably upon delays to *R.101*. Cardington had the only mast in Britain suitable for extensive trials and *R.101* blocked the way to Cardington and to that essential masthead.

Early in June 1929 news reached Howden which, though it came in the midst of a wildcat strike, flared off a new sense of optimism among all who worked on *R.100* except her Chief Designer. The Air Ministry intended to ask the Airship Guarantee Company to tender for a successor to the prototype ship.[10] Wallis, for his part, saw this as, yet again, a signal set against his move to Weybridge. There was no one else in the employ of the company and probably no one else in the whole of Britain who could fulfil the Ministry's requirements and prepare within twelve months the data, drawings and information demanded. If Burney were to point out to McLean that the only hope of saving Vickers' investment was to continue Wallis at Howden, then, according to Wallis's prognosis, McLean's business sense would outstrip his interest in heavier-than-air developments which, after all, could with some justice be regarded as already safe in the more than capable hands of Pierson and Mitchell.

There was, however, in the Air Ministry's invitation, a rare suggestion of flattery towards the work already done, and in it more than a hint that Bairstow and Pippard were coming close to signing the Airworthiness Certificate, for it was unlikely that the Ministry would be preparing a successor had the inspectors expressed any new or serious doubts about *R.100*.

The Certificate was in fact signed on 3 July 1929 and, immediately Wallis submerged his own doubts and all connected with *R.100* shut their minds to the future and concentrated their attention upon his brain-child in the shed at Howden. Gassing began almost immediately.

The process of gassing was complicated and more than a little dangerous. Any false move could mean either disaster to the frail skin of the bag (the largest of the fourteen had cost £6,000) or, at best, deflation and therefore, conceivably, the loss of £500 worth of hydrogen. In Wallis's opinion the Works staff was not competent to supervise such delicate work; instead he placed one team of riggers under Norway and another under the Chief Draughtsman, and he himself danced about on the floor of the shed supervising the whole operation with the aid of a megaphone. He was up each morning at 6.30, started work before 8 and seldom finished before 9 at night. Frequently, after supper, he would return to the shed, taking Molly with him. She reported to a friend: 'It's most eerie climbing about the shed with just a little lamp,' and again:

It's such an eerie process in the dark save for the Watchman's two little lights. Barnes is a positive monkey as regards climbing. It sends my heart into my tummy to see him climbing a wire ladder with a lantern in one hand.[11]

165

For two weeks they worked like this, and at the end of that fortnight every bag was in place and only one had suffered a tiny tear. That one error had exploded in Wallis a show of temper entirely suited to his extrovert function—and, according to his peculiar diagnosis, brought on also an attack of lumbago.

Now the true shape of the ship was visible; she was actually floating on air and the new gassing could continue with less supervision. For a few weeks Wallis returned to thoughts of aeroplanes and then the time had come to ballast-up *R.100*. Molly was away from Howden for a few days and Philip Teed had come to stay to make purity tests on the hydrogen and to watch the ballasting. They lived a hilarious bachelor existence, laying all meals the night before for the next day, breakfast at one end of the dining table, tea in the middle, supper at the far end, moving like the Mad Hatter from one end to the other. For their innumerable cups of tea Wallis invented a system more efficient than most bachelors can contrive:

You have two cups, one for milky tea, and one for unmilky—thus you never need to wash either and still your unmilky tea is not made cloudy. They are referred to as 'thick' and 'clear' respectively.[12]

The comfortable casualness at home and the happy labour in the shed were dislocated by the inevitable presence of the Burneys. Mrs Burney's hair-style and her overpowering perfume brought home to Barnes the loneliness he felt separated from Molly's unaffected presence.

'Do you know,' Molly had written eighteen months earlier,

'I've never yet powdered my nose . . . If I did I should use boracic powder to save the stink . . . Barnes always says how he hates dancing with a scenty-powdery woman.'[13]

But even the 'stink' from Mrs Burney was as nothing when compared with the repugnance always aroused in Wallis by the closeness of Burney himself. In the shed he was forced to put up with his master but back at the bungalow he was determined to keep Burney at bay. He and Teed, whose love for Burney was no greater than his friend's, unscrewed the bell from the door and wedged the wheels with a pencil. Then, so that they could later excuse themselves for not hearing Burney's knocking, they turned on the radio and gave it full volume. The news blared out; on her world cruise *Graf Zeppelin* had reached Los Angeles and before midnight would be leaving again for Lakehurst, New Jersey.[14]

Shed trials began early in September. It is a sad comment on the delays to which the building of the ship had been subjected that the plan for these trials had been prepared in the greatest detail as long ago as December 1926. Fortunately, even at that early stage, thirty-three months before the first trial was run, Wallis had foreseen that at the outset of *R.100*'s engine trials a difficulty must be faced that had never before been encountered. *R.100* fitted her parent shed with an exactness that might prove disastrous when her propellers were started, for the disturbance of air caused in an enclosed building by a propeller slipstream could start excessive rocking on a lighter-than-air ship—and 'excessive' was only four feet at its widest and fifteen inches at some points.[15] If *R.100* was not to bounce herself into disaster against the walls of the shed then the restraints upon the ship must be highly sophisticated and precise. Wallis designed for her a bow-frame nosecap of girders to distribute the thrust into two of the door-principals of the Howden shed. For the stem he prepared a symmetrical system of wire-guys arranged in such a manner as to permit only a small degree of easy movement at the stem, any such movement bringing into play large damping forces to the point where—still within the limits of safety —the movement would be arrested. There still remained the most important precaution of all: careful supervision. This was something that Wallis could not and would not delegate. What is more, the satisfactory conclusion of the shed trials without mishap to the outer frame would not be the end, for a similar set of problems would arise when, for the first time, *R.100* was walked out of the Howden shed. Only intimate and ruthless supervision of the kind that he felt himself uniquely capable of providing would see her safely out of the tiny clearance at the shed doors.

On 30 September 1929 at Cardington *R.101* began her lift and trim tests, and the grape-vine to Howden quivered with the news that she would be flying in a fortnight.

Barnes Wallis

On 10 October 1929 the young American publishing house of Alfred A. Knopf, as part of its too short British adventure, published Burney's book *The World, the Air, and the Future*. This was the work which in Wallis's view, grimly held and roundly expressed even forty years after the event, anthologised all Burney's sins of arrogance, ignorance and obstinacy, and there can be no dissent from the view that, apart from a bow to the excellence of Howden's system of propulsion, almost every technical proposal now put forward by Burney ran counter to Wallis's advice and experience. But to accuse Burney, as did Wallis, of bad or even malicious timing, seems to undervalue his knowledge of publicity. Burney knew that for the year which is about the limit of time in which a book can continue to generate publicity, airships would be much in the news. And through the impending din there would be frequent references to the latest book on the subject, a book written by a man who was one of the founders of the industry and, according to public repute, rare if not unique for his combination of engineering knowledge, business acumen, international experience and political ability. But there were considerations other than the commercial in Burney's book and to these—notably to the call to Britain that she come face-to-face with the implications of the new Air Age —publicity was no less important; Burney's timing cannot be faulted.

Wallis saw the technical delusions which are clear and undeniable though a comparatively small part of *The World, the Air, and the Future*. He saw the apparent treachery of Burney's unequivocal (and one might have thought equally clear and undeniable) statement that in his view both *R.100* and *R.101* had proved themselves commercial failures before they ever flew, and of his no more equivocal conviction that 'the airship enthusiasts [had] overstated their case' and that now 'there were two courses open: one was to confess failure, the other to say nothing and get down to the real problem of finding a solution'.[16] Surely those who had followed Burney through a decade of bombast could not regard this as a gratuitous attack on Wallis: for in these passages it appears that there is torn from Burney, for all his swaggering egotism, a confession of *mea culpa, mea maxima culpa*. True, even this confession, if it is genuine, is, like the technical theorising and posturing, only incidental to the book. The rest, per-

168

versely (and with a few details changed) might, much of it, have been written by Wallis himself. In fact, with those few details amended to fit altered circumstances, twenty or thirty years later Wallis was to propound Burney's main thesis in lectures, articles and interviews: sea routes could no longer serve to buttress Britain's economic and diplomatic strength, and from now on the only chance that Britain had of maintaining her Empire, bolstering her own economy and combating the economic super-strength of the United States depended upon her development as a commercial and military air power. The creation of long-distance, non-stop air routes would prevent the disruption of the bonds of Empire that might otherwise be susceptible to the whim of every Britain-hating despot or by the accidents of local dis-affection or enmities.

In some sense Burney's understanding of *geo-politik* was in 1928 further advanced than could be claimed for Wallis even forty years later. Cynically perhaps, but certainly pragmatically, Burney offered an alternative to economic competition with the almost unbeatable Americans: a system of Anglo-American collaborations which would give reality to the dream of a unified West.

For Wallis, however, the publication of Burney's book was unmitigated insult. In black and white it added the force of blows to the conviction that needed no addition. He must get away from this man and all his works.

On 12 October 1929 *R.101* at last left her shed at Cardington. Two days later (although she still had only a provisional Air-worthiness Certificate) she flew for the first time, around Bedford and on to London. She was in the air for five and a half hours.[17] Four days later, with on board her 'onlie begetter', Lord Thomson, she made another and longer flight (9 hours 38 minutes) over the Midlands, at the end of which the Secretary of State informed correspondents that he had every hope of going with *R.101* to India at Christmas. His hopes—and those of the Howden team waiting with such scant patience for use of the Cardington mast —were dashed by forecasts of bad weather. *R.101*, too precious to risk in a storm, was hurried back into her shed and there she remained until the first day of November when, as if to show the world the truth behind the fiction of His Majesty's Loyal Opposition, the Shadow Secretary, Sir Samuel Hoare, was on board for a flight over the Royal home at Sandringham.

Nobody commented on what was for England the unnaturally good weather in which these early trials had been conducted; not even when, in a short flight staged in the second week of November for the express delectation of a group of Members of Parliament, *R.101* revealed her aggressive buoyancy—and dangers to come—by lurching so violently as she left the mast that she smashed crockery, tipped cutlery from the tables and Members of Parliament from their seats. But in circles more knowledgeable than those in which the decanted Members moved, doubts about the ship's stability, equipment and performance were growing from whisper to whine. One of *R.101*'s officers reported officially that the gauges in the ballast tanks 'are not satisfactory, and cannot be relied upon'. Colmore commented on the chafing of the gas-bags caused by contact with the radial struts and, on this same major defect, the Chief Coxswain, G. W. Hunt, was more specific and far more alarmist:

> In the case of numbers 3 to 14 bags inclusively a very considerable move was taking place . . . and at times the surge of the bags in a forward and after direction was considerably marked. . . . the plates on top of the radial struts rubbed and chafed the bags, and in places such as Number 8 starboard fore end tore the bag 9 inches in a jagged tear. Number 8 thus became deflated to 60 per cent and on inspection taking place it was noticed that on every roll the valves opened to the extent of a quarter to half an inch. The holes on the top of Number 14 bag were caused by the bag bearing hard on O girder, where several nuts project, and combined with the movement of the bag caused puncturing.[18]

There was perturbation, too, about the condition of the outer skin and over certain comparatively minor matters such as the inefficiency of the ventilation system and the impossibility of clearing the bilge-water which seeped into the control-car when the ship was at the masthead. (There is no record of either of these faults being corrected before *R.101* set off for tragedy.)

Nevertheless on 17 November *R.101* went on an endurance flight, her designers and crew apparently confident and the nation roused to new enthusiasm by the drum-beating of the Press and the posturings of Lord Thomson. On that flight, which lasted for thirty hours, again in better than average flying conditions, she passed directly over her shed-bound rival. In a letter written at the time from her brother-in-law's home Molly Wallis wrote:

> We heard last night that *R.101* had been flying over Howden; I could have wept at not being there to see how Barnes liked it.'[19]

So, too, could all who relish a good moment in the scenario. But at the time Wallis wrote nothing of his feelings as he watched the first prize in the great race pass as it seemed to the opposing team.

However, the successful endurance flight of *R.101* gave hope to Howden. *R.100* was now officially Air Ministry property although still under the immediate control of her constructors. Now, it seemed, Cardington must pack its ship back into her shed and leave the mast clear for *R.100*. The weather gods had other and persistently malicious ideas. Suddenly the calm was broken that had persisted all through *R.101*'s flight trials. *R.101* clung precariously to the Cardington mast, buffeted by every wind that blew across the Bedfordshire flats so that for two weeks there was no hope of moving her to the shed. Up at Howden allied storms proved to the *R.100* team that even had Cardington cleared they, in their turn, could never risk the delicate business of removing their own ship from her metal sheath.

Now for both Wallises there were frustrations more immediate than the postponement of their physical move and for Barnes problems more emotional than delay to his activity on aeroplanes. He knew that he must have a break from work. He was again exhausted, almost continuously suffering from migraine and insomnia. He feared that if he did not have a holiday he might drive himself into a nervous breakdown and he knew that each postponement to the flight trials of *R.100* would make it that much more difficult for him to find time for the break between finishing with airships and beginning a full-time career with aeroplanes.

There was a danger that the first calm would coincide with Christmas, and to both of them Christmas was important. Barnes was at his family best amidst the ordered disarray of the festival. He was not, as a general rule, easy in the company of his own children, nor they with him; his own fiercely Victorian notions of discipline and his eternal preoccupation with his work strained the relationships beyond the possibility of comfort. His affection he had lavished openly on his mother and on Molly but he seldom showed any warmth towards his children (so seldom that Mary was to say that she would have been amazed had he ever kissed her or held her on his knee). But his devotion to tradition—and the momentary break which it provided from professional pressures—allowed him to relax at Christmas. He loved organising family games, singing carols, supervising the handing out of presents and marshalling the whole family to church. And for this Christmas of 1929 he and Molly had planned to take the children to her home in Hampstead where Mr Bloxam, for all his one-time severity with his daughter and son-in-law to be, was in truth not unlike Barnes, a man who relaxed best if he could organise the relaxation, a man who believed that the old games were the best games and the old traditions worthy of deliberate preservation.

Chas. E. Browne had become a frequent visitor to Howden and in his company Barnes usually found it easy to relax, to fall back into that pleasant relationship that can exist between much-loved, much-admired teacher and bright pupil who has proved the worth of his master's teaching. Uncle Chas. had just retired from Christ's Hospital, but late in November he brought to Howden from the school an invitation to Wallis to give a lecture next term on airships. Wallis was elated; he regarded this as an honour beyond any so far conferred upon him even by his peers among engineers, but even the invitation and even the visit from Uncle Chas. could not dispel his edginess. There was nothing that he could do at Howden except wait. He could not concentrate on his plans for aeroplanes while his career in airships was still unproved.

He decided upon a change of scene and chose the Cairn Hydro at Harrogate, close enough to Howden so that he could be back at short notice and yet, in its luxury, utterly unlike the severity of the sheds or the cramped conditions of their bungalow.

The move was an entire failure. Molly joined Wallis as a nerve-stricken invalid. He, for his part, added nausea and loss of appetite to the migraines and insomnia that he had brought with him from Howden. As ever, he hated to sit idly indoors but he would not leave the hotel in case the all-important telephone call came through while he was out.

That call came on Sunday, 15 December, and the cure was immediate. The migraine vanished. With a Drake-like calmness Wallis ate a large meal while Molly packed and within an hour they were on the road for Howden.

It was a beautiful, moonlit night, cloudless and with scarcely a breath of wind; the promise for the next day rich. Molly slept fitfully for a few hours but Barnes joined Norway in the shed at 3 a.m. There also he found Scott who, by the extraordinary arrangement which prevailed, had charge of all flying operations for both ships. Soon buses arrived carrying the handling party: 400 soldiers from the Depot at York. Soon too the newspaper reporters poured in, the officials who had a right to be present and the officials who were curious and no more. Wallis had little love for reporters and less for officials but, despite his strenuous reservations about Scott's intellect and distrust and even dislike of the captain's gin-consumption, for Scott the flier he had entire respect based on a decade of observation. With complete confidence he left to Scott the business of preparing the ship for flight. Just before 6 a.m. he returned from pacing the apron and it was Wallis himself who supervised the nice operation of removing *R.100* from her shed. A centre line had been painted on the floor and continued out onto the aerodrome; plumb bobs were hung from bow and stern. Slowly, carefully, using these aids to keep the ship straight, the handling party walked the *R.100* out into the open. The fiery red ball of the rising sun broke through the mists of the December morning and shone like the arc-lamps in a theatre onto the bow—the hull—the stern. The chorus of watchers let out a great yell, part triumph, part relief, as the whole ship cleared the shed. Wallis was too absorbed with this meticulous effort to notice Molly at the edge of the crowd. Forty years later she wrote, 'I can't think of it even now without trembling with excitement.'[20]

Wallis joined Scott, Norway and Booth in the control car. With one of those primitive-seeming actions which gave to the operation of airships a touch of humanising simplicity that contradicted their massive and ominous shape and the complexity of their construction and mechanism, a half-ton bag of water was emptied from the bow and another from the stern. The handling party released the holding ropes and Wallis's great work, begun, it seemed, so very long ago, was in the air.

In flight *R.100* behaved impeccably. Everything that Wallis had planned for her she performed as he had predicted. She handled as easily as a well-built liner and bucked and rolled far less. It was clear that *R.100* was much closer to contract specifications than was *R.101* and probably ten miles an hour faster in the air. The only setback to *R.100*'s first flight came at the very end: it took several attempts and three hours of effort to bring her into the Cardington mast. On further trials certain defects appeared, minor in themselves but sufficient to persuade Wallis and the authorities that she must be put back into a shed for repairs before she attempted her full speed trials.

Wallis could now enjoy his Christmas in Hampstead, but a question mark still hung over his future. Would the very success of *R.100*'s preliminary flights spell *finis* to his thoughts of change? During the holiday he went to see McLean and was much relieved by the assurances he received. One of Wallis's assistants, Jimmy Watson, a colleague from wartime days at Barrow, was entirely capable of dealing with last-minute problems on *R.100* and if, as now seemed probable, the Air Ministry implemented its proclaimed decision of contracting the Airship Guarantee Company for a new ship then, in McLean's view, as Wallis had already laid down in *R.100* the principles on which her successor should be based, Watson and others were by now quite capable of following these precepts. If necessary Wallis could serve as an adviser even while working at Weybridge and from time to time he could go back to Howden to oversee design and construction. Meanwhile, a contract could be drawn up which would seal Wallis's transfer.

That contract, still in provisional form, was signed on 1 January 1930.

But his first months as an aeroplane designer were as gloomy and as frustrating as any he had experienced for years. For weeks on end in 1930 he was separated from Molly and forced to live for most of the time in hotels in the Weybridge area. In the past separation had but served to heighten their affection; this time the strain came close to being too much for their love.

Much as Wallis had learned to admire McLean, in negotiation he found him no less difficult than Burney and it seemed as if the details of his agreement with Vickers would never be settled. Worst of all, he who at Howden had grown accustomed to pre-eminence now found himself nominally among equals and actually surrounded by men who knew far more than he, many of them having worked on aeroplanes almost from their inception. Despite his high-sounding title and his consciousness of originality he was to his colleagues a neophyte with all to learn and no authority or knowledge which could permit him to break the Weybridge habit of talking through every problem for hours on end—'they are the greatest argufiers I ever met', he wrote to Molly. In order to set down on paper the ideas that had been in his mind for the last two years he was forced to work long hours into every evening.

There were other interruptions to professional progress. First, the need to find a permanent home. Just as in the past he had seldom thought of financial reward as the motivating force behind his work and had at times taken professional decisions that were in pecuniary terms naïve and even foolhardy, so now, when both security and affluence were his, the habits of parsimony drilled into him by the circumstances of his childhood remained unshakable. His salary as Pierson's equal was £2,500 a year, of itself no mean sum particularly in a time of economic depression. With bonuses on sales in his first year at Weybridge his earnings came close to £7,000, but still he did not—and did not wish to—indulge himself or his family in luxury.

One possibility that was now open he was determined to secure: a house that could be a home for a large family, something more expansive and more private than a bungalow on the edge of an airship-station. The situation that was eventually selected was in part determined by chance. Young Barnes had suffered a double mastoid and the surgeon had advised that he live on high and dry ground. Wallis drew a line on the map due south from Weybridge, and one Saturday in their two-cylinder car he and Molly set off for the point where the line cut the Surrey highlands. There, close to Effingham, 450 feet above sea level and on chalk, they saw a partially-built house backing on to a golf course. Immediately they drove to the club-house, where Barnes enquired the price of the house and asked too about the cost of living in the area. ('After all,' as he said years later, 'I had to be careful, I was only earning £2,500 a year.')[21] Wallis had securities worth

£2,500. The price of the house was £2,500. He sold his securities and bought the house in Molly's name.

Either from determination or from perspicacity Barnes and Molly instructed the builders to make seven bedrooms in the space intended for four.

Because White Hill House is set back from a lane that has never quite abandoned the bucolic for the suburban, because the garden (which was created entirely by Molly and Barnes) runs down to the golf-course, and as there are good views of the Surrey hills from the back windows, there is about the house a sense of privacy and spaciousness. It is none the less no more than a comfortable middle-class house typical of its period and area, its architecture solid and uninspired; the gables and leaded windows an unhappy but unique concession to aestheticism. Over the years it has taken on the quality of a home, the sprawling casualness that is the hallmark of a large family, but it remains inescapably what it was by design, 'stockbroker Tudor', a home 'for the managerial class', and it is difficult to read its history as the ivory tower of genius.

Having found his home at Effingham, even that achievement interrupted his attempts to get to grips with his new profession, for he had to supervise the necessary alterations. And each time he felt himself close to a free period in which he might master his new trade he was summoned back to *R.100*.

The full speed trials on 18 January revealed what seemed to be a serious weakness which demanded further basic work. At speeds over 70 m.p.h. the outer cover wrinkled. Wallis would not accept that there was any fundamental weakness in his design but ascribed this phenomenon to harmonic eddies set up by the slipstream and, for once in agreement with Burney, pointed out that 70 m.p.h. was the ultimate contract speed. The discovery imposed a necessity for further trials and for all of them Wallis had to be at hand.

On 12 March the Air Ministry announced that *R.100* would be ready to fly the Atlantic at the end of May.[22] New engines, built to the old specifications, were installed in preparation for this flight. When they were tried out in the air they proved just as efficient as the originals but during these same trials, and for the first time, a serious fault developed. The light tail fairing of the hull collapsed under high aerodynamic pressures. Much earlier

Sir Dennistoun Burney with Sir John
Sandeman Allen, M.P.

Cartoon of Sir Robert
McLean

R. K. Pierson

Captain 'Mutt'
Summers

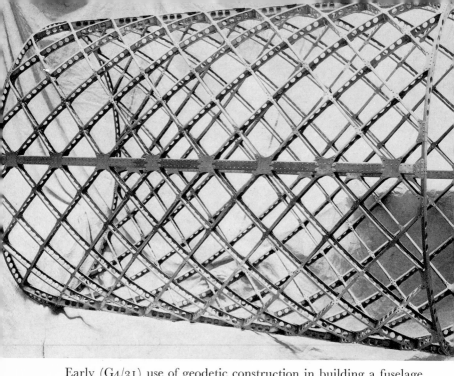

Early (G4/31) use of geodetic construction in building a fuselage

Wellesleys of RAF Long Range Flight on their successful attempt
to break the world long-distance record, November 1938

in the history of *R.100*, wind-tunnel tests on a model had seemed to reveal suction forces which might be excessive over the after-part of the hull. When the matter had been discussed with aero-dynamic experts they had insisted that there was no basis in theory for the existence of these pressures and it had been assumed that the wind-tunnel tests had been incorrectly prepared or that there had been an error in reading the results.[23]

Now, when the true facts were revealed, Wallis had lost his unique authority. *R.100* was at least nominally in the jurisdiction of the Royal Airship Works and he accepted with surprising equanimity the solution proposed—which involved removing the pointed tail—although that solution destroyed the aesthetic perfection of his conception and consequently, according to his engineering *credo*, its technical perfection as well.

Meanwhile the *R.101* team, finding themselves falling so far behind in the long-established race to achieve distant flight, began tentative negotiations for postponement of both maiden voyages, *R.100* to Canada and *R.101* to India. Both ships, they argued, were not as yet fit for the arduous journeys planned for them; a disaster to either might well end all hope of an extended airship service. The Airship Guarantee Company, now with a new con-tract assured[24] and with confidence enhanced by the general success of *R.100*'s trials, refused so much as conversation on the subject and would not be moved even by the extraordinary and sinister behaviour of *R.101* during the Hendon Air Display at the end of June when she showed herself subject to overcontrol, plummeting when she should have dived gently, bucking when the downward movement was corrected and pitching as much as 25 degrees from the horizontal. Her gas-valves leaked badly and her gas-bags were found to be riddled with small holes.

In the spring of 1930 Wallis received from a source that he had not suspected a rebuff that added perversely to his sense of frustra-tion. He wanted to avoid interruptions from *R.100*, but the one concession to his old career that he dearly wished to make was that he be on board his ship when she flew to Canada. McLean would have none of it. Firmly, irrevocably indeed and with no show of respect to Wallis's pride as a designer, he gave his instruc-tions: Wallis could kill himself if he so wished, but in one of the aeroplanes he was going to build, not in this airship contraption.[25] Thus it was that instead of flying in triumph to Canada, Wallis found himself in Southampton attempting to act as back-stop to Mitchell. Supermarine had an order on their books from the Guinness Company for a flying-boat yacht. Mitchell, for all his undoubted genius as a designer, was no authority on structures; the wings of the Guinness flying-boat flapped like a bird's and brought on aileron reversion. Wallis was to put the matter right but he was to do more: Mitchell was also no organiser and McLean hoped that Wallis could bring some order into the system at Southampton. Unfortunately, either deliberately or by default, McLean omitted to tell Mitchell the extent of Wallis's authority.

This failure apart, Mitchell, like Wallis himself, was suffering from frustration. His early optimism over the fast experimental 'plane $F7/30$ was ebbing. He had in his mind a killer-fighter and he hated wasting time on luxury flying yachts. There was, too, oppressive upon him knowledge that he would not share with anyone and certainly not with the interloper from Weybridge: he knew that his time was short. Cancer would not wait for the Spitfire.

So, as Wallis worked on the Guinness flying yacht and wrote in his private notebook detailed comments on the personnel at Supermarine, Mitchell grew more and more bitter and turned his bitterness on Wallis. At first Wallis took Mitchell's attitude for professional pique and was prepared to ignore it but soon he realised that, whether caused by pique or by something more profound, the tensions between them made the arrangement impossible. When they were together they seldom spoke, but after a few weeks they were seldom together in the office that they were supposed to share, for one or the other of them was up in London complaining that the situation could not be allowed to continue. Finally McLean agreed, and to the relief of both designers recalled Wallis to Weybridge. Just as at Southampton he had been set to correcting Mitchell's exercises, so now at Weybridge he was put to work to cure the fuselage flexibility of a high-speed fighter designed by Pierson. Mutt Summers, the test pilot, had been so appalled by the tail-flutter when the prototype was put into a dive that he had declared the 'plane useless. Wallis successfully redesigned the fuselage and, happily for him, Pierson was more generous than Mitchell had been for he recognised Wallis's skill and great potential and began to look upon his colleague as something of a prophet.

The End of Airships

It was while Wallis was considering Pierson's fighter that he hit on the idea of applying geodetics to aircraft construction. The only metal structure used by Pierson was extruded sections for the wing spars. These were crossed by wooden spars over which fabric was stretched. The rectangular fuselage was made up of tubes and wires and, in the first instance, this too was clothed crudely with doped flat-sided fabric stitched on to wooden battens. During the process of construction Pierson had become impressed by the reduction in resistance that could come with streamlining and had attempted to achieve this by the simple process of adding a streamlined plywood form to the original rectangular frame. This arrangement rendered the whole volume of the fuselage abaft the wings unusable and wasteful. Wallis regarded this with distaste and, as is so often the case, in considering one question—how to construct streamlined form effectively—he came to an answer that was irrelevant and yet sensational. Geodesics, not necessarily of constant curvature, could be drawn on the streamline surface. Better still, if two similar but opposite handed geodesics could be rigidly joined at the point of intersection and if then shear or torsional loading were to be applied to the structure as a whole the opposite handed geodesics would bear equal but opposite forces. There would follow a great improvement in strength and a great saving in weight.

Still only on his private drawing-board, entirely untested in laboratory or workshop, he established to his own satisfaction the possibility that space-frames could be built in curvilinear form, the whole contriving an articulated structure without internal chords, diagonals or bulkheads in which all the members are placed as geodesics in the boundary surface. Wallis was convinced that with wings—and indeed with fuselage—by geodetic construction as well as with his old favourite, the use of light alloys, he could make a phenomenal reduction in the weight factor of aerostats without involving the design in any contradictory loss of 'stiffness' or safety. Unfortunately even in his primitive geodetic designs the number and form of the parameters involved made it virtually impossible that he could prove his theory by compact mathematical formulae. Nor could he establish any workable comparison with frames built in what was then the conventional manner. But as he drew, calculated and considered, his conviction became more certain and his determination more intense that he must make for himself the chance to turn his theories into practice. This was, he was sure, the way of the future and his drawing-board speculations the key, not only to his new career but also to a revolution in aircraft construction.

Before this work had progressed from a gleam in the mind the past came back to disturb him. *R.100* set off for Canada.

Despite his new excitement it was galling for Wallis to have to read in the newspapers of the success of his ship, vexing to have to wait for the return of Norway for a full account, and most infuriating of all to realise that Burney was on board posturing as the genius who had created the ship.*

When finally Norway came back to England his report did in some degree make up to Wallis for his years of slavery to Burney and to *R.100*. Wallis had reservations about Norway's intelligence and integrity yet seldom had any peace-time exploit been so fortunate in its chronicler as was this, *R.100*'s only long-distance flight. The long account in Nevil Shute's autobiography is written with a novelist's pen out of an engineer's mind; even the excerpts that he includes from his diary have that rare and almost unique quality that combines the humanity of an artist with the percipience of a participant who was also an expert.

It must have been in style not unlike this that Norway recounted the adventure to Wallis when *R.100* came back to England. The description of the long hours of virtually sybaritic ease, sherry in the lounge, three-course meals and a good night's sleep disturbed only by the snores of the occupant of the next cabin: all this must have come to Wallis as justification for seventeen years' devotion to airships. The manner in which *R.100* had survived a series of violent storms in the St Lawrence estuary was vindication of Wallis's capacity as a designer. The passengers in *R.100* had made the crossings of the Atlantic in comfort almost equivalent to that enjoyed on the *Mauretania* and in half the time.

R.100 went into a shed at Cardington. The *R.101* team and those who supported the Cardington ship were now more than ever committed to attempting the flight to India, for the success of *R.100* forced upon them the need to emulate, even to go one better—and soon.

Wallis, the prime creator of *R.100*, was scarcely noticed by the

* Higham, in what is otherwise a most accurate account, is in error when he includes Wallis in the complement of *R.100* on her flight to Canada.

Press or by the public. While *R.101*'s builders fought to obey Thomson's instruction that the ship must be ready for her journey by the end of September, Wallis went back to Weybridge and set himself once more to considering the future of the heavier-than-air alternative. He was not then aware that his achievement in securing victory for the 'Capitalist' ship had earned him a small but secure place among the private hates of Stafford Cripps and that this, among many other facts, was to cause the long postponement of his knighthood.

It seems that in September 1930, Wallis had none but the most superficial knowledge of the expedients that were being hurried through on *R.101* in order to comply with Thomson's instructions.

In a sense the whole airship programme had always been a slave to political considerations. Most immediately the transatlantic flight of *R.100* had been allowed to take precedence over *R.101*'s flight to the Orient only because the Government, although it resented the notion that the Capitalist ship would be first across the starting line, nevertheless preferred some British glory in Imperial skies to further postponement of achievement. There was an Imperial Conference due to meet in London, the first since that historic Conference of 1926 which had adopted Balfour's doctrine of Dominion status. Ramsay MacDonald's Labour Government hoped to show that it, too, could bring happy drama to the conference table. Trumpets off: enter Lord Thomson fresh from a return flight to India—and the Dominion statemen gathered in London could but applaud the ingenuity of the Mother Country and could but recognise their responsibility to give practicality, by way of bases and mooring-masts, to the bonds of empire. Their enthusiasm and their support would make those links far more secure and would tie their countries to Britain far more firmly than had been achieved by Balfour's doctrine.

The dramatic persuader would not be the only advantage to be gained from the Indian flight. The long-term economic benefits of Imperial flying routes were incontrovertible and a vision of the long term might well have more immediate consequences, for if confidence in Britain's economic future could be restored, the worst effects of the Depression might be halted. The Cabinet was unanimous in its approval of Thomson's urgency. But Thomson alone was fully aware of the technical hazards, and for reasons that are easily explicable he had no intention of passing on to his colleagues any doubts that were in his mind.

He had for too long regarded *R.101* as his ship, for too long he had travelled the road of confidence in full view of Parliament and people; this alone would have made it difficult for him to turn a somersault into caution. But dissension within the Labour ranks fed the fires of his ambition. The Labour Government seemed utterly helpless before the rising tide of unemployment, and impotence set Labour leaders at each other's throats. If Thomson could bring off a great coup, face-saving to the Government, to the Party and ultimately of genuine value to the nation, the opportunities for his advancement were beyond measure.

He was in no mood to accept the advice of those who urged caution and he could well argue that there had been some risk in *R.100*'s flight to Canada and that indeed no great adventure could be begun if its champions waited upon certainty.

There was still some chance that the decision would be taken out of the realm where even the Secretary of State could force a decision. McWade, the Inspector in charge of the Aeronautical Inspection Directorate at Cardington—and therefore the official with the ultimate responsibility for issuing a Permit to Fly—had written a devastating report on the modifications carried out on *R.101* and on the dangers implicit in the rubbing of the gas-bags against the main longitudinals and the heads of the taper-pins at the points of the main and inner struts at the inner girder ends.[26] So perturbed was he that he had addressed his report to the Director of Aeronautical Inspection rather than risk the delays and obstructions of the 'proper channels', but the Director, Colonel Outram, like most of the Air Ministry's top technicians, had come up the way of aeroplanes; he had a reputation for speciousness which he was to confirm at the Court of Inquiry, but even had he wished to risk the displeasure of the Secretary of State he had no professional knowledge with which to support his stand. Inevitably McWade's comments were passed back to Colmore and the *R.101* designers. As judges in their own case they could hardly be expected to find themselves guilty of incompetence and by this time the Cardington team seemed no longer capable of any clear thought: a sense of inevitability had gripped them and they went about their work as it were with perpetually shrugging shoulders. McWade's perspicacity and courageous impertinence were brushed aside as of no consequence. He had done all he could for *R.101*; but he was so certain of his facts that he could see nothing but folly in sacrificing himself to the foolishness of others. He contrived an excuse so that he would not have to fly in the ship. His place on board was taken by Bushfield, the Inspector who had gone to Canada in *R.100*, but who had never before been in *R.101* and could not know all her aerodynamic defects.[27]

One man still stood firm against Thomson. Sir Sefton Brancker, the Director of Civil Aviation, argued with his chief in the corridors of the Air Ministry, in the bar of the House of Lords, anywhere he could waylay him, and for his pains was accused of 'showing the white feather'. Even up to lunch time on Friday, 3 October, Brancker was attempting to find telling arguments for postponement.[28]

But Lord Thomson would have none of it. At 6.36 p.m. on the evening of Saturday, 4 October 1930, *R.101* slipped the mast at Cardington.

Scarcely twelve hours later the telephone rang at White Hill House, Effingham. Wallis answered and was for a moment bad tempered with the Weybridge colleague who seemed unable to bring out his reasons for a call at such an hour. Then truth broke through the stammerings: *R.101* was down at Beauvais, only 7 hours 24 minutes out from Cardington, and all but six of her complement of fifty-four dead or dying. Wallis clung to the 'phone, saying nothing, so that his informant thought he had not heard and started to tell his story all over again. Wallis thanked him, hung up and sat on the edge of his bed staring blankly into his memories.[29]

That *R.101* could not be a success he had always known and in the long years of criticism founded upon calm calculation he had known too that disaster was possible, even probable, but until now he had never opened his mind to the human mathematics of tragedy. Richmond he had despised as a designer, but death was too high a price to pay for ignorance; too high also a price for the pride and obstinacy that he knew to be Thomson's failings. Brancker, the unshaken, unshakable aristocrat, he had never met, but mutual acquaintances spoke well of his dignity and courage. For these three Wallis's sorrow was impersonal. He could not forgive them the arrogance that had cost him so many friends: Irwin, so often Wallis's pilot; the little Scot, Sandy Bushfield, who should never have flown in *R.101*; Johnston, the navigator who had taken *R.100* to Canada; Atherstone, for so long one of the best officers in the Airship Service; but even for these his grief was somewhat tempered by the fatalism that is part of the equipment of pioneers. The death of others worried him more profoundly. Now that it was too late he wanted to turn back the pages of history, to ignore the years of bitterness that had separated him from them, to revert to those happy days when Colmore and Scott had served with him in the cheerful camaraderie of war time. The bitterness evaporated. He thought of Colmore, weak perhaps but gallant and one of the few who had done his best to hold the airshipmen from dissension. He remembered Scott, now once more in recollection 'Scotty', gay, extroverted and the finest pilot in airships. These were the representatives and almost the last survivors of his youthful experience. It was as if two more familiar names had been added to the war memorials; for Wallis the consciousness of surviving beyond the hope of his generation was now virtually complete. Self-recrimination soured his grief. Had he but accepted, so long ago, inclusion in the *R.101* design team then this tragedy could have been averted. Later, had he but been more forthright in his criticisms and given them due publicity then again he might have found listeners and *R.101* would not have flown before she was ready.

That Sunday morning he went as usual to church and for the rest of the day sat silent in his armchair. Early on Monday morning he drove himself to Weybridge, cancelled the three public lectures he was due to give in the last months of 1930 and, as if shaking off the past, began to work furiously on the design of a bomber.

The bitterness so long prevailing between the two airship teams was not softened even by tragedy. The men of *R.100* were offered no official representation at the funeral of the *R.101* victims. Norway, still bruised by the derogatory manner in which he had been treated on his last visit to Cardington only two weeks earlier, nevertheless waited for several hours among the half-million who lined the streets of London to pay sad tribute to the dead from

Beauvais. Wallis and Teed chose to go to Bedford,[30] thus identifying themselves with an even more intimate gesture of respect,
for this was R.*101*'s own town, the procession that passed as
Wallis and Teed stood unrecognised at the roadside carried
Bedford's friends who had also been the friends of Wallis: with
the cortège there vanished for a whole area hopes that Wallis had
once shared.

As neither Wallis nor any other R.*100* man was invited to the
funeral, so was Wallis's evidence never asked by the Court of
Inquiry which, under the presidency of Sir John Simon, investigated the causes of the disaster. In books and articles written
subsequent to the tragedy much has been made of the fact that
this exclusion applied not only to Wallis but to all the R.*100* team.
Nevil Shute, writing entirely from memory, not only states the
exclusion of R.*100* personnel as a fact but justifies it on the
grounds that the rivalry between the two teams was so deep-set
that his own side could not be dispassionate, and so well-known
that no Court would expect dispassion from them. In fact Booth,
now the most experienced airship captain in England, presented
a statement and Philip Teed gave unequivocal evidence that
was designed entirely for one end: to protect the reputation
of the Captain of R.*101*, Flight-Lieutenant H. Carmichael
Irwin.

Wallis, however, with Richmond dead and even by the reckon-
ings of those most partisan to the Cardington way of thinking,
now Britain's most experienced designer, was never called nor was
his opinion sought. The suspicion must remain undispersed that
Wallis's knowledge was regarded as inconvenient by the authorities and that it was feared that his well-established forthrightness, his lucidity and his oft expressed objection to the design
conception of R.*101* might disrupt the intention to 'whitewash'
those responsible for the disaster—an intention that was identified and attacked even at the time by several technical journals.[31]
True, much did come out before the Court of the haste, botching
and political pressures which combined to bring about the catastrophe, but the political pressures continued even into *post-
mortem* and with them a decent attempt to avoid condemning
individuals; the more damning evidence was either glossed
over in the *Report* or presented in a manner that must be
regarded as deliberately confusing. Even at the time Wallis was

certain that the disaster had been caused by fundamental errors in designing. While the Court was still sitting he wrote to a friend:

> I think it will be definitely established . . . that the failure of the *R.101* was due to inherent defects in certain parts of her design,

and, still prickly in his defence of airships as a whole, he added,

> [this] rather than anything fundamentally associated with the rigid airship as such.[32]

A few months later he added comments about *R.101*'s poor lift efficiency and this was the only technical criticism he deigned to add to his destruction of the occult evidence which, perhaps for the lack of other more substantial witness, was admitted to the Court proceedings:

> [It bears] a striking resemblance to the clever imaginative work of Rudyard Kipling's publication under the title of *The Night Mail*.

R.101, he pointed out, when she took off was not lighter-than-air in the strict sense of the term:

> The ship was being flown in a heavy condition (that is, as a sort of elementary combination of airship and aeroplane) in the hope that by this device she would be able to carry enough fuel to enable her to complete the first stage of her journey to India.[33]

Time, much thought and much experience with aeroplanes did not alter this view that overloading was the prime cause of the crash. He came to regard *R.101*'s structure as 'inferior' to the framework of the Naval Ship No. 1, the girders of which were designed by the Works Manager who was not a technologist in any sense of the word. The parachute wiring which 'Richmond and Rope thought clever' he had always known to be thoroughly unsatisfactory, their ultimate decision to let out the wiring so that the gas-bags came into contact with the many sharp points in

North's structure as 'almost criminal' and their placing of the gas valves as 'a piece of folly which cannot be too thoroughly condemned', and even four decades later he insisted still that his first impression had been correct but that now he could refine them from afterknowledge.* And to his technical explanation he added a more personal and psychological explanation:

> I attribute the *R.101* disaster firstly to my refusal to work with Scott, Colmore, Richmond and Nixon; secondly to Richmond's overweening vanity; thirdly to Scott's lazy self-assurance; and lastly to a certain lack of moral courage in Colmore. None of them had the moral courage to confess that their ship was a mass of mistakes from beginning to end and was in fact demonstrably unfit to fly over any distances.[34]

The crash of *R.101* destroyed for all time Britain's rigid airship programme. The destruction of *Akron* in 1933 and *Macon* in 1935 brought to an end United States' ventures with rigids, and then in May 1937 a disaster to the *Hindenburg* at Lakehurst, New Jersey, in full view of the newsreel cameras, seemed destined to take even the Germans out of the race which they had begun and which, except for the weeks after *R.100*'s transatlantic round-voyage, they had never looked like losing. However, the Germans persisted. To take the place of the *Hindenburg* and the still successful *Graf Zeppelin* they built *Graf Zeppelin II*, a ship that it was their intention to inflate with safe helium. The refusal of the United States Secretary of the Interior, Harold Ickes, to countersign the State Department's authority for the export of helium to Germany brought to an end the forty-year-long story.

---

* 'There is no doubt in my mind that the disaster to the *R.101* is that these unfortunate fellows relied on dynamic lift since she was so much too heavy, a thing which should *never* be done in an airship. Dynamic lift can only be produced by putting on a lot of up-elevator, thus inducing a large *down-load* on the tail and causing the ship to fly pitched up in which attitude, if her speed is sufficient, the dynamic lift upwards will exceed not only the static heaviness but also the downward load on the tail. If now, in this condition, the angle of incidence of a sharp-edged fin, such as that of *R.101*, becomes too great, the fin will stall, leaving the trailing area of the elevator unloaded. That is to say, the heavy down-load of the tail is instantly removed with the result that the tail will suddenly rise and the bow will sink, since it was this down-load on the tail which was keeping the ship pitched up. The result is, of course, a sharp dive which cannot be corrected.'

Barnes Wallis

As with the years he became more and more a public figure noted for his originality of mind and occasional eccentricity of behaviour so with ever-increasing frequency Wallis was approached by devotees of lighter-than-air craft who demanded of him that he should not only share their devotion but demonstrate its validity by turning his attention back from his worship of speed and noise to the sensible, decent and comfortable airship. Although Wallis never denied that for him airships possessed romance unknown to aeroplanes and were second only to the poetry he had found in ships of the sea, although he held to the view that his years on airship designing were not wasted and that without the experience that he gained from *No.9* to *R.100* his aeroplane designing would have lacked originality and even competence, he never faltered in his view that he left lighter-than-air construction at almost the right moment.

Had history been different, had Lord Thomson enjoyed his hoped-for triumph at the Imperial Conference, it is conceivable that the development of *R.100* and *R.101* would have continued and that new British rigids would have been ordered, but all the evidence seems to indicate that even so the renaissance would have been short-lived. As far back in time as time is recorded the viability of any transport system has been measured by its efficiency as a mail-carrier. Even before *R.101* plunged to destruction airships in this respect and in comparison with aeroplanes were slipping off the scale.

As passenger carriers airships do seem to have demonstrated advantages that even to this day are not shared by aeroplanes. To their habitual steadiness in flight there are many supporting stories: how Burney dropped his watch on to the inner side of the cover of *R.100* from where it was rescued by a rigger after several hours; how a passenger in *Hindenburg* set a fountain pen on end on a table in which position it remained for ninety minutes; and, perhaps, the most telling testimony to their equilibrium, that of Wallis himself who claimed that in many hours flying in all sorts of airships from 1915 to 1930 he never knew one to roll at all.[35] Those who travelled in airships were not deafened by engine noise—as bear witness Nevil Shute's complaint that on *R.100* he was kept awake by snores from the next cabin—and airships were almost entirely innocent of the intrusive and impertinent loudness which both prop. and jet-planes inflict on the land-bound.

The End of Airships

In terms of luxury *R.100*, *R.101* and *Hindenburg* came close to challenging ocean liners, as yet Tourist Class rather than First but comfortably expansive. The passenger could move about freely from lounge to dining-room, to observation-deck, to bar—and so to bed on a comfortably sprung mattress in a private cabin. Nor were airship passengers subjected to a regimen of synthetic foods served on synthetic trays such as have become the customary cuisine of the airlines. Nevil Shute, a man with cheerfully sybaritic tendencies, comments on the excellence of breakfast on board *R.100* Canada-bound. The last meal served on *R.101* would not have disgraced a Lord Mayor's banquet, even if a cheese compounded of twenty varieties, like so many more serious failings in the ship, savours of desperate ingenuity.

Nor can the record of catastrophe prove that airships could not be made safe. In their defence it must be urged that with the exception of the *Hindenburg* all of the airships that flew and crashed were prototypes. Had time and money been given for experiment, correction and redesigning, even in the elementary conditions of aerodynamics then prevailing, it seems likely that the safety factor could have been vastly increased, and as the science developed to the state that it reached in the 1950s it is almost certain that passenger airships could have been built no less safe than their contemporary 'planes.

Wallis persisted in his romantic affection for airships and never recanted his belief in their especial virtues, but, once he had given up his primacy among airshipmen and though he was, from time to time, tempted by those who hoped to see airships once more in the skies, his refusal to reverse the logic of history seldom faltered. He accepted as indisputable the fact that airships cannot come close to the speed of planes. The magnificent achievement of his own *R.100* did not blind him to arithmetic: the ship's outward journey reduced by less than twenty-fours the time set for the sea-going Atlantic Blue Riband. Even, as the years went by and more and more innovations became available for their potential improvement, still he recognised that airships must remain sadly susceptible to the vagaries of the weather and that their theoretical load capacity was not equal to that of a war-time bomber. Forty years after *R.100*'s maiden flight Peter Masefield extended the conceivable line of airship progress by adding to the record of *R.100* all those technological advances that might

have been available to an $R.200$. Wallis aggreed with his conclusions: provide stressed-skin, turbine-power and axial flow, fill
her with helium and even so, and in good weather, $R.200$ could
not fly from London to New York in less than thirty-four hours
nor make the eastbound trip in less than twenty-eight, while in
unfavourable conditions the time might well be doubled. At very
best $R.200$ would achieve sixty-four round trips a year. The
modern jet-airliner makes 200 and carries far more than the
optimum of 100 passengers envisaged for this fairy tale $R.200$.[36]
Silence, steadiness and comfort close to luxury there could be in
rigid airships, but neither in 1930 nor thereafter was it likely
that, in the teeth of the rapid development of aeroplanes, there
could be found the huge capital sums necessary to support the
uncertain and at best minimal profits that might come from
rigids.

The Service authorities did not give up so easily. Within days
of the end of $R.101$ the Chief of Air Staff was writing to Air Vice
Marshal Dowding under 'Very Secret' cover explaining his personal conviction that $R.100$ should take over and make the trip
to India that winter.[37] Dowding replied that such an effort was
out of the question. His reasons were not those that the Chief of
Air Staff had expected. Dowding said nothing of the danger of
running a hydrogen-filled ship on petrol engines in hot climates,
nor did he insist that for such a long flight $R.100$, like $R.101$,
should have one bay added. His principal objection revealed how
much officialdom had been conspiring against $R.100$:

> You see Richmond wanted to put $R.101$'s type of cover on
> $R.100$. Burney objected and said (a) that it would be unduly
> heavy and (b) actually unsafe for the faster ship. I was prepared
> to back Richmond's opinion when he was alive and ready to
> design it; but now that he's dead and we don't know where to
> turn for a designer . . .[38]

Happily for his equanimity Wallis knew nothing of these
exchanges (and remained ignorant of them until he read this
passage) for the thought of Richmond the ignoramus tinkering
with his own ship would have roused his horror and his temper.

The Air Force abandoned the chase, but still the political
powers were not entirely silenced. The Prime Minister continued

in public the ancient political game of cliché. The 'mishap' at Beauvais was a 'temporary set-back',[39] but the plain truth was that even the Government could not find reason, money or technicians of sufficient experience to revive the programme.

In August 1931 the Labour Government fell, victim to a further financial crisis. The task of the new National Government (not a Coalition in the ordinary sense of the term but a co-operation of individuals) was to attempt to stem the flood-tides of public expenditure, and it was with something of a sense of relief that Ramsey MacDonald—with sitting beside him on the Front Bench Sir Samuel Hoare, once the principal parliamentary spokesman for the Capitalist ship—could put before the House a 'reduced programme of expenditure on airships'.[40] 'Reduced' was yet another debater's cliché, for all that was voted was £20,000 to support a watching brief on airship development in other countries.

Wallis took no part in the correspondence in the public and technical press over the future of airships which continued throughout 1931. Although his friend Philip Teed was one of those who insisted that the country should accept as irrevocable the failure of an intelligent, lengthy and expensive effort,[41] already in 1928 Wallis had wakened from the dream of Imperial airship routes. In 1930 he grieved for his one-time companions; in 1931 when the breakers' men tore apart the remains of *R.100* and set a steam-roller to crushing a half-million pounds worth of technical ingenuity, he did not mourn nor indeed did he so much as comment, although the brutality symbolised the nullification of the whole of his adult career.

11 Wellesley and Wellington

There were other breaker's men at work in Europe tearing at the structure of Western civilisation, preparing to drive their steam-roller of hate over the hopes of all mankind. In the Reichstag Elections of 1928 the Nazis won twelve seats; in 1930, 107; and in 1932, 230. Even before Hitler took over unique authority, his virulence, his determined expansionism and deliberate flouting of peace treaty and disarmament agreement had started the world upon a new weapons race.

At the beginning of the 'thirties there was in this race only one runner of consequence: Germany. British statesmen remained obstinately rooted in the pacific habit of a decade earlier and blithely convinced that their policies must be directed still to resolving problems created by the First World War rather than to preparing for the Second. They followed the pacifism of the people and, with the additional excuse of economic depression, did nothing to warn the electorate of the dangers of the policies that the electorate demanded. These were the days of the Peace Pledge Union, of the 'King and Country' debate in the Oxford Union, of *Journey's End* and *All Quiet on the Western Front*, the days when in a by-election an advocate of rearmament managed to jettison a majority of 15,000 votes.

Britain was now only the fifth air power in the world; a shameful situation from which the politicians managed to eke out much glory, setting themselves up as men of virtue who stood by the principles of their predecessors which other nations were deserting. When, in 1933, the Under-Secretary of State for Air announced yet another postponement of a proposed ten-year programme for the Royal Air Force he did so with the triumphant flourish of a herald announcing a great victory. Even for those who questioned the decline in British strength there was a salve that has been applied frequently in Britain during the twentieth century: Britain's 'planes might be few in number, the Royal Air Force undermanned and the money short for future development but Britain's inventiveness and technical ingenuity were unequalled. Had not Britain demonstrated the superior quality of both pilots and aeronautical engineers by winning outright the Schneider Trophy—the third and conclusive victory in 1931 by a Supermarine Rolls Royce S-6B flying at 340 miles per hour? Did she not hold the speed record of 357 m.p.h.?

If Wallis was in any way conscious of the conflicting auguries that made the times at once inauspicious for a designer of weapons and yet inevitably and hideously promising, he did not reveal his knowledge in his correspondence: there is no mention of Hitler earlier than 1938 nor, perhaps more surprisingly, any direct political reference to disarmament. One cannot claim for him any greater foresight than was shown by most of his compatriots and their political leaders; indeed, in a manner that is to a later generation almost inexplicable, even as he worked on revolutionary designs for bombers, he followed the contemporary fashion of regarding himself as a pacifist.

Even at that time a pacifist working for Vickers was a paradox beyond resolving, for Vickers had been pricked as the principal obstacle to peace, and the firm's most intimate secrets—some of them fabricated but unchallenged—had been paraded in the full glare of a United States Congressional Committee of Inquiry under a witch-hunting isolationist, Senator Gerald P. Nye of North Dakota. The Nye Munitions Committee (with which, incidentally, Alger Hiss served as assistant legal adviser) set out in 1934 to prove the comfortable and fashionable thesis that wars are caused not by disputed boundaries, nor by problems over racial minorities nor international economic problems but by the bloodthirsty rapacity of arms manufacturers and the heartless greed of international bankers. 'Public Enemy No. 1,' shrieked Nye to the Senate, 'should be the munitions manufacturer who wants to sell his powder and poison gas . . . The result of this act will inevitably drag us into war.'[1] By using its power to impound documents, the Nye Committee had brought sensation where generally there was only boring invective. Personal and confidential letters from Craven of Vickers to high officials of the American Electric Boat Company were read into the record; in versions edited with heavy-handed cunning so that it appeared that Vickers were not merely indulging in international price-fixing (which was probably true) but also (which was almost certainly untrue) that they were bribing and in other unscrupulous ways influencing senior officers of the United States Navy. The most sensational accusation was after this fashion: Britain represented by Vickers—and the Nye Committee made little effort to distinguish the nation from the firm—had a vast commercial embassy in Turkey, which used a platoon of superior harlots who kept armaments contracts virtually—if that is the word —under their pillows. Better still for the Senator from North Dakota, one witness, an American arms salesman, insisted that he had lost a huge order because his prospective clients had been suborned by King George V acting as a Vickers' agent.

Like so many witch-hunts, in time the Nye Committee destroyed itself by its own ridiculous excesses. But Congressional attacks on Vickers were useful also for the opposition in the House of Commons, and Clement Attlee repeated the Turkish harlot story, though he felt bound to clothe it in some parliamentary respectability by elevating the ladies to the rank of 'women of doubtful character'. This and many more serious allegations made against Vickers before the Congressional Committee were rehearsed on the floor of the House and in the British Press by Labour Party members and pacifists who wanted legislation to prohibit private manufacture of arms. Their efforts led to the setting up of a Royal Commission which, if it behaved with more decorum than its American counterpart, none the less pursued Vickers with extraordinary vigour. By May 1937, when the Commission issued its report, there had been some changes in the political atmosphere and comprehension of the true facts of the European situation was no longer unusual even among politicians, the Civil Service and the General Staff. The Royal Commission followed judiciously in the path that others were now treading: theoretically a state monopoly of arms manufacture might be desirable but in practice a shift made at this moment towards the creation of such a monopoly would destroy Britain's last hope of re-arming in time to meet the threat from Nazi Germany. The Air Staff agreed for, although against its inclination, it depended upon Vickers and its competitors to fulfil Scheme F which planned to bring eight thousand new 'planes to the Royal Air Force by the end of 1939. But expediency did not fill with rose petals the chasm between Vickers and Whitehall. When, in October 1937, Mutt Summers returned from one of his frequent trips to Germany his report, full of gloomy statistics about the rapid expansion of the German aircraft programme and its technical superiority to Britain's, was gloriously inaccurate for he had been fed bloated information by General Milch, but its conclusions were correct and so depressing that even the new Chairman of Vickers, Sir Archibald Jamieson, felt bound to send it on to the Ministry. The reply of the Secretary of State, Lord Swinton, to Jamieson on the Summers report was in such terms as could only pass between friends but it revealed no change of heart towards Vickers: 'Kindly tell your pilots to mind their own bloody business.'[2]

Happily for Wallis, the self-styled pacifist, and, as it was to turn out, happily for the nation, one man in Vickers, Sir Robert McLean, continued to mind his 'own bloody business' to considerable effect. McLean made an almost unique contribution to the eventual destruction of Nazism and made it at a time when even Churchill was helpless, ignored by the nation and by his fellow members of Parliament. McLean listened to the thunderclaps over the Continent and with remarkable accuracy forecast the time when the storm would hit Britain. Undoubtedly McLean was concerned for the profits of his two aircraft companies, but his conviction that the coming war would be won by 'planes such as the Spitfire and the Wellington, and the almost desperate energy with which he pursued the Air Ministry and the Air Staff in the attempt to force them to share his views, had inspiration far beyond the commercial. Fortunately for his designers, McLean was cast from a mould that was fast becoming obsolescent; he believed that it was the task of a leader to discover subordinates of originality and thereafter to give them free rein and his full support. In this he was at odds not only with the Air Ministry but even with Sir Charles Craven who shared some of the Ministry's suspicion of individual genius. Against positive opposition from the Air Ministry, and with only grudging support from the Vickers Board, McLean argued, bludgeoned and tricked his way through the 'thirties. He cajoled the Air Staff out of its infatuation with biplanes and thus made the Wellesley into a practical proposition. He thrust the successes of the prototype under the sniffing noses at the Air Ministry, weaned the purchasing authorities from their obstinate preference for the Handley Page Hampden and thus presented to Wallis and Pierson the opportunity to develop the most durable of all British bombers, the Wellington. With no less courage and no less vigour he nursed and championed Mitchell and so, out of almost thirty designs completed at Supermarine between 1932 and 1935, there came one which was the prototype of the greatest of all fighters, the Spitfire. More than any other one man it was MacLean who, against all opposition, in five years shifted the Royal Air Force from devotion to wooden biplanes and gave it the metal monoplanes with which, against all odds, it hammered the enemy in the opening months of the war and, when all else failed, held him back from the last fortress of hope.

Wallis's first effort in the total design of an aeroplane was the M.1/30, produced in response to a specification for a biplane torpedo-bomber issued in March 1930. As a heavier-than-air machine its conception was novel but the influence of *R.100* was palpable and admitted in the Vickers tender which without inhibition boasted for the design rare lightness from the incorporation 'of structural methods similar to those recently used so successfully on H.M.A. *R.100*'. Duralumin was employed for wing-spars, longerons and fuselage-struts and the riveting of the longerons was organised after the manner that Wallis had developed for *R.100*.[3] M.1/30 with Summers as test pilot flew for the first time from Brooklands on 11 January 1933, and, after several further test flights and minor adjustments, the prototype M.1/30 ended its short life on 23 November 1933 when, for the first time diving at speed, it broke up in the air. Mutt Summers' parachute opened at once but his observer, John Radcliffe, suffered a few moments of terror hanging by his parachute back-strap to the machine gun in the cockpit whilst the fuselage and portions of fabric and structure disappeared from his arc of vision, and then the two parachuted safely to earth.

Meanwhile Wallis was at work on two alternative answers to one question which continued the debate over geodetic construction. In November 1931 the Air Ministry had issued another specification for a torpedo bomber. In his first response to this specification Wallis envisaged a monoplane, but the Air Ministry favoured a biplane, and Wallis humoured their preference with a design which was accepted in April 1932. However, he managed to persuade his Vickers masters to persist with the building of a monoplane, and so it came about that there were two versions of G.4/31, a biplane and a monoplane, both of them groping towards a geodetic conception and neither of them achieving it in full. The few who could read the signs were aware that in his monoplane Wallis had come close to establishing proof of his conviction that, for the first time since the Great War, an entirely new method of aeroplane construction was available to designers. Unfortunately, by 1935, the Air Ministry was committed to the familiar, had ordered 150 biplanes, and indeed had inflicted upon the favoured G.4/31 biplane certain modifications which set it even further back than the original design from the full achievement of geodetic construction.[4]

McLean's persistence equalled and even exceeded that of Wallis. He nagged at the Air Ministry, and, in this more acute than his designer, elided the construction of the two forms and thus avoided the consequences of Service timorousness and innate conservatism. Two months later McLean's obstinacy had its reward: the contract for biplanes was cancelled and for it the Air Ministry substituted an order for ninety-six monoplanes to be used not as torpedo-carriers but as medium-bombers.

Now Wallis could develop the geodetic construction to its full advantage. Within months he was explaining for his Vickers colleagues and for the *cognoscenti* in the Air Ministry the dream fulfilled in the newly named Wellesley, and incidentally adding to his boasts a quality—'long-range'—which had not been demanded by the specification.

'The Wellesley,' he wrote, 'is metal constructed on an entirely new principle—the Vickers–Wallis "Geodetic" system.'

All parts of the structure are formed as geodetics in the streamline shape of the fuselage, and also in the curved profile of the wings . . . This method of aeroplane construction is the most important contribution to aircraft engineering since the completion of the first successful metal aircraft. For example, it permits each wing to be hollow and entirely free from any kind of obstruction—the additional space thus gained can be utilised for extra tankage or other loads, and the complete structure is one of extreme lightness combined with great strength and rigidity, thus making possible a range and load carrying capacity that has hitherto been considered unattainable.[5]

It was heady stuff. The coupling of his own name with the world-famous name of Vickers seemed to trumpet his arrival centre-stage in the drama of the history of aeroplanes. There was also a codicil to the paper which reiterated the text that can be taken as the theme for the whole of Wallis's life:

The range would be sufficient to fly to any part of the Empire without landing on foreign soil to re-fuel.

The life-history of an aeroplane design is inevitably long. By the time the Wellesley had proved its long-range capabilities it was obsolescent and as a service machine well-nigh obsolete. Almost it can be said that the formation flight to Australia in 1938 was both the final test and the last important adventure of the Wellesley, although some flew on into active service during the Second World War in support of Wavell's advance into the Western Desert and Slim's battle for Keren. Similarly, because progress in design-theory runs at a rate which outstrips by far the practical possibilities of putting a 'plane into the air, the history of one species begins long before its parent-species has matured. So it is that the story of the Wellington opens even before the first flight of a Wellesley.

In October 1932, at a time when there were available to Wallis only the sensational test-bed figures for the Wellesley's air-frame strength, Vickers received an Air Ministry specification for a twin-engined medium day-bomber. In their tender of February 1933 Vickers banked all on geodetic construction and so B.9/32 was the ancestor of the Wellington.

Into B.9/32 Wallis and Pierson poured the fruits of their vast and complementary experience and, as design-studies and experiments progressed, not only their own work but also the implicit development of the whole aircraft industry over the years since the First World War, so that in many respects the prototype Wellington was no mere adaptation of previous 'planes but a new *genus*, embodying novel concepts not only in structure but also in the application of knowledge acquired over two decades about aerodynamics, motive power and metallurgy.

Wellesley and Wellington

In all these matters the designers were far ahead of those who ordered and used their 'planes, the Air Ministry and serving officers in the Royal Air Force. For example, if Wallis and Pierson had followed the demands of the original specification and obeyed, as had hitherto been the invariable custom, the tare-weight requirement of 6,300 lb they would have been frustrated in their plans to install the most powerful engine available, the structural weight would have been limited and the result would have been a machine much slower than the Wellington with weight-carrying capacity much reduced. Instead, by argument and demonstration and occasional evasion Vickers pushed the tare-weight requirement from the original 6,300 lb of 1933 to 11,500 in 1936.[6]

A pilot contract was received in September 1933. At that time the tare-weight requirement was still in force but already the original specification had been amended from a high- to a mid-wing configuration, a change that delighted the designers for, though it was motivated by the Air Force wish to improve visibility for pilots flying in formation, it served to enhance the aesthetic and aerodynamic properties of the 'plane. During 1934 the Air Ministry asked for revisions of the bomb-door system and of the arrangements for oil supply. Vickers countered with a request to use a heavier and more powerful engine than the specified Goshawk. The Air Ministry accepted that the 'plane could be fitted with Bristol Pegasus engines and variable-pitch propellers but in turn demanded a greater fuel-load so as to provide a range of 1,500 miles at 215 m.p.h. and a height of 15,000 feet.[7]

The design inhibition of fixed tare-weight had by now been eroded and from 1936 it was the Air Ministry which made most of the demands and which pressed upon the willing designers ever greater requirements for weight-carrying capability. Range, speed, ceiling—all had improved at a rate which at the time set the Wellington first among the bombers of the world. If necessary the 'plane could fly on one engine and the extraordinary resilience of geodetic construction was apparent to an intelligent minority in the Ministry and the Service.

At this period in his career (and not for the last time) Wallis was almost obsessively involved in his work. Then, and in the hectic years to come, because of his undeniably Victorian attitude to children, he was spared from the major diversion which most family men enjoy or suffer. He was the unchallenged head of the household but as such seldom, if ever, involved in the *minutiae* of existence. He paid bills (and too often not only for his immediate family but also for his father and sister). He discussed with Molly the education of their offspring. But to the children themselves he was stern and unapproachable, his silences to be returned with quiet and his infrequent gaieties to be repaid with liveliness. Once a year, on family camping holidays, he would become by his own lights one of the group, but the pitching of tents was a technology no less exact than geodetics and family walks as deliberate as a test-bed experiment. As for so long even after his mother's death he had been above all things a son so now he was completely a husband, and a father only to the bounds of duty. His was the responsibility for large questions of morals; the trivialities of existence were kept from him by Molly. To his children he was the Jahweh of their lives, an awesome personality who seemed outside their understanding except in those moments when they broke one of his unwritten Commandments—all of which had something to do with manners—and then he would descend from his throne, as quick to punish as he was slow to praise. His wrath, when it came, was uninhibited by progressive educational considerations, for his attitude to corporeal correction had slipped back fifty years to something more reactionary than his own ideas when he had been young. He had no intention of spoiling the child by sparing the rod.

Many activities he continued because they had long since become inescapable habits. On Sunday mornings he attended early service both because he had been reared as a churchgoer and because somewhere in the recesses of his inherited conscience was the conviction that any break in his communion with his God might disrupt his God-given genius. He took exercise, played golf, went for long walks and tended his garden, but now no longer with the pleasured enthusiasm of his days at Cowes, for now exercise was a means to an end and not the end in itself; he was set upon holding himself physically to resist mental overstrain. One new activity he did accept: with Molly he joined a madrigal choir—and almost weekly cursed the demands of rehearsal which interrupted the leisure he could give to work.

Wellesley and Wellington

It was an austere life dedicated exclusively to the pursuit of his own particular truth. Wallis, at this time, was once more a man without a twinkle in his eye, unwilling to be lured into sociability and sombrely, even desperately, egocentric. Invited to a dinner—a works dinner at that—he replied:

> I have made it a rule now for many years not to attend late dinners of this kind as I find owing to my advanced age and other troubles that I am invariably laid up as a consequence of a departure from the very rigid diet on which I exist.[8]

At the moment of writing that letter he was forty-seven years of age!

He dealt carefully with administration, was meticulous in meeting the problems of his staff and replied with generous amplitude and full courtesy to appeals for help from bright young men and requests for information from his peers, but such appeals and such requests he considered an inevitable concomitant of his professional responsibilities; replying was a duty, there was no more to it and little more that was personal in his occasional letter to his old mentor, his old senior, his old companion, H. B. Pratt. When, prematurely, in the early twenties, Pratt had given up hope for the future of rigids, he had returned from whence he came, to Barrow, to the shipbuilding yards, and there with time he had become Vickers' expert on the design of sea-mines. Once or twice a year the two exchanged letters, generally about some candidate for employment, and as a gesture to a vanished past those letters usually ended with a few lines of family gossip, but between Wallis and Pratt the full-blown formality of address remained as always: 'Dear Wallis,' 'Dear Pratt,' and 'Yours sincerely, B. N. Wallis' or 'H. B. Pratt'.

Then suddenly the quiescent and by now seemingly unimportant relationship burst around Wallis's head. The opening scenes in what was to be the first act of a tragedy were in the convention that had grown up between the two men. Pratt had been elected President of the Barrow Association of Engineers and, as he had done in the past, he wrote to Wallis asking for a lecture. The subject chosen by Pratt was 'Aeroplane Design', but unfortunately he added the rider that the talk should be on 'general and elementary lines'. Obsessed as he was with geodetic construction Wallis hoped to use the occasion to proselytise for an extension of his theories with which he was already toying: the application of geodetic construction to shipbuilding. Therefore in his reply to Pratt he skirted the true boundaries of the invitation and wrote that he had 'at his fingerends' a lecture on a 'new departure in structure which I have already developed here and we are at present constructing two experimental machines which, if successful, should give most exceptional performances as regards load carrying capacity and radius of action.' The information was gratuitous for Wallis had felt bound to consult McLean who had been adamant that there must be no publication or publicity about geodetic construction until what was still a theoretical conception had proved practical in flight. In effect Wallis was saying to Pratt that he would not give the lecture he was asked to give and could not give the lecture he wanted to give.

Pratt was not easily dissuaded. If the journey to Barrow was not for Wallis then what about one of his juniors? Wallis stayed obstinate: there was no one else at Weybridge capable of lecturing to such a gathering of 'highly trained technical people'. This second letter in the series contained a brutal truth disguised as helpfulness (and such was his single-mindedness, disguised perhaps even from the writer). Wallis prefaced his list of those outside Weybridge who might lecture with the phrase—'If you are not yourself sufficiently acquainted with the personalities of the aircraft industry.'[9] This to one of Britain's aviation pioneers!

For a while correspondence between the two old friends reverted to its spasmodic inconsequence and then, early in 1936, Wallis re-opened the subject of geodetic construction. The embargo on lectures remained, although in an odd repetition of history that, had they known about it, would have given much scope to those who were even then attacking the international machinations of Vickers, all the secrets of the Wellesley had been revealed to a prospective enemy, the Japanese, in much the same manner as the few secrets of British airships had been presented to the Germans just before the First World War. (The Japanese Naval Aeronautics Department rejected geodetic construction as 'too complicated' but thought it worth studying for its capability of long-distance flight.)[10] Wallis would not lecture at

Barrow: indeed he had no wish to give Pratt any information about aircraft but he was now so certain of the worth of his innovation that he felt ready to return to his idea of widening the application of the principle to shipbuilding. He addressed a long and as usual carefully drafted paper to Sir Charles Craven and, having suffered in the past from dissensions between one Vickers group and another, set himself to the task of acquiring at the same time an advocate at Barrow. Pratt was his choice, for Pratt had the ability and the experience to grasp the principles as Craven never could.

His letter to Pratt was met with the coldness which, perhaps, it deserved. Pratt wrote that even consideration of the suggestion was outside his province but that he was sure that the 'new system of construction is likely to be most effective *for its purpose*'. Wallis was not put off: he insisted that Pratt come to Weybridge to see the miracles that were being wrought.

Pratt visited Weybridge and the consequence was quite other than the intention—and devastating. Pratt understood little of what was going on but the dynamism around him was inescapable. This was the atmosphere that he had once shared, the excitement of pioneering that had once been his and that he had tried to forget. Before he was thirty he had been Britain's leading airship designer. Wallis had been his protégé and for long his junior and the two men were the same age—still only forty-nine—yet here was Wallis, white-hot under the stimulation and toil of great innovations while Pratt laboured wearily as little more than a technical salesman for well-tried and basically uninteresting naval weapons. The dramatic contrast ground misery into his mind and discontent thrashed out into frantic expressions of frustration. His was a 'mental living death'. He blamed himself because fifteen years earlier when post-First World War redundancies had hit the airship industry he had settled for 'a then safe and easy job with immediate profit instead of sticking to aircraft with faith in the future'. As he listened to Wallis's technical explanations and as he savoured once more the smell of genesis all around him, Pratt felt himself fired with new optimism. He knew himself to be a designer of outstanding ability and saw himself still as memory reminded him he had once been: an innovator of genius. He could return to the road from which he had strayed, wilfully and lunatically: at forty-nine there was still plenty of time. The man to give him this second beginning was the man whom he had taken up so readily all those years ago in the Isle of Wight, the man with whom he had worked in the cheerful secrecy of Victoria Street.

At Weybridge he said nothing of the hope that was now clear in his mind, but as soon as he returned to Barrow he talked to his wife and found her already alert to the desiccation of brain and spirit that he was suffering. Then, without a word to his superiors, he sat down to write a long letter to Wallis. This was a letter quite unlike anything else that had ever passed between the two.[11]

Unlike Wallis, Pratt had no affluence of vocabulary, none of that ease in expression which gave to Wallis yet another mark of rarity among their fellow-professionals, but now, under the strain of hope and despair, all literary inhibitions vanished. The words poured out, excited and not always correctly used, but spilling over page after page of hideous self-revelation. He wanted a job in aviation. He must have that job and, surely, his record proved that he merited that job. Money did not matter; all that he cared about was a fresh beginning. There was no pride left to Pratt except the pride in a past that he had betrayed, until the very last sentence of the long letter when, as if as an after-thought forced upon him by convention, he drew back from arrogance and hysteria. Even this disclaimer he coupled with a grim metaphor— partner to many that he had used on the previous pages but otherwise almost unique in Pratt's generally dry correspondence. 'If you cannot see any use for me', he wrote, 'do not hesitate to say so and I shall have to reconcile myself to stay in the hole I have made.'

Wallis was shocked. The frenzy apparent in Pratt's letter embarrassed him but still worse he knew, instinctively, that if there were any conflict within himself between friendship or charity and single-minded dedication to his work, friendship and charity would have to be sacrificed. Certain that he was right, still he drilled himself to consider that his immediate reaction might be wrong and that Pratt might indeed make a contribution to current work at Weybridge. He almost hoped that others would be ready to accept Pratt's offer, and as the two whom he must consult—McLean and Pierson—were both away for a few days he contented himself with a purely formal acknowledgement.

Now thoroughly roused, Pratt seized upon the empty courtesies in Wallis's letter and wrote again in similar if even more excitable terms than those of his letter of only four days earlier. Now he underlined his willingness to come down the ladder in order to climb again. He begged Wallis to ignore the positions he (Pratt) had once held. 'I would much prefer to work at the drawing-board for a year or two of intensive work and study.' Into this second letter there was injected a new strain of attempted cunning, a reminder of an obligation once incurred and with it flattery, undoubtedly genuine, entirely comprehensible in the circumstances of his dependence upon Wallis's goodwill, and yet perhaps a revelation of some weakening in Pratt's fibre and some justification of the rejection upon which Wallis had already virtually decided.

> I have always thought that if chance had originally made me your assistant instead of vice versa we probably would have progressed together. In addition to your exceptional inventor's ability you have more and larger guts than I have.[12]

Wallis's consultations with Pierson and McLean were sadly formal. All three were sorry for Pratt but only Wallis could have served as advocate and he had no stomach for the cause. Instead and inevitably it was left to him to serve as executioner. This he did in a letter[13] that spelt out in terms firm, clear and almost without compassion the triumvirate's certainty that Pratt had lost his way and could not be put back on the path by any action that they were prepared to take. Only after many years could Pratt recover the fifteen he had mislaid: indeed it was doubtful if time lost could ever be replaced. Vickers had other men who had knowledge more recent and, by implication, better than Pratt's, of organisation, of the treatment of duralumin—and the treatment of Government inspectors. How could Pratt expect the keen young men in the Drawing Office to relish the arrival as an equal in their midst of a distinguished ghost from a past that had proved a dead end? Since Pratt's heyday even drawing-office techniques had changed dramatically. And were Pratt to be promoted over the heads of those same young men could he not see that their resentment would be explosive, justifiable and—the implication was clear—detrimental to the important experiments on which all at Weybridge were concentrating.

Barnes Wallis

Wallis's only concession to past friendship and collaboration, though reasonable enough, must have appeared to Pratt as paltry consolation, for Wallis suggested that Pratt might apply to one of the automobile firms, Rootes, Humber or Austin, who were laying down shadow factories to produce the machines designed by others. There he could learn about the modern aircraft industry. Almost the only softening in a harsh letter, almost the only recognition of Pratt's past greatness, was the recommendation that Pratt must not consider a salary less than he was receiving at Barrow and even this can but have seemed to Pratt as a gratuitous underlining of hopelessness, for if it was difficult for him to change professions such a change without financial sacrifice was unthinkable.

Nevertheless Pratt gathered around him his tattered dignity and made no reply to Wallis.

Shortly, it seemed that Pratt's persistence had brought its reward. When McLean sacked his manager, Knight, for swearing he lost also Knight's superior, Maxwell Muller, the Works Superintendent at Weybridge. To take his place McLean brought up from Supermarine an exceedingly able young organiser, T. C. L. Westbrook and, at the suggestion of Craven but this time without consulting Wallis or Pierson, moved Pratt to Southampton as General Manager. It was not the design job for which Pratt longed but it was work with aeroplanes and at one of the centres where the British war machine was at last being brought to some kind of readiness. Mitchell was close to death but his Spitfire was a reality and for some years Pratt was allowed the privilege of organising the harvest of another man's creativity.

But, if Pratt's tragedy began in 1923 when he refused to join the Airship Guarantee Company and if it was still to develop its final and most awful chapter, in 1936 Wallis failed to turn back the pages to the bright beginning. It can be urged that he had no alternative: that all his arguments against employing Pratt at Weybridge were valid and indisputable; that obligation is no substitute for shattered promise and that progress is more important than loyalty. But what cannot be denied is that by furthering the tragedy Wallis laid upon his conscience a doubt that, despite rationalisation, was to remain with him throughout his life.

In refusing Pratt, Wallis also cut what were close to being the last strands in a bond that tied him to his younger self. Now he could set the blame with Fate just as he had done when first rivalry and then death separated him from Scott and Colmore. Now, as then, he could justify himself to himself by arguing that professional standards must never bend to the needs of friendship, but no sophistry could alter the certainty of isolation. Wallis, a man who had never found intimacy easy, became more and more certain that for him intimacy was impossible and that, being impossible, it was also undesirable.

There was, however, at about this time, one attempt at sociability—made not so much by Barnes as by Molly with Barnes as a conscripted ally—which ended not in tragedy but in farce.

In October 1935 Molly Wallis took her daughter Mary—now eight years old—to a children's party. From the mob of neatly-bowed girls and scrubbed boys one stood out for rare beauty and for eccentricity of dress, but whether this handsome young creature, long-haired and wearing a knitted and pleated woollen skirt, was boy or girl even Molly, the mother of both boys and girls, could not tell. Molly Wallis had a quick way with a mystery: she put the question direct to her hostess. To the answer that this was Harry Stopes Roe, the eleven-year-old son of Marie Stopes, there was added a gratuitous explanation of the odd garment. The great pioneer of birth control would not suffer her son the risk to his genitals that she foresaw in the wearing of trousers. (Later Molly came to know that for the same reason Harry was forbidden a bicycle.)

Molly Wallis was never a collector of celebrities, but when she was told also that Marie Stopes herself was due at the party she determined to make contact with a pioneer whose work she had long admired. Barnes had been the first to read *Married Love*, and at the moment of their engagement had lent the book to Molly and she had become an enthusiastic disciple of Dr Stopes and an energetic supporter of her birth control movement.

The regal arrival of Marie Stopes at the children's party coincided with a dance in which her son was partnering Mary Wallis but the easy conversational opening thus provided to Molly proved an illusion. Marie Stopes had no time to spare for impertinent enthusiasts who happened to be, to their everlasting disadvantage, mothers of daughters. Molly Wallis refused to be snubbed and at last forced from the *grande dame* a tiny flicker of interest: when she heard that Molly had a son close to Harry's age, her eagerness to provide suitable male companionship for her own boy persuaded Marie Stopes to order that Barnes Junior (but not Mary) be brought to the Guy Fawkes Day party at the Stopes Roes' elegant eighteenth-century house, Norbury Park.

This summons accepted and fulfilled there followed in the Wallis household some discussion as to whether the courtesy should be repaid at all and if so how. If Wallis shared his wife's admiration for Marie Stopes' crusading work for women, he was unlike Molly in that he was aware of her other attainments and cared for them not at all. Her claim to creativity as palaeontologist, biologist and coal-chemist he knew to be no more than pretensions; as for her literary efforts, he saw them for what they were, affected drivel made even more sickening by her out-of-character obsequiousness towards men of real authority in the world of letters.

Nevertheles he agreed that Marie Stopes should be invited to Effingham and also, entirely against his social habit at the time that he would not make some excuse to absent himself when she came. Presumably because curiosity formed not a small part of her extraordinary make-up Marie Stopes accepted the invitation.

The gods met and there was thunder.

They could not spend the entire evening talking of birth control, the one topic on which her authority was indisputably superior to his own but also one in which his practical experience might have interested her. He tried music, and Marie Stopes dismissed as frivolous all musical experience. In other places, at other times and in other company both Marie Stopes and Barnes Wallis showed themselves as skilful duellists in defence of their own views about education and the rearing of children, but on this occasion and within moments of broaching this subject which fascinated them both it was clear that their theories were based on such disparate foundations that they could not agree even on a battle-ground.

Wallis, in his own home, was at a disadvantage because the severe rules of courtesy which he set for himself could not make him into a patient audience but would not allow him to interrupt or contradict a guest, but when finally and with her unshakable conviction of divine authority she came to aeronautics, an end to politeness was close. The rules of hospitality be damned, and with them all care of his wife's eagerness, his son's hopes of

Production Wellington

'Only another thousand miles, Charlie, and we'll be home.'
A 1941 cartoon extolling the durability of Wellingtons

Left: The spherical
dambusting bomb. *B[...]*
The Möhne Dam br[...]
Guy Gibson's autog[...]
can be seen close to t[...]
break in the Dam, an[...]
of other members of [...]
Squadron in the top [...]
hand corner

friend and his own respect for the author of *Married Love*.
Wallis knew that his knowledge and experience was, in this
one subject at least, so far beyond that of his guest as to make
argument between them ridiculous, but the misconceptions and
heresies that she was mouthing demanded correction. He would
have exploded into forthrightness had not Marie Stopes mis-
taken his angry expression for bewilderment and decided that
a man who could not so much as appreciate the finer points of
what was supposed to be his own profession made an audience
unworthy of her talents. She could not leave until her husband
came for her with a car, and so, as with a child who is beneath
the possibility of intelligent conversation, she decreed games.
Chess it was to be, but even this to rules of her own devising—
'quick chess' with no pauses for thought—a pattern which Wallis
regarded as antipathetic to the spirit of a game that he relished.

Molly had long since realised the seething antipathy between
her husband and Marie Stopes, but with a seemingly quiet game
of chess in progress she felt that the worst was over and that she
could relax sufficiently to fetch her youngest son, Christopher,
for his evening feed.

Wallis had always enjoyed watching Molly breast-feeding. The
sight pleased him aesthetically, bringing with it memories of
mediaeval paintings of Virgin and Child, but it aroused also his
admiration as an engineer and he had claimed more than once
that no man-made arrangement is so efficient, economical, neat
and hygienic. The two sources of appreciation held him from
any sense of prudishness over breast-feeding and he had never
objected to Molly suckling their children in front of friends at
home or even in full view of strangers on a long train journey.

Not so Marie Stopes. The author of *Married Love* was shocked
when Molly fed Christopher and made no effort to hide her displeasure that such coarse behaviour should continue in her
presence. Her furious disgust did not pass unnoticed by Molly
but even she did not see the wonderful irony of the situation.
Christopher had made his entrance into the world strictly according to Stopes. When his birth was imminent Barnes had written
to Molly:

I have a peculiar feeling of satisfaction over this, partly because
it is really and truly our first 'made to order'.[14]

As for Barnes, faced now with Marie Stopes' sounds and gestures of disapproval, he chose to interpret these as signs that Marie Stopes realised and disliked the inevitability of her defeat in the chess game. At that moment Humphrey Roe arrived. Two or three more moves and the game was over. Marie Stopes swept out of the house screeching over her shoulder that she had let him win the chess game only because she had to leave. She never again visited Effingham and she and Barnes Wallis never exchanged another word in conversation, but the meeting with Marie Stopes was to have considerable effect upon the later history of the Wallis family.

As he had lost Pratt so soon Wallis was to lose direct contact with another who had come to figure largely in his professional life, a man for whom his respect was unbounded: Sir Robert McLean. McLean's resignation from Vickers in October 1938 can be traced back to the early 'twenties. It is much involved with the long-standing animosity between Britain's largest arms manufacturer and the Government departments which bought the arms that Vickers made and to the sturdy suspicion of all armament firms which infected the minds of the public and which had been much exacerbated during the years when disarmament seemed the only respectable policy. By the mid-'thirties many who wished to curb the malevolent influence of Vickers had come into philosophical alliance with McLean and had been forced to accept his thesis that the next war, when and if it came, would be won and lost in the air. Uneasy viewing of the two curtain-raisers, in Abyssinia and in Spain, made the possibility into a near-certainty. However, once the thesis was generally accepted, McLean was virtually isolated for there lingered in the minds of some the hope that war might be avoided if the machinations of the arms manufacturers could be curbed, and to them now the outstanding villain in the galaxy of public enemies was the manufacturer of bombers and fighters. The Air Ministry and the Air Staff were naturally content that in their hands lay the future, but they hoped to be masters of their own happy fate and felt the need to free themselves of the overweening influence of the Vickers aircraft companies. Within the vast Vickers organisation itself feeling was no less intense and after much the same pattern. The central Board was inclined to resent the independence of Vickers Aircraft and Supermarine, and Sir Charles Craven took objection to the manner in which McLean gave himself plenipotentiary powers in dealings with the Secretary of State. McLean seldom attempted to make himself or his firm popular with the Government, the Air Ministry or his Vickers superiors. Indeed, he was loud in his distaste for what he regarded as the ineptitude of the Air Ministry and the complacency of the Air Staff, and his forthrightness, far from pleasing the Vickers Board, instead made them feel that the time must be near when he should be cut down to size.

Each time that the moment for discipline seemed imminent some achievement by one or other of the aircraft companies brought both kudos and orders to Vickers and postponed the clash between McLean and the Board. When the monoplane which had been designed to Wallis's geodetic principles, and which Weybridge had built without Government support, outflew the favoured biplane and in 1935 forced a reluctant Air Ministry to cancel its order for 150 biplanes in favour of Wellesleys, the triumph was irrefutable, but the laurel-wreath contained thorns. After a visit to Weybridge a representative of Fairey Aviation wrote to Wallis congratulating him on the success of his Wellesley designs, but added:

> The machine is a winner . . . but unless Sir Robert is told the truth the job is a failure . . . for there are a lot of spies in the camp.[15]

Wallis promised to 'keep as closely in touch with things' to 'see how they are going'. He did not tell McLean but McLean did not need to be told for he knew full well that some of his subordinates were forecasting his downfall, were assuming that his disciples would be destroyed with him, and were doing all that they could to ingratiate themselves with the eventual victors. Still he founded the security of his own position and policies upon the genius of his designers and still they gave him reason for confidence.

He had shown his obstinacy and risked his future for Mitchell's fighters. The Air Ministry's impoverished notions of aircraft-potential were enshrined in a document issued with the full authority of the Air Staff, which called for a fighter with a maximum speed of 250 m.p.h. When Mitchell attempted to fulfil the specifications set down as F.7/30 he could muster a 'plane with a top speed of no better than 210 m.p.h., just over half as fast as his final Schneider Trophy machine. Mitchell protested to McLean and McLean banged Air Ministry tables and then with his opposite number at Rolls-Royce, A. F. Sidgreaves,

> . . . decided that the two companies together should themselves finance the building of (a real killer fighter). The Air Ministry were informed of this decision, and were told that in no circumstances would any technical member of the Air Ministry be consulted or allowed to interfere with the designer.[16]

This was no way to win the affection of the Service or the Ministry, and even after the Spitfire proved its worth in March 1936 the Air Ministry continued to grumble that its wing structure made the 'plane too complicated for general use. (By the end of the War the aircraft industry had built 21,000 of these over-complicated structures!)

That there should have been any equivalent problem for McLean, for Vickers, or for the designers with the B.9/32, seems incredible and it is true that its selection as Britain's front-line bomber was certain even before the first flight of the prototype, but the struggle for recognition of the virtues of their design had been intense, so much so that at one moment Craven in some perturbation passed on to Weybridge the sour complaint of Air Marshal Sir Wilfred Freeman, the Air Member for Research and Development, that if McLean did not stop plaguing the Air Ministry with his unfounded boasts about the patent superiority of the Vickers' plane over the Handley Page Hampden submission to the B.9/32 specification, there would be no chance of any orders whatsoever for the Vickers bomber.

Happily, on that first flight, with Summers as pilot and Wallis and the General Manager at Weybridge, T. C. L. Westbrook, on board, the prototype Wellington carried double the bomb load for twice the distance presented in the pilot contract specification. For McLean and his designers there could scarcely be clearer justification than this and even his opponents on the Vickers Central Board could hardly hold against McLean what was to them the most effective of all proofs of success, an entry in the order-book. Within two months of the maiden flight a contract for 180 bombers had been bludgeoned out of the Scrooges at the Air Ministry.

The 'plane that they ordered had but recently been christened Crecy. In September 1936 it was renamed Wellington, thus succeeding Wellesley and preceding Warwick in a series which by the use of his initial paid tribute to Wallis's great contribution.

With its future secured it was possible to envisage refinement of the Wellington design. The fuel capacity was to be raised to 696 gallons, the bomb-load set at 4,300 lb and the all-up weight for production models estimated at 21,000 lb. It was realised that the geodetic construction of the wing promised a bonus that in earlier designs had not been possible. Outboard of the engine nacelles between the front and rear spars there was an unimpeded space and it was decided to use this space in each wing for three separate fuel tanks, all of them capable of being isolated in the event of fire.[17]

To McLean's enemies their moment seemed to have arrived in 1937. They had always urged against geodetic construction, that it would prove difficult to produce in large numbers and they regarded McLean's boast that he would turn out one a day on each day of the year as yet another example of his overweening confidence. During 1937 Weybridge did in fact fall behind with deliveries and, with full Cabinet backing, the Air Ministry seized the opportunity presented to force the two Vickers aircraft companies into a position more directly subservient to the Central Board. The reorganisation was not completed until early in 1938, but by then Jamieson had taken over as Chairman and he, even more than Craven, relished the chance to reassert the authority of the Board and, again even more than Craven, was certain that Vickers' future depended upon establishing better relations with the Air Ministry. His own close friendship with Lord Swinton seemed to him to promise much in this direction and McLean's continuing independence of thought, action and voice to threaten acid in this sweetness that he planned.

Once more, however, it seemed possible that, as so often in the past, achievement would save McLean. The energetic supervision of the General Manager at Weybridge, T. C. L. Westbrook, not only made up the leeway on orders, but actually delivered the first Wellington—to 99 Squadron—on 10 October 1938, ahead of schedule.

A month later the Wellesley came once more to the forefront of events and added another feather to the cap that the Air Ministry and Vickers Board was attempting to pull from McLean's head. Vickers, this time with full and enthusiastic support from certain elements in the Royal Air Force, set before the eyes of the unwilling another inescapable proof of their superior skill. By way of McLean Wallis's certainty of the Wellesley's long-range potential had been borne upon the Air Ministry as early as 1933 when a Long Range Development Unit was established under the command of Wing Commander O. R. Gayford. Five standard Wellesleys—with minimal adaptations—were assigned to this unit, and in July 1938, as a preliminary to an attempt on the long-distance record, four of them under the command of Squadron Leader R. Kellett flew in formation from Cranwell to the Persian Gulf and back to Ismailia, a distance of 4,300 miles, in thirty-two-hours.

The world record, at that time held by the Russians, was now within Britain's grasp and an attempt on it was planned for November. It was decided to add to the severity of the test the self-imposed handicap of a formation flight, thus forcing upon all the 'planes taking part the discipline of flying at a mean speed below the optimum of any one 'plane. Even so McLean was optimistic, Squadron Leader Kellett (who was to lead the flight once more) was certain of the result and Wallis, too, prophesied that there would be no difficulty and calculated that theoretically and given good conditions the flight could achieve a non-stop record of 9,000 miles.[18] Then, just as ambition soared, disaster struck and for a short time even the confidence of Wallis was shaken. Back from a test flight with Mutt Summers as pilot, the observer, R. C. Handasyde, reported that the wings of the adapted Wellesleys were far too flexible, so much so that whenever Summers put on any 'G' Handasyde could see large wrinkles on the top surface of the wing. Wallis was incredulous; Wellesleys had already flown thousands of miles in service without revealing any substantial defect, but he could not ignore the report of a highly-experienced observer. Calculation and experiment supported Wallis's certainty but still Handasyde held to the evidence of his eyes. The resolution of the paradox was simple and almost ludicrous. For the flight Wallis had designed a pressed celluloid hood to cover the observer. Each time Handasyde's body sank slightly in his

padded seat with an increase in his effective weight the imperfec-
tions in the celluloid pressings were sufficient to give him the
impression that the wing fabric was moving upwards.[19]

With this tragi-comedy over, all was ready for the attempt,
and on Guy Fawkes Day 1938 three Wellesleys took off from
Ismailia for Australia. Take-off weight was 18,400 lb and the
planned operating height of 10,000 feet was reached in forty-five
minutes. Unfortunately weather conditions were appalling and
although all three 'planes exceeded the Soviet achievement one
had to land at Singapore and the other two came down to tree-
top height and to 90 m.p.h. for the last 1,500 miles. Nevertheless their record, set officially at 7,157·7 miles, stood for nine
years.

The achievement was tremendous and for the future of Britain
as an air power of greater significance than the outright winning
of the Schneider Trophy, but the reluctance with which officialdom at this time received all news that added to the credibility
of McLean, Wallis and their colleagues, can be judged from a
remark made by a senior member of the Air Staff when he heard
of the Wellesley's success. 'It will encourage that fellow Wallis
to go on with geodetic construction,' was the best he could offer
by way of praise.[20]

As for McLean: before the long-distance record could be
written into the credit balance of his perspicacity, he doubted if
Jamieson and his allies at the Air Ministry would allow him the
opportunity for further triumphs. In October 1938 he was forced
to resign from Vickers. As soon as the decision was taken McLean
drove to warn Wallis and Pierson. That Wallis was capable of
an occasional flurry of fury is undeniable; hot anger is sometimes indistinguishable from powerful loyalty; and when Wallis
heard the news he came close to quarrelling with McLean
because Sir Robert refused to allow him to resign with his
chairman.[21]

Wallis stayed, but he had lost his most stalwart and most powerful supporter and at just the moment when his mind was burgeon-
ing with another vital project—one that had the enthusiastic
approval of his departing superior: his plans for a giant bomber.
McLean's last note to Wallis on this subject (written after his
resignation had been accepted) contains two lines which, though
ostensibly they refer to the plan that was immediately in Wallis's

Barnes Wallis

thoughts, can be taken as some measure of his bitterness at his own rejection:

> Can little people see big things? I suppose the nit in the child's hair thinks the head it is on is the biggest thing in the world— and a good living.[22]

By this time many had come to see war as inevitable. Wallis, it would seem, seldom thought about the future in the theoretical terms that are the common parlance of statesmen, journalists and darts-players in the public bar; aeronautical problems he must solve even if Chamberlain wrought the miracle of 'peace in our time' which he had promised on his return from Munich in September 1938. However, as 1938 turned into 1939 Wallis's attitude suffered a slight but perceptible change. Still he laboured at a thesis because it opened up a fascinating technological prospect but now he identified the enemy and dedicated himself—and his theories—to its destruction. Intellect had been the spur but now he was riding with the whip of patriotism.

12 Wallis goes to War

Wallis had seldom concerned himself with the moral implications of his work: his conscience was untroubled by the fact that from his earliest days as a shipyard apprentice he had worked on machines designed for war or adaptable to a warlike purpose. True, he had at one time called himself a pacifist, but his pacifism seems to have been no more than a negative attitude, a statement of the order of 'I do not much wish to kill my fellow human beings'. Both his religion and his patriotism were deeply felt and both were enthused by an Old Testament God, but of the two, patriotism was the more compelling. As Hitler's brutalities and the arrogance of the Germans made war almost inevitable Wallis abdicated any thought of turning the other cheek. Becoming certain of the advent of war, he snapped the shackles of immediate responsibility and, with an access of energy that had as yet touched few in Britain, prepared to initiate his own battle with Germany by extending his thinking and his knowledge far outside his previous competence.

He came to the conviction that he could best support the war effort by concentrating on the possibilities of penetration bombing, and by developing the largest bomb which could be carried in existing or potentially available bombers. To this end he set himself to making a profound study of high explosives and the detonation of large charges. Then, as often in his life, Wallis had a rare genius for extending the line of his immediate work into the future; thus, his belief in larger and larger bombs was conditioned not only by strategic considerations but also by his faith in larger and larger aeroplanes. This faith informed his design policy for at least three years before the outbreak of war. Originally his arguments favouring size had ostensibly been directed towards economy in passenger transport, but the theories urged for peace were easily convertible into the currency of war. Already in May 1939, in a letter which, for his purpose, conveniently confused the distinction between passenger and bomber 'planes, he was pointing out that the best six-engined machine flying offered a surface loading of only 27·6 lb sq. ft.[1] In all this he had the support of Pierson who had himself presented a paper demonstrating that Vickers' proposed six-engine geodetic bomber with its span of 235 feet and 20 ton bomb-load would have the offensive power of a whole squadron of Wellingtons, could cruise at 55 m.p.h. more than the Wellington and would require a crew of seven as against a Wellington squadron's forty-eight.[2] Air Ministry and civil aviation experts had treated these ideas with indifference; thus Wallis was back where he started before he issued his papers, with no takers for his scheme; and no McLean to enforce it, with or without government support. He turned for persuasion from carrier to weapon. Here, had he realised it, the whole history of the RAF was against him: most of its short battle experience had been in the Middle East or on the North-West Frontier where the Air Force was little more than airborne artillery for which small bombs were ideal. A few perspicacious officers were preaching a gospel which would soon give the RAF a battle philosophy unique among the air arms of the world, and were already considering the idea of shaking off the artillery-in-the-air, cavalry-in-the-sky mentality and using air power as a strategic force independent of land or sea operations. To them Wallis's big 'plane–big bomb thesis would have been acceptable, but most of them were still of junior air rank, and out of England commanding the very operations in India, Iraq and Palestine which were obfuscating the logic of RAF development.

White-hot with, to him, irrefutable proof of the validity of large bombs, Wallis was astute enough to know that the existence of a big bomber design on his drawing-board blocked one potential official objection: they could not plead against him the time it would take to develop a bomber to carry his big bomb. His large bomber could be flying sooner than any other new bomber of which he had heard so much as a rumour.

However, as that 1939 summer drew towards its hideous conclusion, Wallis found himself once more forced to revert from invention and foresightedness to responsibility for the immediate.

Wallis goes to War

The RAF set about compensating in a few months for the handi-caps imposed by twenty years of disarmament and appeasement; and the Civil Service and its masters now attempted to erase their own follies which had left Britain virtually defenceless and incapable of carrying battle to an enemy ready and able to thrust the consequences of war into the very heart of the Common-wealth.

Orders for Wellingtons mounted, and then for Wellingtons with innumerable adaptations or additions, intended for specific tactical or strategic purposes. With such demands ever increasing before him, there was little time for the theoretical work still necessary to create big bombs and bombers. Nevertheless there were moments in the first weeks of September when Wallis's mind went back to those humiliating moments in August 1914 when, at Weymouth, he, the civilian out of place in a uniformed mob, had suffered the bitterness of youth not dressed for war. If all that he was to be allowed to do in the search for survival and eventual victory was to act as a superior foreman for building Wellingtons, might he not be better employed with the RAF in some administrative but military capacity? It was a romantic notion; forced on him no doubt more by frustration recalled than by conviction; but it drove him back to his determination to add originality to the seemingly sterile supervisory function upon which he was engaged.

Others of his generation suffered similar heart-searching, and for one close to this story the end was tragedy: H. B. Pratt, Wallis's one-time companion, mentor, colleague, began the Second World War charged with hope such as he had not known for a long time. As General Manager of Supermarine he was supervising the construction of Britain's only fighter which could match the enemy's machines in the air: for until daughter-factories could be set up, Southampton controlled the output of the Spitfire. Unhappily, within a few months, war was his downfall. Trevor Westbrook had been snapped up by Beaverbrook, and among the tasks allotted to him was the hastening of the Spitfire construction programme. His knowledge and tireless zeal put him into the position of seeming to countermand Pratt's orders. Pratt complained to Craven but for him there was no easy way out: through Beaverbrook Westbrook was all-powerful; and Pratt's complaint became a resignation. For months he canvassed the Ministries and aircraft industry for some opening in which he could use that originality which, despite all rebuffs, he still felt in himself. There were jobs for everyone; but, unlike Wallis, Pratt had no palpitating ideas to shock others into taking notice of him. Repeatedly rejected for the posts he thought he should have; unable, now, to 'stay in the hole I have made'; in Britain's most ill-omened hour when she needed every spark of experience and originality that she could strike off from her people, H. B. Pratt, one of the great pioneers of the aircraft industry, shot himself.

Wallis did his best to ignore Pratt's death, but other war-casualties he could not escape: on 7 November 1940 Molly's sister Barbara and her husband were killed on one of Goering's first raids on centres of civilian population. They left behind two sons, John aged ten and Robert aged eight. Barnes and Molly did not hesitate; they immediately offered to adopt the children, without argument over pros and cons. More even than Molly, Barnes was adamant: the boys must come at once to Effingham to be part of his family, and their education should be continued just as it had been planned by their parents.

Happily for Wallis and the country he was too busy to brood for long on that accident of age which had deprived him of his second chance for military fulfilment. If he was not, at the outbreak of war, immediately given the chance to prepare his big bomb–big bomber programme, there were immediate and frequent calls on his versatile ingenuity. The loss of the *Athenia* on the very night war broke out, and of fifteen more merchantmen before the end of September, presaged a repetition of the First World War U-boat campaign. But there was another threat to British shipping: magnetic mines laid by U-boats. Admiralty forecasts were gloomy; and miserably justified by events: from November 1939 to April 1940 losses to mines exceeded, by a considerable tonnage, losses to U-boat attack. There were not enough minesweepers, nor men to man them, nor even time to spare for sweeping shipping lanes in the conventional manner.

Admiralty turned to Vickers, Vickers to Wallis: could some kind of mine-destroying apparatus be mounted on an aircraft? The idea of an electric coil fitted below a Wellington to detonate mines seemed to have possibilities and it was planned to strip three Wellingon IAs of all unnecessary fitments and have them equipped with coils carrying 310 amps at 110 volts DC. The Wellingtons would have to transport their own generators, and even as he produced his plans Wallis insinuated a word for his large bomber: such pay-loads as were now imperative could not be achieved with a normal safety factor in any 'structure now in production'.[3]

As ever, problem progressed to solution which posed another problem: the coil would produce a strong magnetic field which, disorienting the 'plane's compass, would make navigation virtually impossible. There was no room for a course-setting gyro-compass and Wallis had to rule out the alternative of putting a neutralising coil round the magnetic compass when he discovered certain magnetic characteristics in the landing undercarriage which, hitherto insignificant, now invalidated such an arrangement. Wallis could find no solution more satisfactory than the provision of a pilot aeroplane far enough ahead of the Wellington to be out of range of the detonating coil.

During this research Wallis foresaw the possibility that the coil-carrying 'plane might be damaged by the explosions of the mines it detonated. Experiment showed that when a mine exploded at ten fathoms depth the bubble did not reach the surface for $1\frac{1}{2}$ seconds, by which time the Wellington would be a hundred yards away. That information was filed away in his mind: it was of some significance for the work which led to the dam-busting exploits.

By December 1939 it seemed that a way could be discovered to minimise navigation difficulties caused by the coil. Admiralty experts found that if the 'plane's compass was adjusted after the aircraft had been subjected to the full strength of the coil's magnetic field, then compass readings were sufficiently reliable for the pilot to reach home even in fog.[4] The first test-flight took place just before Christmas with Summers as pilot and Wallis as a crew-member.[5] Experiment continued and by January 1940 six D.W.I. Wellingtons were operating. Sweeping at only forty feet above water, they were responsible for an eighth of all magnetic mines detonated or swept before May. But the method was too random and Wellingtons too much in demand for other work. New methods—degaussing and the LL sweep—mastered the threat and by summer the D.W.I. was obsolescent, although it was used later in the confined waters of the Mediterranean and the Suez Canal.

In one respect the effort to produce a mine-sweeping Wellington gave Wallis cause for optimism. Gone was pre-war indecisive-
ness among the authorities, gone the miserliness, industrial
inefficiency and labour troubles which had disrupted so many
of his schemes. Six weeks of consistently amiable co-operation
between the authorities and industry, including Vickers, had
carried conception to achievement.

That exhilaration was soon erased. News leaked through to him
that the Air Ministry would accept no more geodetic construction.[6] Wallis was utterly convinced of the great development still
open to this form of construction. He suspected that his designs
were being condemned for the disasters suffered by 99 Squadron
over the Schillig Roads on 14 December 1939, when more than
half the twenty-four Wellingtons had been lost to enemy action.
But RAF analyses did not criticise Wellington design principles.
The conclusion—that the Wellington could not defend itself
against a beam attack from above—was excused: it had 'Never
previously been thought that a beam attack could be developed
in view of modern speeds and the consequent deflection-shooting
involved.'[7] There was no reflection on the Wellington; what was
needed was self-sealing tanks on all bombers. And when, early in
the New Year, Air Ministry asked Wallis to give consideration
to improving the fabric covering of Wellingtons, its reasons were
genuine: in war conditions of usage and exposure wear and tear
were much more severe than in peacetime. That the Ministry was
not influenced by the Schillig set-backs is now obvious, for their
first memorandum on the subject had been written in the first
week of November before those disasters occurred.

Wallis, eager in defence of his construction principles, was now
faced with an almost impossible task. Geodetic construction he
felt bound to vindicate and he had knowledgeable champions.
Thus, *The Aeroplane* in November 1940:

> Wellingtons have returned from raids so damaged that they
> would appear to be about to collapse at any moment. Yet the
> geodetic structure spreads the loads so well that even though
> large portions might be shot away the machines have been able
> to return to their bases . . . The distribution of loads and the
> high degree of redundancy in the structure makes the geodetic
> system of great military value in keeping losses to a minimum.[8]

In Wallis's view, failures could not be scored to enemy action; he must put the blame down to poor installation or, more frequently, to improper handling in service. Those fabric failures in flight that he had been able to inspect could be proved to result from previous failures on the ground. No fabric, nor the thin plate advocated as an alternative, could withstand indefinitely the strain of walking or kneeling on it, and the time-honoured service custom of painting over small defects—in this case with extra coats of dope—heightened the fragility of undamaged parts of the dope-film and disturbed aerodynamic smoothness.

And he defended his Wellington against rumours that, being fabric-covered, it was dangerously liable to destruction by anti-aircraft attack, showing that fabric was, in fact, exceptionally successful in escaping total destruction by gun-fire. A Wellesley wing had remained aerodynamically sound after being peppered by a naval two-pounder and, because the fabric was able to yield to the effects of blast, both Wellesley and Wellington wings had suffered no permanent damage from the transient pressure waves caused by exploding shells. He resisted, with asperity, the suggestion that new Wellingtons be covered with thin metal plate; and even when he bowed to Air Ministry belief that an all-metal skin would reduce the chance of fire, his concession was tactical: the additional skin he regarded as 'a very inefficient and expensive form of covering' and he hoped that in the new, experimental, wing commissioned by 'an unexpectedly enlightened Air Ministry', the emphasis on covering even a portion of the wing with twin-gauge metal 'will be allowed to be forgotten'.[9]

But he did not and could not deny the susceptibility to fire shown by the Wellingtons. A method of covering petrol tanks with a self-sealing skin was borrowed from the French and installed in most British bombers by the spring of 1940, but Wallis concentrated on non-inflammable fabric dopes and throughout the first months of 1940 carried on a vast amount of correspondence on the subject with experts in Britain and the United States. Only in the first months of 1940 was Wallis informed that Imperial Chemical Industries were trying to imitate the best of all dope—the German—[10] and by then he had ordered supplies of the best dope he knew about, from America.

Working simultaneously, with Pierson, on a multiplicity of

projects Wallis had overall responsibilty for modifications to the Mark 1 and Mark 2 Wellingtons; and throughout that aircraft's long history he retained some supervisory function. It is testimony to the superb adaptability of his design philosophy that the all-up weight of the latter-day types approached 40,000 lb as compared with the 6,300 lb of the prototype. His work kept him from twelve to fourteen hours a day at his drawing-board during the first months of the war. He was also involved in perfecting the repair system for Wellingtons; a method of local surgery by which damaged geodetic members could be repaired or replaced in the field.

But Wallis was driven to superhuman efforts whenever his mind settled instinctively on a solution to a problem which must be supported by evidence if it is to persuade those who were, to his way of thinking, too puffed up by authority to accept the expert's wisdom or too stupid to go straight to the QED without labouring the theorem. Overworked at Weybridge, still he felt himself cheated of his opportunity to get at the enemy's throat. His active participation in the battle against Nazism was begun not at Weybridge but from his home at Effingham in spare time that, mathematically, did not exist. He wrote to his old chief, Masterman:

> Life is almost unrelieved gloom—worse than 25 years ago, except that this time I can feel that I am doing something useful whereas last war I certainly was not—in spite of your efforts to convince me to the contrary . . . Tremendously busy —on big developments, which if they had been put in hand two years ago would have won us the war by this time. Too late as usual.[11]

His busy-ness was a one-man conspiracy to persuade policy-makers to accept his 'big developments', his proposals for penetration bombing with great bombs carried by large bombers.

There was much that he had to learn if he was to teach others the validity of his own ideas, and throughout the winter of 1939 and the spring of 1940 he continued the studies begun before war broke out. He built up for himself a substantial profile of the German economy. (Later he added a similar study of Italy.) He plotted the distribution in enemy territory of oil-storage tanks and dams. He applied his acute engineer's understanding to learning all he could about the winding-shafts of German collieries and the techniques of building gravity—multiple-arch and earth-dams. He continued trying to perfect his knowledge of the behaviour, chemistry and physics of high explosives; the propagation of waves in all types of soil; the effects of subterranean explosion of large charges at camouflet depths. He considered the visibility of targets at great heights and was encouraged to experiment with the possibility of designing a bomber to operate at 40,000 feet. All he studied confirmed that his big-bomb thesis was valid.

Whatever else might seem fantastic in his aspirations, his conclusion that he must design a 'plane to fly at 40,000 feet was no longer a dream, for this height had been achieved through his work and Pierson's with an adapted Wellington. But high-altitude flying was only a part, and a small part, of reaching the goal which Wallis had before him. Still, between him, the proof of his thesis and the redirection of national policy, stood a programme of calculation, invention, construction, adaptation, design and persuasion to give full-time occupation to a team of intellectual giants; yet to Wallis the need to complete the programme was obvious and, when Pétain deserted and left Britain as the only bulwark against universal Fascism, his determination to present his arguments in irrefutable form became frenetic. He would allow no-one to stand between him and what he regarded as his responsibility to bring down the Axis Powers.

It is upon his wartime exploits that much of his fame with the general public has been based. It must be admitted that a considerable body of mythology has grown up around the true story of Wallis during the Second World War; and it cannot be denied that to that body Wallis has added a few delightful fables of his own. Fortunately history no less than fairy-tale is flattering to his genius, as is the quantity and quality of his contribution to eventual victory. One can dispense with the fiction of originality thwarted at every turn by stupid authority and supported only by men as unorthodox as himself. In wartime the little bureaucrats were no longer omnipotent; genius and high skill had been brought in from many places. Where there was opposition to Wallis it can now be seen generally—though not always—as founded on sound reasoning that had its origin outside the radius of his direct and unequivocal intentions. With one scandalous exception the opposition was seldom mean-minded. His conviction that for the first eighteen months of war it was virtually unanimous belongs to a conventional pattern—there is justification for it in his life and those of other inventors—of originality abused and rejected. But as history it is as far from the truth as the subsidiary fiction that all opposition was swept away by the understanding of another genius, Lord Beaverbrook.

Some of the myths became enshrined as facts because at the time Wallis obfuscated the distinction between the big bomb–big 'plane theory and his plan to destroy the Axis by attacking its industrial power. This may not have been deliberate, for in his own mind at the time the two notions were interwoven and it is possible that they remained, to him, interdependent for ever after. In a TV broadcast as late as 1967 he answered a heavily-loaded question—'Why didn't anybody take up the idea?' with a no less biased answer—'Nobody liked it, nobody believed in it, nobody thought it possible',[12] without troubling to clarify whether the idea was the ten-ton bomb, the big bomber, or the attack on the Dams. But when Wallis first presented his proposals for hastening victory by aerial warfare some in authority responded favourably to one idea, some to another. Sir Henry Tizard, for example, was as ardent in support of the Wallis theory of strategic bombing as he was, for some years, adamant in refusing him facilities for building his big bomb and big 'plane.

The true story of the early meetings between Beaverbrook and Wallis is unlike the legend and belongs to farce, rather than epic. From the beginning of the war Wallis had added fire-watching to his many activities and at their inception he joined the Local Defence Volunteers (later the Home Guard). All the zeal, experience and acumen that he was even then applying to his great plans for striking at the heart of Germany he gave also to the task of producing a scheme for sterilising Effingham Golf Course. He designed a series of trestles and devised a plan at once effective and economical for their positioning. He called upon Canadian Gunners encamped at Effingham and used his personal charm to persuade them to undertake, outside their normal military duties, the manual labour involved in putting his plan into action. Then, working as ever from the particular to the implication, he decided to offer the country at large the Wallis–

Effingham system of defence against airborne landings. As with any of his major schemes he produced a portfolio of calculations and drawings, added an explanation written in his habitually lucid style, and forwarded the dossier to Craven.

This took most of June 1940; the month when Italy entered the war and in which Wallis was experimenting with moulded wings for Wellingtons and, despite discouragements, began preliminary designs for the strategic bomber; the month in which he had three serious attacks of migraine, spent several hours rehearsing with the Effingham Choir for a concert of the works of his favourite composer, Vaughan Williams; and added a somewhat surprising subject to his lecture repertoire: Mothercraft.

Two weeks after delivering his 'Effingham' defence plans to Craven he was summoned to see Lord Beaverbrook. To Wallis the conjunction seemed obvious, and with a second copy of the dossier he went up to the Ministry of Aircraft Production. His appointment was for 11; he arrived at 10.45 and was kept waiting three hours. On being called into the presence and before Wallis even sat down, Beaverbrook shouted at him, 'Will you go to America for me?'[13]

'Yes. But I'd rather stop in England for you.'

'And what would you do in England?'

'Build you a monster bomber to smash the Germans.'

'What engines would you use?'

Unconsciously imitating Beaverbrook's staccato manner Wallis set out his requirements and one by one Beaverbrook dismissed them until Wallis reached the fourth and fifth in his imaginary list of utilisable engines when Beaverbrook changed his abrupt 'Impossible' to a slightly more encouraging 'Just could be,' and asked, 'Got any drawings with you?' Sensing the negative he went on, 'Come and see me; any time; tonight; the middle of the night; tomorrow.' Wallis agreed to come again to the Ministry the next day and then, as if there had been no vital interpolation, Beaverbrook returned to the suggestion that Wallis should go to America. He flipped a newspaper cutting across the table: 'See, the Americans have got a 'plane that can go up into the stratosphere. I want one too.'

'But we have one. My Wellington with a pressurised cabin has already gone up to 40,000 feet.' The Minister of Aircraft Production was almost as surprised to hear that Britain had such a 'plane as was its joint-designer when he discovered that the Minister had never heard of it.

Next day Wallis and Pierson went to the Ministry to go over plans for the giant bomber. Beaverbrook was interested, even intellectually excited, but he would not and could not commit the Government to a project on this scale. After two hours of listening and questioning he grunted that he would have to ask the Air Staff.

Wallis was not content to leave to Beaverbrook and chance the task of advocacy. He persuaded the Vickers–Armstrong Board to put more formally to the Minister a proposal that they be given a contract for a 'Victory' bomber to carry a ten-ton bomb. He redoubled his energies at the drawing-board and began his own programme for persuading the Air Staff. The Director General of Research and Development at the Air Ministry, Air-Marshal Arthur Tedder, was one of the young officers who, already in peacetime, had envisaged an independent role for the RAF and in him Wallis soon discovered an enthusiastic ally who would serve as his spokesman. But when the formal letter reached Beaverbrook on 1 November 1940 the whole situation had changed. Tedder had been posted to the Middle East; the Battle of Britain had been won but with devastating losses in 'planes and pilots; the more recent variants of the Wellington were proving their worth in the first attacks on enemy-occupied Europe and the Minister had no intention of allowing its designer to divert his energies from the task of producing still better adaptations.

This time Beaverbrook's answer was a hedged negative: he had talked with the Air Staff and, with Tedder now away, had found them unanimously against Wallis. No reasons were given, but there was one which, even had there been no major considerations of military and economic planning, would have justified the Air Staff's decision: as yet there was in use no stabilised bomb-sight; bomb-aiming was still a primitive art and the chances high of missing the target. A bomber carrying only one bomb that did not hit its target meant a sortie wasted. It is unfortunate that this was not explained to Wallis; had it been he would have been given the chance to follow his usual practice of working back through a proposal to remove all the obstacles raised against it. He might have produced a new bomb-sight long before the stabilised bomb-sight came into use.

But, in truth, Beaverbrook had been impressed, if only by Wallis's information on high-altitude bombers. He would have no other activity interfering with his determination to arm the RAF with this weapon in which he had entire faith. On 9 January 1941 he wrote to Vickers:

High-altitude bombers are to be developed intensively. I wish you to undertake this work.

The Wellington V is to be fully developed with Hercules and Merlin engines. The Merlin to take preference. The B1/35 is to have a pressure cabin; the work is to be pursued urgently. The Centaurus engine will be developed for use with this aeroplane.[14]

So the fiat embodied a defeat for Wallis: he was bound to have his time taken up with Wellington developments and not only the Air Ministry but the Vickers Board were likely to be against him if he spent his energies on other matters. Indeed, even the one concession which Beaverbrook admitted to the last sentence of his letter on high-altitude bombers was half-hearted and served to underline the Minister's firmness:

Subject to the above work taking precedence, you should continue research on your 50-ton bomber.

Still, for Wallis there was a tiny gesture of encouragement; Beaverbrook gave authority for the officials of his Ministry and of the Air Ministry to feed Wallis with such information and intelligence-data as he might need in building up his case.

Wallis had failed to win his way by presenting in theoretical terms the large hypothesis on which he based his big bomb–big bomber ideas: a year earlier he had shifted the emphasis of his argument from carrier to weapon; now he would try to persuade by shifting it to objectives. He would change the minds of the obdurate Minister, his dim-witted officials and his reactionary officers by pin-pointing the targets against which the big bomb could be used.

Wallis's *A Note on a method of attacking the Axis Powers* took almost a year to produce and was a closely-reasoned argument liberally embellished with mathematical tables, but its thesis was simple: the Axis could wage successful war only while its industry continued to provide the materials for war. Industry depends on power, power on fuel, on thermal generating stations, hydro-electric installations and buried storage tanks of hydro-carbon fuels. So he came back to his ten-ton bomb and thus once more to his big 'plane; for he argued that all these sources of supply were susceptible to attack by a large penetration bomb.

The richness of intelligence data in the *Method of Attack* is in itself some refutation of the travesty that Wallis was treated with discourtesy and disbelief by the authorities, for most of it was gathered on his behalf by officers working to Whitehall instructions, and notably by Wing Commander F. W. Winterbotham. Just such another of those originals who fit the pattern of genius recognising genius, Winterbotham was sensitised to receive with sympathy the wildest-seeming dreams of a man like Wallis and equipped to respond to them with useful and well-informed support. A one-time Oxford law student, one-time Yeomanry officer, one-time Royal Flying Corps pilot and one-time farmer, he had returned to the RAF to a desk-job that served as cover for high-grade intelligence operations which had taken him into the presence and close to the confidence of many among the Nazi leadership. Winterbotham it was who, with his French opposite number, originated early in the 'thirties the technique and practice of high-altitude spying.[15]

Wallis and Winterbotham first met at lunch at Leo D'Erlanger's in autumn 1939.[16] Their mutual liking was immediate and from that time they saw each other quite often and Winterbotham early achieved a distinction rare among Wallis's colleagues in being allowed to call him by his Christian name. Not only did Winterbotham do what he was told in providing Wallis with intelligence data, he set himself up as one of the most vocal of the few active champions of Wallis's theories. In the late summer of 1940 he thrust a paper supporting Wallis into the brain-centre of Britain's war effort: the Prime Minister's Office. The answer was not what he hoped but much what he expected:

I have not only read your interesting paper on the ultimate aim of bombing warfare, but have consulted certain good-willed experts without disclosing your identity.

The view held is that such a project as you describe could

not come to fruition until 1942, even if then. This may not be a complete bar since the war may still be going on in that year.

It is suggested, however, that if the plan is to be put into effect in a reasonable period the best thing to do is to take it up with the Boeing Company or some other American firm used to work of this type.[17]

Winterbotham helped to elevate Wallis above the gaggle of lunatic inventors who in wartime plague ministries with their recipes for immediate victory, but Wallis was not always an easy collaborator, and when he circulated no fewer than a hundred copies of his *Method of Attack*, four of them in the still-neutral United States, it was not only Security, and Wallis's opponents, who accepted that here was another mad scientist. But the accusation could not be raised against him for discussing the embryo paper with those senior officials who could contribute to its completion and adoption. Sir Henry Tizard, the Scientific Adviser to the Ministry of Aircraft Production and next to Lindemann probably the most influential scientist in the country, was, unlike Lindemann, a man whose generosity equalled his originality of thought. Dr David Pye, the Ministry's Director of Scientific Research belonged to that brilliant Cambridge circle which included the Trevelyans and the Leigh-Mallorys. At the same Ministry, as Director of Armament Development, there was Air Commodore Patrick Huskinson, a man of quick sympathy and quicker intelligence, who would have made a poor model for the common caricature of the bone-headed conservative serving officers. All these and many others gave Wallis of their experience and, if in various degrees, of their enthusiastic support; but it was in March 1941, when the paper was finally delivered, that Tizard showed the full measure of seriousness with which he regarded Wallis, for he set up an *ad hoc* committee to look into the proposals and saw to it that the membership was of such authority as had not often been gathered together, even in war-time, in one technical committee. In addition to Pye as chairman, there were no fewer than four members who were or would soon be Fellows of the Royal Society—Andrade, Bernal, G. I. Taylor and W. H. Glanville. There was also Huskinson, who was never slow to accept new ideas and never reluctant to press them on his superiors.

The Committee met for the first time on Good Friday, 11 April 1941. Some mystery surrounds the circumstances of this meeting. Writing after the war Wallis argued an extension of the myth of rejection:

> Although no official intimation was sent to me, I was given to understand that there was something to my ideas and although the notion of the 10-ton bomb was consequently (subsequently?) rejected, the suggestion for the destruction of the Dams led to the formation of a special committee called the 'Air Attacks on Dams Committee'.[18]

His personal diary makes no mention of his presence at the Ministry on 11 April, but his attendance is listed in the official minutes,[19] and according to the same minutes, written on the day of the meeting, the decision taken was not quite as definite as Wallis came to remember: 'those present agreed to recommend that some means of attacking the German and Italian Power Installations be considered'. It is, however, implicit in the minutes that the Dams should be the prime and possibly exclusive target and it was on the Dams that a more formal committee soon concentrated its attention.

But there was at the time one public figure, well-nigh omnipotent, who, consistent in little else, was unflagging and immovable in his opposition to Wallis. Frederick Lindemann, Professor of Experimental Philosophy at Oxford, was well-placed to make his prejudices serve as vetoes. An old and close friend of Winston Churchill, whom he had first met in the First World War when Lindemann had carried out some daring and fruitful investigations into the effect of spin on aeroplanes, from 1932 onwards he had served as Churchill's adviser on scientific matters. Lindemann had developed his own beloved schemes for aerial bombardment and his own fantastic proposition for safeguarding Britain by 'dropping bombs hanging by wires in the path of attacking aircraft'.[20] Churchill followed Lindemann blindly wherever his science fiction led, and seems to have taken no account of Lindemann's zest for bringing the dubious pleasures of academic feuding into national policy-making. In the spring of 1941 Lindemann did not yet know Wallis, but damned him because of Wallis's friends. He was frenetic in his disagreements with other scientists:

he detested Tizard, and Professor Blackett, who was also showing interest in Wallis's schemes, was not far behind in Lindemann's litany of distaste. So, where Wallis said 'Yes', Tizard and Blackett 'Perhaps', it was inevitable that Lindemann would say 'No'. It is almost certain that Lindemann had been behind the rejection of Winterbotham's first approach to Downing Street on Wallis's behalf.

In the years that immediately preceded the outbreak of war there had come to Wallis from more than one seemingly authoritative source rumours that his name was going forward for the Honours List. Now, early in the war, rumour became certainty, and he could not deny to himself that a knighthood would be some compensation for what he regarded as the humiliations of his childhood and disappointments of his maturity. He was, too, sufficiently a man of the world to know that a distinction of this kind would add weight to his powers of persuasion and open doors still closed to him. Half in jest he allowed himself to doodle designs for a new Wallis coat-of-arms. The game he shared only with Molly: a tiny shoe, perhaps, against a background of wings; and always Icarus. But even the private and playful nature of the game does not hide the depths of its motivation. Honours lists succeeded each other; nothing for Wallis, until early in 1941 came the customary letter from Downing Street:

The Prime Minister wishes to inform Mr B. N. Wallis that His Majesty . . .

There followed the usual courtesies and—the offer of an OBE.

It is difficult to understand the mentality of those who organised this affair. If it was intended as a bribe to silence Wallis in the midst of his irritating campaign, it was hardly big enough! It could be interpreted as a malicious joke, but the only possible perpetrator was Lindemann who had no sense of humour. For lack of evidence one must set the blame on Civil Service incompetence; certainly it was an insult to offer the designer of *R.80* and *R.100*, of Wellesley and Wellington a decoration commonly given to non-combatant Wing Commanders. It is easy to imagine with what hurt pride and fury Wallis read that letter. His refusal was certain, quick, short and remarkable only for its dignity. As so often in the past it seemed to him that whatever heights he scaled there was waiting some enemy eager to hurl him back into the depths.

By the time the Dams Committee first met Wallis had convinced himself that the destructive power he sought to direct against the Dams could be released only in the form of shockwaves. Winterbotham, who was no scientist but the leading champion of the Wallis cause, was eager to accept the theory. All investigation, he suggested to Pye, and all discussion, while failing to find enough evidence to bolster Wallis's arguments, had certainly produced nothing to disprove them.[21] Pye replied cautiously that Wallis's figures needed confirmation. Tizard, too, was sympathetic, but felt that much more investigation was needed and was prepared to encourage all who might help to make facilities available for it. On one point both scientists and strategists were sceptical: Wallis proposed a fifteen foot bomb; how could it be detonated so that all its length exploded at the same instant? Even Wallis agreed that without that the shockwave would be insufficiently powerful to produce the required effect.

His failure to walk the paths of persuasion step by step; his persistence in confusing some interest in his thesis with total acceptance, bemused his friends and angered even the most powerful among those prepared to become his allies. Within weeks of the first and indecisive meeting of the Dams Committee he was pestering Tizard for 'definite instructions' about work on both big bombs and big bombers. Tizard answered unequivocally: he thought he had already made himself clear; the Air Staff had no interest in a specialised bomber designed solely to carry one big bomb; Wallis's view that it could win the war was not accepted; there was, however, some interest in a more versatile big bomber and Tizard had understood that Wallis had offered to design such a machine:

The Air Staff want not only to have the Wellington V in operation as soon as possible, but also want the utmost energy directed to the design and production of the high-altitude Warwick. I have told them that nothing that is being done or will be done on the proposed big bomber will affect the priority of work on the Wellington V and the Warwick. Please confirm this too. I don't want to let the Air Staff down.

As for the big bomb itself, I am certainly in favour of continuation of the work. Let me know what you mean by 'definite instructions to go ahead'. In other words, what further instructions and facilities do you want to settle finally (if it can be settled finally), without full-scale experiments, the particular advantages of the 10-ton penetrating bomb.

I may say that on our part we are trying to collect further evidence on the effect of underground shock-waves.[22]

Wallis was unabashed: he had always known that members of the Air Staff were against him but he could not believe that a man as great as Tizard would remain for ever or for long in that darkness where Air Staff decisions were made. He seized eagerly on the last paragraphs of Tizard's letter. With the help of Dr Glanville of the Road Research Laboratory he had made a series of models of the major Dams; the first was the one Wallis had chosen as his principal target, the one Ruhr dam which held sulphur-free water, the Möhne. When the dam had been opened by the Kaiser in 1913, the Germans were so proud of the achievement that they had spread, through the world's press, general and technical information about it, down to minute detail. So Wallis was able to build at Harmondsworth an exact scale reproduction of the Möhne Dam. Even the tiny blocks used in the model were in every detail faithful to the original. But this delicate method of making scale models was time-consuming, too much so for Wallis's patience. So a method was developed which involved sweeping-up the contours of the Dam in concrete There followed months of experiment; and the conclusions were less favourable than even the sceptics had imagined. To achieve the result Wallis needed his bomb would have to carry a charge-weight of about 30,000 lb and this, when cased, would give a bomb-weight of more than 60,000 lb.[23] Not only was such a weight far beyond the carrying capacity of any bomber in service, but it was unthinkable, even were he given authority to build a plane to carry such a bomb, that it could be brought into operation in conscionable time.

Despite this devastating disappointment Wallis's attention now became concentrated on the target: having accepted the propaganda he had devised for others, he was determined to find a way of destroying the Dams. For the time being he set aside the big bomb notion and sought other ways to bring a sufficient charge into actual contact with the Dam. Most of the Dams, including the Möhne, were protected by large double-boom defences lying on the surface of the water, from each of which hung a web of the heaviest torpedo-netting. But the solution to that tactical problem could wait until he had the technical means for destroying the Dams. He had long been interested in the ballistic properties of spheres; years before, to the consternation of cricket authorities, he had offered to design a cricket ball apparently undistinguishable from the regulation model, but unplayable by batsmen.[24] He knew from his reading that spheres not only have good ballistic properties, and are not susceptible to disturbance by under-body turbulence of the carrying aircraft, but have a more accurate flight path than the ordinary bomb. They are especially good for underwater bombing where rapid deceleration and good water-stability are required.

And the past gave Wallis a hint for the future: naval gunners had long made use of the ability of the sphere to ricochet on water; Nelson had used the property to extend the effective range of his guns. Wallis recalled reading that German mathematicians had enshrined these antique practices in a mathematical law. Eventually he tracked down this material to a paper published in 1921 by Cranz and Becker[25] who had estabished that if the angle of incidence is less than $7°$ the angle of reflection from the water is always less than the angle of incidence. Applying this knowledge to his problem Wallis came to the notion of a spherical missile which if dropped on the water at some considerable distance upstream would reach the Dam in a series of ricochets and then, after impact with the crest of the Dam, would sink in close contact with the face of the masonry and there be detonated by hydrostatic pistol. Experiments were begun in the garden of his home with his children, Mary, Barnes, Elisabeth and Christopher as terrified research assistants. A small catapult shot marbles at the surface water in a tub and from the results obtained Wallis was able to draw a series of curves by which he could place the theoretical range which would be obtained were his bomb dropped from an aircraft moving at a given speed.

His faith in the Air Staff being shattered, this time he turned to the Navy, to Professor Blackett, Director of Naval Operational Research, with a paper outlining his new theory.[26] But from previous experience he had learnt cunning, and his paper contained no reference to a supplementary theory as yet untested by experiments: the addition of spin at the moment of launching the bomb. If a spherical missile be set spinning about a horizontal axis and be then projected horizontally in the direction of the underside's movement, it will 'fly by itself' in a greater or lesser degree. The length of the initial flight before hitting the water is extended; where ricochets are required the angle of incidence can be increased above the 7° limit; the number of ricochets is increased and therefore the range of travel on the water after the first impact.

Though this important addition to Wallis's thesis was not revealed, the DNOR fully justified Wallis's certainty that his response would be more sympathetic than the Air Staff's. Unfortunately, as it seemed to Wallis, Blackett's enthusiasm took the form of passing the paper to Tizard. Happily, Tizard did not take exception to what looked like an attempt to by-pass his authority, but on the day following his reception of the paper visited Wallis at the secret establishment he had been provided with at Burhill, Walton-on-Thames. He was sufficiently convinced by what Wallis had to say to obtain for him authority to make more elaborate tests, using a ship model tank at the National Physical Laboratory.

Wallis designed a catapult able to project a lead sphere at the necessary scale velocity. He now introduced spin into the experiments; but, unwilling to show his hand at first, arranged to carry out a series of experiments on a reservoir near his home. At the N.P.L., with spheres ranging in density from lead down to light wood, his theories seemed to be sustained. If extrapolation was justified then the contact weight required to demolish a dam such as the Möhne was only 7,000 lb, well within the carrying capacity of British bombers. But extrapolation from tiny models is an unsure way of establishing a theory: experiment must be initiated in conditions approximating closely to reality. Even if all other obstacles could be overcome, still the whole project would be rendered worthless should the enemy discover even a hint of what was in store for him.

It is one of the strange circumstances in the history of the attack on the Dams that, though for almost three years Wallis's theories and experiments were known to a large and ever widening circle in Britain, German Intelligence remained comfortably ignorant. But that is hindsight: in the first months of 1941 the risk of penetration by enemy agents had to be taken, by experiments in the open against a real dam, and by investigation of the best means of releasing from a 'plane a large sphere spinning with high angular velocity. Wallis made innumerable ground tests with spheres made of welded steel pressings spun in a rig, dropped on greased steel plates and arrested by an emplacement of sandbags, but he was still worried lest there be some serious effect on the controls of the 'plane caused by the strong gyroscopic moment exerted by the spinning spheres.

There was yet a third possibility of opening his scheme to enemy observation. The Royal Navy had been quick to recognise the new weapon as potentially useful against naval targets such as pocket-battleships hiding in the Norwegian fjords. Wallis was worried that the Navy might use the weapon prematurely. *Scharnhorst*, *Gneisenau* and *Tirpitz* were small targets and the chances of hitting them by the normal processes of air attack were slight indeed. They were heavily defended by *flak*, smoke and fighter cover. A ship, like a dam, is most vulnerable near its bottom and if the naval authorities, continuing to be more perspicacious than their Air Staff colleagues, launched an attack, then his secret would be out.

But that risk, too, must be taken. Dr Reginald Stradling had pointed out that there was at Nant-y-Gro in Wales a disused dam which conformed, in general configuration, to the Möhne, and which, because the flood water could escape into a larger dam, could be treated with impunity. Although this Welsh dam was only one fifth the size of the Möhne, it was ten times as big as the largest model yet used and would therefore provide a satisfactory, and, indeed, furthest practicable, point in a series of extrapolatory experiments. But the Nant-y-Gro dam belonged to Birmingham Corporation and, in seeking the Corporation's consent, some indication of what was afoot must be spread to a new group of officials.

Meanwhile, and contrary to the legend, Wallis was given authority to convert one of the latest and fastest Wellingtons to his purpose, so that it could carry four spherical bombs, each 4' 6" in diameter, and the small hydraulic motors which would rotate the bombs at high speed.

Wallis goes to War

The growth of confidence in Wallis now demonstrated by some in high places brought to his side several more junior but none the less useful and energetic aides and allies. The Director of Armaments at the Ministry, Air Commodore Pidcock, and his deputy, Group-Captain Wynter-Morgan, appointed Squadron-Leader Green to assist Wallis in the large-scale trials; the Director of Special Weapons at Admiralty, Admiral E. de F. Renouf, attached to Wallis Lieutenant-Commander Leo Lane, who was to prove one of his ablest assistants; the Royal Aircraft Establishment provided the services of Mr J. Woolls, a skilful high-speed photographer. And always with him were his two old colleagues, Summers and Handasyde, as test pilots.

13 The Attack on the Dams

Providence plays its considerable part in the winning of wars, and looking back at the history of Wallis's efforts to defeat the Axis one is struck, not so much by the irksome presence of opponents as by the convenient arrival upon the scene of those who would eventually give to him the encouragement that he desired and the opportunity that he needed. Thus Beaverbrook, Tizard and Winterbotham had all entered the cast at the right moment. In 1941 Norbert Rowe became Director of Technical Development at the Ministry of Aircraft Development —and Rowe was one of the very few civil servants whom Wallis liked as a man and respected as a technologist. Although Tedder had been removed before ever his patronage could be useful his role as advocate among serving officers was more than filled when Ralph Cochrane was given a senior post in Bomber Command, for Cochrane was not only an old friend from RNAS days but also one who had already shown his faith in Wallis as a designer when, serving as Chief of Staff to the Royal New Zealand Air Force, he had written the first orders for Wellingtons.

For the future most important of all: in 1942, at just the time when Wallis's cause was reviving, there had been appointed as Commander-in-Chief, Bomber Command, Air Marshall Sir Arthur Harris, and although the effect of this appointment was not immediate, its long-term consequences were entirely to Wallis's advantage. Harris was one of the architects of eventual victory and his support of Wallis became in time as near ungrudging, as a man of Harris's temperament could manage. But at first his attitude to the inventor and his inventions showed no more enthusiasm than that of his predecessors.

Unlikely as it may seem on first reading of their characters, there is a considerable similarity between the two men that made

Above: H.M. King George VI looks at scale-model used for briefing 617 Squadron, 17 May 1943. *Left to right* A. V. M. Cochrane, Wing-Commander Gibson, H.M. The King, Group Captain Whitworth. *Right:* Wing-Commander Guy Gibson, V.C., D.S.O. and bar, D.F.C. and bar

Ten-ton *Grand Slam* bomb being taken from store

Wild Goose on rail-trolley at Predannack

it all too easy for their enemies to brand them as models cast from the same mould, a mould which, in the eyes of those enemies, should never have been made. Both mistrusted politicians, disliked senior civil servants and despised the mob of obstructionists, whom Harris habitually called 'jacks-in-office'.[1] Both men were loyal to their subordinates but critical of their equals and superiors who did not look upon problems with the same acuity as was their own habit. Determination and originality both men had far beyond the vast majority of their contemporaries and they shared the ability to work for long hours at high pressure; and between them they had about as much diplomacy as a circus prize-fighter. So it was that in the simple arithmetic of the Honours List Harris ended the war with a rare distinction among Britain's principal Commanders: he was not made a peer. Similiarly, Wallis was rewarded with an honour less significant than was given even to such as the designer of the civilian ration book.

Back in the spring of 1942, however, there was already good reason for Wallis and his supporters to welcome the arrival of Harris at Bomber Command for he was known to be a leader who might have occasion to cast Wallis in the role for which Wallis had long cast himself. One of the few senior Air Force officers who had been obstinate in his preference for the Wellington over the Handley Page Hampden, Harris had also been a lonely prophet of the large bomb doctrine. For several years he had argued that the standard 250 lb general purpose bomb was in his own uninhibited phrase) 'a ridiculous missile', and, having seen the bomb in use in the early stages of the war, his criticism had become even more open and even more forthright. The bomb seldom reached its target, he complained, and when it did then it wrought very little damage.

Most significant of all for the eventual blossoming of some understanding between the commander and the inventor was the consonance between the theories of warfare that the two had arrived at independently. Much damage was done to Harris's reputation by the circumstance that ultimately it was his duty to order most of the great attacks on German cities, and these raids have also led to much misunderstanding of the true nature of his bombing philosophy. Under the direction of his political masters he did order the thousand-bomber raids, but unlike those masters he did not intend them primarily as thrusts at

German morale. He knew full well that the enemy's raids on London, Coventry and other British cities had not destroyed British morale, and he could see no reason why the Germans should react differently from the British. What he intended by the thousand-bomber raids was the disruption and if possible the destruction of German industry. Like Wallis he knew that this could not be done with pin-prick attacks on enemy shipping or lines of communication, and like Wallis, once having decided to go for German industry he had no difficulty in choosing the Ruhr as the battleground for Bomber Command. There are therefore, as seen by the glow of after-knowledge, many similarities of experience, conviction and even prejudice that could have brought about a coincidence of interest between Harris and Wallis from the very moment of Harris's entry into office. But in 1942 there were also forces holding them apart, and for the moment these forces were the greater.

In his days as Deputy Chief of Air Staff Harris had learnt an almost frenetic mistrust of inventors. Although he does not name him in his autobiography, it is clear from the context that even Cherwell's gadgetry for the air defence of Britain Harris had dismissed with his usual devastating bluntness (and this most probably is yet another harvest sown by honesty that was to be reaped by lack of honour, and that was to prove yet another link between Harris and Wallis). But for the moment, and it would seem until he was persuaded by Cochrane that Wallis was cut from a different cloth than Lindemann or any other inventor, Harris persisted in looking upon Wallis as yet another scientist crazed out of his peace-time sanity by the urgencies of war, and as an engineer who was deserting his proper task of designing bombers in order to give himself up to impracticable schemes for destroying indestructible and unreachable targets.

If this were all, his critics would be justified in complaining that Harris himself was no more perspicacious than the 'jacks-in-office' he so much despised, but Harris had motives for not supporting Wallis that were far more rational than his suspicion of inventors. His lack of enthusiasm was founded upon information that to him made recurring nightmare; information of which Wallis was for the most part happily unaware. The two men were in fact at the outset separated by the very thesis that they held in common; the thesis that Germany could be defeated

over the Ruhr, for while both men believed in striking at the
enemy's industries with a heavy weight of bombs, Harris knew
only too well the inadequacy of Britain's bomber force not only
for this task but for the many others that it had to perform. He
knew the shortage of suitable 'planes and Britain's poverty in
trained bomber crews. He knew too that in early attempts to raid
the Ruhr only a tiny proportion of the committed force had found
its way to the target area and that of those who reached the area
very few indeed had succeeded in hitting the target. He knew that
precision bombing was beyond the capacity of the Royal Air Force
or of any other air force on either side in the war, and that precision bombing against the Ruhr was made more than ordinarily
difficult because of the industrial haze that hung forever over the
region. Thus, Harris, who had no great faith in the perspicacity
of many of his Air Force colleagues and no patience at all with
some of their decisions, nevertheless, if for different reasons,
arrived at the same conclusion that had persuaded the Air Staff
in 1941 to reject Wallis's big bomb–big bomber proposals. He was
not content with the ridiculous weapons that had sufficed in pre-
war sorties against tribesmen and rebels, but he had drawn conclusions from the German raids on the British that the Germans
themselves failed to note. Harris favoured large blanketing raids
by big forces of bombers. He was not yet ready to recognise
the feasibility of a pin-point attack such as that which Wallis
envisaged against the Dams.

However, during the latter part of 1942 and early in 1943 there
were developments, economic, strategic, tactical and technical,
which prepared Harris for another and more sympathetic look at
the Wallis proposals. Although at first America's entry into the
war had served to debilitate the expansion of the Royal Air Force
because the United States had been forced to turn its industrial
production to the task of making up in months for the isolationist
and pacifist illusions of two decades, still by the middle of 1942
the USAAF had based in Britain a bomber force, almost equal
in strength to the Royal Air Force, with behind it the vast potential of American military reserves, man-power and industrial
might. Both for America and for Britain the sensational tragedies
of the war in the Far East wrought a paradox upon the war in
Europe, for the Allies were forced for the moment to regard
operations in Asia as little more than prophylactics against

further disaster, and were thus able to release some energies for the war in the West.

Hitler's folly in attacking Russia had also served to break the onus of uniqueness which hitherto had been suffered by Britain. More intimately, the efforts of Dominion Governments were bearing fruit; for example, it was on 1 January 1943 that the Royal Canadian Air Force brought a whole Group, Number 6 Group, to Bomber Command. At about the same time Britain's own training schemes were reaching a peak and as bomber crews were produced so too were the 'planes for them to fly.

The Lancaster, the heir to a disastrously unsatisfactory type, the Manchester, by the end of 1942 had been nursed through teething troubles, and the Lancaster added to the Royal Air Force what was probably the most successful and least vulnerable heavy bomber produced by any of the belligerents in the Second World War.

Also by the end of 1942 new navigational aids had been introduced which simplified the process of reaching and identifying targets, and with them more sophisticated measures than had hitherto been known for countering the effectiveness of German air defences.

Never before, not even in the bustling days when, virtually alone, he was responsible for *R.100* and never again, not even when he was frantically involved with *Wild Goose* and *Swallow*, did Wallis work at such high pressure as now in the months of 1942. His determination to prove his dam thesis and to establish the viability of his 'bouncing bomb' added to his already arduous duties at Vickers the roles of advocate, author, designer and director of experiments, observer and—for him the most difficult of all—diplomat. He produced five lengthy, closely-reasoned and carefully-documented papers. Week after week he travelled to London for meetings with Winterbotham, Merton, Blackett, Rowe, Renouf, Lockspeiser or Craven. During June and July he spent at least two hundred hours at the National Physical Laboratory. Twice he visited Nant-y-Gro and, after it had been decided that the first dropping tests would be carried out on the South Coast at Chesil Beach he was often based for days on end at Weymouth, and during that time spent many hours flying with Summers and Handasyde.

Twice during the year he was seriously ill (the convalescence from one of these illnesses gave him the chance to read Francis's *The Battle for Supplies*), but medical investigators may find significance in the fact that this year of frenetic activity was comparatively free from migraines. Even, it may be noteworthy that the only bout recorded in his meticulous diary was in the September week when he attempted once more the almost impossible task of persuading to his side Lord Cherwell. Cherwell's antagonism remained inviolate. At the time Wallis noted that Cherwell 'doubted if the Dams were of any consequence'; later, when the war was over and Wallis was trying for an Inventor's Award he set down Cherwell's persistent opposition in terms that were, for Wallis on Cherwell, remarkably mild, describing his attitude as 'somewhat unresponsive'.

Throughout 1942, and indeed for the rest of the war, Wallis allowed himself little relaxation. The man who in peace-time, for the illogical reason that by so doing he would encourage others to work on the Sabbath, would not even read a newspaper on a Sunday, broke his life-time habit of church-going and made of Sunday just another twelve-hour working day.

That there were dangers in addition to the possibility of revelation of his intentions to the enemy implicit in the series of less secret experiments was frighteningly demonstrated on 4 December 1942 during the first test over Chesil Beach. For the very reason that it was essential to keep knowledge of the programme within the smallest possible circle it was thought undesirable to give notice to the ground defences. The diameter of the spheres was such as to make it impossible to fit bomb doors, and, despite the great height at which Summers flew (with Wallis as passenger), the spheres spinning at a high rate in the 'plane's underbelly were clearly visible from the ground. A bomber such as this was not listed in any of the aircraft recognition manuals; its contours had been so grossly altered as to prevent all but the most sophisticated observers from identifying it as a converted Wellington. 'When in doubt: shoot', and the gunners around Portland Harbour opened up all unknowing that had their aim been better they would have shot down Britain's most original designer and one of the best test-pilots of all time and would have brought to a premature conclusion the plans of which the enemy was still strangely ignorant.

Although the 'plane and its occupants escaped the spitting

distaste of the anti-aircraft guns this first test was a gloomy failure. All four of the welded steel spheres shattered on impact with the water.

An attempt was now made to reinforce the thin shells by fitting them with a light mixture of granulated cork and cement, and as by now the experiments at the National Physical Laboratory had shown that there was little inherent danger to the 'plane, for the next series of trials, from 12 to 15 December, Summers was instructed to dive the Wellington at top speed and to release the spheres at a height of only sixty feet. Despite the reinforcement provided the casings were again damaged but on these occasions Wallis took some encouragement from the fact that on impact they changed shape but did not shatter.

Meanwhile, Wallis set about preparing a new paper synthesising all that he had written earlier on the structural characteristics of the Dams, the catchment area, the rate of rainfall, the calendar of the rise and fall of water, the economic importance of the proposed target, and adding for the first time a full account of the weapon itself and how it might be used both against the Dams and against enemy shipping.[2]

These arguments were clear in his mind, when, in November 1942 at the instigation of Winterbotham, Wallis was summoned to appear before the newly-established Tribunal of Scientific Advisers to the Ministry of Supply. Once more Wallis seemed fortunate in his peers. Thomas Merton, the Chairman of the Tribunal, was himself a man of genius whose vast knowledge was coupled with originality that responded readily to Wallis's unorthodoxy. His fellow-members were men of comparable quality, Sir Ian Heilbron and Sir William Stanier. The Tribunal listened with much sympathy to Wallis's case and questioned him with care and authority, but could not act against Cherwell's unmitigated opposition.

By now Wallis imagined an opponent under every conference table and his doubts were heightened by the uncertainty that was causing those who worked with him to seize upon and repeat to him every rumour of opposition that came their way. Squadron Leader Green reported that one senior scientist was deliberately blocking progress even while pretending to support Wallis. This whisper confirmed suspicions held by Wallis; suspicions that came as much from his instinctive dislike for the scientist's 'leftish' views as from any evidence connected with the actual project, and all added to set off an extraordinary episode. Wallis called in the Secret Service officer in charge of the security of his experiments and accused 'a very distinguished scientist' of aiding the enemy. When finally he named the subject of his tale even Wallis was shocked by the response. 'My God. I have been following him myself for months.' It is but fair both to Wallis and to anyone who (correctly or incorrectly) may be identified as the scientist involved that both the Secret Service and Wallis later came to accept his entire innocence of any subversive activity, though Wallis remained uncertain of the man's proclaimed enthusiasm for his efforts. That there were those who pretended more support than they actually gave is clear both from the sequence of changing decisions in the January and February of 1943—the weeks that followed upon the first successful runs at Chesil Beach —and by the claim made by Winterbotham a quarter of a century later that David Pye (who was not the scientist of the Secret Service episode), whom Wallis during the war and for long after regarded as one of his few constant allies, had in truth been as antagonistic behind the scenes as he was co-operative to Wallis's face.[3]

Whatever the reality, by the end of January 1943 at least those responsible for naval tactics were so convinced of the potential utility of Wallis's weapon that they applied for and received permission from the Ministry of Aircraft Production to convert two Mosquitoes to carry small spherical bombs. Vickers were to produce 250 of these bombs. Though Cherwell remained adamant in his opposition even after he had interviewed Wallis once more, on 2 February 1943, and had read his new paper, on the very next day Lockspeiser telephoned to Wallis that permission had been given for him to go ahead with the preliminary design work for installing in the Lancaster apparatus for carrying and launching his bomb. Wallis was not satisfied. From years of study he knew that the time for attacking the Dams was only three months off and that therefore a decision as tentative as this was no decision at all. With impatience that is understandable he asked for all or nothing and received instead the habitual temporising answer of a bureaucrat: Cherwell had to be persuaded that amendment to the Lancaster would not stand in the way of the development of more advanced bombers, notably the new Wallis–Pierson 'plane, the B.3/42. He wished to have a file prepared for circulation to all parties.

On 10 February came the daunting news that no action should be taken, not even with preliminary designs for the Lancaster adaptation. Despair but strengthened Wallis's obduracy. He set about making a film showing the whole operation on the model scale at Teddington. He was still confident that a demonstration of this kind would persuade even the most obtuse and would shame into acquiescence even the most obstructive. Fortunately for him the veto against further activity either had not been communicated to the authorities at Teddington or else was by them conveniently ignored, and the N.P.L. staff gave to Wallis speedy, energetic and intelligent collaboration. Two air tanks were submerged in the testing tank. In one of them there was placed a powerful arc light and in the other a lady from the Physics Department with a high-speed camera. Spheres were fired up the tank to make contact with a scale model of a dam projecting just above the surface, and the subsequent underwater path of the spheres was recorded as it crawled down the submerged face. The film was finished just in time to have its world première on 19 February 1943 at the Admiralty before the First Sea Lord, Admiral Sir Dudley Pound, and the Chief of the Air Staff, Air Chief Marshal Sir Charles Portal, and a second showing on the 22nd at the Headquarters of Bomber Command at High Wycombe.

That Wallis was so much as invited to Harris's headquarters against the drift of official opinion he owed to the pertinacity of Winterbotham, to the friendship of Cochrane and, most powerful of all, to the interest of the Chief of the Air Staff, Air Chief Marshal Sir Charles Portal. But once arrived he could take no comfort from his reception. As Wallis stood in the doorway of the room of the Commander-in-Chief Harris bellowed at him, 'What is it you want? I've no use for you damned inventors. My boys' lives are too precious to be wasted on your crazy notions.' Either Harris had determined to set Wallis from the beginning to the limits of his powers of exposition and persuasion or else he had met his match for after a moment for recovery from this assault Wallis went into his lucid exposition—intelligent layman version—and, once he had delivered himself on his initial tirade, Harris listened with patience and cross-questioned Wallis with skill and understanding. He even admitted—and the admission is significant of the jealousy and antipathy that existed for Wallis in some quarters—that he had not been fully or accurately informed of the details of Wallis's proposals. Wallis asked Harris to see the film made at Teddington and they went immediately to the Headquarters' projection room.

That Harris did not underestimate the importance of their discussion is made obvious by his insistence that even the carefully screened personnel manning the projection room be excluded from the showing. The film projector, he insisted, must be worked by Air Vice-Marshal Saundby. As a projectionist Saundby was an excellent senior staff officer and he was soon enmeshed in yards of celluloid. Finally, however, Saundby managed to work the projector, and though Harris's only critical comment on the film was a series of grunts his eventual farewell to Wallis, if non-committal, was at least less abusive than his welcome, and Wallis left High Wycombe feeling that if he had not tamed a lion at least he had lain down in a lion's cage and had not been eaten up. That evening, as he thought back over the interview, his hopes rose. One item of information that Harris had let drop seemed to indicate a green light where hitherto there had been a red following upon many ambers. Harris had admitted that the Chief of the Air Staff had authorised the conversion of three Lancasters.

Next morning Wallis went to Weybridge to report to the Manager, Hew Kilner, and was told that together they were to go immediately to London to see Sir Charles Craven. Wallis's optimism of the night before burgeoned. Palpably Harris's grunts had been translated into orders for rapid action. He was to be taken off all other work so that he could hurry through the mass of preparations for a raid in May. However, the moment he arrived in Craven's office he knew that he had misjudged the situation. Wallis was left standing in front of Craven's desk like a soldier up on a charge and the orderly room atmosphere was heightened by Kilner at attention beside him as prisoner's escort while Craven barked out the list of Wallis's crimes. He was making a nuisance of himself at the Ministry of Aircraft Production. He was damaging the interests of Vickers. The Air Staff was tired of his behaviour, and Air Marshal Linnell, who as Controller of Research and Development at the Ministry was *ex officio* a member of the Air Staff, had specifically asked Craven to instruct Wallis 'to stop his silly nonsense about the destruction of the Dams'. Without giving Wallis a chance to interject a word Craven went on: these were the orders of the Government, and his orders as Chairman of Vickers.

Wallis whispered just one sentence. If he was acting against the interests of the firm then his resignation was at Craven's disposal. At this Craven lost all control. Over and over again he shouted the one word 'Mutiny' emphasising his fury by each time crashing down his fist on to the top of his desk.

Wallis was so taken aback by this violence from a man normally as even-tempered as he was courteous that he stumbled out of the room and stood for some minutes in the corridor attempting to recover. When he was joined by Kilner he reiterated his intention of resigning.

Still shaken by the unexpected onslaught Wallis went from Vickers House to the Royal Air Force Club for lunch with Winterbotham and then, in the afternoon, to Richmond Terrace to pour out his troubles to Merton and his assistant Sydney Barratt. He was so desperate that he did not appreciate the importance of this meeting. Merton had come to realise that Wallis was one of 'the greatest engineers of all time'[4] and Barratt shared his enthusiasm. They had access to the War Cabinet by way of Oliver Lyttelton, the Minister of Production, and their pointed and lengthy cross-questioning of Wallis was no mere gesture of comfort for a fellow-scientist who had been humiliated. They were at work, deliberately and efficiently, gathering evidence which would justify circumventing the opposition of such as Linnell and Cherwell, the lukewarmness of Pye and Lockspeiser, and the irascibility of Craven. Given enough technical evidence—and both were qualified to assess Wallis's schemes— they could go above the opposition, to the Cabinet and to the Prime Minister himself.

Wallis answered their questions with his habitual cogency but he had given up hope. For the next two days he was at Weybridge working at his routine activities. The clash with Craven had left him dispirited, the more so because he did not know if his resignation had been accepted, but he was certain still that his Dams thesis was beyond rebuttal and that those who attempted to frustrate it were fools, villains—even traitors.

In this mood he returned to Weybridge once more on Friday,

The Attack on the Dams

26 February, determined to close his mind to everything except the work that he had in hand on Mosquito fabric. There he found a message waiting for him instructing him to report that afternoon to Linnell at the Ministry of Aircraft Production. He was sure that the Controller intended to reinforce the orders that he had already passed to Wallis by way of Craven, and the conviction heightened his fury for he took it as an insult that he should be treated like an obstinate schoolboy.

Craven was present when Wallis arrived in Linnell's office and Wallis was so indignant at what he took to be an alliance to humiliate him further that he did not at first notice his friend, Norbert Rowe, and his feeling of resentment towards Linnell was such that he could not bring himself to listen with care to the Air Marshal's opening remarks. Then, suddenly, the fantastic truth shattered his inattention. The Dams were to be attacked in May. Lancaster installations must be rushed through and the refined design, testing and manufacture of his extraordinary bombs completed in eight weeks so that the special squadron which was to be formed for the raid within Cochrane's Bomber Group could have time to use them in practice runs. Four years of thought, research, hope and frustration had at last brought acquiescence, but only when acquiescence carried with it such necessity for haste as to make achievement almost inconceivable.

Conflicting evidence in contemporary records and, even more, oral and written comments made—some of them—long after the event by many of the principal protagonists and by historians, serve to confound any attempt to unravel the circumstances which changed Tuesday's 'mutiny' into Friday's benediction.

Even the most sympathetic biographer must set down as sign of persecution-mania (understandable perhaps, but unacceptable) the explanation which Wallis himself put forward at the time in his private correspondence and to which he held, at least half in earnest, for many years after 1943. It was, he argued, a logical consequence of the enmity to his ideas in certain quarters, that his opponents were determined to silence him once and for all by setting him a time-table that they knew he could not meet. That he had enemies is undeniable, but the more powerful of them (both in terms of personal antagonism and of national importance) had achieved their ends at the moment when Craven gave to Wallis orders to stop work on the Dams. If there were

251

villains among them not one was so irresponsible as to urge the waste of money, machines and even the lives of the most experienced crews in Bomber Command on the task of bringing to heel one obdurate inventor, and even if his nightmare suspicions had any justification it is inconceivable that the lunatic urgings of the few would have carried weight with such as Cochrane or Harris.

On the other hand, once the impossible had been achieved, several of his friends and even some he had categorised as enemies claimed to the credit of their own advocacy the change of heart.

Most frequent among the many interpretations that have been published ascribe the sudden decision to the all-powerful and infallibly adventurous intervention of the Prime Minister but there is no supporting evidence in Churchill's public papers.

One hypothesis stands out as seemingly more acceptable than all others because it is founded upon experience that is shared by even the humblest who have been forced to deal with Government departments—in Britain or elsewhere. It is that the left hand did not know what the right hand was doing: that Tizard and Merton were consistent in their support of Wallis, that he had converted into a fervent but as yet unrecognised admirer the Vice Chief of the Air Staff, Air Chief Marshal Sir Wilfred Freeman, while others, Linnell among them—and Cherwell to an almost pathological degree—were consistently in opposition, and that, until Wallis told Merton of his interview with Craven, his supporters had not been aware of the distance to which his opponents were prepared to go to stop him, and so, in this moment of crisis rushed to get the decision revoked and found a surprising but effective ally in Harris, the one man other than the Prime Minister whose alliance was capable of immediate translation into action.

There is no doubt that, at their meeting at the beginning of the week, Harris had been more impressed than his grunts had given Wallis cause to suspect. Had he known that one of his Air Force colleagues was about to pass to Wallis orders to end the whole project he would not have told Wallis that another of his fellow-airmen, no less than the Chief of the Air Staff, Air Chief Marshal Sir Charles Portal, had issued instructions for the Lancaster conversions. Indeed, as further support for the left hand–right hand theory, it seems that not only Harris but even Portal was ignorant of Linnell's intentions.

The Attack on the Dams

An attempt to appreciate the situation as it must have appeared to Harris at the time tends to confirm his role in making the decision. If one accepts that in the case of Wallis he had been persuaded out of his habitual mistrust of inventors then it is not difficult to imagine him looking at the proposed project with ever-increasing favour. He had for long been an advocate of defeating the enemy by attacking the Ruhr: the method that Wallis proposed was not his but in the realistic manner that a commander must adopt he would see this as a comparatively inexpensive experiment that might achieve much with only one raid. He was not asked to reduce the number of aircraft at his disposal; the Lancasters would be additional to strength; with luck, if the Dams Raid was successful, many would survive and could be brought into service for other purposes. Even the very fact that it was essential that the raid be carried out on a moonlit night could be said to recommend it to Harris, for on such a night as the battle between fighter and bomber then stood, it would be unlikely that he could commit to action any other part of Bomber Command, and though he was not inclined to risk men or machines without justification, he was also averse to allowing any respite to the enemy. Similarly, the severe demands that Wallis would make on bomber crews could be set to the credit side by the Air Officer Commanding-in-Chief. Because they must be experienced crews they must be men who were either 'time-expired' or at the very least close to being withdrawn from the fighting line.[5] Thus (with men as with machines) their period of training would not deplete the fighting strength at Harris's disposal.

Whatever the causes and whoever was responsible for the decision so suddenly and so surprisingly passed to Wallis on 26 February, the immediate prospect was more terrifying than exalting. Time was so short—only two months—and so much remained to be done. Perhaps this was the first occasion in his career when he was conscious of the limitations implicit in his habit of accepting for himself the total responsibility for every detail in a project. As with Norbert Rowe he walked down the corridor from Linnell's office he muttered, 'If only I had someone to lean on.' Rowe, a Catholic, took the remark as addressed to him. Whenever he felt the need for support, he told Wallis, he offered up a prayer to St Joseph; the form that he used he would send to Wallis immediately.[6] Though it is likely that Rowe had given spiritual implications to what was in truth no more than a murmured supplication for the impossible, for a team of Wallises to help the one who carried the burden, Rowe knew his man. Wallis dearly loved a saint and, as a man who revelled in making things with his own hands, he had a particular affection for the carpenter-saint. Every day until the raid Wallis offered up the prayer that Rowe copied out for him; the prayer that seemed to have been written to Wallis's own specifications .

O glorious St Joseph, chaste spouse of the Virgin Mary, be mindful of us, watch over us, help us to work out our sanctification. O thou whose power doth make possible things which are seemingly impossible, look to our present needs, come to our aid in the distressing and difficult circumstances in which we find ourselves and take under your protecting wing the direction of these important and difficult matters, which we recommend to you, so that their happy issue may turn to the greater glory of God and the good of souls.

St Joseph, helper in times of difficulty, pray for us.

Neither at the time nor later did either Rowe or Wallis notice the fact that St Joseph was at that moment especially well-placed to help Wallis make possible the impossible; both of the feast days of 'this just man', 19 March and 1 May, fell within those few weeks before the raid.

Eight weeks to go and almost nothing was ready; not men, not weapons and not machines. It would be a miracle if all were completed in time but happily in war-time miracles are sometimes wrought by very ordinary mortals A bald recital of the specifications of the paraphernalia that was used against the Dams on the night of 16–17 May shows that almost every item was designed and made in those eight weeks, that in that time many principles, both technical and tactical, were substantially altered and some long-held theories abandoned.

In time for the raid twenty Lancasters were modified for Wallis's purposes. On 26 February Wallis was still dedicated to the notion of a spherical weapon; the bombs dropped were cylindrical, 60 inches long and 50 inches in diameter with three hydrostatic pistols set to detonate at 30 feet and with a 90-second time fuse

The Attack on the Dams

(initiated at the moment of release) intended to destroy the weapon should the pistols fail to function. The total weight of the bomb was far more than had been envisaged: 9,250 lb of which 6,000 lb was charge weight. Wallis had given much thought to the method of installing, spinning and launching the bombs, but even for this the detail had to be fixed in the final weeks, and eventually the aircraft installation consisted of two V-shaped arms each hinged about a fore-and-aft axis and so arranged that by means of disc-wheels the cylindrical case of the weapon could be rotatably held. The external diameter of the discs was minimally smaller than the internal diameter of circular tracks at the ends of the weapon and power for rotation was provided by a hydraulic motor and belt drive to one of the discs, the spin being transmitted by contact between the internal track and the driven disc. Wallis had thought to control rotation at about 700 r.p.m. but settled eventually on 500 r.p.m. In February he had no design for the calliper arms; as he finally built them they were supported inwards against stops by a straining system held by a bomb-stop.

His whole thesis had been based upon the knowledge that the velocity and range of a bomb dropped from a low height would be greatly increased by impacting back-spin and that it would either bounce over the defensive-netting or else have sufficient momentum to break through, and that either way it would still be spinning at a rate sufficient to fulfil his requirement: when it hit the dam the spin and velocity of sink would compensate for the bounce-back. This thesis was never changed, but Wallis's calculations had been based on a flight speed of some 350 m.p.h. and a drop from a height of 120 or 150 feet, whereas in the weeks of final trials it was found difficult to dive a Lancaster at low heights beyond 250 m.p.h. and the change from a spherical to a cylindrical bomb forced the decision to attack at a height of 60 feet. In those eight weeks he was forced to re-work all the relevant calculations and also to discover and provide for the pilot's means for maintaining the exact height.

Even on 26 February Wallis could not close his mind to the imminence of those weeks in the middle of May when the Dams must be attacked. With St Joseph as spiritual ally and now with many human but useful supporters bustling to his assistance nevertheless the odds against success remained high. And if time was in short supply materials were in shorter.

255

Barnes Wallis

Starting at 8.30 in the morning which followed that miraculous Friday when authority was at last given him and working not less than twelve hours a day—and often sixteen or even seventeen for seven days a week—he set out on a long and frantic series of meetings, experiments and journeys to ministries in London, to Woolwich Arsenal, to Reculver and to Chesil Beach. Drawings that in peace-time conditions would have taken weeks of preparation were rushed through in twenty-four hours. (The first full-scale drawings of the bomb proposed for the raid were begun at 11.30 a.m. on that first Saturday, 27 February, and were finished by 6.30 p.m. on the Sunday!) He was fortunate in that the designer of the Lancaster, Roy Chadwick, himself took in hand the task of preparing the Lancaster conversion, and fortunate too in the staff officer, Group Captain Bufton, who was detailed to build a tactical framework upon the theoretical foundation provided by Wallis.

But the first set-back came almost immediately and was of such severity as might have driven to despair both Barnes Wallis and St Joseph. Except for a momentary hesitation in June 1942 when he had considered the possibility of a cylindrical weapon,[7] Wallis had held consistently to the principle of a sphere. Now, no sooner was he told that his concept was in general acceptable than he was also informed that he could not have the many tons of steel needed to make the dies for spherical bombs. It was as if he had been given a car and then told that he must drive it without wheels. He was forced to rethink and redesign the weapon as a cylindrical core padded out to spherical shape with wooden casing. He knew this to be a compromise and, immediately, he had cause to think it damnation to his plans; when first Summers dropped the new weapon the casings shattered on impact with the water, just as had the prototype wooden spheres a year earlier. Some other and more enduring padding had to be discovered, and the search for this more satisfactory material continued well into May. (The bombs that were eventually dropped had no padding.)

Reports from the armaments experts added to Wallis's despair; they were having the greatest difficulty devising a hydrostatic pistol robust enough to resist detonation at the moment of impact with the water and yet sufficiently sensitive to go off when the bomb reached the required depth.

The Attack on the Dams

There were tactical worries to add to the technical. The Air Force had begun a series of daily reconnaissance sorties over the Dams flying a Mosquito at great height. The results of these flights when interpreted by the photographic unit at Medmenham revealed that the Germans were strengthening the anti-torpedo boom at Möhne and were placing anti-aircraft guns on top of the Dam's two towers.

On 22 March Wallis experienced an upsurge of optimism, when it was reported that a loaded Lancaster could operate to a distance of 585 miles from base; 150 miles further than was needed.

There were other problems to be resolved by theoretical calculation, for example, the effect that a misplaced bomb would have on the surface of the water and the time that must be allowed for waves set up by a bomb to die down before the next bomb could be dropped.

Ground-based experiments must continue even while preparations for action were put in hand. Wallis designed, and his assistants built the huge arms which served as supports for the store, which by this time had grown to a weight of almost 12,000 lb. The bomb was spun by a Vickers–Janney variable speed gear and the first ground tests at the reduced speed of 150 r.p.m. proved entirely satisfactory, but there was still the possibility that when the sphere was spun at its full speed of 400 r.p.m. it might leap out of its supports. This potential danger was not finally erased from Wallis's mind until 7 April.

It was also essential that there should be designed a mechanism for destroying the bomb should the hydrostatic pistol fail to operate. This too Wallis took in hand.

In all the years that Wallis had given to planning his assault on the Dams he had buried deep in his mind the knowledge that ultimately the success of his schemes would not depend solely on his technical ingenuity, that no perfected application of theory to practice could remove the appalling risk to the lives of the crews who must deliver the bombs from low altitudes deep over enemy territory. The news that a special squadron was to be formed to fulfil his purposes he had accepted in the same spirit as the information that Avros were to adapt twenty Lancasters. Even when he was told—on 20 March—that the squadron would be based on Scampton the information was but confirmation of triumph over the opposition and incitement to more measuring, calculation and consideration of technical needs. But on 23 March a telephone call from Cochrane's Senior Air Staff Officer, Group Captain H. V. Satterley, interrupted Wallis's fury of abstraction. For the first time a name was forced into his consciousness that had no connection with design or decision-making. Next day, 24 March 1943, the name became a human being, the incalculable sum of skill and courage that would, in the last resort, confirm or confound his years of hypothesis, argument and experiment.

At 4.30 on that day Mutt Summers brought Wing Commander Guy Gibson to Wallis's office. As Wallis had for long respected and liked Summers so he came to like and respect this young veteran, matured by the brutal experience of 173 missions; even in a perverse way, to stand in awe of him. Wallis's brusque manner on this, their first meeting, was more than a demonstration of his habitual calm when launched upon an exposition of technical details; the Wing Commander's rings of rank, the D.S.O. and D.F.C. medal-ribbons bridged the thirty years age-gap and, as always when he met men of action, aroused in Wallis twinges of envy. The thinker faced the doer, and it was the thinker who felt himself reduced in scale.

There was other cause for embarrassment on this occasion. Gibson was commanding officer of an élite squadron and as such invested with entire authority to select pilots and crews from the total strength of Bomber Command, but no-one had thought to add his name to the list of those who knew for what purpose the squadron had been formed. He was aware that he was to train men of considerable experience beyond the limits of their tried ability and undeniable courage. He knew that theirs was to be a rushed programme, that they must be made especially proficient in low-flying and that their target was considered to be of supreme importance. But the target had not been identified, and Wallis did not feel that he had the authority to breach the security precautions even for the benefit of the leader for whom, in principle, those precautions had been devised. Therefore this first meeting Wallis devoted to a lecture on the theory of his bomb; the Dams were never mentioned, and though Gibson listened politely and with growing comprehension and left certain that he had met a genius, still—in this not unlike his distant superior,

'Bomber' Harris—he was not at all sure that he trusted inventors even if they were geniuses.

The story of the selection and training of 617 Squadron has been told on many occasions, and notably with telling and dramatic effect by Gibson himself and by Paul Brickhill. The antics, achievement and the names of Gibson's subordinates have deservedly become part of folk-lore. Wallis was their *deus ex machina*, the manner of their training and the grave demands on their skill and courage were almost superhuman responses to his intellect, his was the inspiration that sent them out to survive or to die, but even so what went on at Scampton in April and May is only tangentially part of the life-story of Barnes Wallis. It was not until 11 May that he had an opportunity of watching Lancasters of 617 Squadron at practice and not until the day before the Raid that he visited Scampton and met members of the Squadron other than Gibson. His involvement with the air crews was in time to mean so much to him that he was later to refer to 617 Squadron as 'his squadron', and this feeling was reciprocated by the young men who used his weapons in action so that those who have survived the many hazardous exploits of 617 Squadron and have lived on into middle-age have come to regard him as one of themselves.

There was, in truth, little time for Wallis to involve himself with the human element in the programme, so many were the demands upon his technical ingenuity and so great the pressures upon his mental and spiritual resilience. The notion of attacking the Dams had been in his mind for years, and the prospects were by now so certain in theory that even he had come to regard the practical application as irrefutable, and it was not until the early part of April 1943 that he was forced to realise that there were still many question-marks written against his hypotheses and many handsome theories that must still be translated into arte-facts. Worse still, when theory became practice, although the process he had planned worked to perfection when it was tried out on the ground at the Royal Aircraft Establishment at Farn-borough, once the first adapted Lancaster was put into the air, for one reason or another, either because the pilot flew too high or because the bomb shattered on impact, practice did not match theory. (Experiments running concurrently with the much smaller and still spherical bomb designed for use by naval

Mosquitoes were facing no such difficulties.) As so often with major innovation scale effects were proving to be the great imponderable and, even with the spherical bomb, some effects undeniable to observation remained (and remain) inexplicable by calculation.

It was, however, the cylindrical bomb for the Dams that was now uppermost in Wallis's mind. If he could not get it to work in time for the Raid then even the success of the naval weapon would be no consolation at all. His diary for April is full of entries which, despite their curt nature, do not hide the disappointment and ever-present knowledge that time was running out. On 16 April, with only a month to go before the date set for the Raid, he set about a fundamental investigation of the stresses on the hoops that bound the casings. Two days later Summers took off from Manston in Kent and dropped off Reculver three bombs each treated in a different way. Gloomily Wallis recorded the results of the experiment:

1. Varnished—held up and sank complete
2. Plain—exploded and sank complete
3. Varnished and filled—held up but cylinder came out.

Generally the diary for April and early May is a mad sequence of journeys by train ('April 22nd. Caught 11.50 a.m. to town—fare 2/9'), by car ('April 19th. Total mileage 234 miles') and, by 'plane, of conferences, discussions and tests. There were moments that hindsight sees as comical as for example when on 17 April Wallis stripped to his underclothes and waded out into the cold sea in a fruitless effort to recover parts of a broken sphere. But at the time there was little for laughter, only long hours of work, continuous absence from home and family and the consciousness of the pages ripping from the calendar.

He knew, too, that the chances of the enemy discovering what was afoot grew as more and more consultants were brought in, as the number of manufacturers involved became greater, and as Gibson's pilots intensified their low-flying training.

Even in the midst of war 'planes flying up and down the Midlands at a height of 150 feet were bound to draw public attention and when Wallis decided that the height must be exactly 60 feet attention became complaint. (It is a legend worthy of acceptance that one Midland mayor wrote to Cochrane reporting that he had seen motorists duck as the Lancasters hurtled over them and that he received a courteous reply stating that 'our pilots have now been instructed to show due regard for other road users.')[8]

Maintaining exact altitude when flying at church-spire heights was difficult even for the most experienced fliers; once Wallis had insisted on tree-top flying the task was virtually impossible. Gibson, Cochrane and Wallis all produced ideas for assisting the pilots but none worked in practice. Technicians, set to solve the problem by Wallis's old chief, Sir Robert McLean (by now at E.M.I.), came up with an electronic apparatus which seemed promising, but in flight it proved too sensitive. The solution did not come until the third week of April and then it was Lockspeiser who resurrected a First World War device, based upon the elementary notion of triangulation: two spotlights, one under the nose and the other under the belly of the 'plane, so set that they coincided on the water when the 'plane was flying at 60 feet. It was simple even if it added another dimension of risk—lights on the 'planes—to a task already hazardous beyond belief.

Since first he had set his mind to the problem of destroying the Dams, Wallis had been concerned lest the Germans hit upon the same principles that informed his work and then reasoned back from their own proposals for a bomb to be used against Allied targets to identify the vulnerability of their Dams. British Intelligence reassured Wallis that nothing of the kind was afoot in Germany but now, once Gibson had been informed of his target and had switched the Squadron's practice-runs to reservoirs and lakes, his concern for security became obsessive.

Security was in hands more qualified than his, but the years of frustration had persuaded him to regard every detail in the project as his intimate responsibility and there was in his mind, in addition to his conviction that the Germans must hit upon evidence of his experiments and the training-programme of 617 Squadron, a wakening of conscience as he forced himself to remember that two years earlier he had sent to the United States copies of his very first *Method of Attack* paper.

On 21 April 1943 Wallis took his worries over security to Winterbotham.[9] He did not mention his own indiscretion, but the meeting he recorded in his diary in a seemingly hysterical form:

'Called on F.L.W. to discuss rate of leakage of news from U.S.A. to Germany.' Winterbotham was still certain that the Germans had no knowledge of the bomb (which both he and Wallis still called 'the sphere') and he was adamant that, even if on that very day an enemy agent stumbled on some significant information, it would take one month for the news to reach Germany, there to be interpreted into comprehension and action. Winterbotham's answer was comforting but hardly comfortable. There was still almost a month to go; not enough for all that needed to be done but far too long for security to be certain.

The last days of April brought hope that the problems with the bomb were close to resolution: on the 28th Wallis drove to Reculver and there watched as the first reinforced bomb was dropped on to a rough sea from 130 feet. Next day at 9.15 a.m. there was staged for him a further test run, still over a rough sea. The Lancaster came in across Reculver at a height of 60 feet, the rotation of spin was produced at a rate far higher than the 500 r.p.m. which Wallis had set as the optimum and, although the 'plane was flying at a speed greater than the 240–250 m.p.h. which by now had been established as the appropriate diving-speed, the cylinder behaved as the paper calculations had predicted and the case was undamaged.

Next day, the last of April, again began well. In the morning Lancasters dropped two cylinders; the first was satisfactory and the second 'a very good show'. There followed a Mosquito dropping an ash-covered sphere and reporting this Wallis came close to the ecstatic:

A very fine run—1,600 yds. 13 secs. Speed 360 m.p.h. Revs. 700. Real tank-style! 12 bounces.

But came the afternoon and it seemed that St Joseph, Wallis, Gibson and the Air Staff had all left out of their calculations a fickle element, the English weather. Gale-force winds made flying impossible and even when they eased two days later the sea stayed unusually rough so that it was impossible to experiment. Over Germany, too, the weather was antagonistic; as late as 10 May air photographic reconnaissance above the Dams was out of the question.

Although the Dams attack was uppermost in his mind Wallis used the days of deprivation to complete other work: on future Wellingtons and on the bomb as a naval weapon. But at the end of the second week St George took over from St Joseph, the weather in Britain turned fine and the meteorologists predicted for the next few days conveniently clear nights over Germany. Nor was it only the elements that were set fair; on the 11th three aircraft from 617 Squadron gave Wallis a grandstand view of immaculate drops on the Reculver range—the theoretical and the tactical were, for the first time, in overt coalition and promise seemed close to fulfilment. Wallis's pleasure and the ease of mind of all concerned were strengthened when reports from our own agents in Germany and those from the interpreters of aerial photographs confirmed the opinion of Security that the enemy had not fathomed British intentions. There was no evidence that he was making any new effort to strengthen defence-systems in the Dams area.

Certainly not only German Intelligence but also the whole organisation under the Commissioners for the Defence of the Reich failed to prepare for an attack on the Dams. For almost a year a local commander was consistently brushed aside when he plagued his superiors with complaints about the vulnerability of Möhne, but it is not unusual that junior officers imagine that they hold the position of greatest danger nor rare that their seniors maintain a different appreciation of the situation.

Unlike Cherwell the Germans knew the Dams to be an important target. With him and with most British authorities the majority of German experts believed them to be inviolable, but the Germans were forced to add one consideration which did not appear in British calculations. If the Dams were susceptible to attack and as there were not available possibilities of adding powerfully to the defence system there was one other precaution that could minimise the consequences of a successful attack: they could lower the level of water in the Dams. But, not unnaturally, German economists reasoned just as Wallis had reasoned for three years: the maintenance of high productivity in the Ruhr was of paramount importance to the Nazi war effort and, if this productivity was to be maintained, then, in the summer months,

Barnes Wallis

the rivers must be dammed to a dangerously high level; the Möhne at 133·5 million cubic metres, only 5 million cubic metres below maximum. If safety were the only consideration then, the German experts agreed, the water-level must be reduced by as much as 50 million cubic metres. But if the British could bring this about by a whisper then they would not need to mount a raid; for the Germans it would be tantamount to surrender before ever battle had been joined.

Although twenty-eight years later it still seems miraculous that the particular secret of Wallis and 617 Squadron was not uncovered by the Germans until the Dams were attacked, the reasons that prevented the enemy from making in 1943 more general provision for defending such seemingly vital targets are more easily discernible. Battered on all sides and routed on some, for the first time since Hitler had begun his programme of attrition the Axis was floundering. In January the siege of Leningrad had been raised and in February von Paulus had surrendered at Stalingrad; for the Germans an unprecedented occurrence and an inconceivable example that nevertheless seemed likely to be emulated in North Africa where great Axis forces had been in full flight since November 1942. German and Italian airfields and the ports of Southern Italy were under constant bombardment and the invasion of Sicily was both inevitable and imminent. The German High Command had to reckon with the possibility that the efforts of the Russians would force a Second Front on the Western Allies. Daily and nightly German cities suffered from powerful reminders of the growing strength of Allied bomber-forces. Berlin, Wilhelmshaven, Hamburg, Frankfurt and Mannheim were all hit in the early months of 1943 and, even closer to the Dams, from early March it had been obvious to the Germans that Bomber Command was engaged in a major campaign against the Ruhr. Essen—the headquarters of Krupps, the United and the Rheinische steel works—the commercial and industrial capital of the region, had been attacked on the night of 5 March by a massive force of 442 and a week later by 348 bombers; on the night of 3 April 348 'planes attacked the same city and on the last day of April another large force returned to Essen inflicting what the Germans themselves described as 'total damage on gas, water and electricity at Krupps'. Duisburg, the second city of the Ruhr, was treated with similar ferocity on the 26 April and once again only four days before the Dams raid.[10]

Humiliated abroad, threatened with invasion from South and West and pounded at home the Germans were virtually forced to down-grade the importance of the Dams.

The battering of the Ruhr towns had still a more immediate and tactical consequence, for when 617 Squadron flew in over Germany the ground defence system was convinced that this was just one more raid directed at the great centres of industry and population in the Ruhr. Thus, although in the full moon of the night of the Dams Raid there were over Germany only the bombers of 617 Squadron, the function of diversionary attacks had been amply fulfilled for weeks by other night-bomber squadrons, and the enemy was kept guessing until the very moment 617 Squadron attacked the Möhne.

Since the beginning of the war scarcely a day had passed, not even a Saturday, a Sunday or a Bank Holiday, without Wallis entering in his diary at least one note which showed him active on a project. For the 13 and 14 May and although these were working days, a Thursday and a Friday, the diary is blank. Many years later, when in other respects his memory of the period was both vivid and minute, he could remember nothing of those two days; it was as if as prelude to battle he had escaped from both the mundane and the consequential into a trance-like vigil. But on Saturday 15 May, he was back to brutal reality. At three o'clock that afternoon, with Kilner as his companion and Summers as pilot, he took off from Weybridge—in a Red Cross Wellington! —for Scampton. Gibson met him when he arrived at the Base and, as they looked around the Lancasters, the Wing Commander fed Wallis the latest information. There seemed now no doubt that the next night would be fine for the operation that had been given the code-name 'Chastise'. (The code-name for the successful breaching of a dam was to be 'Nigger' in honour of Gibson's dog.)

At six o'clock Wallis spoke to all the 'plane captains. Time and time again he had given a talk like this. He had lectured the sophisticated but antagonistic, the highly-informed who were sympathetic, Cabinet Ministers and senior officers who understood the strategical implications of what he said but not the scientific theorising. Beaverbrook, Cherwell, Portal, Harris, Renouf, Pound, Merton, Tizard, Pye, Lockspeiser, Linnell, Craven—a list of those who had heard various versions of the lecture that he now gave to nineteen young airmen reads like a *Who's Who* of Britain's war-time leadership. But never before had he faced an audience such as this and never before had his lecture-hall been the ante-room to battle. By the measure of his years and experience these boys were not much older than his own children; not one of them had been born when he was a war-time serving officer. If they remembered the crash of *R.101* it was only as a moment of excited gossip in their early school-days, no more tragic than the disputed goal that lost Arsenal the Cup to Cardiff City, in their memories far less vivid than the body-line controversy or Obolensky's try against the All Blacks. Yet these were the men who would run the final and irredeemable test on his great theory; their lives were his responsibility and his career was in their hands.

At 10 p.m. he and Gibson met once more in the C.O.'s office and it was while they were going over final details that the news came that Gibson's dog had been run over. As was his custom before he went to bed Wallis wrote up his diary. The entry 'Nigger Killed' is the first reference to an animal in any of his personal papers since those days at Cowes forty years earlier when he had complained of his landlady's flea-bitten mongrel and, even against his vigorous protests, it is difficult to shake off the conviction that at the time he feared an omen in the death of Gibson's dog just twenty-four hours before its name would be the one word which all concerned waited to hear from over Germany.

Wallis slept well and was still in bed at eleven on the morning of Sunday 16 May, when the last of the Lancasters that were to raid Germany that night was delivered to 617 Squadron.

All that afternoon Wallis bustled round Scampton, inspecting the 'planes, their bombs and bomb-spinning installations. At six he briefed the crews and at 9 p.m. he watched them take-off.

Weeks earlier Wallis had asked for permission to fly as a member of Gibson's crew. Without so much as suggesting that the request be passed on, Norbert Rowe had turned it down, giving as excuse the possibility that Wallis might be captured but patently needing no justification beyond common sense and Gibson's ease of mind. Now, as Gibson left without him, Wallis had nothing before him but the agony of waiting, the possibility that the whole operation might end in disaster that was his creation, and the certainty that however good the news that came back eventually from Germany it must be leavened with tragedy. He could not know that by 11 p.m. when he set off for Cochrane's headquarters, one 'plane with its seven-man crew had been lost to enemy *flak* over Holland, and two more were on their way home (one having obeyed so literally the instruction to fly low to avoid fighter interception that the bomb beneath the Lancaster had been ripped off by a wave). Before Wallis arrived at Grantham at least one more 'plane had been shot down.

In the history books battle is precisely ordered; a movement here, there a withdrawal, now a decisive charge and elsewhere a fatal error; all can be reduced to a conflict of shaded and stippled rectangles, and a thousand lives lost can be represented frugally by the head of an arrow on a printed page; but any man who has ever been through a battle and then sees it described knows how little consonance there is between what he remembers and what he reads. It is the inconsequential which is etched most deeply into the remembering mind; a tree revealed by the flash of a gun or a moment of wonder at the beauty of tracer-patterns stays clear in recollection long after the logic of event, cause and consequence that at the time was but dimly understood, has with the years been erased forever. The human being at the business of war is a highly-trained machine which watches the enemy, orders man-œuvres and pulls levers, and this machine is to all intents separate from the sensitive and terrified mind which functions in the same body. There are at work in the fighting-man at least three disparate and even contradictory energies: inconsequential observation, technical concentration, and fear, which make it difficult for him to produce after the event a conclusive and comprehensive account of his own part in a battle. Because any one battle is a composite of the activities of all those who take part any attempt to reconstruct the story as a whole must be a synthesis of contradictions or, at the very best, a hypothetical reconstruction based on near-agreement.

A battle such as that over the Dams is of short duration, is fought at great speed, and, more even than land or sea battles is in many respects not one but many fights in which each 'plane

is an army to itself connected only by crackling radio to the other
armies, suffering its own disasters, and never certain of the extent
of its own triumphs nor indeed sure which triumphs are its own
work.

It is not surprising, therefore, that though the raids of 16–17
May 1943 have been much reported by men on both sides, still,
even after more than a quarter of a century, there can be little
certainty about what happened. The Germans on the ground
were taken by surprise and surprise is never a steady collaborator
with accuracy. They, and the British bomber-crews, suffered from
the physical circumstances which conventionally make battle
reporting difficult. Smoke is an obfuscator, noise deadens the
senses, a flash or an explosion is the event of a second.

As for the British: they had been rigorously trained for this
task and as they roared over the Dams, if sight had been their only
sense, it could have seemed as if once more they were looking
down upon a scale-model or as if yet again they were practising
over a reservoir in Wales or a lake in Cumberland. But if their
reactions had become automatic with training nevertheless no
drill nor yet previous experience could erase the knowledge that
the country below them was not the Lake District, and, although
the hand would react automatically to messages trained into the
mind, still these were men and not robots, and when radio
calls to comrades remained unanswered this too was an inescapable message that shifted the scenery and turned neat preparation
into confused reality.

With men on both sides thus handicapped it is nevertheless true
that there is a degree of coherence in the accounts that have come
from both sides, but it is the coherence of a kaleidoscope rather
than a continuum of drama.

The brightness of the moon and excellent visibility on the night
of 16–17 May more than fulfilled the predictions of the weather
experts but, if a raid on a night such as this must have seemed to
the Germans surprising and indeed unprecedented, their belief
that it was none the less directed against the Ruhr towns appeared
to be substantiated when some of the attacking 'planes—in fact
the second wave—circled high over Düsseldorf, Essen and
Duisburg. The first wave, having flown at low altitude round the
Northern edge of the Ruhr anti-aircraft ring, penetrated the
defence system between Münster and Dortmund flying below

the zone of fire of heavy anti-aircraft guns and then came down even lower: to tree-top level.

The blindness of the Germans persisted even to the moment when Gibson and his 'planes approached Möhne. Soon after midnight the observers watching the skies above the Dam gave warning of British bombers. A few minutes later the duty engineer at the Möhnetal power station telephoned to his superiors at the headquarters of the Dams organisation in Neheim and Niederensee: a raid on the Dams was about to be launched. His alarm was treated with arrogant disbelief; at headquarters they were heartily sick of the nervousness of the men on the spot. Beyond the ordinary air-raid alert no particular warning was passed on to the local inhabitants and the subsequent loss of life can be ascribed almost entirely to this circumstance because most of the inhabitants were in their air-raid shelters when the truth—and the Dam—burst upon them and by that time two mishaps for the British had added to German confusion: the 'plane of Gibson's second-in-command crashed on the power installation which provided local electricity supplies, and one bomb (probably from this same 'plane) must have been dropped when the 'plane was yawing for it flew off the water at an angle and crashed into the centre of telephonic communications, thus substantiating Wallis's hypothesis about the failings of cylindrical bombs. At Möhne itself the Germans had only six 2 cm guns, one each on the sluice towers, one on the right-hand extremity of the wall-surface and three in the meadows below the Dam. Only three of these guns could have any substantial influence on the battle because Gibson's 'planes were hidden behind woods for most of their approach run, so that the line of attack could not be ascertained by the gunners on the wall, and the British flew at such low altitudes as to bring them below the levels of practical deflection of the guns. It was only after they had dropped their bombs that the 'planes were lifted to heights at which they were in any real sense vulnerable to the guns on the Dam and even then the time available to the defenders was minimal, and for much of the raid 617 Squadron kept up a ferocious fire against the gun crews.

In the skies above the Dams and on the ground close by there was shock, smoke, noise, mist, danger, heroism—and death. Back at Grantham there was uncertainty and, for too long, silence.

There in the Group Operations Room Wallis, Harris and Cochrane waited for the coded Morse signals from Gibson's 'plane that would spell out success or failure. As each hour that was in truth only sixty seconds long ticked by Wallis's sense increased of separation from the commanders, and when the first message came through his momentary hopefulness collapsed almost to despair for it revealed that Gibson's own bomb had exploded only a few feet from the Dam without causing any breach. He knew that the attack was on and that his thesis had failed at its first trial in battle-conditions. Now each second was an hour and it seemed to Wallis that Harris and Cochrane were already condemning him. 'Gonner', the code-word for bomb dropped without result, came three times more and Wallis knew what was in the minds of the two senior airmen: the crews out there were theirs, the lunatic certainty that had sent them there was his. Nothing was said. Wallis sat on the steps of the operations platform and could not even pray. Then suddenly the Morse began again. Wallis rose to his feet and as the Signals Officer called out excitedly the code-word 'Nigger', in a gesture that was for much of his adult life the nearest that he could come to exuberance or an overt expression of the release of pent-up emotion, he pumped his hands up and down violently. Cochrane, who was also not one to show his feelings, was quick to congratulate him, and even Harris, whom some thought to have no feelings to show, smiled upon him with unusual benevolence.

After the Möhne Dam, the Eder and the undefended dams at Sorpe and Bever were attacked by Gibson's reserve flights. The first bomb was dropped on Möhne at 0027 hours on 17 May and the last more than three hours later at Ennepe.

If, as is desirable so that Wallis can be judged as inventor, all passion is extracted from an account of the raid, then also among the major issues to be resolved is whether events justified his long-held confidence that one bomb properly placed would be enough to destroy even the Möhne Dam. At Grantham all believed that this conviction was vindicated; as late as 6 July 1943 when Field Marshal Milch held a post-mortem on the raid German opinion coincided with the British: for many years after the war Wallis, too, held to the belief that Möhne was breached by only one bomb and it is the view that has been generally accepted by narrators.

The Attack on the Dams

Yet the break in the Dam was enormous: a rectangular wedge almost 250 feet wide and 112 feet deep was torn away from a 50 foot thick wall and some 45,000 cubic feet of masonry was washed away. As the Möhne wall was built in a steep curve the section thus destroyed exerted a strong downward pressure on adjoining wall sections and this pressure added to the damage so that eventually more than 60,000 cubic feet of masonry needed replacing.

The possibility that not one but two bombs combined to make the fantastically large breach was in fact implicit in air reconnaissance reports written on 17 May 1943, and at least one commentator has implied that the interpreters of air photographs knew on that very day that two bombs had struck the Möhne.[11] However, what appears to be the most substantial and, in technical terms, the calmest of all accounts of the raid, although it was written by German experts in September 1943, seems not to have been used as evidence by any previous historians, British or German, but points to the possibility (if no more) that though one bomb, the last of four used against Möhne, actually breached the dam, two of the three bombs dropped earlier had caused some damage.

This report[12] supports most other accounts, both British and German, in the assumption that four bombs were dropped at Möhne and that, of these four, only three need be taken into account—the fourth having cleared the Dam and exploded about 40 yards from the open side. The first bomb exploded on the water-side (the very first of the raid, dropped by Gibson himself) was no more than 30 yards short but somewhat left of the centre of the target. It tore its way through the torpedo netting but otherwise had little effect; even the anchor weights on the barrage were shifted by only a few feet. The second of the relevant bombs was a little more off target; it exploded close to the left bank almost 100 yards from the wall and the swell that came from the explosion caused the loose earth on the left bank to collapse over a considerable distance and brought such a cascading of water that the occupants of the left-hand sluice tower believed for a while that the dam had been breached. It was the last of the four bombs dropped on Möhne which struck the centre of the dam and it is more than likely that it was this bomb, and this bomb alone, which did all the damage, but there remains a slight possibility, which can never be removed or made into a certainty, that one or both of the other two water-side bombs cracked the dam-wall. Certainly these two comparatively errant bombs set up a violent extension of the impact of explosion which was recorded as far away as Göttingen, and this would imply a substantial effect on the rocky bottom, certainly when the Dam was drained there were some cracks visible that could not be credited to the fourth bomb; and at Eder, which was attacked an hour after Möhne, the wall was undoubtedly and substantially damaged by two bombs some distance off-target before a third direct hit made the final breach. But evidence from Eder is inconclusive to argument over Möhne for the Eder Dam was a less substantial construction and was not, as Möhne, protected on its water-side by a layer of earth.

It would seem then more plausible to hold to the general conviction that the Möhne was breached by one bomb and to claim that Wallis's hypothesis was validated. Tragically at Eder another theory was substantiated, one that he had held at the beginning of his planning but since discarded: Maudsley's 'plane blew itself up by the force of the explosion of its own bomb.

Less than half-an-hour after Gibson dropped the first bomb at Möhne and only four minutes before the Dam was breached one Lancaster approached the undefended but mist-wreathed Sorpe Dam. The captain had been instructed to use his bomb as a conventional weapon (without spin) and he made no less than ten runs before he was satisfied with his sighting. The bomb threw up a column of water to a height of 600 feet but made little effect on the earth and rubble dam. More than two hours later— and the time spent in the battle-area is of itself a measure of the valour of Gibson and his crews—the Wing Commander ordered up two of the reserve bombers for a further attack on Sorpe. One 'plane made several attempts to establish through the swirling mists a clear sight of the target but eventually gave up and returned home safely. Almost the last of 617 Squadron's bombers to be called to attack the Dams was piloted by Pilot-Officer Burpee, a Canadian. Because he did not answer Gibson's call it had been assumed that he was already dead before he was ordered to Sorpe but, according to the German report of September 1943, soon after 3 a.m. a solitary 'plane dropped a second bomb at Sorpe. Although it was on target and although the concrete wall of the Dam was stripped by the explosion, the earth dam was not breached. Yet there is, even at this late date, a strange kind of comfort that comes from being able to assume that Burpee *found* his target before he was killed.

The last bomb dropped in this magnificent raid was dropped at Ennepe at 0337 hours. By then the visibility was poor and the bomb was almost half a mile off target and did no damage.

At Grantham as dawn broke Harris made what was for him a rare gesture. He took Wallis and Cochrane out on to the apron to meet the returning crews, and it was while they waited there that he announced to Wallis that after this success he would be prepared to buy from him 'even a pink elephant'. One other comment made that morning by Harris must be recorded. His mind was on his crews and it was consistent with the pride in his service that compelled this gruff-seeming commander that he was already planning as reward for a unique achievement an unusually long list of decorations, but he had not forgotten the author of the achievement. He turned to Wallis and said, 'For this, I'll see to it that you get a K.'[13]

The arithmetic of war is beyond calculation. It is possible to record and to make some assessment of the devastation caused by the raids and possible to describe but not easy to evaluate the shock to the enemy's confidence and the stimulus to our own; but ingenuity such as that practised by Wallis cannot be measured and there is no equation for the skill, the heroism and the sacrifice of 617 Squadron. Even so a recounting of what happened to the Squadron on that night in 1943 set down as in some god-like score-sheet does serve to justify Wallis and the men who made the decision to send them out and, in the last resort, adds the force of dispassion to the many and properly emotional tributes that have been paid to those who manned the 'planes.

Of the nineteen 'planes that set out on the raid eleven returned safely to base. Only one 'plane was destroyed over Möhne and from that 'plane one member of the crew parachuted to safety.

Casualties are not numbers but men. It is testing to the human spirit to have to write that, despite the exorbitant demands that were made upon their skill, despite the hazards of the full-moon, the absence of diversion, the multiplicity of the targets and the time spent over the Dams, the loss of fifty-five men was less than had been feared, and it is both painful and tasteless to set against that figure 476 Germans dead and 69 missing, 593 foreign workers dead and 156 missing.[14] But the raid was not designed to inflict casualties; in terms of its real objectives the record runs thus: Both the Möhne and the Eder lakes were emptied. The vital Mittelland Canal was disrupted. At Bringhausen the storage power station was submerged. The main railway line between Kassel and Hagen was washed away and the floods broke into the city of Kassel itself—forty miles from Möhne. The ferro-concrete bridge at Neheim was utterly destroyed. And, for those who attempted to clear the disaster-scene, mud, the most obstinate element, swept over the whole area and disrupted many industries for months. Crops were ruined. Many hydro-electric plants were destroyed. Most serious of all for the Germans, the waters behind the Möhne supplied the needs of four and a half million inhabitants and its destruction halved the quantity available. Immediately the enemy had to deploy thousands of troops, police and labourers to rescue work, to evacuation and to the task of restoring communications. For months after the raid frantic energy, skills that were needed for the Atlantic Wall and valuable manpower had to be diverted to repairing the damage, and although, by an effort that must be accepted as superhuman, the Germans had the Möhne in operation at the end of September 1943 the Dam was not fully repaired until August 1944. Meanwhile, out of fear of a second attack, the defences of the whole Dams area were heavily reinforced; a diversion of strength that the Germans could ill-afford and, for the Allies, a bonus that was not inconsiderable.

Had the Sorpe Dam and the lesser targets gone with the Möhne and the Eder the Ruhr might have been utterly removed as the manufactory of war and that could have brought the Germans to the end two years earlier than actually happened. But, if the victory was not complete, nevertheless the triumph of Wallis, of Bomber Command, of Gibson and his crews, is undeniable. The genius and obstinacy of one man in his mid-fifties had been linked to the hard-won experience, the skill and the bravery of 133 men in their early twenties, and together they had won a battle that must stand with the great victories of armies or battle-fleets.

Merited recognition came immediately to Gibson and to thirty-two officers and men of 617 Squadron; Wallis received a sheaf of congratulatory messages—but nothing else. Harris had kept his promise; his recommendation that Wallis should be knighted was written within days of the raid;[15] but for this kind of manipulation Harris was a mere child among jealous adults. Stafford Cripps at the Ministry, who had been one of the first to write a fulsome letter to Wallis, saw some danger to his own dignity if he accepted a recommendation from a serving officer; members of the Vickers Board were against the honour, some of them because they had not as yet themselves received the accolade, and almost all because they feared that a knighthood for Wallis would serve to encourage his habitual indiscipline; and neither senior civil servants nor senior airmen would risk their own chances of honours by pressing a case upon the Patronage Secretary or the Inner Cabinet.

Honour of a kind did come to Wallis—but in a backhanded way and from the enemy. The first communiqué, issued from the Führer's headquarters on 17 May, was both laconic and surprisingly honest: the Dams had been breached, flooding was serious and there had been many civilian casualties. Even the number of British 'planes shot down was underestimated. However, within twenty-four hours the habitual vileness of the German propaganda machine was at work erasing the damage to national confidence wrought by the shocked professional honesty of the German Intelligence Service no less than by the gallantry of 617 Squadron. For Goebbels and his subordinates there was available one possibility for turning slings and arrows into whips driving the nation to greater effort, for persuading a gullible race that defeat was not disaster but instead just one more item of self-justification; what must be admitted and endured could with profit be blamed on the Jews. Goebbels, who one day was confessing to his diary that the Dams Raids had taken the Luftwaffe by surprise, had inflicted heavy damage and many casualties, disrupted production—and made the Führer very angry—on the next had his tale ready: 'the plan for the attack stemmed from a Jew who had emigrated from Berlin.'[16]

On the 20th the *Völkischer Beobachter* confirmed the report (in words that are patently Goebbels' own) that 'a Jewish doctor formerly resident in Berlin' was the intellectual originator of the 'terror attack'. Under a Stockholm by-line the report was suitably and obediently embellished. International Jewry, said the newspaper, 'feels that a calamitous mistake was made'. British circles, too, were 'extremely embarrassed by this Jewish error' and the

Svenska Dageblader was quoted in support of the thesis that the Dams Raid 'will be seen in many places as a mistake of the first magnitude'. To all this the newspaper added a note:

> The German people need no further evidence of Jewish unholy guilt. Anti-semitism is greatly feared in Britain and is growing among the British . . . who feel that Jewish refugees welcomed as guests will use the war to damage and threaten their existence.

In German the grammatical transition which links this passage to what has gone before is so clumsy (or so devious) as to make it difficult for even the most sceptical reader to distinguish whether the phrase itself is a quotation from Sweden or German editorialising. To a huge majority of newspaper-readers, the implications must have been clear: that their own hatred of the Jews was beginning to spread among their enemies was confirmed from neutral sources.

Goebbels' crazed imagination could conjure up a Jew behind every dagger-thrust at Germany, but it could be that Goebbels was trapped by the implications of German-Jewish origins in the name of Lindemann, and if so it is a nice twist of fate that the outstanding opponent of the Dams project should be credited by the enemy with its successful prosecution; but whatever the origin of the identification, within three days of the raid Goebbels had available a complete dossier on 'the Jewish doctor'. All this devil-dancing with truth was according to a pattern and is not surprising. What was surprising and remains extraordinary is that if Goebbels' dossier was fabricated it did at least exist, whereas his more sophisticated, more realistic and less easily self-intoxicated colleagues in the German Intelligence Services had no dossier at all. So far as can be discovered the true author of the project, remained, to the Germans, anonymous.

14 The Big Bombs

Achievement followed upon achievement, experiment was continuous and effort overlapped with effort. Wallis was a one-man army and at last his genius was recognised by the Royal Air Force. If Cherwell, the most powerful of all decision-makers in the world of science, still disliked Wallis the man and held his ideas in disdain, there were many others scarcely less influential who had discovered that they and the nation could not afford to ignore or to despise a Wallis thesis. But at White Hill House and at school his children continued to be almost entirely unaware of the extraordinary part that their father was playing in the battle with Nazi Germany. Nor was this lack of communication entirely thoughtless or utterly the product of Victorian remoteness. Wallis was confident in his work, determined in his desire to press it to a conclusion, but he was also a simple and devout Christian who regarded his gifts as God's blessing, who allowed himself no pride but only gratitude to God; a man who, for all his seeming arrogance towards his opponents, practised a sincere humility. At home he kept silent, because he had always been silent at home and because he would not and could not boast in front of his own family.

The gifts of which he might have boasted, the genius which, after the Dams Raid, provided for him a special relationship with Bomber Command and a continuing and intimate connection with its ace squadron were by now most obviously directed towards the invention and design of bombs; later, in the highly emotional publicity that followed eventual victory it was the bouncing bomb, its naval equivalent, Tallboy, and Grand Slam which incised his name into the consciousness of the nation. Because these rare products of his imagination and ingenuity at the time meant so much to the Air Force it is well-nigh inevitable that his biographer must take such time and length to describe activity on the bombs as is bound to distort the proper arithmetic of his life and work. But even in that period when he was working for up to sixteen hours a day on preparations for the Dams Raid he found also the time and the intellectual energy to invent a new range-finder for Mosquitoes (though he stole the time, and perhaps again the intellectual energy, from a committee-meeting on the B3/42), but for the most part even in the war years the creation of bombs was a self-imposed addition to a busy working-life which was itself far from conventional. It was by no means surprising nor entirely to their discredit that both Government and Vickers showed frequent signs of perturbation that Wallis's mania for inventing new bombs would take him from his principal professional duty to design the machines that would deliver conventional or unconventional bombs. For the successful prosecution of the war new varieties of the Wellington were essential and so, too, were the complementary and supplementary Warwicks and Windsors. Wallis, with Pierson, was responsible for them all.

Although theirs was the original conception much of the story of the Warwick lies outside the history of Pierson–Wallis collaborative ventures and it was fears for the future of the B3/42 which aroused the suspicions of Whitehall whenever Wallis went off on some bomb-designing excursion. In a sense the Windsor stood in relation to the Warwick as the Lancaster to the Manchester, for both were four-engined emendations of an originally twin-engined concept, but more particularly the Windsor was the logical outcome of the big bomber principle, expounded so often and so cogently by Wallis, coupled with a natural desire on the part of both designers to exploit to the full the advantages of geodetic construction.

In their design programme Wallis and Pierson achieved a step towards fulfilling the big bomber–big bomb philosophy, but the air offensive of 1943 (including the Dams Raid itself) had proved that the Lancaster was already capable of bomb-carrying performance that the Windsor could do no better than equal even on the drawing-board. Although in 1943 and 1944 Wallis paid much attention to the 'plane only three Windsors flew (not one of them on active service). The fascinating notion of using Windsors for long-range civil aviation was discarded and if it need not be accounted a Wallis failure, nevertheless in the history of Wallis designs the Windsor is most interesting only because its wing-structure represents what is possibly the most sophisticated use ever made of geodetic construction.

In the year of the Dams Raid Wallis was named a Commander of the Order of the British Empire. A C.B.E. was some compensation for the refusal of the knighthood that Harris had promised and if the accolade was withheld at least this honour stopped short of being a slap in the face like the earlier offer of an O.B.E.

Why, despite one moment during the Anzio battle when 617 Squadron was prepared for a raid against an Italian dam, the bomb as used against the Dams was never again employed after May 1943 remains a mystery. Within days of the Dams Raid Wallis produced a catalogue of suitable targets in enemy-held territory that included several hundred items. He favoured above all other possibilities some of the innumerable viaducts in Italy; and had they but known of the possibility, all those who for almost two years fought their dreary way up the Italian peninsula would have been loud in their support for his preference; but he included targets in Holland, France, Rumania as well as many in the German homeland. In general terms and in particular Cochrane seconded Wallis's proposition. But Harris would not buy this particular pink elephant, Tizard and Merton made no attempt to intervene on Wallis's behalf, Cherwell did not even deign to oppose it and, so far as can be ascertained, there is no official document extant which argues the pros and cons of the case, and no subsequent historian has so much as noticed that, though Renouf and his naval fliers were now free to use the smaller spherical bomb against enemy merchantmen and did so with vigour and success, the bomb that had breached Möhne and Eder, the bomb that was in time to become better known than any other weapon of the Second World War, was used for less than four hours.

The nearest one can come to verifiable evidence for the reasoning that lay behind this attenuated history is based upon a letter from Sir Arthur Harris to the author of this biography[1] in which the Commander-in-Chief implies that as the Dams Raid had reinforced his long-held respect for Wallis, as he knew already at the time of the Raid that Wallis had in mind other and even more potent weapons, and as all Wallis weapons were likely to make substantial demands upon the courage and skill of air-crews, he decided to reserve 617 Squadron for the delivery of future Wallis bombs. The weakness in this argument lies in the fact that the Squadron was ordered into other operations before there was another Wallis bomb available. Nevertheless Harris's recollection does seem to hint at a more substantial hypothesis. Targets more important even than those that were in the list provided by Wallis were already in Harris's mind for Intelligence was beginning to accumulate evidence that the enemy, too, had in process a new weapon that could neither be resisted in the air nor destroyed upon the ground by any means then available to the Allies, a weapon that if it were not neutralised might well turn the course of war once more in favour of the Axis. Wallis's idea of a 'penetration' bomb could be the answer of providence, but before it could be used Wallis himself must give much time to its design, Chadwick would have to produce further adaptations to the Lancaster, and, most important of all, materials and industrial labour would have to be diverted to its production.

Meanwhile, as the conflation of intelligence reports progressed which was to confirm the existence of the V.1 rocket, Wallis like all those involved with the bouncing bomb had to be brought back to dealing with another problem that, accidentally, he had created. It was known that at least one of the bombs carried on the night of 16–17 May had fallen intact into enemy hands. The thought of our own dams breached by replicas of our own bombs, of the coalfields flooded and the Sheffield steel works out of action, set even Wallis and his supporters to long hours of near-frantic deliberations and added the spice of terror of retaliation to Cherwell's unquenchable opposition.

It was not until 1945, when the war was won, that British authorities came to know that this disastrous consequence of achievement was averted not because of the precautions set up as a result of the many conferences of the summer of 1943 but because the Germans, with their customary thoroughness, had stepped several paces backwards from the bomb that they had in their hands, and, instead of using it almost immediately (as was well within their understanding and their competence), had insisted on reworking the calculations and reconstructing all the experiments that Wallis had carried out over more than two years. It was only after eighteen months that the Germans were satisfied that they could build and use a bouncing bomb and by that time the tactical possibility had passed.

But not all German engineers were similarly cautious; the enemy no less than the Allies had their inventors whose lunatic-seeming ideas could be translated into devastating weaponry, and it was the whisper of information about one of these ideas, communicated to Wallis on 12 July 1943, which took him away from full-time aeroplane designing, away even from the attempt to develop counter-measures to the bomb he had, as it were, presented to the Germans, and set him off once more on a frantic effort to convert in short time a long-held theory into a practical weapon.

On that day at the Air Ministry he was told that German plans were far advanced to launch rockets or flying-bombs against Britain.

British Intelligence, an arm of the Service whose part in the Second World War it is hard to overestimate, had, by November 1939, full information on German progress in rocketry. However, it was not until the winter of 1942 and the spring of 1943 that evidence, accumulated from spies, resistance workers, aerial reconnaissance sorties and the interrogation of prisoners-of-war impressed upon the British Chiefs of Staff the horrific possibility that the Germans might soon have at their disposal a weapon of a kind which they could not as yet identify but which, if it was the rocket they suspected, could be launched against British cities at such a rate as could kill one hundred thousand every month. Because they did not know the specifications of the weapon they were also powerless to prepare counter-measures. The one hope left to them was to discover the centres of research and the launching-sites and to obliterate them by massive bombing attacks.

Some British scientists insisted that the rockets were a myth because no fuel existed which could propel them the required distance. Even in February 1943, when the War Office was suffici-ently sure of its facts to issue a directive to its own Air Photo-graphic Interpreters to watch for signs that would substantiate the belief that the Germans were planning to use 'some form of long-range projectors, capable of firing on this country from the

French coast'[2] and even after intensified aerial reconnaisance
had verified the suspicion that, if there was rocket mischief in
train its brain-centre was at Peenemünde on the Baltic and its
strong right arm in the Pas de Calais, there were some in authority
—the ubiquitous and omniscient Cherwell as ever noisy in the
van[3]—who claimed that Intelligence was diving into a trap built
for it by the cunning Boche and that the whole complex of
information had been spread to mask some other and more
feasible operation.

Fortunately, fear of the unknown and realisation of the hideous
consequences that might follow upon complacency were too powerful for the sceptics. A special committee was set up under Duncan
Sandys, Parliamentary Secretary to the Ministry of Supply, and
was given as remit a wide range of investigation into the viability
of rockets, the state of their development and the practicality of
various proposals for counter-measures. The Sandys Committee
was allowed the unusual privilege of being answerable only to
the Cabinet.

Increased reconnaissance over Peenemünde turned rumour
and Intelligence hypothesis into certainty: the enemy was far-
advanced in his rocket programme; and the certainty brought
with it the no less desperate conclusion that the Allies had immediately available no suitable defensive system. The best that could
be extemporised was a mass attack against the brain-centre at
Peenemünde.

The first such attack was not launched until 17 August 1943,
but in that very week the shadow of the rocket took on even more
sinister proportions when it was discovered that the Germans were
also far-advanced in their efforts to produce 'a pilot-less aircraft'.

The struggle against rockets and flying-bombs continued for
the rest of the war, but it is that first raid in mid-August 1943
which highlights the decision taken a month earlier to admit
Wallis to the cognisance of the enemy's progress and to give to him
a free hand to develop TALLBOY, the big bomb of which he had
dreamed for so long and which appears always in his notes rich
with the enthusiasm of block capitals. On that night 597 planes
led by Group Captain J. H. Searby loosed against Peenemünde
1,937 tons of bombs. The results were satisfactory; even Goebbels
was forced to admit that 'preparations were set back by four or
even six weeks';[4] but this was not obliteration, and there still

remained to be attacked the intimidating sites in the North of France. Long before he gave the orders Harris had appreciated the impossibility of the task that he was proposing to his squadrons. He was asking for precision bombing against targets encased in seemingly invulnerable emplacements. From all his squadrons, 617 was the obvious choice for such a role, and the name of Wallis was now synonymous with the Squadron. What is more, Wallis had been preaching for years not merely the doctrine of a ten-ton bomb but of a ten-ton bomb with penetration capacity that could set up in the target an 'earthquake' syndrome.

The basis of Wallis's sermon was his 1940 paper *A Note on a Method of Attacking the Axis Powers*. (The casual implication of the description is deceptive; the 'Note' runs to sixty typed foolscap pages of text, thirty complicated tables and twenty pages of appendix.) The text of the sermon is the quotation from Thomas Hardy which Wallis used as an epigraph: 'Experience is as to INTENSITY and not as to duration'.

Even those who in 1940 had been sceptical of the force of Wallis's big-bomb theories, when they came to re-reading his paper in 1943, must have felt some sense of awe. So much of what Wallis had written in 1940, at a time when actual experience of bombing was still limited, had by 1943 been empirically justified. The trumpet of prophecy rang out most clearly in Chapter VI of the *Note* in which Wallis seemed to have already in his crystal ball the outlines of the targets that were now at last given to him as objectives.

These targets are unfortunately of the most massive nature, and are practically invulnerable to attack by existing aerial methods. They are, however, concentrated in character, and cannot be moved or dispersed.

For the destruction of such targets the technique which he had postulated in 1940 and which he began to develop with the utmost energy in July 1943 involved two departures from general practice: first, the utilisation of far larger unit sizes of bombs than had hitherto been contemplated, the increase of size being roughly proportional to the great size or mass of the target; and secondly, and by 1943 far more important but still a notion that was to Wallis *sui generis*, instead of relying upon a direct hit to destroy the target, he proposed the use of the pressure wave set up by detonation in the surrounding medium.

In 1940 Wallis had been convinced that this shock wave effect was minimal if the surrounding medium was air but that it was developed to a high degree in water and to an even greater degree in earth. The targets he now had in his sights were all earth-encased. He had also argued that in order to obtain maximum penetration and release maximum kinetic energy the bomb must be released from a great height (40,000 feet had been suggested); in 1940 it was the absence of a front-line bomber which could carry a sufficient weight of bombs to such a height that had given excuse to those who rejected his proposals. Now, in 1943, the pressurised cabin, the weight-carrying capacity of the Lancaster and the development of high-flying techniques and efficient bomb-sights had turned the whole proposal from fantasy into possibility.

However, as the project had been dismissed long since, no one, not even Wallis himself, had undertaken any considerable experiment to vindicate his penetration-bomb theory. A few weeks before Wallis had been initiated into the still small group of those with knowledge of the threat of rockets, into a meeting that was primarily devoted to considering the use of the 'bouncing bombs' against German canals and the Rothensee Ship Lift, Cochrane had inserted a parenthesis that can now be seen as significant when he suggested an investigation of the possibilities of the deep penetration bomb but, either as cover for his real intentions or because he was genuinely hopeful that the camouflet bomb could be used most effectively against targets which three years earlier Wallis had selected as notably vulnerable to this kind of attack, Cochrane had given as his possible objective the coal-mines of the Ruhr.[5] Most of those present at the meeting were agreed in their doubt that the Lancaster could bomb from a height sufficient to create a camouflet, and although Wallis had undertaken to produce details of the estimated effects of a ten-ton bomb released from 22,000 feet, the letter which came to him with the Minutes, whilst drawing his attention to several other responsibilities that devolved upon him as a result of the meeting, did not so much as mention this particular task.[6]

So that in his ready acceptance of the orders that he received on July 12 there seems to be an element of bravado, an inspired optimism that he could work out a feasible proposition for the camouflet bomb. Nor is this impression weakened by the account of his meeting the very next day with Roy Chadwick[7]—about further adaptations of the Lancaster—for it seems to have been no more than an Oriental bazaar haggle between two friendly dealers, Wallis trying to bid up the weight-carrying potential of the Lancaster against the dutifully histrionic protests of the 'plane's designer until, after extravagance had been curbed and concession accepted, they arrived at the bargain which both men had in mind before ever the auction began. The hammer came down at 20,000 lb.[8]

If the potential of the bomb was still highly speculative, Wallis's freedom to establish that potential was in happy contrast to most of his previous experience. For the rest of the war, even after bombs of this general kind had been used, experiments continued to discover the most suitable designs, the best tactical methods and the effectiveness of the bombs, against concrete, sand, earth, armour-plate; in all these experiments Wallis played a principal role and, in the sense that a penetration bomb of some kind was never abandoned, suffered comparatively few frustrations except those that are commonplace to all scientific experiment.

Progress on Tallboy was in fact remarkably fast. Scaled-down calibration trials were in train before the end of August and on 12 September Wallis had a prototype available for his inspection, but if considerable production was to be organised some materials must be shipped from the United States and, though Chadwick for his part had set about designing the adaptations to the Lancaster with alacrity, in September the Ministry of Aircraft Production issued a fiat of some significance: when Chadwick's designs were ready they were to be applied first to fourteen Lancasters of 617 Squadron. Ambitious still for his earlier bomb, Wallis resisted the decision and temporarily won his way but the signs were there to be read, the 'bouncing bomb' had had its day.

Even Wallis could not resist the logic of another decision communicated to him on 2 October 1943. The halcyon days of Tallboy were over even before the bomb had ever been dropped, not because of any recalcitrance on the part of British decision-makers but because the Germans had learnt a lesson from Searby's August raid on Peenemünde and were now preparing for their secret weapons dispersed sites and comparatively mobile launching equipment. Wallis could continue theoretical planning for a ten-ton bomb, but its production was no longer imperative and priority must be given to a scaled-down penetration bomb. The code-name Tallboy was continued for the 12,000 lb penetration bomb, but for Wallis it had lost its magic—and its block capitals.

As if he needed some private battle-ground for his war against the Axis, Wallis began to cast around for new arguments to revive the Air Force bouncing bomb and, when they were rejected, he turned to the Naval version and tried, without success, to persuade the Army that it would be effective against tanks. However, from the moment in October 1943 that Tallboy was reduced in size and importance until the end of the war, there is visible a change of tempo in Wallis's life. By the standards of ordinary men and even by the standards of ordinary men at war he was still busy, his days fully occupied and his weekends seldom given to relaxation. Still he used his rare appearances at family meals not for communication with his children but for reading papers and books. There were still to be moments of high excitement—as when Tallboy and eventually Grand Slam (the revived ten tonner) were dropped in action—but the near-maniac enthusiasm had evaporated and with it the single-mindedness.

In a book written not long after the end of the war in which I considered, among other things transatlantic, the American ideogram of Englishmen I wrote:

> Foreigners have told us that reticence is a British characteristic, and although reticence appears to be the antithesis of those qualities of imperialism, intellectual as well as political, that have been outstanding in British history, we believe the foreigners and let them hold to their myths.[9]

My own experience in the year that followed VE Day when I had access to War Office publicity files for the whole of the war should have told me that what I wrote of Britain at peace was a half-lie, for Britain at war and, certainly from Dunkirk on, the British Government collectively and the three services independently made strenuous efforts to reconcile the two irreconcilable needs: to inform allies and neutrals of the huge endeavours of Britain without revealing to the enemy the dangerously useful *minutiae* that were the foundations of so many of those en-

deavours. On some issues the efforts of the information organisa-
tions were either too feeble or else fell upon disbelieving ears.
But service eagerness to tell a tale if that tale was to our credit
was unquenchable in the midst of war and so it was that within
weeks of the successful attack on Möhne and Eder the P.R.
Section at the Air Ministry was casting about for means of bringing to the American public news of this magnificent achievement
in which British technical genius and the superlative skill and
bravery of British bomber-crews had combined to strike a formidable blow at German industrial might and German morale.

It was a difficult problem that faced the publicists. The
Germans had a 'bouncing bomb' in their possession—this much
was known—but whether they had all its secrets was still unsure.
Both American and Russian military experts were, during the
autumn of 1943, made privy to the principles upon which Wallis
had founded his bomb, but this was something quite different
from revealing them to a wider public in America or at home, for
such revelation would be tantamount to publication to the enemy.

It was decided that Gibson would be sent on a lecture tour in
the United States, and then the P.R. Section announced that the
Americans had been persuaded to make a film about the Dams
Raid. P.R. had not appreciated the perversion of truth into
fantasy that was inherent both in the limiting rubrics that were
added to the permission to make a film (Wallis's identity must not
be revealed, nor the true nature of the bomb) and in the custom
of American movie-construction. The draft script was completed
in a remarkably short time, perhaps because it was little more
than an anthology of Hollywood clichés. By way of the British
Embassy in Washington, the Air Ministry and the Security
Branch of the Ministry of Aircraft Production, this draft script
reached Wallis in the first week of November and on Guy Fawkes
Day he exploded in a letter to David Pye:

I have asked Wing Commander Arnold to show the script to
you, as perhaps I am so intimately connected with the whole
undertakings that my feelings in the matter may be misleading
me in the opinion I have formed.

I appear in the film under a false name and under such a
caricature that I do not think any exception can be taken to
the matter on personal grounds, but what I do feel is that the

whole presentation forms a disgraceful travesty of the work of distinguished English Scientists in general, and the presentiment [sic] of a gaga professor as representative of a large body of scientists must be repulsive to all of us, and probably harmful to the reputation of technicians in this country. On these grounds I feel most strongly that some action should be taken in high quarters to cancel the permission that has been given by the British Air Attaché in Washington, and at least to insist upon the scientific side of the work having some adequate though possibly quite erroneous background.[10]

Whether Wallis's objections to the script were quite so impersonal as he pretended and whatever Pye's earlier attitude to the Dams project, Pye's response to this letter was immediate and active. As enthusiastic for the good reputation of British science as was Wallis and more competent in the devious ways of governments he eschewed a frontal attack on the film and launched instead a series of delays by questioning details in the script. For almost a year the correspondence continued; it was never decisively concluded, but that particular film was never made.

In the last two years of the war, though he worked with undiminished zeal at the task that was his by right of professional training, Wallis made comparatively few sorties into those areas that belonged customarily to the planners of military and economic warfare, and accepted with unusual meekness the decisions of those who had the major responsibility for making military decisions, even when their decisions reduced the effectiveness of his own genius as designer and inventor.

In 1944 the scaled-down 12,000 lb penetration-bomb proved itself a weapon of formidable utility in the hands of 617 Squadron, now under the command of Wing Commander Leonard Cheshire. The first were dropped on the Saumur railway tunnel only a few days after the invasion of Normandy; all but one bomb found the target and of these one in particular bored its way through eighty feet of earth, exploded in the tunnel and cascaded onto the railway line almost 10,000 tons of earth. A Panzer division on its way north by rail from Bordeaux to attack the Allied bridgehead had to be diverted and by the time that the Germans had the railway working again the Allied forward troops were close to Saumur.

The Big Bombs

A week later, 617 Squadron was in action again with Tallboys, using them this time to cause havoc by water on 14 June at Le Havre, and 15 June at Boulogne, and using them to such effect that the German E-boat force, which had been sniping with considerable diligence at Allied follow-up convoys, was decimated and was never again a danger to the supply lines of the invasion.

On the morning of 13 June 1944 the fears that had first caused the British Government to allow Wallis an opportunity to go ahead with Tallboy became reality when at a quarter past four the first flying bomb landed at Swanscombe in Kent. Six minutes later another bomb fell at Cuckfield in Sussex and another reached London, destroying the Grove Road railway bridge in Bethnal Green, killing six people and seriously injuring nine. The Chiefs of Staff were now in a quandary. Forty-two launching sites had been identified in the Pas de Calais and close to the Somme but it was estimated that it would require no less than 3,000 heavy bomber sorties to wipe them out, and such a diversion of strength from the support of the invasion forces in Normandy was unthinkable. What could not be changed must be ignored: 'The Chiefs of Staff are not unduly worried about Crossbow'[11]— so the Chief Intelligence Officer, Allied Expeditionary Air Force, to his superior, Air Chief Marshal Trafford Leigh-Mallory. But within days almost 150 flying bombs had crossed the English coast and half that number had fallen on the capital. What could no longer be ignored had to be countered, and although Eisenhower's instruction that bombing attacks be given priority 'over everything else except the urgent requirements of the battle'[12] shifted the emphasis only slightly from the previous decision of the Chiefs of Staff, that shift was sufficient to permit the use against V.1 launching sites of some bomber units, both British and American—among them, for the first time on 19 June, 617 Squadron armed with Tallboys. Despite indifferent weather the Squadron made successful attacks against sites at Watten, Wizernes, Rilly la Montagne and the rocket-stores at Siracourt and Creil. On each occasion the bomb-aiming was magnificently accurate and, even though the Lancasters had not been able to fly at the optimum height envisaged by Wallis, his penetration bombing thesis was amply justified. Watten was so shattered that the Germans were forced to abandon the site; the 10,000 ton dome on top of the tunnels at Wizernes was hurled from its foundations and the tunnels reduced to rubble; at Creil and Rilly la Montagne the underground shelters had collapsed; at Siracourt a Tallboy pierced a sixteen-foot concrete roof, and two of the four lower walls were reduced to rubble.[13]

In this particular sequence of raids perhaps the most important was on 5 July. The objective Marquise-Mimoyesque, one of the first sites identified by Medmenham as a rocket-launching site, was in fact something even more sinister: a vast emplacement for a projected long-range gun installation which was to house, in three shafts sunk deep into the hillside, 50 barrels each 400 feet long designed to spew up each day 600 tons of explosive into the centre of London. One Tallboy tore off part of the twenty-foot concrete roof of one shaft, another caused the total collapse of the second shaft and so disturbed the third as to make it unusable. 300 workers sheltering 500 feet below the surface were entombed by the bombs. Although it was not this disaster alone which persuaded the Germans to abandon what was to have been the V.3—subsequent experiment proved the projectile unstable in flight—Marquise-Mimoyesque merits a place among the battle-honours of 617 Squadron and should rank high on the list of Wallis's achievements.

Four months later, Wallis and Tait (Cheshire's successor) with 617 Squadron and Tallboy wrought a victory even more sensational—and Wallis did not so much as note it in his diary.

The 42,000-ton battleship *Tirpitz* was for most of the war the largest capital ship in Western waters. Armed powerfully with eight 15-inch guns, twelve 5·9-inch, eighteen 4·1-inch, sixteen 37-millimetre and fifty 20-millimetre machine guns and eighty-four anti-aircraft guns, she was also formidably armoured with side-plates up to fifteen inches thick and—most important to this story—an eight-inch thick deck shielding her magazines and engine rooms and, covering the upper deck, armour plate of thickness sufficient to detonate bombs that might otherwise have exploded inside the ship.

As part of the preparation for resisting what Hitler believed to be an imminent invasion of Norway, *Tirpitz* had been stationed in Northern waters since January 1942. She put to sea only twice, but the presence of an enemy capital ship in a Norwegian harbour added a nightmarish unknown quantity to the careful calculations of Allied leaders. Churchill made no secret of his fears;

within days of *Tirpitz* arriving at Trondheim he was writing to the Chiefs of Staff:

> The destruction or even the crippling of this ship is the greatest event at sea at the present time. No other target is comparable to it.[14]

Most immediate was the threat which *Tirpitz* presented to convoys bound for Russia. Once, in March 1942, she put to sea against a convoy, sank a straggling merchantman, was almost caught by the British Home Fleet, but sailed back to Narvik and thence to Trondheim. This unpretentious exploit had enlarged the nightmare for the Allies, and both Churchill and Stalin began to use dramatic language as if to shout down their own fears ('We are resolved to fight our way through to you,' wrote Churchill in reply to a desperate plea from Stalin. 'On account of the *Tirpitz* . . . the passage of every convoy has become a serious fleet operation') and, just as earlier the existence of *Tirpitz* had weakened the Pacific Fleet, by denying to it reinforcements from the West, so now it forced a reduction of protection for Atlantic convoys.

In June 1942 Russia was facing a new German offensive that might open up to the enemy the road to Moscow, to the Ukraine and to the Caucasus. Supplies from the West were more vital than ever and 200,000 tons were loaded in the merchantmen of Convoy PQ17 which sailed from Iceland on 27 June. Covering forces from both the Royal and United States Navies included two battleships, an aircraft carrier and seven cruisers. On 5 July *Tirpitz*, with the battle-cruisers, *Hipper*, *Scheer* and *Lützow* sailed from Norway. The advent of these heavy ships so bemused the Allies that the covering vessels were ordered back to their home ports and the merchantmen instructed to disperse and make their way as best they could to Archangel. The German ships hurried back to Norway; it was all somewhat reminiscent of the old story about the man who met a bear and both ran away. But *Tirpitz* and her consorts won the day without firing a shot. Shore-based aircraft and U-boats sank twenty-one ships and only 70,000 tons of supplies reached Russia.[15] By her very existence *Tirpitz* had won for the Germans their most important naval victory of the War, and what *Tirpitz* had achieved once she could repeat at will.

In fact German naval thinking had also been disrupted by this adventure. *Tirpitz* had come close to disaster from the torpedoes of a Russian submarine, and the Germans shivered whenever they considered what might have happened had she come within range of the guns of H.M.S. *Duke of York* or U.S.S. *Washington*. It was considered no longer possible to implement Raeder's conviction that all forces available should be used without reserve to disrupt supply routes to Russia. The alternative and far more economical course was to defeat the Allies by menacing their lines of communication.

In the months after the PQ17 holocaust almost the whole of the submarine force available to the Allies, large numbers of destroyers, the capital ships of the Home Fleet and sizeable units from the Fleet Air Arm and the Royal Air Force were dedicated to the task of guarding convoys against possible attack by *Tirpitz* and her companions. The Norwegian Resistance movement, the Royal Navy using manned 'chariot-torpedoes', and submarines from three Allied navies all tried unsuccessfully to eradicate the threat presented by her existence. She survived conventional bomber attacks, protected always by her heavy anti-aircraft fire-power, her ability to make smoke, her massive armour-plated deck structure, by the enveloping mass of the mountains around her fjord fastness, and by the comparatively minuscular size of target which she presented to attacking 'planes. The failure of all these attempts contributed largely to the sensational decision, taken in April 1943, to abandon the Arctic supply route for the summer months of that year. At just the moment when the Russians seemed about to destroy the German armies in the East, and again without firing a shot, *Tirpitz* had won a battle of enormous importance.

Then, in September 1943, *Tirpitz* put to sea once more, and for the first and only time in her career, fired her full complement of eight 15-inch guns. It was a farcical episode: an overblown Goliath battering at a tiny David—the minute Norwegian garrison at Spitzbergen. At last, however, in the week when *Tirpitz* returned to Altenfjord from her glorious victory at Spitzbergen, the Royal Navy succeeded in an attempt to incapacitate the ship. Two midget submarines out of a force of six penetrated the defences of the fjord and detonated mines against the hull of the ship. The damage caused was extensive: one of the ship's turbines was lifted from its bed, a gun-turret was jammed and all the range-finders, the starboard propeller-shaft and armament-control gear put out of service. Now, once *Scharnhorst* was presented as a Christmas box to the Allies by Admiral Fraser, the only major threat to the Arctic route could be measured in terms of the capacity of the enemy to repair *Tirpitz*; it was essential that she be given the *coup de grâce*. The Fleet Air Arm, operating from carriers, registered several hits without once piercing the lower armoured deck.

In the late summer of 1944 when Tallboy had proved herself against the flying bomb emplacements, the E-boat pens and against the Dortmund–Ems canal, it was decided that at last we had a bomb that could penetrate to the heart of a ship. 617 Squadron were the specialists in the use of Wallis's bombs and in precision bombing. For the attack on *Tirpitz* Bomber Command detailed in addition No. 9 Squadron, another unit equipped with specially adapted Lancasters. But the Altenfjord was out of range of heavily-laden Lancasters flying from British bases. Accordingly the two Squadrons flew to Russia, refuelled and bombed-up, and on 15 September took off from Yagodnik to make a daylight attack on *Tirpitz*. They arrived over the target area just a few minutes too late, for the Germans had made day into night with a most effective smoke-screen. Nevertheless the Lancasters bombed through the smoke and then flew on back to Britain, hoping but not knowing if any Tallboy had found the mark.

In fact one bomb had struck the ship's bows and had caused such havoc as made it virtually impossible that she could ever again be seaworthy. Still the extent of the devastation was unknown to British Intelligence and, when air reconnaissance reported *Tirpitz* fled from Altenfjord, the old nightmare revived of a daring enemy sortie. The Germans had laboriously towed the *Tirpitz* to Tromsö, planning to moor her in shallow waters for use as a fort against Allied land forces engaged in liberating Norway. There she was identified by a member of the Norwegian Resistance who radioed her position to his contacts in Britain. 617 Squadron had just proved the value of Tallboy once more by shattering the embankment of the Dortmund–Ems Canal so that this important link in German communications was never again available to the enemy during the war, but the move to Tromsö brought *Tirpitz* just within range of Lancasters providing they were once more adapted. 617 Squadron and their colleagues of

9 Squadron were alerted; Rolls-Royce Merlin 24 engines were taken from other 'planes in Bomber Command, armour-plating was stripped from the bombers of the two squadrons, the mid-upper gun-turrets were removed and overload petrol-tanks originally designed for Wellingtons were retrieved from dumps all over the Command and installed in the Lancasters. All this was completed in less than a week, and the squadrons were ordered to Lossiemouth, the bomber-base closest to Tromsö, to await good weather. An attempt to destroy *Tirpitz* for ever was made on 28 October 1944 but was thwarted by low cloud and the 'planes returned to Lossiemouth.

617 Squadron could not be kept idle in the North of Scotland. There was work to do in support of the Allied advance towards Germany and so they came south and set off once more against the kind of target that had made their fame. The Americans were held up in the Belfort Gap but there was every chance that they would break out soon and attempt to cross the Rhine. At that moment, it was feared, the Germans would open the flood-gates on the Krebs Dam. Best therefore to do it for them before Allied troops were in the flood area. But with what? This would have been an ideal target for Wallis's bouncing-bomb, but the Lancasters of 617 Squadron had long since been so altered as to make a return to this method impossible. Conventional bombs were useless against a dam and the chances of a hit slight with a Tallboy dropped, as a Tallboy should be dropped, from high altitude. Wallis was consulted and it was decided to send in 617 Squadron once more in a low-flying attack but with Tallboys armed with delay-fuses. The Krebs Dam went the way of Möhne and Eder and within a day the level of the water in the Rhine had fallen so low that river barges far into Switzerland were left grounded on the mud.[16]

And so, for 617 Squadron, at the end of the first week of November, back to Lossiemouth. On 13 November 1944 the squadron took off for Tromsö.

The Germans had not had time to reconstruct at Tromsö the elaborate smoke-making machinery that had shielded *Tirpitz* so successfully at the Altenfjord and, at 14,000 feet, the bombers had a clear view of their target. The first bomb to hit struck almost amidships and a second abaft the main gun-turret. The bombs smashed the lower armoured deck and opened a gap between the side of the ship and the deck. Fires were started and a magazine exploded. Twenty minutes after the first hit there was an enormous explosion which tore a hole 120 feet long in the port side from deck to keel; *Tirpitz* turned turtle, rolled through 140 degrees and her superstructure became embedded in the sea-bottom.[17] 1,200 Germans were entombed in the ship. The *Tirpitz*, the most powerful unit in Hitler's navy, had for almost four years won victory after victory by the very fact of her existence. In her last hours not even the fighters at Bardufors came to her assistance and she was destroyed by the heroic efforts of the crews of two tiny submarines and of two RAF squadrons nobly assisted by the Norwegian Resistance. But ultimately her destruction can be set to the account of the ingenuity of Barnes Wallis.

As the strength of the German air defences waned so did Allied bombers range ever more freely and strike ever more ferociously at the bastions from which the enemy might launch his last desperate counter-attacks. In this phase of the war Wallis's Tall-boys were notably effective for they gave to Bomber Command the possibility of destroying comparatively small but heavily fortified targets such as viaducts and bridges which were essential links in Germany's communications system.

Conscious though he was of his own identification with 617 Squadron and proud though he remained of the men, and of the bombs that he had designed, the successes of 617 and the consistency with which Tallboy hurled aside concrete and shattered bridges and viaducts was so regular as to carry with it the quality of the inevitable. Even when Grand Slam was finally brought into service it was an anti-climax for Wallis. This was in effect the ten-ton bomb as it had been conceived from the beginning and the successful conclusion of a programme of persuasion that had lasted as long as the war. When it was dropped for the first time, on 14 March 1945, inevitably by 617 Squadron (now under the command of Wing Commander J. E. Fauquier) it was fantastically successful. One ten-ton bomb demolished seven spans of the double concrete viaduct at Bielefeld.

By this time the Germans had no effective answer to the enormous destructive power loosed against them by the Allies and in a last flurry of activity, using both Tallboys and Grand Slams, Wallis's agents, 617 Squadron, contributed far more than one squadron's share to the disruption of communications which, in the last three months of the war in Europe, brought German war production virtually to a standstill.

In time of war even victories offer few satisfactions to the men who achieve them. But for the remote architect of triumph such as Wallis, there are frustrations beyond those common to the fighting man—for the proof of his success he can grasp only through his intellect; rarely, if ever, can he see it and never know it. Thus, in the moment of his most sensational achievement, the successful attack against the Dams, though Wallis had pored over the intelligence reports and aerial photographs, he was inevitably deprived in that he could not at once satisfy his scientist's curiosity and pride by going out to Germany there to sense upon the ground the effectiveness of his years of argument, experiment and effort. Although Wallis was elated by the courtesies accorded him when he made a one-day excursion to Northern France on 3 April 1945, his inspection of the damage caused by his big bombs was noticeably casual and considerably impeded by appalling weather and by the onset of a bad cold, but the Dams Raid was still to him the high moment of his war. Therefore, as the front-line troops of the Allies approached the Möhne he plagued the Air Ministry to send him to Germany. On Friday 22 April 1945, when sporadic fighting was still continuing in the Ruhr, Wallis was flown out from Hendon. Bomber Command had even taken the trouble to seek out for the occasion a navigator who was a survivor of the Raid.

On the way to Paderborn the 'plane circled low over the Möhne and, perhaps for the first time, Wallis knew what it was that he had done and felt the full force of the demands he had made upon 617 Squadron. But at Paderborn the courtesies were swept aside by the confusions that came with invasion. However, while he was waiting for the British Town Major to produce a car, Wallis had an opportunity—the first of his life—to see at close quarters a defeated enemy. Only weeks before Paderborn had been devastated in one air raid that lasted only twenty minutes and there was left standing in the town but one undamaged building; the Town Hall. Dead Germans were still buried in the ruins of the town and Wallis noted in his diary that there was 'A good old stink'.

Eventually a car was found for Wallis, but at Gütersloh he discovered similar confusion and similar horror. Here the Town

The Big Bombs

Major was an American; he knew nothing at all about this middle-aged British civilian wearing a dirty raincoat who claimed that he was the true conqueror of the region. Although the Town Major's efforts to contact SHAEF Advanced Headquarters came to nothing, he exercised the conventional hospitality of his countrymen and, because in comparison to Paderborn, Gütersloh was a town that still possessed some amenities, he was able to find for Wallis a billet in a hotel. The hot and cold system still worked, but there was no bedding for it had all been removed by the retreating Germans, by advancing Allies or by looters. After dinner with the Town Major a sleeping bag was found for Wallis and he went to bed, but not to sleep, for all through the night the convoys rolled past that carried Allied Forces forward to the last battle. Wallis listened to them almost contentedly; at last he was in a war.

At nine the next morning the Town Major called for him to take him to breakfast at his own billet. Once again there was no car that could be placed entirely at Wallis's disposal; the weather was appalling, and all day Wallis was aware of an imminent migraine which hit him with devastating effect during dinner and did not leave him even after a dose of extra-strong pills and a night's sleep. However, when at last his car arrived at 8.30 a.m. on 22 April his curiosity overcame his sickness and he set off for Bielefeld. For two hours in bitter winds and icy rain he inspected the crumbling masonry of the viaduct. His elation at the 'marvellous bombing' was considerably reduced on the way to Möhne along roads lined with predatory gangs of Poles, Russians, French and Belgians released from prisons or slave labour camps. Most of them, he noted, were pushing anything that they could find that moved on wheels, and loaded onto these perambulators, soap-box carts, and milkman's drays, were piles of food, clothes, books and furniture. From time to time he stopped the car so that he could speak with Allied soldiers or surly German civilians and thus, to the evidence of his own eyes, were added tales of pillage, rape and murder. This was not war as he had understood it with his intellect; this was not his prized destruction of the sources of power, industrial and military might. It was certainly not war as he had always imagined it with that part of his mind which loved uniforms, discipline and personal courage. It was not Tennyson but Goya. By the time he reached Möhne all elation had evaporated and the migraine had returned in full spate. With two RAF companions he inspected the Dam and was satisfied, but the satisfaction was sadly anti-climatic. Dutifully he set off to question the residents in the little Gasthof above the Dam, but found it boarded up. Sensing that he was being watched from inside, he banged on the door, a portion of the barricade was removed and a villainous-looking middle-aged woman glowered at him. In his halting German he tried to discover the reasons for the defence system, and was told that a gang of Poles and Russians had rampaged through the area, looting and raping. His reply was typical of the man: 'But we are just simple Englishmen', and then his technical curiosity overcame his distaste for all that he had seen and heard. 'On the night of the great raid how many bombs had hit the Dam?' The answer was immediate and unequivocal: 'Two.'

He had had all the experience he could take, and although his tour of inspection continued, it was not until three days later that his interest rose again to anything like its habitual level. By that time he was in Cologne and, looking at the damage to the Cathedral, he commented:

> It is very noticeable that a pure Gothic building will withstand modern bombing well—it is, of course an artificial structure of members being in compression, and as we found in the experiments how to determine the charge required to destroy the piers of Bielefeld viaduct, being heavily loaded, are therefore resistant to shock.[18]

Even so he was more excited by the fine mosaic floor and by the lovely figures decorating the shafts of the main pillars in the nave than by any engineering circumstances, and more delighted by the fact that the beauties of Cologne Cathedral were substantially intact than he had been by any demonstration of his own technical perspicacity.

The penultimate entry in his diary is typical:

> Much time was wasted here by the irrepressible instincts of our two senior Air Officers to loot—they descended into the deepest cellars . . . and after some two hours succeeded in securing 6 $\frac{1}{2}$-bottles of bad unnamed red wine. It was not amusing to

see them haring off at each new scent as rumours arrived of wine here and wine there.

This was a man who for all his vast contribution to victory and despite experience in two wars could not shake off his censorious custom, a man who could not understand or would not accept the human fallibility of men at war.

Back home and for the moment Wallis had had enough of looking back. Now his eyes were fixed firmly upon the future. On 8 May 1945, the day which for so many men and women was a day set apart from history, a day for memories, for jubilation and thanksgiving, Wallis made only one entry in his diary: 'Work on supersonics'. Three months later when the Americans unleashed against Hiroshima a bomb that made even Grand Slam seem like an Agincourt arrow Wallis was on holiday and made no comment either in his diary or in letters. A week later on VJ Day the diary entry was almost exactly as on VE Day: 'Supersonic work'.

15 *Wild Goose*

Barnes Wallis had contributed to the eventual victory on a scale that sets him apart from all but a very few. His score-sheet comes close to being fantastic. A sequence of devastating blows at the enemy's economic potential; the elimination of the major capital ship in the German Navy; substantial counter-thrusts against the last desperate assaults aimed at Britain in the terrifying shapes of V.1, V.2 and V.3; telling ventures in support of the forces engaged in liberating Europe; all this and more can be ascribed to the sequence of bombs devised by Wallis. His pre-war Wellington droned its way over enemy-held territory for most of the war and already by 1942 was the only aircraft with Bomber Command that had been in service at the beginning of the war. More Wellingtons were produced than any other British bomber and their diversity of operational role was extraordinary; Wellingtons served in every theatre of war and with every flying command except Fighter. Its early susceptibility to beam attack from above when used in daylight was no fault of the designer and the magnificent durability of the Wellington was attributable entirely to Wallis and his geodetic construction. The lives of innumerable Air Force crews had been saved by a 'plane that could fly, so it seemed, so long as it still had an engine.

The importance of this work was always recognised by the men who used the weapons he gave them. Wellingtons, the beloved 'Wimpys' of Bomber Command, took on mythic qualities for the men who flew them. The squadron chosen to drop Wallis's bombs came to regard him as one of themselves. Despite his reputation for austerity this élite group was consistently proud of its own mad 'Prof.' and fully alive to his rare sanity. He in his turn abandoned, if only for them, his censoriousness and does not appear to have noticed the hard-drinking, the wenching

300

and the bawdiness which are the unfailing customs for today of young men who risk death on every tomorrow. It was his belief in the closeness of his relationship with the young men who had risked and often given all to prove his theses that led eventually to what he himself was to describe as the greatest of all his achievements, the creation of the Royal Air Force Foundation. And the very fact that he did see himself—as in a sense the men of 617 Squadron saw him—as belonging to the squadron was an enlargement of his life-long capacity for being more easily contented by self-identification with an institution than by any association with individuals.

The acceptance that he won from 617 Squadron delighted him above all because these were young men. So, too, in comparison with those who barred his way, were the senior officers in a young man's service (Cochrane, for example, was only forty-eight at the time of the dam-busting raids) and they too came to add affection for the man to the respect which they showed for his ideas. Cochrane always, Tedder when he was in the right place so to do, and after the Dams Raid, even the habitually gruff Harris accepted Wallis as one of themselves. Portal wrote for all the Royal Air Force when at the end of the war he sent him a holograph note

> No small part of the credit for what the R.A.F. has been able to do goes to you . . . Thank you for all your efforts on our behalf.[1]

During the war, and despite the persistent antagonism of Cherwell and the ambivalent attitude of some others, Wallis had won the admiration which he coveted from his peers among scientists. Merton looked upon him as 'the paramount engineering genuis of the age'. Tizard, always his friend even when he felt bound to thwart him, spoke often and wrote sometimes in terms that were adulatory, for example, after the Dams Raid, 'I have no hesitation in saying that yours is the finest technical achievement of the war.'[2] Blackett had given to Wallis his unqualified support.

In 1945 he was made a Fellow of the Royal Society, the first engineer to be so honoured in modern times, and was given the Ewing Medal. These high honours provided for Wallis the comforting excuse that he needed when it became clear that he was to be passed over once more even in the torrent of public recognition that poured out at the moment of victory. The affection of air crews and Air Force commanders and the generosity of scientists had not touched those who had the ultimate authority for the Honours List. Wallis blamed it all on Vickers. In a letter to Trevor Westbrook he wrote:

> It was very nice of you to expect to see a knighthood for me, but I have been told on very high authority that this was twice turned down by Sir Charles Craven and until some change of policy is adopted by our directors I do not think that you will find that any technical official will be permitted to receive a knighthood until the whole hierarchy of directors has been suitably rewarded . . . Now that I have got the F.R.S. I do not really care what happens, but I would not change that for a dukedom and it is the only scientific distinction in the world which is really worth having and which cannot be bought either by fear or favour.[3]

He had forgotten or chose to ignore the fact that two years earlier he had set the blame for the rejection of Harris's recommendation at the feet of Stafford Cripps. Wallis's exclusion from all national honours did owe something to the petty policy of the Vickers Board; but a man may be known as much by the enemies as by the friends he keeps, and Wallis's enemies were many. Cherwell was implacable and Churchill was persistently loyal to his scientific adviser; in his history of the war, although he mentions every one of the Wallis bombs and describes their use in some detail he contrives to do so without once using Wallis's name. Attlee and Cripps remembered the triumph of the Capitalist *R.100* over the Socialist *R.101*, and Attlee, in particular, had not forgotten the distaste that he and his Labour colleagues had for Vickers, 'the merchants of death'. Harris was for Wallis, but Harris had even more enemies in high places than Wallis. Tizard, Merton and Blackett concentrated their attention on having Wallis elected to the Royal Society.

Wallis maintained his protest that he was satisfied by the tributes of his peers and wanted no 'more spectacular political recognition', and held to it with ever increasing acerbity for the next twenty years. He convinced himself more easily than he convinced his friends, for he was undoubtedly and understandably disappointed. Nevertheless, bitter though it was, this exclusion of Wallis from the inner circle of smugness had some beneficial consequences. It emphasised his independence, even from the full responsibility of unquestioning loyalty to Vickers, and, now that he was freed from the inevitable pressures of war-time, also set him free from the shackles of success which swept most others in Government and in the industry itself into excited and excitable plans for the post-war expansion of the aircraft industry.

There were other and more private and emotional reasons for his feeling that the end of the war brought with it a new and this time a comfortable isolation from involvement and an enhanced sense of freedom to work at those tasks which he chose for himself. His children were approaching adulthood, not yet beyond the need for care or expense but the older of them close to an age which Wallis found more interesting and more amenable than childhood. In this, not unlike many a man who has achieved much in his professional life, he had hopes that one at least among his children would follow him as an engineer. In May 1945 he tried to persuade Barnes Junior to go to Barrow. Instead, Barnes Junior went up to Cambridge and after a year doing more or less what his father wished him to do changed from reading for the Engineering Tripos to his real love, Mathematics. Wallis accepted the disappointment with good grace, and though he never went so far as to admit to his son that he had courted Molly in lyrical mathematics, did more than he need have done—and more than student-sons or their university mentors like to accept—by bombarding the boy's tutors with questions and advice.

The death of Dr Charles Wallis in January 1945 relieved him of a duty that he had carried willingly enough for almost three decades.

Freed from the hysterical pressures of war-time working conditions; from bustling here and rushing there; from the drab endlessness of committee meetings; from the exhaustion of the mental juggling required so that several and diverse projects could be held in being at the same time; from the uncertainty and fear caused by air raids and buzz-bombs; and freed too, it must be accepted, from the continual presence of children,

Wallis was once more at liberty to enjoy the relationship which he found most comfortable: he was alone with Molly. There was so much that they had been forced to sacrifice during the years of war; so much that they had abandoned after the idyllic days at Howden. Now, once more, they read aloud to each other. They worked together in the garden and he made ingenious improvements in the house. Again, as at Howden, he shared with her his 'thinking times', waking her often at six in the morning, or even earlier, to tell her of some new idea that had come to his mind.

In their years at Effingham, Wallis had come to identify his Christianity not merely with ethics but with regular attendance at the village church. Here his unsophisticated, unquestioning theology came into consonance with his zest for belonging to an identifiable unit. As ever eager to serve even in the most humble capacity where his enthusiasm was engaged, he had acted as Secretary of the Parochial Council. There are in existence minutes written by him and embellished with drawings of airships and aeroplanes which seem to justify his opinion that he would have exchanged, without regret, his life in the twentieth century for existence as a monk illustrating manuscripts. Now, as soon as the war was over, Wallis could return to church-going and church work.

So eager was he to avoid any renewal of commitment to authority, be it governmental or commercial, that he received with eagerness and the utmost seriousness a suggestion from Tizard—made already before the war was won[4]—that he should consider a professorship. In his reply to Tizard, Wallis enlarged on his pleasure in lecturing and showed himself well aware of his own ability as a teacher. The stipend of a professor would be insufficient to meet Wallis's many responsibilities and at face value would represent a substantial reduction in his earnings, but, as Tizard pointed out, few professors in the applied sciences lived on their university salaries and some, of whom Wallis would undoubtedly be one, more than doubled their income by accepting consultancies. For several years Wallis continued to look somewhat wistfully towards the academic life. But that dream faded, driven into twilight by practicalities and the bright sun of new, exciting ideas.

In 1945 there were reasons, more potent than reaction after war-time frenzy, why Wallis might have been tempted to retire

Above: Swallow-model; sub-sonic altitude, transparent fuselage. *Left:* Barnes Wallis with a working model of the projected airliner derived from *Swallow*

Exterior of White Hill House, Effingham, Surrey

Interior of White Hill House

had he not been obsessed with his consideration of a novel approach to design. Change at Weybridge and in the overall control and atmosphere of Vickers served to isolate him from his colleagues. R. K. Pierson, another great designer who had not been given his due reward, was retired and his place as Chief Designer taken by a man who had once been a very junior member of Wallis's team. There were similar changes at board level and it seemed likely that Vickers would concentrate their aircraft production capacity on the Viking and its successor, the Viceroy (later, in deference to the disappearance of the Raj, renamed Viscount). These were not the 'planes that Wallis wanted to develop.

However, at the moment of Pierson's retirement Sir Hew Kilner, the new Chairman of Vickers, offered to Wallis a position as Special Director and head of an independent Research Department. It was an anomalous role; there were no terms of reference laid down, nor was there set out with any clarity the relationship between Wallis and his colleagues at Weybridge, but in the looseness of the arrangement Wallis saw his advantage. He could undertake any work which interested him and need not outline his objectives.

And the work which interested him was the development of variable geometric designs, his objective the design of a wing-controlled aerodyne.

The rest of the aircraft world set off in search of higher speeds, longer range and greater pay-load by designing more powerful engines and more stress-resistant frames. Wallis had other ideas. The advisability of securing speed, range and pay-load he recognised, but he was eager to rethink the accepted principles of flight, and in the process of rethinking he groped back over his whole experience as marine engineer, airship builder, aeroplane designer and bomb constructor. From this rethinking came variable wing-span—a mathematical theory not an invention— but a theory which Wallis the mathematician could pass on to Wallis the engineer and Wallis the designer.

Over forty years, great advances had been made in the theory and practice of the stability and control of aeroplanes, but already the hand of convention was upon aeroplane design. The pioneers had flown on a chair set within the open framework of their craft, their flying-machines made stable by an auxiliary aerofoil placed either before or behind the primary organ of flight: the wing. Their 'planes approached the two-dimensional. Then, as aviators and their passengers demanded protection from the elements, the 'plane became more and more enclosed, more and more three-dimensional.

The history of successful aviation is in terms of world history so short that it can be contained in the memory of a living man. (It is all in the memory of Barnes Wallis.) It is no longer easy to accept the notion that what one might call the 'mediaeval' period of aviation lasted almost to the Second World War. In superficial profile the Hawker fighters built in 1935 were much more akin to the fighters of the First World War than to their successors, the Spitfires and the Hurricanes. But, because this mediaeval period ended with seven years of war when scientists had no time for theoretical research that could not be turned to immediate military advantage, aeronautical engineers gave little thought to what they had done to 'planes by making them into the aerodynamic equivalent of a solid.

As Wallis looked out over the whole range of aircraft designing and set it against the background of his own experience, certain questions and doubts entered his thinking. There was, for example, uncertainty about the necessity for a tail. Even at subsonic speeds the increase in tail volume compelled by multiple engine installations added something between three and five per cent to the all-up weight of the complete aeroplane and as much as twenty per cent to the total profile drag of the aircraft. Could this inefficiency be removed? Was the seeming indispensability of the tail mere convention driven ever further into the convictions of designers by the circumstance that the mathematics of stability and control which most aeronautical engineers used went no further than reducing the generalisations of rigid dynamics to the particular anatomy of the conventional aeroplane? Were aeronautical engineers the victims of their own sophistry, basing their conclusions on evidence that had been designed solely for the purpose of supporting those conclusions?

There was also in his mind some doubt about the practice of lateral control by means of ailerons. This brilliant notion, a development of the Wright Brothers' wing-warping, was first used by Santos-Dumont in 1906, then by Blériot, and by Glenn Curtiss in 1908 on the 'plane *Red Wing*, built in the United

States for the Aerial Experiment Association. Since then it had been a basic control on all 'planes, but as speeds soared so did the aileron type of control become increasingly uncertain. Could it be abolished?

Soon for Wallis the various questions began to resolve themselves into an answer. In the problem lay the solution. From the beginning airship designers had been working with solid bodies in flight. They had had to contend with pitching and yawing and consequent effects on stability and control. While hopes for the airship were high the Aeronautical Research Committee had paid much attention to the problems of three-dimensional flow over elongated bodies, but the hideous awakening from the airship dream and the concurrent fulfilment of the aeroplane had persuaded most experts to thrust airship research into the dark cellars of libraries.

Yet in aerodynamic quality the modern 'plane was close to the discarded airship. Wallis was rare in that he had come to aeroplane designing after years spent contending with the enormous difficulties of controlling airships. As he now realised, those very difficulties formed the basis of the solution he now sought. As soon as he was given his head—and his Research Department—Wallis began a series of design studies. Almost a year later, in the early autumn of 1946, he completed a monumental paper, *The Application of the Aerodynamic Properties of Three Dimensional Bodies to the Stabilisation and Control of Aerodynes*.

Few scientists and no engineers have equalled Wallis for skill in the composition of technical papers, and in the corpus of his work not even his great war-time compositions had the didactic force of this, the first-fruit of peace, which set out to demonstrate how, at one stroke, he could abolish both tail and aileron, reduce profile drag and all-up weight and give to aircraft the desirable but seemingly incompatible properties of high fuel-carrying capacity, great speed and long range.

On close inspection Wallis the writer, like Wallis the lecturer and Wallis the conversationalist, could be guilty of using his own ability to disguise the fact that his premises were not always as sure as by bland assertion he made them appear to be. Thus in *The Application of Aerodynamic Properties*, although undoubtedly he had good reason for urging that the anatomical plan of the conventional aeroplane of the time was not well-adapted for speeds approaching the speed of sound, to assert, as he did, that this was 'evident' amounted to cavalier dismissal of the authority of many reputable designers who were still working within the convention, and when he made the bland statement that it was 'indisputably' an 'unsuitable technique' to increase the size of 'planes in order to achieve long range and large pay-loads he was brushing aside most of his peers who accepted this technique as both inevitable and desirable. Certainly there were several leading designers in all the aircraft-producing countries who, had they been given the opportunity, would have rejected with asperity his proclamation that

> ... It is a matter of doubt whether a satisfactory solution can be found to the difficulty of producing an empennage which will be efficient under the great variety of conditions encountered in sub-, trans-, and supersonic flight.

But the unequivocal statement of premise was no more than a debater's trick; the presentation of hypothesis as fact, was merely limbering-up, the postulatory preface of Euclidian geometry, and there was nothing arrogant or dubious in the quintessential logic which followed. Clearly, fluently, with ample reference to historical evidence and substantial mathematical exegesis, Wallis argued his way to the conclusion that he should be allowed to translate design study into practical experiment.

From his reading of nineteenth-century mathematicians and from his airship experience he drew what was in this case a genuine irrefutable conclusion: that even in the simplest of mathematical forms an ichthyoid body has the property of producing powerful moments at small angles of incidence with the potentially valuable characteristic that these moments are not accompanied by large resultant forces in any direction. The time was ripe, he argued, for a fundamental change in the anatomy of aircraft and the logical direction for change was in the application to the stabilisation and control of aeroplanes of the aerodynamic properties of solids.

> The bare anatomical form which evolves ... comprises only three organs, namely a body and two wings. The wings may be

moved at will relative to the body on which they are mounted, the movement of the wings relative to the body being used to control the motion of the aerodyne in flight; while body and wings acting in conjunction render it stable.

At one stroke he would abolish tail and aileron, reduce profile drag and all-up weight. This would not be a development of the aeroplane but a new type of aerial vehicle.

It seems preferable, therefore, to refer to the resulting flying machine as an aerodyne rather than an aeroplane, since the latter term has come to be associated with flying machines the wings of which are fixed either to the body or to each other; and as 'aerodyne' itself is a broad generic term it is convenient to distinguish this new species of the genus as a 'wing controlled aerodyne'.

He could not know it but this bold claim for generic originality, clear though it is and justified, marked the beginning of confusion which was to bedevil *Wild Goose* and *Swallow* and which still invests debates over the eventual fate of his attempt with variable geometry aircraft to place Britain once more in the van of aerial development. Some, among them, even the official historian of Vickers,[5] argue that what he had in mind at first was an unmanned interceptor missile to take its place in the front line of British rocketry. Wallis himself and his supporters insisted that from the beginning he was considering a long-range aircraft 'from which aircraft to meet military requirements could be developed'.[6] And this debate made Wallis a shuttlecock between the military and civil aviation.

More perhaps than any other industry the aircraft industry suffers from two substantially related influences that inhibit innovation: the phenomenal cost and duration of design, experiment, building and testing of prototypes is one, and the other the need to accept as a unique palliative to the high price and exorbitant gestation period adaptability to military purposes in the eventual product. Both influences make it virtually inevitable that aircraft designers and those by whom they are overtly employed must bow to the only patron whose book-keeping processes are not fully subject to financial reality; the only purchaser who has need of military 'planes: Government. This implied the need to consider any craft not only for its passenger, goods and mail-carrying capacity but also for its possibilities as a weapon.

Wallis's attitudes to the forces which moulded his own destiny and which set the patterns of use for the aircraft he created were in some ways insensitive. His principal concern was to design and build; to what use his airships and aeroplanes were put was to him only of secondary importance. But the accusation of insensitivity is reduced in force by the naïveté of Wallis's ethical code. He loathed the State but he loved Britain with an uncomplicated fervour that blinkered him to what might otherwise be considered a dichotomy of loyalties. From the end of the First World War he had been obsessed by the notion of long-range flight and if, in pressing this cause, he felt bound to argue strategic advantages then, once more, he could with no great difficulty submerge his peace-loving conscience and raise in its place his enthusiasm for the unity of the British Empire.

If there is apparent an inconsistency in Wallis's ethical and political attitudes to his work there is none in his design-philosophy. From the beginning of his aeronautical career he had been passionately devoted to one purpose: the achievement of economic long-range flight by the application of engineering skill and originality. In this context efforts to achieve his end with airships may be seen as a journey down a *cul-de-sac* but, in the sense that *R.80* and *R.100* were designed to provide light-weight structures of great strength and rigidity that reduced the structure-weight of an aircraft and made available for pay-load and fuel a proportion undreamed of in other craft, Wallis's airship ventures were not even a detour but rather a preliminary exploration on the direct road to his geodetic structures for heavier-than-air machines.

There is consistency too in his search after clean aerodynamic forms; that the streamlining of his airships and the fine lines of Wellesley and Wellington are aesthetically satisfying is no coincidence imposed upon a series of engineering concepts by the intrusion of an artist's vision. As an artist Wallis did revel—and instinctively—in the attempt to bring shapes to perfection but, as an engineer, he knew too that the best lines are the most efficient and if he resented any attempt to amend the shapes that he envisaged for his craft it was not merely because such amendments made his airships and 'planes less beautiful, but because in tampering with their aesthetic qualities the efficiency of his craft was reduced.

Wild Goose and, in its turn, *Swallow,* the developments of the decade after the war, followed the logic of all that had gone before in Wallis's aeronautical career. Frank Whittle had invented the jet engine and in so doing had opened up possibilities of speed and range that had hitherto been inconceivable. Now supersonic long-distance flight was a practical proposition, and Wallis could extend the logical progression of his design career by seeking to eliminate from aeroplanes all those surfaces which contribute little to lift but add much to drag. *Wild Goose* and *Swallow,* both tailless aircraft, were essays in aerodynamic efficiency of a kind that no other designer and no other nation had attempted.

In the years when he was first wrestling with the notions of variable geometry, Wallis paid little attention to the fact that his daughter, Mary, was spending a great deal of time in the company of Harry Stopes-Roe, her one-time dancing partner, the son of his erstwhile chess opponent, Marie Stopes, and he was utterly unprepared for the news that Harry had asked Mary to become his wife.

When Harry informed his mother of his intention she, the energetic exponent of women's rights, arrogant as any Victorian paterfamilias, insisted that such decisions were for her to make and that she had in mind two or three candidates who, being eugenically sound, would pass to future generations her own magnificent genes. Mary Wallis was the daughter of 'that obstreperous engineer-fellow' and her eugenic unsoundness was palpably demonstrated by her wearing spectacles. Harry refused to accept the role of the dutiful son but instead prepared to announce his engagement. Unabashed, Marie Stopes wrote to Wallis informing him that the marriage was out of the question. Wallis ignored her and Harry ignored her, but when the engagement was formally announced in *The Times* Harry appeared simply as the son of his father; his eugenically superb mother was, at her own insistence, spared the shame of a mention.

Several young couples, Mary Wallis and Harry Stopes-Roe

among them, planned a continental holiday. Marie Stopes, on hearing of this, told her doctor that it was part of a vile scheme to lure Harry into a compromising situation so that he would be forced to marry Mary, and the doctor, who was also the Wallises' general practitioner and an old friend, passed to Wallis a full account of Marie Stopes's accusations. Now Wallis was roused. For hour after hour he and Molly thrashed over the situation, and eventually Wallis put the story to his solicitor with the suggestion that he should take action for slander. Wisely, the solicitor advised instead a dignified silence and, though it was against his nature to accept insult without retaliation, Wallis refrained from taking the matter further. Invitations to a wedding on 27 July 1948 were sent out. Harry's father accepted but Marie Stopes did not reply. Nor did she send a wedding-present though a few months later she gave Harry a cheque for £100 with strict instructions that every penny of it was to be spent on himself. Harry bought Mary a piano. In her will Marie Stopes left nothing of her considerable fortune to her son and daughter-in-law though she relented sufficiently to bequeath a house to their son, Jonathan.

But variable geometry and its application to the future of aeronautics was more absorbing than quarrels with a stupid and vicious woman, more exciting even than a wedding in the family. When Wallis presented to Sir Hew Kilner his paper *The Application of Aerodynamic Properties* it was already clear, even to him, that Vickers could not on its own account sponsor the development of a wing-controlled aerodyne: economic circumstances had changed so that it was no longer possible for any firm—even Vickers—to finance a huge project on a gamble that it might some day bring home huge profits.

For the next thirteen years *Wild Goose* and *Swallow* were in effect two creations in search of an angel. At various times Wallis tried the Ministry of Supply, British Overseas Airways Corporation, the Air Staff, Mutual Weapons Development Program, National Aeronautics and Space Administration, and the Royal Aircraft Establishment—some of them coincidentally and others several times over. Though every design study proved his thesis to be technically justified, the project skittered into desuetude so that to this day no plane has been built in Britain that fulfils Wallis's requirements, and the only American attempt to use variable geometry, the F111, has been a financial and technical disaster because its designers ignored or did not know some of the basic precepts which Wallis had established.

Yet the first approaches to the British Government were wonderfully encouraging. Wallis's war-time colleagues, Lockspeiser and Tizard, read his paper for the Ministry of Supply and with unqualified enthusiasm passed it to a committee of distinguished aeronautical engineers, Tizard adding the comment that the new project might be of such importance as would make it 'in the end, comparable to the introduction of radar'. Funds were made available for Wallis to begin experimental work.

Still Wallis hoped that he could ensure the future of his schemes by arousing immediately the interest of an eventual purchaser. He discussed the notion with another of his war-time allies, F. W. Winterbotham, and in the summer of 1948, Winterbotham arranged for Wallis a rendezvous at Taormina in Sicily with Whitney Straight, then Managing Director of BOAC.

This rare adventure into the exotic seems to have touched Wallis very little. He had not been in Taormina for more than four days when he was writing back to Molly his plans for the journey home three weeks later: he could last the three weeks and must if he was to have 'some heavy talks with Whitney Straight on aeroplanes', but then he would take the flying-boat from Augusta and be back in England in a day, overflying the architectural glories of Italy and making no effort to visit St Peter's, the masterpiece which he had never seen but which had been the subject of his enthusiasm in so many conversations and lectures.

Meanwhile, in Sicily, he avoided sight-seeing; partly because he was too busy preparing his 'lectures' for Whitney Straight and partly because he had developed a zeal for schnorkelling, but principally because his habitual pleasure in hard-living did not extend to bouncing along primitive tracks in a jeep. The sun he enjoyed, and the heat did not dim his powers of observation nor his pleasure in the didactic:

The bay during the morning exhibits a sort of hierarchy in the order in which sunshades are put out on the beach. The Marchese's villa adjoins the Villa St Andrea to the East and the Marchesical sunshade is consequently planted next to the foundations of the ruined Greek temple. Then come our three chairs covered by 2 sunshades and after that lower orders that we do not know. Fred and Peter cultivate the acquaintance of the Marchese and Marchesa, more particularly as they generally seem to have a Principe (you know the pronunciation—phonetically, giving English values and consonants, Principe is pronounced Preenchipe, accented on the 1st syllable and and Marchese is Markaise accented on the 2nd syllable. All final e's are sounded, generally rather lightly and with the open 'ai' sound) and his Principaessa (accent on 3rd syllable) staying with them or else an odd Duchesa or two.[7]

But no amusements, no sociological investigations and no lessons in Italian were allowed to deflect him from the prime purpose of his visit: long meetings with Whitney Straight 'unhampered by the jealous intervention of stupid people'.

Whitney Straight is an example of that strain in American society, and particularly in American high society, which threads comfortably into British life. Almost entirely English-educated (including a spell at the progressive school founded by his family at Dartington Hall) he had begun his career as a professional racing motorist and had then moved into civil aviation and thus, at the beginning of the war, into the Royal Air Force. He had ended the war as a Group Captain and an A.D.C. to the King.

A man with such a record was almost inevitably acceptable to Wallis. But he had reservations about the ability of Straight and 'his so-called experts' to comprehend 'the revolution that I can produce in air transport'. This weakness Wallis set himself to correct. At his own departure from England he had not dared to risk bringing with him any secret papers nor even books that might betray to a clever observer the tenor of his invention. Therefore at Taormina he had to spend much time re-working his formulae from first principles. 'I have nothing', he wrote to Molly, 'but my pen, my paper, my slide rule and my head.' Yet, with the exception of 'one single cryptic formula that would have been too long to derive here' in less than a week, though self-interrupted by swimming, schnorkelling, sun-bathing and not a little eating and drinking, he reconstituted the whole novel concept and developed a number of sketches of enlargements of the

Wild Goose theme that might serve BOAC. For hour upon hour
he lectured at Straight:

> Imagine us [Wallis wrote to Molly] sitting after dinner at his
> hotel on a terrace about 1000 feet above the bay, with the
> great bulk of Etna outlined against the velvet blue of the
> western sky, while the precipitous face of the bay up which we
> had climbed was picked out in fairy-lights winking from the
> white masses of the hillside-villas glowing coldly in the light of
> the moon at the full; and all the while me, lecturing hard on
> future developments of aircraft, taking sips at intervals from
> a glass of Italian liqueur, and doubling my optimism at every
> sip![8]

His optimism seemed justified. Straight was suitably impressed
and promised that he would take the matter further with Tedder,
now Chief of the Air Staff, in the hope that BOAC and the
RAF could get together and to their mutual advantage develop
Wild Goose. The thought of an alliance on his behalf between the
giants of civil and military aviation set Wallis off on the journey
back to England in high spirits. At Augusta his optimism was
enhanced. A dinner-party had been arranged by the Station
Commander, and one of Wallis's fellow guests was Air Marshal
Sir John Baldwin. Baldwin reminded Wallis how they had first
met when he had been Commandant at Cranwell in 1938. 'I
thought you were a bit of an old professor when you lectured to
us, but when I commanded No. 1 Bomber Group in the war and
we all used Wellingtons, I saw that you were right.' This set Wallis
to thinking about others who had come belatedly to accept the
accuracy of his visions. Bomber Harris on the morning after the
great Dams Raid: 'I never believed a word you said, Wallis; now
if you want to sell me a pink elephant, I'll buy it.' And Sir
Wilfred Freeman, in July 1943: 'Do you remember that ten-ton
bomb you talked about in 1939? How soon could you let me have
some?'

It was just the kind of musing that was bound to make him
hopeful that once more he would convince the doubting:

> Little triumphs, perhaps, but how pleasing to one's vanity, to
> move over the world amongst all these aeronautical people and

315

to be recognised among them. What will it be like if I live to see my *Wild Goose* come into general service?[9]

Nothing came of the Taormina discussions and there followed a series of changes in high places which were to deprive him of 'all those aeronautical people' who recognised him as an equal. Within four years, for one reason or another, Lockspeiser, Tizard, Tedder and Straight had all left the seats of power from which they might have helped Wallis to bring *Wild Goose* into general service.

Nevertheless, Wallis was not downcast. If Britain could not find the money then there was still some hope that he would win support from the Americans, by this time the benefactors from whom all blessings flowed. In October 1948 he set off on what was for him an even more exotic pilgrimage than the journey to Taormina. He had never before crossed the Atlantic.

His long experience of watching from afar American efforts to build a successful rigid airship and closer knowledge of American aeroplane design had given him little respect for that part of American achievement which the Americans themselves prized most highly: their technology. In 1948 he felt himself and his nation to be humiliated by the shortage of dollars which afflicted the British in the United States. His economics were always emotional and he contrived in his mind a strange conjunction between Britain's sacrifice in two wars, his own vast contribution to victory in the second of those wars, the sacrifices of 617 Squadron—and the comforts now enjoyed by the Americans.[10] His was the anti-Americanism that is not unusual in a middle-class Englishman of his generation, but in an odd way it was also something far more egocentric: a latter-day repetition of the resentment that, in his youth, his branch of the Wallis family had shown for their more prosperous relations.

In the first days of his visit, in Washington, D.C., and for the sake of *Wild Goose*, Wallis allowed himself to be treated hospitably. He was taken to Mount Vernon by his American hosts and was suitably polite, though he found the place 'small by our standards'. But, as conversations droned on with American aeronautical experts and it seemed that no support for his plans would be forthcoming—certainly not until he had much more to show them—Wallis found many new reasons for disliking America. The hotels were 'awful' and the drivers on the road 'lunatic'.

Wild Goose

Later Wallis was to insist that F111 was born out of these tentative discussions in 1948. The Americans, he argued, had listened to his theories with care and had found them so good that they had decided to exploit them for themselves. But he, in his 'infinite cunning', had held back from emphasising that the absence of tail was central to his design doctrine. F111 was built with a tail.[11] Even for the amateur it is difficult to see how the Wallis theories could be expounded without revealing the theme of taillessness and yet, while it is impossible to disprove that work on an American variable geometry 'plane had begun before October 1948, it is equally impossible to confound Wallis's conviction. What is certain is that in 1948 Wallis received nothing from the Americans—and that eventually Britain was forced to go to the United States for variable geometry 'planes.

Returned home from the United States without encouragement, money or cause for optimism, still Wallis insisted upon starting trials with *Wild Goose*. He was now more than sixty years old and he had come to imagine that his role in an experiment had changed. No longer, as in the days of his airships, of Wellingtons and the war-time bombs, did he see himself as the all-seeing, all-arranging central figure of a project. Now he was the philosopher, the inspiration and the manipulator. Throughout the early days of *Wild Goose* Wallis continued the pretence and persuaded himself that 'with infinite cunning' he had withdrawn into the background 'as a visitor and not as chief of the whole show'. It was a slight and amusing delusion: in truth the readiness with which others turned to him for the toppling of obstacles and the alacrity with which he accepted their invitations, set him up as still the unchallenged and unchallengeable leader.

By 1949 his theories had been substantiated with a multitude of calculations and by hundreds of experiments with model 'planes, but the large-scale proof was yet to come, and hence Wallis's 'horrid anxiety' at the end of the year. He knew, none better, the difficulties of forecasting scale-effect. Wallis himself explained scale-effect in a letter to his wife (a letter, incidentally, which he never sent):

A common plank will bear you safely across a stream. Multiply the width of the stream five hundred fold and an immensely

317

elaborate structure, supported on four or five intermediate piers, must be contrived, after hundreds of years of evolution, to carry you safely across the Thames. That is a purely static problem. When enlarging a model aeroplane we have to deal with both static and dynamic scale effects.

A model, he knew, does not prove, it merely raises hopes.

He had before him in these first large-scale experiments in variable wing-span a yet more confusing side issue: the problem of ground-effect. The aerodynamic characteristics of a swiftly moving aeroplane flying (as the experimental 'planes would have to fly) close to the ground are in many and important respects utterly unlike those experienced when it has reached even a normal commercial cruising height. Further, Wallis's chosen method of launching from a power-driven trolley would, he thought, have many eventual advantages but immediately and in the process of testing it involved an additional and especial consequence, for it caused erratic disturbance to the air-flow above the trolley and thus rendered the experiments atypical to the general tenor of his calculations. Indeed, the first *Wild Goose* reared-up on take-off, stalled and crashed. After adjustment, the second put her bow down and dived into the ground without ever clearing the region of major disturbance above the trolley. Consequently, before he could go any further, Wallis had to invent a modification. He hit upon the jump-start. The 'plane was to be held on the trolley in an attitude that would suit the peculiar air-flow over the trolley until such a time as the lifting force exceeded its weight by something like one and a half times. At that moment it could be released automatically and because of this large excess lift would jump clean through the area of disturbed flow. Immediately the wings could be set for flight and the plane would go forward in the freedom of undisturbed air.

There were disappointments at each stage, and there was also restlessness, even amongst his closer associates who felt that he was chancing eventual success by refusing to accept the minimal risks involved in going immediately to man-controlled test flights. It was a test-pilot's business to use his skills and his courage to abbreviate the long process of experiment, investigation and correction. A highly-qualified man in the air with the new 'plane could provide information which otherwise could only be achieved after months and even years of experiment with models and radio-controlled prototypes—and perhaps not even then, for the trained human observer is equipped with sensitivity and instinct that is far more acute than the most delicate instruments, and his powers of association and correlation exceed by far the capacity of the most advanced machine. Geoffrey Quill told Wallis that the moment he decided to man his new 'plane a queue of all the best pilots in Britain would form outside his office, headed by Quill himself. But Wallis, rarely the most patient of men, was in this patient beyond other men's bearing. His mind went back and his conscience reacted to the long history of disaster upon which the progress of aviation had been wrought. Even the dam-busting raids had become for him a horrifying example of too precipitate squandering of life in the cause of proving an equation. Now in peace-time while he was responsible for a project Wallis was determined that not one life should be risked. Experiment and failure, adjustment and new experiment, all must go forward with scrupulous caution, using models and radio-controlled flight until such time as he could feel morally justified in entrusting a human being to his invention.

The opposition of his friends drove him back into the despair of loneliness. He began to feel a schizophrenia not unlike that which he had suffered throughout the 'thirties when he, a self-styled pacifist, was gaining prominence as the designer of efficient weapons of war. Now he, the author of this sensational advance in aeronautics, felt alone in the conviction that no advance was worth the price of a man's life.

His Vickers paymasters were becoming exasperated with his prodigality and exasperated too by the unwillingness of Government to support with adequate funds Wallis's dedication to unmanned experiment. The direction at Weybridge had no objection to Wallis playing with little models by the dozen. A model could be built in a few days and at tiny cost. Crash one model and another could be built to replace it. But each time that he crashed a full-size machine he destroyed or seriously damaged something that had taken months to make at a price of several hundred thousand pounds. And each delay for the creation of a replacement postponed into a seemingly inaccessible future the moment when Wallis's employers might earn the rewards of their support. They knew, as Wallis knew, that if he persisted in his refusal to use a test-pilot, he would have to solve not only the immensely difficult problem of getting his full-size *Wild Goose* into the air but also the problem of learning to fly it from the ground. They knew, as he knew, that there could be no gradualness, no possibility of half-flying the 'plane. Either it was safe on the ground or else it was careering through the air at one or two hundred miles an hour, potentially a complete victim to the slightest miscalculation.

Despite the pleas of his employees and the grumblings of his employers, Wallis persisted.

In the gloomy winter months that began 1950 he drove himself and his 'children' close to the point of exhaustion. Week after week he made the journey by car through fog, snow or rain to the National Aeronautical Establishment at Thurleigh in Bedfordshire, camped there in a hut at the side of the aerodrome, rose each morning at seven and worked frequently until midnight.

The weather that winter continued viciously cold—until one of Wallis's assistants presented him with a duffle-coat, and then, immediately, the temperature rose—but even when the thermometer soared to ten degrees above freezing it could not alter the fact that livings conditions were crude. Huts left over not from the Second but from the First World War could never be luxurious, and the comfort of Wallis and his staff was not improved by a canteen-service that was surly to the point of indifference. But an entirely male community has means of caring for itself that might surprise its womenfolk. At Thurleigh distinguished radio engineers exercised a genius for cooking, meteorological experts proved themselves scroungers no less competent than army batmen, and pilots saw to it that eggs were always available for Wallis, the quasi-vegetarian.

Wallis had doubled the thrust of the trolley. The test run for 17 January 1950 was a locked-on run; *Wild Goose* being committed to all the motions of take-off except the final parting. Wallis and his colleagues watched from a small control tower, waiting optimistically for the signal that the 'plane had reached a speed of the order of 90 miles an hour, but the signal never came. When *Wild Goose* passed the control tower her speed was up to 120 miles an hour and she was developing a lifting force at least three times her own weight so that there was even some danger that she would fly away with her trolley—as Wallis wrote 'like the

great Roc that whiffled off with poor Sinbad the Sailor'. The rest of
that day was spent upon investigating faults in the signal system.

The disappointment of the day and the bitterness of the
weather were somewhat relieved by a telephone call early in the
evening from Weybridge. There they had attempted the first suck
at Wallis's newly constructed stratosphere chamber. Although, as
had been expected, there were a number of minor leaks the great
door had closed perfectly; this despite the fact that Wallis had
deliberately omitted the joint bolts that conventionally are used
to hold such a door to the open end of a cylinder.

Thursday, 19 January 1950, was even colder than the preceding
days, with a wind rising steadily as the hours went by and blow-
ing always from the north. Wallis went out to the testing zone
dressed, as if for some antique Arctic expedition, in a cotton vest,
a woollen vest, three woollen sweaters, the old Burberry that had
been his uniform in the days of the dam-busting. Somehow, over
all this he dragged a mackintosh. He wore a scarf, a hat, two pairs
of thick socks, stockings and gum-boots. Even so the wind pierced
Wallis, and his companions were frozen stiff. As they walked off
to their observation station Startup, his cameraman said, 'I've just
made a discovery; I've lost my feet.'

It seemed as if they had lost more than feet. The first locked-on
run was a failure: long before the moment of simulated take-off
the trolley-jet expired. Wallis ordered another locked-on run,
this time with 25 per cent more fuel, and was rewarded with a
signal flash after 560 yards.

Now he decided that he would attempt a real take-off. The
wind was still leaden with snow and the light poor. Nevertheless,
although he had previously said he would not permit a free flight
to take off down-wind, he now felt that he must find out if the
jump take-off would really happen. At 3.30 p.m. they fired the jet
and were rewarded with a splendid run, a perfect take-off and a
'plane climbing exquisitely. Nash, the 'pilot' on the ground,
flattened out the 'plane at approximately fifty feet, she flew perfectly and gracefully, but the 'pilot' was much too slow on his
pull-out. Ignominiously *Wild Goose* dived into the ground.

Fortunately Wallis had insisted on putting in a control-stick
orders recorder. He had asked for it three months earlier but his
'naughty children' had not bothered so that they had had to work
the whole of the previous week-end to get it ready in time. Now

his obstinacy reaped its reward because he was able to see exactly where Nash's directions had erred.

There was nothing wrong with the theory and nothing wrong with the practice. *Wild Goose* could fly.

Wallis's first reaction was not unnaturally an enormous sense of relief. He had risked the whole of his professional career and with it the welfare of many of his loyal helpers. He knew now that he was on the right road. He was confident (over-confident as it transpired) that never again would he have to endure the worries and anxieties of the past years which had come to such a hideous climax during the difficulties and seeming failures of the previous six months. His team collected up the bits of *Wild Goose*, drove back to workshops, and then Wallis went immediately to his cabin where he 'spent the first five minutes on my knees praising and blessing God for his mercy to me'. That night as he lay in bed he recited over and over again his favourite collect for the Third Sunday after Trinity:

Oh Lord, we beseech Thee mercifully to hear us; and grant that we, to whom Thou has given an hearty desire to pray, may by Thy mighty aid be defended and comforted in all dangers and adversities; through Jesus Christ Our Lord.

Next morning he had doubts, not about *Wild Goose* nor yet about the future of his great project, but doubts about his *Laus Deo* and the justification for his thanksgiving.

I have since thought that what one should more properly praise and thank God for is the encouragement to persevere rather than any measure of success, and a Christian's chief difficulty lies in his uncertainty of God's wishes. Hence I suppose our tendency to interpret success as an indication that in our persistence in the face of difficulty we have been in fact on the right road. How is one to distinguish between cases in which failure indicates God's will to desist and those in which a feeling of stubborn determination in the face of failures indicates God's intention that we should persist?

In the past and on many occasions he had protested the disabling pressure of age but always to thrust it from him with youthful activity; now, for the first time, he felt that the years could not be denied. He was by no means certain that he could survive the strains imposed upon him by his zeal for *Wild Goose* and by the compulsion which, now as always, he felt to set the pace for his 'children'.

It was not until the summer of 1951 that *Wild Goose* was ready for more expansive trials, and the centre of Wallis's existence moved to Predannack Aerodrome near the Lizard in Cornwall. Here the sense of loneliness, of isolation which he had known so often since the late 'twenties and which had begun to diminish at Thurleigh, fell from him entirely. Now, as never during the Second World War, he was not only leader of a team, he was part of that team. Confidence and authority revived an essential boyishness long-suppressed.

The popular view of Wallis as an austere man not far short of bigotry on such matters as teetotalism and vegetarianism is an entire misrepresentation founded upon casual and short-term interviews. With friendship it vanished entirely, but even those who were not admitted to his close acquaintance can erase the impression by comparing Wallis with devotees of the more puritanical cults for there was in Wallis none of the condemnatory superiority and none of the missionary fervour that such men find inescapable. His teetotalism is an utter myth. He was not a drinking man as are those who take a bottle of whisky a day. Indeed he seldom drank at all outside his own home, but only because, by his own confession, he had a poor head; at home he pressed the sherry and the beer on his friends and drank with them glass for glass. His reasons for abandoning tobacco in middle-age were, as we have seen, not what he imagined them to have been, but he did not deny that he had smoked and enjoyed it. He did not much like meat but he was not in the true sense a vegetarian, and, although he was not slow to react to bad language and had an unworldly incomprehension of what he still described as 'filthy talk', there were among the anecdotes which he told with fine histrionic flourishes several that were innocently Rabelaisian.

On close inspection, then, the austerity evaporates, but in its place one must put something that is pleasant if somewhat outmoded and therefore surprising to the majority who have been brought up in a more caustic environment. The words that Wallis used to describe the lighter pleasures are themselves antiquated and apt to arouse derision, but they are the words which we too must use if we are to thrust aside the impression of severity. A gathering was 'jolly'; his colleagues 'a bunch of good fellows' (if they were not 'unmitigated and ignorant villains and rogues'). His so-called austerity was a deliberate anti-sybaritism and undoubtedly as the years advanced, when he might have been expected to relish both the comfortable armchair and the pedestal due to his seniority, he enjoyed instead—more even than he did in his youth—every opportunity to live and work in simple and even primitive surroundings and, most particularly, in all-male company. So at the age of sixty-four, he found himself wonderfully elated by camping out at Predannack.

Predannack had stood empty and decaying since the last wartime Coastal Command pilots had taken their handle-bar moustaches and their high spirits back to insurance offices or tutorials. Even in war-time Predannack had been a grim station, virtually overhanging the sea and enclosed by peat bogs which had more than once spelt disaster to a pilot returning exhausted from an Atlantic patrol; now gorse and heather were recapturing the runways. Still, Wallis enjoyed his visits to Predannack, for around him there was activity, enthusiasm and the quality he prized above all others: loyalty.

The trials at Predannack and at Weybridge dragged on through 1951 and on into 1952. Sometimes Wallis flew down to Cornwall in an old biplane piloted by Cheshire and flew back the same day. Sometimes he stayed for weeks on end. His theories were right, of that neither he nor any of his closer associates had any doubt, but before theory could become reality there were hundreds of experiments to complete and at every stage tribulation, set-back, fallibility and even ludicrous error. Not only was it necessary to invent, adapt, build and test within the main project—the programme for transferring *Wild Goose* from the drawing-board to the air—but also the very process of testing demanded ingenuity far beyond the ordinary.

On 21 September 1951 (St Matthew's Day, as he noted in his diary, and therefore of particular significance to anyone educated at Christ's Hospital, for it is the day on which every year Christ's Hospital celebrates its ancient connection with the City of London) all seemed set fair for a good trial but after two hours of careful preparation the trolley's jet engines failed to start. The fault had to be found. Every major part was checked but all seemed in order. The tracing went on and eventually one of the fitters found a cracked union nut, and therefore a leak on one of the high-pressure pipes used to force hydrogen peroxide from tanks into the combustion chamber. Still the investigations had to thrust back one stage further to discover why the nut had cracked. The answer was simple: the nut was made of brass instead of steel. A stupid mistake, or so it seemed, and yet because both brass and steel nuts are cadmium-plated an error that could be identified only by a man with a magnet or else by disaster.

The actual trolley Wallis had changed substantially. The first successful launching at Thurleigh had been from a rubber-tyred trolley; now they were using a railway-type trolley and the method of holding and releasing the aircraft had been so modified as to jump the aircraft on take-off much higher above the ground. This should have made for vast improvements in performance, but fact did not match prediction.

There was always in his mind the nagging worry that some error in calculation would crash the 'plane back on to its own trolley-way for he knew that a crash of this kind would mean delays for a year or longer. But there were other and even more disquieting troubles. Locked-on runs during which pitch, roll and yaw were measured showed the aircraft behaving in a manner quite unlike that predicted from careful wind-tunnel tests made at the National Physical Laboratory. He had only one auto-pilot, a new and excellent model but much heavier than those he had used previously. Indeed this, with extra radio equipment and stronger fuselage and wings, raised the weight that had to be lifted to over 800 lbs, more than twice the weight in the successful launching at Thurleigh. If the National Physical Laboratory's calculations were correct and the wings set according to those calculations, this increased weight was feasible, but observation at Predannack made it uncertain.

Despite this set-back Wallis had to make some demonstration of progress. He was well aware that enemies were not far off and critics all around him—many of them powerful in Vickers. Caution might bring its own disaster for there were some who would see themselves proudly in the role of guardians of the public or corporate purse. A major disaster and all his work would be ended, the victim of an easy cry that 'the old man had lost his touch'. Even his own confidence was ebbing; his only certainty was the loyalty of his staff.

Early in February 1952 he organised a delaying demonstration at Predannack for Stewart Mitchell, an ex-Naval gunnery expert who was now Controller, Guided Weapons and Electronics, at the Ministry of Aviation, and for his old friend Cochrane, now Vice Chief of the Air Staff. Mitchell pressed the suggestion that a test-pilot could solve many of Wallis's problems for him. This was no novel proposal but what was novel—and to Wallis temporarily shattering—was the unanimity of agreement from his own staff. Even Cheshire agreed, and only Cochrane stood by him; some of the rest in their eagerness to press the point went much further than they had originally intended and expressed lack of confidence in the whole project.

Cochrane and Mitchell flew back to London, Wallis remained obdurate and Predannack sulked for forty-eight hours, the social climate matching a hurricane that blew in from the Atlantic.

Then the skies outside cleared and Wallis determined to restore his own confidence and the confidence of his staff with an actual launching. The little craft rose to 200 feet. But the success was modified by the fact that for this test the weight of the glider had been reduced to 350 lbs, no more than had been lifted at Thurleigh; and still the conflict between the National Physical Laboratory and Predannack calculations and observations had not been resolved.

For two months Wallis wrestled with the problem. He put it to other experts, and none of them, not even Ernest Relf, one of the greatest aeronautical theoreticians in the world (himself a one-time National Physical Laboratory official and until recently Principal of the College of Aeronautics) could find an explanation.

There was only one way out. He must ignore the experts of the National Physical Laboratory and risk all upon launching a heavy glider on 29 April 1952, and he had this glider prepared to suit the conclusions drawn at Predannack and Weybridge. He knew what was at stake: if the flight failed then, at very least, the trolley would be destroyed, but he was by now so certain of the eagerness of his enemies that he was sure that the ruin of the trolley would be the preface to his entire ruin. Even to hold the fading loyalty of his own team he must have a sensational success.

But when the day came cross-winds were so high and so gusty that there could well be disaster even in success for *Wild Goose* might do all that was asked of her and then be blown off-course and ram their own workshops or hangars. He was tempted to cancel the great experiment; but cancellations, for whatever reason, would be interpreted as failure. The wind must do its worst as he had done his best. The test must go on.

All of that late April morning he supervised the last checks. Early in the afternoon the RAF Security Police arrived and began to patrol the surrounding countryside. The inhabitants of houses on the potential crash route were brought in to aerodrome dugouts. Cameramen were posted to record the flight, and with one of them, Peter Farr, once his responsibilities were over Wallis took up his own station.

Now he could only watch—and pray.

The seconds ticked on like the days of eternity. Suddenly the jets fired. *Wild Goose* hustled down the track, leaped into the air and flew magnificently. At the first touch from Nash's controls she turned right and for three-quarters of a circuit she answered every touch.

Wallis had drilled himself for years to maintain calm in the critical moments of scientific experiment. But the exhilaration of this stupendous achievement destroyed his practised calm. He found himself shouting a delighted running commentary to the air, to the gorse bushes and to his one companion.

Then, with success complete, unnecessary disaster followed. Nash must have decided to bring the 'plane down. He was flying her only a few feet above the ground and at a speed of 150 m.p.h. Deceived by the lack of perspective in a flat countryside he did not appreciate the closeness of some of the aerodrome buildings. *Wild Goose* hurtled within a few feet of the fire-engine standing close to the runway and shattered her beauty against a concrete shed.

Wallis cared nothing for the crash. This was his moment of triumph and it is significant that when he wrote to Molly at the end of the day he began his letter with a reference to the Wright Brothers:

The greatest contribution they made to the art of flying was . . . lateral control, brought about by the means of the aileron—a brilliant and novel invention, still 44 years later in universal use. And forty-four years later gallant men's lives are still being lost because the behaviour of new aeroplanes is not exactly predictable as far as their controls are concerned. In particular as speeds become higher and higher the aileron type of lateral control becomes more and more dubious . . . Now I have in one great change abolished the aileron and all other conventional controls as well, transforming the complexity of the type that has persisted for nearly half a century to the endearing simplicity of the Wild Goose—just one body and two wings and no other controls at all.[12]

He knew that there was much still to do, but he was delighted that, against all advice, he had achieved this vast demonstration of novelty without risking one life. Certainly he imagined that for the work of that day his name, still uncertainly entered in the histories for his work on airships, on geodetic construction and on the bombs, would stand forever equal to the Wrights among the great pioneers of aviation.

Wallis slipped off to his cabin to book a telephone call to Weybridge. He was eager to pass on the magnificent news to all who had helped.

He was kneeling by his bedside when the telephone rang. Habit brought him to his feet and he found himself excusing to himself this act of seeming discourtesy to his Maker. 'Surely, in His infinite Majesty, God would not resent being hastily cut off, for is not the conservation of human energy in itself an act of worship?'

That night Wallis ordered a celebration party. There were more than fifty present. With the aid of innumerable bottles of beer, four of whisky, six of gin, three of rum and several strange bottles which Wallis recorded as 'peculiar, like Peppermint Cordial guaranteed alcoholic' the celebrations became uproarious. He himself drank one glass of beer and his habitual caution set his mind to working like a till. Twenty pounds, thirty pounds, almost forty pounds—all out of his pocket. But historic occasions did not happen every day.

For the men at the bar a decade slipped away. Many of them had served in the war. For them, as for Wallis himself, the surroundings were too strong for time. The relief of success had on them the well-remembered effect of arousing boisterousness. It was as if they were all just back from a bomber-raid, a fighter-sortie or a tank-patrol in the desert. Almost spontaneously they began to sing: the old service favourites but in versions suitably bowdlerised out of respect for Wallis. Then, so heightened was the atmosphere—and so magnificent the supply of alcohol—that they did something which in ordinary circumstances no gathering of Englishmen could do without suffering communal embarrassment. They began to sing 'Land of Hope and Glory'. One of the foremen, an older man, a Welshman with all his nation's enthusiasm for song—and common lack of knowledge of music—stood by Wallis and insisted on his joining in. 'It's good. You must sing. Gilbert and Sullivan, you know.'

Wallis had proved a theory, and now expected that others with greater authority and infinitely expandable bank-balances would take his proof as cue to total support and future action. Forty years of experience had not taught him all that there was to know about the obduracy of ministries and great corporations. But his optimism was short-lived and soon he was back to finding an enemy behind every Whitehall door. The few exceptions, Tizard and Lockspeiser for example, were men who backed his genius without asking too many questions about where genius was leading, and it may be doubted that many among the rest were in truth 'anxious to see his experiment fail' (his own words). But now that he had proved the validity of the swing-wing principle they wanted from him some conception of precise embodiment that could justify huge development expenditure. Instead, or so it appeared to them, he brushed aside requests for specific prognosis, spoke consistently of the revolution which he had wrought and which they must support for the glory of Britain and the future of aviation.

Wiser men or men unhampered by political overseers and national economic instability might have allowed his genius to leap unhampered from idea to idea whilst they established in parallel some systematic project to translate his brilliance into a definite shape. But these were ordinary hard-working officials, fearful of making a mistake and in effect powerless to risk the grand gesture that Wallis demanded. Their timidity he took for jealousy, even for hatred, their lack of immediate enthusiasm for deliberate obstructionism. Here they were once more, the spiritual heirs of the men who had set their silly pride to the destruction of the British rigid airship, who had opposed his big 'plane and his big bomb, who had tried to interfere in his private war with Germany, and as he came again to resent their blindness so did he betray himself into peevishness. 'He would never again darken the doors of the Royal Aeronautical Establishment,' the Aerodynamics Division of the National Physical Laboratory had 'insulted him' by sending to the Ministry of Supply (which had paid for it) a report on some aspect of his swing-wing work. The Civil Service was determined to do him down.

A few weeks after the first successful flight another experimental effort ended in disaster, not because of any inherent failure in the prototype but because again a ground pilot misjudged the stick-control and crashed the model almost immediately after take-off. Wallis released a fine display of bad temper, sought to excuse himself without indulging in apology by buying two rounds of drinks at the Old Inn at Mullion Cove ('Thank goodness only £2.13s.6d. instead of £37 odd') and then went off to bed with a violent migraine. He woke in the middle of the night aware of a dimly-held notion that it would be possible to maintain experimental flights for much longer than one circuit. By morning he had worked out his new concept and, before leaving for London at 10.45 a.m. he had explained his plans to his team and convinced himself (and perhaps them) that the previous day's unpleasantness had never happened.

There were further crashes but, so far as Wallis and his team could discover, all of them were caused by circumstances extraneous to his theories. Now, whenever he was at Predannack he was conscious of a sense of complacency for already *Wild Goose* had achieved a lift-coefficient at G's up to 0·7. His satisfaction was not unnaturally touched with some malicious pleasure because the National Physical Laboratory had insisted that the new anatomy of *Wild Goose* could not be satisfactory at G's over 0·3 and Wallis had come to suspect that, once more 'they', the manipulators of power, were against him. 'No wonder I seem to be rather "touchy" to some people,' he wrote in a letter to his wife. Even his wife and his closest colleagues would have set down 'touchy' as an insufficient word to describe Wallis's flaring tempers and occasional huge sulks.

The euphoria of *Wild Goose*'s successful flight soon evaporated. He had not been hailed as the man who changed aeronautical history; instead, he saw himself once more as the unrecognised, unrewarded and jealously obstructed genius. If the role for which he cast himself was only in part his by right, his claim to it was perversely buttressed by the phenomenal public success of Paul Brickhill's book *The Dam Busters*[13] (as later by the even greater public success of the film that was made from it). Wherever Wallis went he was greeted as the great scientist who had been forced to fight the authorities in order to be allowed to fight the Germans: even when he visited Leonard Cheshire's Home for Incurables close to Predannack, although he found there much spiritual comfort, he found too that all the patients admired him for what he had done and pitied him for the lack of acceptance, gratitude or honour which he had experienced, for all were reading 'the inevitable Dambusters'. Because of the book he was famous for having no fame. The paradox at one and the same time heightened in him the sense that he was forever the victim of the Fates and underscored his conviction that the Fates had powerful allies in Whitehall.

16 The Barnes Wallis RAF Foundation

In his own lifetime Wallis became a mythical character: the frustrated genius; the austere scientist; the remote original. Often he added fables of his own devising to the story of his life, and certainly by the time he reached old age he had the saga so much by rote that it carried the authority which comes with repetition to give the sound of historicity even to the less verifiable parts of the tale. But there is one episode—his application for an Inventor's Award and the use to which he put that Award—which has become comparatively well-known in an entirely apocryphal version, although his version was true and unadorned.

Nor until four years after the war was the suggestion first made that Wallis should apply to the Royal Commission on Awards to Inventors for some monetary recognition of his work in destroying the Ruhr Dams. The proposal came from Air Chief Marshal Sir Wilfred Freeman; Wallis rejected it out of hand, not because he was unaware of the warmth of personal friendship that inspired Freeman but because he felt that 'the real credit is not due to me but to the aircrews who did the job'.[1]

The event that persuaded Wallis to change his mind has been used consistently in a sense contrary to the truth, as if it was both coincidental with his rejection of Freeman's suggestion, and spiritual reinforcement for his refusal of that most practical proposition. Fourteen months after the suggestion Wallis heard a sermon by the Vicar of Effingham preached on the text *II Samuel 23*, verses 14–17:

And David was then in an hold, and the garrison of the Philistines was then in Bethlehem.
And David longed, and said, Oh that one would give me drink of the well of Bethlehem, which is by the gate!

The Barnes Wallis RAF Foundation

And the three mighty men brake through the host of the
Philistines, and drew water out of the well at Bethlehem, that
was by the gate, and took it, and brought it to David; nevertheless he would not drink thereof, but poured it out unto the
Lord.

And he said, Be it far from me, O Lord, that I should do
this: is not this the blood of the men that went in jeopardy of
their lives?

However one interprets this story it is not difficult to see how
it came to be associated with Wallis's original refusal to fall in
with Freeman's plans on his behalf. 'Nevertheless he would not
drink thereof' can be taken as, for him, the key phrase, whereas
in truth the line that inspired him was '[he] poured it out unto the
Lord'. Moved by this phrase from his original intention to resist
all monetary gain, Wallis decided that instead he would use the
most worldly of all gifts open to him—money—in the service
of God and of the 'men that went in jeopardy of their lives' to
make that gift useful to their children. He would argue his way to
an Award and with it would set up a special Foundation within
Christ's Hospital for the education of the children of Royal Air
Force personnel.

There followed a struggle that bruised his spirit. He expected
no opposition to his claim; his dam-busting invention alone
merited an Award; the knowledgeable friends he consulted set
its monetary value at around £25,000 and no one, friend, neutral
or enemy, could object to the manner in which he planned to
spend the money. He was therefore much surprised when he
was told that the Ministry of Supply intended to oppose his
application; and deeply shocked when he was advised by friend
after friend that he would 'give much offence in high places'
if the Ministry's opposition was defeated and then, instead of
using the money himself, he subverted it to charitable purposes.

The Ministry's case was malicious but clever: it was founded
upon a series of half-truths or truths that, in the early years of
the war, Wallis himself had used to convince the authorities of
the viability of his proposals. The method of attacking the Dams,
it argued, was not novel; there was no evidence that the Dams
would not have been breached if Wallis had not invented the
bouncing-bomb; the principles of the bouncing-bomb were well

known already in the nineteenth century; at the time when Wallis had been at work on the bomb he was a full-time paid member of Vickers Armstrong, the recipients of a developing contract from the Ministry. For bad measure there were added three objections: that he had never been discouraged by officialdom; that he had been at all relevant times a member of the Committee on Air Attack on Dams and therefore had been privy both 'to the problems and to all schemes suggested to solve it' (an argument implying plagiarism on his part) and that he had already been 'rewarded . . . in the only manner legally open to the Crown, namely by the bestowing of an honour, the C.B.E., on him'.

Goaded to fury, Wallis prepared his rebuttal, and one by one the objections were dismantled. Freeman swore to the opposition; Lockspeiser demonstrated that the Dams Committee was set up only because Wallis had urged an attack against the sources of German hydraulic power. Despite the inhibition placed upon their evidence by the fact that the bouncing-bomb was still on the secret list, Renouf and Cochrane added to their supporting dispositions a hint of the continuing utility of the bomb. All of his distinguished supporters concurred in the view that the conception of the bomb had come from his private consideration, its development had been undertaken and achieved by him as an addition to his normal responsibilities, and the contract to Vickers given only after he had argued his way close to success. As for the C.B.E., that this had been awarded for his work on Wellesley and Wellington was not only demonstrable from letters of 1943 but also sworn by several senior members of the Air Staff.

In March 1951 the case was won before the Tribunal on Inventions. The sum received was £10,000, not, as Wallis had been led to hope, £25,000. This substantial reduction he ascribed, this time, not to the malevolence of the Civil Service but to the objections raised by his own friends to his intention of devoting the Award to charitable, educational and entirely unselfish ends.

The great act of charity on which he now embarked, more even than his huge contributions to aeronautical engineering or his valiant service to a nation at war, enshrined the ideas of a lifetime and drew together into one logical consequence many strains of character, upbringing, career and hopes for the future. His Christianity, his gratitude to the institution that had reared him, and to

the young men who had risked and so often added their lives
to the price paid for the success of his war-time inventions, his
traditionalism, his affection for the Services and his patriotism:
all played some part in bringing about both the fact and the
manner of the Foundation.

Wallis had in his mind two models for his Foundation: the
Hospital's own Royal Mathematical School established by Letters
Patent granted by Charles II in 1673 at the instigation of Sir
Robert Clayton and Samuel Pepys, and Cecil Rhodes's great
educational trust.

The original task of the Royal Mathematical School had been
to produce navigators for the Navy and the Merchant Marine
but as the training of both Royal Navy and Merchant Marine
officers was generally improved so did the prime function of
the Royal Mathematical School evaporate, and just a few years
before Wallis himself entered Christ's Hospital changed circumstances were recognised formally. Thereafter forty places were
reserved within Christ's Hospital for the sons of Royal Naval,
Royal Marine or Royal Naval Reserve officers. But Mathemats
still wore on the shoulders of their blue coats badges modelled
on the 'rare and glorious medallion' struck to commemorate the
foundation of the Royal Mathematical School—'a Christ's Hospital boy being patted on the head by Arithmetic, while Mathematics, Astronomy and Commerce stand by'.

It was the nineteenth century and charitable purpose of the
RMS that Wallis used as model for his Foundation. Transpose
Royal Air Force for Royal Navy and the two interior foundations
are virtually synonymous.

Wallis, busy with so many things and before ever he was
sure of the money, had given much time to considering the
detail of his new Foundation: no restriction should be made
that the children who were to benefit from his charity must be
orphans; the funds provided must not be used to send children
to the Christ's Hospital Preparatory School.

The objection to using the Fund for children as young as nine
years is that this would operate to restrict the 'throughput', and
I think that little advantage is gained by sending a child to a
Preparatory School attached to a great Public School at this
tender age.

In no case should the selection of the children be by competitive examination. Instead,

> I earnestly desire selection to be based upon the service record of the father, as being a man who has shown himself, in the words of Cecil Rhodes, to be a man of truth, courage, devotion to duty and sympathy for and protection of the weak, secondly the exhibition during his school (service) days of moral force of character, and an instinct to lead and to take an interest in other men.[2]

Both the Royal Mathematical School and the Rhodes Scholarships had as a prime purpose the 'benefit of His Majesty's Dominions'. Such too was Wallis's hope for the Royal Air Force Foundation.

The sense of gratification that Wallis derived from his personal 'dede of pittie' was much deepened when, acting in response to his suggestion, the Royal Air Force Benevolent Fund added £10,000 to the capital investment he provided and, when it took over the administration of the Foundation, added also a commitment to pay one-third of the total cost of maintaining and educating at Christ's Hospital all the children admitted under the terms of his Foundation. If he needed any greater compensation for the opposition that his inventions had encountered 'in high places' it came when the serving officers of 617 Squadron volunteered their intention of taking some active interest in the boys and girls of the Foundation, for to him this was comprehension in the highest place of all: among the heirs to the men 'that went in jeopardy of their lives'.

But there was still one detail to be added if all was to be given an immediate tradition: with great care Wallis designed a badge that in its masculine shoulder-version was the same size as the badge worn by the RMS: its central theme he based on the crest of 617 Squadron. His pleasure in this task was in no way diminished by the knowledge that the dies for one of the original badges worn by Mathemats had been presented to Christ's Hospital by another Fellow of the Royal Society and Governor, Sir Isaac Newton.

Joined thus in a happy if accidental conjunction in Wallis's mind, the names of Christ's Hospital and Sir Isaac Newton were

Wood carving of Molly
Wallis by Barnes Wallis

Christ's Hospital, Barnes
Wallis R.A.F. Foundationers
Badge

Sir Barnes Wallis's Armorial
Bearings

Sir Barnes Wallis and the author

soon to come together again in circumstances that, though no
less fortuitous, were for Wallis fraught with difficulties that made
the association far from pleasant.

In June 1952 in the midst of the *Wild Goose* trials Wallis
was ill with a bad bout of influenza—and, as sick-bed relaxation,
turned to other projects which had nothing to do with aeronautics.

I have been able to work all day [he wrote to Molly] on the
Quatercentenary article on Christ's Hospital which the merciless editor of the memorial book tells me must be in before the
end of the month, and all this afternoon and evening on the
new Isaac Newton telescope design for an equally merciless
Astronomer Royal, who says he must have my drawings by
the end of *last* month.[3]

Wallis had been lured into the committee that was preparing
plans for the construction in Britain of a great new radio-tele-
scope by the overt promise that he would be uniquely responsible
for the design of the mount (that part of the telescope which
allows it to point to any sector of the sky and which includes
the drive system) but, as was his custom, he had shown from the
beginning of the project what some others regarded as a poacher's
interest in the design problems associated with other parts of
the telescope. He had settled for an altitude-azimuth mount; in
itself a conventional mount that allows a complete rotation
through 360° about a vertical axis and movement in elevation
about a horizontal axis. To this and to the accompanying drive-
system which permits accurate tracking of celestial objects, Wallis
added certain novel principles. He had it in mind that the lay-
out should be such as to utilise the proposed control system in
which the telescope is constrained to follow the movements of a
small equatorial unit placed at the centre of motion of the telescope. His notions he perfected while he was ill in bed, and the
whole dogma was dictated to his new secretary, Pat Lucas; but
it met with no enthusiasm from the 'nagging' Astronomer Royal.
None the less Wallis kept his telescope in mind, returned from
time to time to his papers, and in 1955 applied for a patent.[4] Then
it was just in time to be used in response to a specification put out
by the Australian Government, and when the Australian 210-foot

Radio Telescope was commissioned at the National Radio Astronomy Observatory, Parkes, New South Wales on 31 October 1961, its mount-system was based upon Wallis's plans. The pointing accuracy was within 1 minute of arc at any orientation, up to wind-speeds of 20 m.p.h. Wallis had in fact exceeded the specifications.

> It is not yet possible [wrote E. G. Bowen in 1963] to give exact figures for the tracking accuracy, but it is already clear that the telescope is capable of tracking sources for many hours to an accuracy better than $\frac{1}{2}$ minute of arc and that the absolute accuracy is within 1 or 2 minutes of arc.
>
> The drive system of the telescope has some unique features which came from the fertile brain of Dr Barnes Wallis of Dambusters fame.[5]

Another project for sick-room completion was not mentioned in his letter to Molly. For years he had been interested in bridge-building. As early as 1932 he had been in touch with the consulting engineers involved in rebuilding Waterloo Bridge. In the midst of the war he had corresponded with the Ministry of Supply about the possibility of applying his theories of geodetic construction to the building of light alloy pontoons. Before the end of the war he had on paper a design for a new London Bridge. Now, inspired by the slightest hint from the Chairman of the London County Council, Mrs Helen Bentwich, he rushed to design a bridge to go across the Thames at Charing Cross.

The bridge has never been built. *The Christ's Hospital Book* did appear but not before its editors had been accidentally responsible for causing Wallis much pain.

Almost as soon as he had been elected to the Royal Society the place fell vacant that the Royal held by right on the Council of Almoners of Christ's Hospital—the school's innermost governing body. Like Armstrong before him, but with the added authority of one who was himself a Blue, unashamedly Wallis proposed himself for the vacancy, was accepted and immediately demonstrated that he had no intention of regarding his new office as an honour without attendant responsibilities. Within weeks of his appointment he was writing to Chas. E. Browne a series of lengthy, quizzing and perspicacious letters about the teaching of science.

(Later he answered a question about his concentration upon the Science School, by saying that this was the side of education that he understood best and that it was also the emphasis that was virtually compelling upon the representative of the Royal Society.) The example of Armstrong and Browne was his Elijah's cloak, and he wore it with a dash, but they had seen science at Christ's Hospital in terms of an educational experiment. For Wallis it was both much more and something of much greater subtlety: the philosophical equivalent of his practical endeavours with airships and a sensational series of 'planes. Good science-teaching he saw as the prelude to the creation of a technologically sophisticated reservoir of leadership which could bring to Britain a new renaissance and which could make Britain once more the head and the centre of a Commonwealth that would share this glory. Like Armstrong before him he recognised the advantages of launching his experiments from a base that was his to command, from a school that, despite the erosion of independence in the twentieth century, was still less than most institutions subservient to Governmental or parental whim. More than Armstrong or Browne his own loyalties were involved with Christ's Hospital, but in 1946, and still twenty and more years later, Christ's Hospital science was to him a prototype to be designed, used experimentally, proved in flight, and then served up as a model for development elsewhere.

Science at Christ's Hospital may be taken as including Mathematics, Physics, Chemistry, Biology, and their associated subjects: but more broadly might be defined as a *method* of *education* that will prepare every Scholar of the House who desires a scientific career, to play a leading part in the life and work of the Commonwealth.

Above all other, this Religious Royal and Ancient Foundation is fitted to be the nursery of those qualities of spirit and mind of which we stand so sorely in need, and to produce from its Science School . . . leaders who *are* men of imagination, men determined to worship God and in so doing to serve their fellow-men.[6]

Wallis could not easily hide even from his friends who were not scientists the truth that was not quite revealed in this as in most of his more politic utterances on the subject. Try as he might to be courteous—and he did not always try very hard—what he was really saying was that a scientific education, and after the heuristic pattern which he had enjoyed, is not only the best of all forms of education but also the one sure foundation upon which the future greatness of Britain could be built.

This certainty some took for conceit, reading the aspiration as autobiography; and it is undeniable that all the qualities listed in the paragraphs just quoted, including religiosity, were qualities possessed by Wallis. But it was not because of his determination to continue to print a battle for science-teaching at Christ's Hospital that his contribution to *The Christ's Hospital Book* brought him soon into bitter and humiliating argument with the school authorities. Were it so the whole episode would belong with institutional history and would merit no more than passing attention; it is of importance to the understanding of the whole man only because as much as any account of opposition endured over airships, bombs or planes, this unhappy incident—occurring, as it did, in a sphere of activity where respect and affection for the man was generally untrammelled and at a time when he had but recently completed his greatest act of charity—may seem to reveal something in the chemistry of Wallis's human relations. If Wallis had been content to write about science at Christ's Hospital few would have questioned his right or skill at riding a hobby-horse. Even his wilder notions of the future of Christ's Hospital as a quasi-university, though they might have caused eyebrows to rise, could not have sharpened many daggers at a time when the establishment of county colleges was a proclaimed part of national educational policy and when advanced thinkers were already discussing the possibilities of sixth-form colleges. But over many years Wallis had been dedicated to the thesis that Britain needs its educated middle-class; this by 1952 was a heresy against the received faith of the nation, and because a Wallis hint is sometimes a bludgeon, the casual suggestion that in a welfare state the role of the only truly charitable public school might well include not merely the defence of the middle-class but even the provision for that middle-class of an élitist education, was heresy vile enough to kindle once more the fires of Smithfield.

It is, therefore, as a substantial development of Wallis's view of British society and not merely as part of a history of filial devotion to the school that had reared him, as verbalisation and practical exposition of theories of social re-organisation and not just as reiteration of long-held beliefs about the role of science in education, that the controversy about *The Christ's Hospital Book* serves both as example and as prelude to all of Wallis's work for Christ's Hospital, and as a typification of much that is central to his life-story.

The narrative of the controversy is simple; the implications sensational. The *Book*, an entirely voluntary contribution to the celebrations of the school's four hundred years of philanthropic existence, had been designed by a small committee of literary Old Blues, as a history of the school in the form of an anthology from the writings on their schooldays and the influence of the school on their own lives and the nation's life by Blues of four centuries. It says much for the affection and respect with which Wallis was regarded by his Christ's Hospital peers that he was the only prospective contributor who was allowed entire freedom of length and subject.

When Wallis had been asked to write for the *Book* he had himself seen the danger-signs and had written to the Executive Editor a letter which contains much of his philosophy and, for the first time, some doubts about the influence of Chas. E. Browne.

Very many thanks for your letter which brings me once more face to face with a difficulty that I have felt for a long time, namely, that I am not in agreement with the educational policy which was initiated under the joint leadership of 'Uncle Chas.', Usherwood and Averill, and has been followed ever since. No doubt they acted under the powerful influence of Professor Armstrong, at that time Chairman of the Education Committee of the Council of Almoners.

The policy has resulted in a tendency to magnify and develop the Manual School at the expense of the Science Laboratories. A contributory cause of the neglect, more particularly of the Physics Labs., is the fact that ever since the foundation of the Science Schools in 1897, the head of the Science School has been a Chemist, a natural reflection of Armstrong's influence, as he also was a Chemist, and moreover one who seems to have cared little or nothing for Physics.

It would however grieve me sorely to write anything that

might hurt 'Uncle Chas.' in his blindness and old age. After forty years' practice as a Scientist, I am convinced that any attempt to specialise or to teach technology in the most formative years of a boy's life is wrong. I believe that the initial excuse for founding the Manual School was Armstrong's idea that *dull* boys could be taught through their hands better than their heads or bottoms; but surely the great social changes which have taken place in our time make the use of Christ's Hospital as a charity, for the relief of parents rather than the education of boys, superfluous. It is therefore my view that the Council of Almoners now control an organisation which should be regarded as a great national asset for the education of those who are by nature fit to become leaders in any profession which they may choose after leaving School, but whose parents would not otherwise be able to afford a Public School education.

I quite realise that it would be a mistake to fill the school entirely with clever competition boys but at the same time it is wrong to present children so dull they can only be taught through their hands. The very idea that Christ's Hospital may be anything *but* a charity for the benefit of parents seems to make octogenarian Almoners angry.

I do not feel able to write in any other strain but that outlined above, with the addition that it is the development of strong individuality rather than mass training which is the important thing for this country in our greatly changed economic condition, and individuality is a virtue that Christ's Hospital knows how to develop above all others.[7]

A parenthetical note is needed if it is to be made clear that whatever reservations Wallis might add to his continuing enthusiasm for his old schoolmaster, his devotion to Uncle Chas. had never wavered nor his gratitude, but, as often happens in enduring relationships between beloved teacher and successful pupil, with the years the terms of reference had changed. By the 1920s the two had been meeting as equals, now, as Browne's health failed, Wallis became the senior, the careful partner. In the last years of a very long life Browne went blind. So that he might continue to correspond with his friend Wallis taught himself Braille, bought and learnt to use a Braille typewriter. Never one to waste knowledge or skills, even after Browne's death Wallis found a use for his Braille. With it he could indulge a rare sybaritic delight: each night he read from the Gospels whilst snugly wrapped in his blankets.

When the Editors of *The Christ's Hospital Book* considered Wallis's proclamations of his intention to write in the strain that he had outlined they failed to see the rocks ahead; instead they encouraged Wallis to write what he wished.

Wallis took up the invitation. The article he wrote and re-wrote over and over again so that it 'occupied my attention and my reading for a far too great proportion of my time'. He discussed it with the Headmaster, H. L. O. Flecker, and twice visited Chas. E. Browne in Sussex 'to make sure that the background was right'.

The article as drafted from his sick-bed reached the Executive Editor on 12 July 1952 accompanied by a letter of rare modesty. The Editor, he said, could turn him out without offence. On 17 July he received a 'heartening letter' (his expression) from the Executive Editor who had liked the article *per se* and who was by no means concerned about the element of controversy which it contained. Certain minor changes were suggested but none that touched sense, argument or phraseology, and such suggestions Wallis accepted meekly. Within a week the article had been rewritten and returned. As a courtesy Wallis sent copies also to the Treasurer, the Clerk and the Headmaster.

There followed: explosion. Flecker objected to being quoted even with his oft-expressed view that the easy entry into Christ's Hospital of 'dull boys' inhibited the School from achieving its full academic potential. The Treasurer (quite accurately) said that he did not know what it was all about but (entirely inaccurately) that it should not be said in an article that was part of the official celebration of a great occasion, and R. C. Evans, the Clerk, wrote a bitter letter in which he accused Wallis of indulging in 'sly manœuvres', of 'using the opportunity to press his own views', of bringing in 'controversial matters which are not particularly related to the teaching of science' and of entirely missing the purpose of the book, which 'is intended to be a thanksgiving for Christ's Hospital'.

On 28 July Wallis withdrew his article. 'I have neither the time nor the will to write any sentimental matter on such an important subject.'[8]

Barnes Wallis

This might have been the end of the unhappy incident had not the Book Committee, like Wallis himself, been exasperated not only by the Clerk's impertinent attempt to censor their efforts but also by his arrogant assumption that piety must be backward-looking and that 'thanksgiving' cannot include criticism and constructiveness. The Executive Editor wrote a personal letter to Wallis begging him to keep his article in the ring 'until such time as we can either defeat the Clerk or else withdraw the whole of the *Book*'. Wallis agreed, admitting at the same time that this support 'restored his self-confidence and self-respect'. *The Christ's Hospital Book* Committee met at the Reform Club on 12 August 1952. All members were present except the poet Edmund Blunden, off teaching in Hong Kong, and such was the agreement of those present that they decided to make unanimity patent by sending to Blunden a long explanatory cable. Philip Youngman Carter released some of the tension when he pointed out that although it was true that many of those who bought the book would be among the class that might be accused of being dullards, not one of them would take that accusation to himself. Two of the Committee went off to seek the advice of the perennial adviser to all Blues, the former Headmaster, Sir William Hamilton Fyfe, and found him entirely of their opinion. Blunden's cabled reply was equally firm: 'We all love Housey too much to love her idly.' He would support any protest and any action on the part of the Committee. A letter was sent to Wallis and he was told that it had been drafted with the intention of being shown to Evans— and to Flecker.

> As members of the committee which is preparing a book to celebrate four hundred years of Christ's Hospital, we appreciate your co-operation in our venture and having read your contribution on Science at Christ's Hospital, we were all convinced that nothing but good could come to the School from publishing it . . .
> We realise that the Clerk's comments spring from his desire to do his duty as he sees it, but we all feel that the assumption is unwarranted that our book should praise the past without ever attempting to prepare the way for the praise of succeeding generations . . . and we all feel, as you must feel and as any observer of English education must feel, that external circum-

stances have forced something of a crisis on Christ's Hospital; the combination of these two facts, and your own unquestionable distinction as a scientist, give to you, in our opinion, a peculiar right to state your views about the future of the School . . . Remembering the stern tradition forged by our predecessors who are honoured in this book, we cannot resist the observation that to this particular venture censorship is especially inappropriate. Fear of loving criticism by one of our own number will only expose the School to spiteful criticism by strangers . . . all you have said has already been said in the *Book*, with appropriate changes for generation, by the greatest of all Christ's Hospital writers, Lamb and Coleridge, and that if we omit what you say, we should, by rights, omit what they have said. I am sure you will agree, and that the Clerk will agree with you, that omitting Lamb and Coleridge would reduce *The C.H. Book* to the level of the ridiculous.[9]

Nothing more was heard from the Clerk or the Headmaster. Wallis rewrote the article yet again but without removing any of his criticisms or constructive dreams—even the crucial passage about 'dull boys' was left untouched. *The Christ's Hospital Book* appeared early in the summer of the Quatercentennial Year, 1953, and was received with enthusiastic reviews (even by a number of reviewers who were not of the fraternity!). It has been through three printings and two editions, and still sells widely even outside Great Britain. There has not been one further word of complaint about Wallis's contribution.

17 By Reason of Strength

By the summer of 1953 Wallis felt
that he had proved that swing-wing was a viable thesis; he had
demonstrated that *Wild Goose* could fly and that its performance
was all that he had promised; he had in mind a solution to the
problem of landing her without disaster. But he could find little
support for his theories, and the opposition, arrogance and
intellectual uncouthness of most of the officials who visited
Predannack goaded him to meeting rudeness with violent explosions of temper. For these explosions he would later apologise—
to his God, to his private diary and to Molly.

His hopes for the future were raised when George Edwards,
a former subordinate in the Vickers hierarchy but now chief
aerodynamicist to the firm, was ordered by the Board to carry
out a design-study for a bomber built to the *Wild Goose* principles
that might serve as successor to the Valiant, only to be devastated
when Vickers issued a fiat to the effect that if, within four weeks,
Wallis could not establish irrefutable proof of the success of his
Wild Goose trials, then Vickers would withdraw support from the
Predannack experiments. The evidence that he had produced so
far Vickers did not regard as conclusive.

Wallis argued his way out of his definitive damnation, but he
saw now that he must fight a battle on two fronts: against his
own employers, and against the 'mean and ignorant little men' in
Whitehall. But there was one considerable weakness in his
opponents' armoury. The Air Staff had to have a successor to
Valiant, no other aircraft firm had come near to finding a suitable
candidate for the succession, and, within Vickers, his competitor-
designers had wrestled for three years with the specifications laid
down by Whitehall and were still no nearer a satisfactory answer
than they had been at the beginning.

By Reason of Strength

That *Valiant* existed at all, and that it should be succeeded by other manned bombers was the consequence of a compromise in a debate about the future of Bomber Command. If one bomb could cause more devastation than all the bombs launched in a thousand-bomber raid, then, it was argued, there was no longer any need for Britain to maintain a large Bomber Command; after Hiroshima there could never again be a Dresden. Instead of a large number of bombers operating at comparatively low heights and therefore unpressurised but equipped with heavy defensive armament, what was needed now was a small force of high-altitude, high-speed bombers, equipped with sophisticated electronic equipment for precision bombing, and, with pressurised crew quarters, but without extensive defensive armament. Moreover, with the arrival on the scene of long-range ballistic missiles, it might be possible to dispense entirely with manned bombers.

Whichever way the pundits argued, the force of their persuasiveness was much reduced by Britain's miserable bank-balance. The nation that had stood alone against the Axis had, in that process, sacrificed its economic well-being. It was palpable that Britain could not afford both bombers and missiles, while sensible accounting seemed to indicate that it could not find the funds for either, but must in future depend for its deterrent upon the United States. This conclusion was to bedevil all political, military, economic and aeronautical thinking in Britain for the next quarter of a century. Economic frustration was to be also a principal cause for the disappointments suffered by Wallis over swing-wing, for ultimately the nation could not or would not risk funds that did not exist for an advance that promised much but that was, nevertheless, hypothetical.

However, within two years of the end of the war, and urged on by public opinion, the Government was persuaded to attempt to provide Britain with both high-altitude bombers and ballistic missiles, and the British V-bomber force was born with the first Valiants.

Once committed, the Royal Air Force set as specifications for a successor to Valiant an aircraft with an all-up weight of 175,000 lb and a much higher altitude and speed performance; it was Wallis's conviction that he could demonstrate the superiority of swing-wing over all the other modes of design, and that he could give to the Air Staff all that it required. He was bemused into thinking that he would by these means persuade his Vickers colleagues out of their tacit opposition to his project. He was determined to prove that his *Wild Goose* was a swan. Very soon his swan-to-be had changed *genus*, and Wallis was at work on the 'plane that came to be called *Swallow*.

Objections to his theories were not all spiteful or jealous, as on occasion even he was prepared to admit. There was, for example, some cause for genuine doubt about the amount of laminar flow that he could obtain with *Wild Goose* and *Swallow*. Laminar flow he thought to be vital to performance, but early in 1954 he set about proving the virtues of his own case by acting as counsel for the prosecution. He revised the configuration of *Wild Goose* so as to achieve high performance even if there was no laminar flow at all, but instead an increase in drag consequent upon flow that was all turbulent. The revision was magnificently reassuring. Even were he wrong in his beliefs about laminar flow (and he was not prepared to admit that he was wrong) still *Wild Goose* would make all other designs theories archaic.

It always interests me [he wrote in another unposted letter to Molly] how wonderfully the terms of a desperately difficult problem become clarified after working on it for several years; and how, in the light of the clarified terms the true solution gradually is revealed, till so clear does it become that we can reduce what was once an amorphous congregation of unreconcilable requirements to the severe and economical form of a syllogism.[1]

Wallis's belief in *Wild Goose* had been unshakable, but he had not achieved the high levels in the ratio of lift to drag for which he had hoped. Now, when he came to reassess the configuration, he envisaged a radical change in the cross-section of the fuselage, making the basic form that of a delta with an enlarged spine running down the middle. This revised geometry allowed him to pivot the wings at the base of the delta so that when in the fully swept-back position they formed a continuous line with the delta forebody. There remained only the problem of designing a joint that could be concealed entirely in the narrow depth of the delta at its base corners.

In this, 'the last really big thing that I shall be privileged to do', all now seemed absolute. As construction *Swallow* was a simple exercise in mechanical engineering; aerodynamically it was perfect, and it could have no competitor in subsonic or supersonic flight. Neither the Ministry of Supply nor Vickers could oppose further experiment, leading as it must to an incomparable aircraft.

For a while, Wallis's ecstasy seemed to be justified. Experts appointed by the Royal Aeronautical Establishment could find no fault with the calculations produced in support of his theory. The Ministry of Supply and the Air Staff went over his projected programme of flight-test research and talked glibly of providing him with the means to transfer his centre of experiment to Australia where more favourable conditions would improve the chances of an early conclusion.

Within three months of the moment when the idea for *Swallow* had first struck him, Wallis had designed and built the first subsonic model—and in so doing had won for himself, not eternal glory as a pioneer, nor even the enthusiastic support of his masters, but a bottle of rum from his chief examiner, Dick Ripper, who had bet that the first model could not be at Predannack in less than five months.

From now on the research programme followed the same pattern of alternating elation and disappointment which had been common to most of Wallis's inventions. One day he was reporting to Molly that all problems had been solved; a week later some catastrophe in experiment or some theoretical quandary set him to desperate reconsideration and to the creation of new designs. Somehow, he was able to divorce the frustrations he suffered at Predannack and in his drawing-office at Weybridge from the more public and eventually more consequential impediments that threatened the future of the whole project.

He did not lose his obstinate enthusiasm for resolving the problems that beset *Swallow*. The first model turned turtle on its maiden flight-trials; Wallis made minor adjustments to the design, and in his mind it became once more what it had always been—'the supreme aircraft'. The 'great hydraulic wing-pivot' which he designed in the autumn of 1954, by the spring of the next year had proved itself unworkable. Disappointed but undeterred, Wallis wrestled with the difficulty through four days of a walking holiday and, back in his office, put to paper 'the ideal solution'.

The process of thought, design, trial, test again and think again was too laborious for Vickers, and so the old debate was revived over manned tests. Wallis was adamant and remained firm in his conviction that he must not risk a man's life even if his refusal to accept this common method of cutting the corners were to delay for years his arrival at the finishing line.

In 1955 *Swallow* had progressed sufficiently so that Wallis could have built an eight-feet long rocket-propelled model. This version of *Swallow* was fired on the artillery range at Larkhill, close to Stonehenge on Salisbury Plain and, once again, Wallis was triumphant. His aerodynamic principles were justified: at great altitudes and at two and a half times the speed of sound, *Swallow* was stable. He went on another walking-tour, this time with his son, Barnes, and for a few days forgot all about *Swallow*. Instead his thoughts went back to some of the happier moments of his life—experienced on other walks but with Molly as his companion—and to that moment that he could never forget but that, in recollection, he remembered still as the saddest he has ever experienced. 'Did you remember,' he wrote to his wife, 'that Monday was the day my mother died 44 years ago?'[2]

Barnes Junior had worked for a short time in his father's Research Department, and had complained then that at Brooklands everything seemed a muddle, and that no one seemed to know what he was doing or why. Wallis offered only a grunt as defence but set down in his diary the philosophy behind his research organisation:

My Research Department is certainly unique and follows no known pattern. Indeed it cannot, for research in modern aeronautical engineering *as it is commonly understood and practised* involves the possession of vast apparatus costing immense sums of money . . . and when all's said and done is capable of dealing only with the narrowest aspects of aeronautical science. Indeed, it may be that I owe much of such success as I have had to *entire lack of specialisation* that leaves me free to roam . . . over the widest fields.[3]

But now an almost unprecedented sense of the need for haste was upon him.

By Reason of Strength

Research of this kind has a time element . . . almost as inexorable as the time element in the playing of a great symphony; only, in this case the Symphony one is conducting? composing? playing? is not only unfinished but *unknown*. But still, in spite of this uncertainty, the tempo at which the great movement must proceed is all important . . . I am indeed comparable to a musician conducting an orchestra of very great complexity, playing a Symphony which the conductor is composing as he goes along. I am fortunate if I can keep a bar ahead of the players! What a magnificent title, 'The Unknown Symphony'.[4]

In September, 1955, Wallis had to compose in a hurry two or three important phrases in this symphony in order to present a sensible performance for the benefit of Air Chief Marshal Sir John Baker, who, as Controller of Aircraft at the Ministry of Supply, had the ultimate responsibility for deciding upon the aircraft requirements of the Royal Air Force. This time Wallis was faced with difficulties relating to the structural design of the forebody in the current version of *Swallow*.

It would not come right. It was a mess, all bits and pieces with no lovely thread of unity . . . I felt myself so worried that I put my difficulty to God . . . boldly asking for his help. That was Monday, I think, and by the afternoon light began to dawn . . . by Wednesday I was able to work constructively at my drawing board and by sticking at it until 7 p.m. had the drawing fit to show Sir John Baker next day . . . Laus Deo and again Laus Deo.[5]

By the summer of 1956, most of the technical difficulties with *Swallow* had been overcome, and it only remained for the production team at Weybridge to take over Wallis's proven theories in order to convert them into a prototype 'plane that would lead in turn to variable geometry 'planes suitable for civil or military aviation.
But by the summer of 1956 the shutters were falling.

It is a truism that it is the busy man who has time for new effort. Wallis, in his mature years, was ever ready to set off on some novel chase, providing always that the quarry excited him. Thus, in

1955, when he was deeply involved in *Swallow*, his attention was suddenly caught by the news of a disaster to two British trawlers in Icelandic waters with the loss of forty men. His persisting love of ships sparked off his thinking processes. Without much encouragement from the British Shipbuilding Research Association, but on Vickers' time and with £1,200 of Vickers' money, he set his research team to make wind-tunnel and simulated tests with models. Protesting that 'this isn't really my business'[6]—nevertheless he came back with an answer: the conventional pattern of top-structure and rigging of trawlers encouraged icing which in turn set the ships out of balance and could lead to them turning over. In its place he advocated the erection of a single forward mast with tripod legs. His report was decently buried by the Research Association in a printed document marked 'Confidential—Not for Publication' and trawlers continued to be rigged as heretofore. Thirteen years later his bitterness exploded onto the television screen after another trawler had been lost and with her all but one of her crew. 'It is', he said, 'a case of the usual inertia . . . to re-rig an old trawler would mean putting her out of service for several months which might result in a great loss to the company which owned her.'[7]

But, as he approached the allotted span of his life, Wallis's confidence in his versatility faltered. It could be that the hesitation was no more than a public rehearsal of a doubt that he needed to have dispelled by public denial, for there was much evidence that his physical and mental powers were as great— and perhaps even greater—than they had been for many years. Migraines were now less frequent and less devastating than they had been in the past, though one attack was of such virulence as to make him leave his car to lie down in a ditch by the side of the road, whence he was rescued by his doctor—who was subsequently reported to the police for carrying a body in the back of his car! Enthusiasms and activities were more widespread and more humane. He had time to spare for his grandchildren such as he had never given to his children. As with his grandchildren, so with a whole new generation of friends, he was more convivial than had been his wont. Seeing them as the contemporaries of his much-loved Royal Air Force crews, in their company he discarded much of the reserve that he had shown to his own peers, even to those few older men such as Dr Boyd, Victor Goddard and the artist,

Egerton Cooper, who had long been his intimates. He gave of the skill in his hands—and infuriated Molly—by rebuilding her kitchen whilst she was away (and without consulting her). He was forever busy, and growing busier, in the service of Christ's Hospital.

Nevertheless, reared as he had been both at home and at school to a ready and almost fundamental acceptance of the sonorities and implications of the Bible, the approach of his seventieth birthday brought with it thoughts of the end.

He spent more and ever more time looking over the way he had come, surrounding himself with mementoes of the heroic years of the bombs and of the magnificence of his contribution to the history of rigid airships. He drove close to distraction his habitually indefatigable secretary, Pat Lucas, by the frequency of calls from his office to hers demanding some ancient file in which he could rediscover a minute detail of a distant past as stimulant to reminiscence. Of much greater consequence: he found himself suddenly aware of the age-gap that divided him from Molly. Soon, he knew, he would be unable to cosset her. Soon, too, his creative spell would be ended: his latest designs for *Swallow* would be the last sequence of alternating depression and elation which combined to produce revolutionary ideas.

The awareness of imminent curtain-fall was short-lived. Though many of the traits revealed at this period—among them the conviviality with friends, the gentleness with his grandchildren and the almost obsessive interest in his own past—remained with him for the rest of his days, it needed only one jolt to set him once again ablaze with ideas that pre-supposed for him an almost indefinite future, only one meeting of the 'antagonistic' Ministry of Supply Steering Committee to persuade him to a closer reading of the 90th Psalm. 'The days of our years are threescore and ten'; true, but the Psalmist went on with a qualification: 'if by reason of strength they be fourscore years . . .' For Wallis nothing provided strength so readily as did opposition. He set the thesis down in his private diary:

If I understand the intention of the mediaeval religious technique that imitation stimulates spiritual growth . . . then I suppose I must also admit that, like a hair-shirt, the dullwitted and unimaginative yet vain and self-important fool forms part of the Divine Creator's method of ensuring scientific progress . . .

He identified his own hair-shirt with precision that was far removed from mystical speculation: 'the very hostile attitude of certain officials of the Ministry of Supply' and the spite and petty jealousy of men in Whitehall and at Weybridge who 'never having made, much less created, anything in their lives, are incapable of understanding how the mind of a "doer" works.'

The years 1957, 1958 and 1959 were the years of nemesis for *Swallow* but even now there is no possibility of handing down a certain, clear and judicious summary of the reasons why judgement went against Wallis and variable geometry. Without being fully conscious of cause and consequence the British people have been aware that in some way the great potential of Britain's aircraft industry has been subverted and there has been a substantial ground-swell of indignation over the manner in which, at a time of economic stringency, the nation was forced to use precious dollars to buy back from the United States what was popularly judged to be the bruised fruit of British technical ingenuity.

In analysing such evidence as is available it does appear that the decision to abandon *Swallow* was not taken by one man, not even by an organisation, and that it was not engendered by any logical series of considerations. There was, instead, a skein of judgements, personal, economic, military and political, so tangled as to be beyond unravelling but together strong enough to strangle the project.

Just as he had done in the days of Wellesley and Wellington Wallis contributed to his own damnation by confusing the issue in that he was not consistent in his ambitions, emphasising sometimes the military and sometimes the civil potential of his innovation. He did so because he was forced to look to military purchasers to support work that he himself regarded as primarily of civil utility, but the ambiguity of intention increased the number of his opponents and added to their opportunities for opposition.

Men cloaked with the political authority that could be translated either into inexorable veto or into benediction were concerned less with the true worth of his proposals than with the certainty and speed of success. A long delay before results could be demonstrated to the electorate and the grim possibility that success might never come would leave them vulnerable to attacks by their opponents. It was their political duty to appear infallible and so for them, as for the civil servants who advised them, it was both easier and safer to refuse support rather than to risk failure or long-drawn-out sustenance for an experiment that was at best a gamble. It was this political need to reject the hazards of speculative adventuring that deprived Wallis of the benevolence of the two key Ministers, Duncan Sandys and Aubrey Jones, although both were personally well-disposed towards him. As late as May 1958, within weeks of suppressing aid for Wallis, Sandys himself told a group of newspapermen that he had always favoured the provision of public funds for Wallis, but had been forced to change his mind by contrary advice from the Vickers Board.

It must be said in defence of both politicians and civil servants that they were faced with the almost impossible task of governing a nation that could no longer afford the luxury of attempting at one and the same time many forms of technological progress. Selection was inevitable; the problem was not simply that of judging Wallis but of establishing priorities. Anthony Wedgwood Benn was in opposition when *Swallow* was abandoned, yet less than a decade later, when he was a minister he defended Duncan Sandys and Aubrey Jones, in part on the casuistical ground that the development of *Swallow* would have impeded essential research directed towards the solution of the problems of urban traffic, and in the course of this defence set the sum proposed by Wallis as required for *Swallow* at £300 million more than Wallis had ever suggested, adding on his own account, for good measure and presumably to make the demands seem even more exorbitant and ridiculous, another £600 million, thus insinuating that it would have cost £1,000 million to perfect a variable geometry plane.[8]

If it is difficult to establish with any clarity the attitude towards *Wild Goose* and *Swallow* of those in authority in Britain, it is virtually impossible to analyse the entire failure of the long-drawn-out quest for American support. Wallis never moved from his position that his own efforts to persuade the Americans to fill the financial vacuum that Britain would not or could not fill for herself did not fail but were in effect so successful that the Americans stole his ideas, and in the process missed a most important element in his notions—the tailless nature of *Swallow*—and thus contributed to the failure of TFX (F111 as it came to be known), though even he came to admit that the comedy of justice was also a tragic farce for which Britain, as well as the United States, was to pay a high price.

The wrangling and evasiveness of those who made the decision to abandon *Swallow* may be difficult to elucidate but the overt story of demise is comparatively simple.

It had begun as early as 1954 when, in order that he might win Government support, Wallis had allowed himself to relate his design to military requirements, for the intention of this decision was within three years confounded by the Defence White Paper which promulgated the Government's intention of turning from manned aircraft and relying instead upon missiles as the best means of launching a nuclear strike.

Still in 1957, and despite the White Paper, there was some hope that support would be found for developing at least a small prototype for research purposes, and on 31 October 1957 a meeting was held between representatives of the Government, of Farnborough and of Vickers–Armstrong (Aircraft), at which two proposals were discussed.

The first was that there should be built a research aircraft weighing a mere 10,000 lb. which could be used to test the aerodynamic qualities and engineering possibilities of variable geometry but applied to the traditional form of an aircraft with a tailplane.

The aims of this first proposal were far from satisfying Wallis's interests: the taillessness of *Swallow* was as essential to his thesis as are fourteen lines to the writing of a sonnet. There was more to his liking in the second Farnborough proposal: that there should be arranged an extensive series of wind-tunnel experiments to test what were in effect the true and essential features of *Swallow*; but again to Wallis it seemed as if Farnborough was preparing to take five steps backwards in order to progress. After ten years of thought, calculation, design and testing he felt himself to be far in advance of the need for wind-tunnel experiments.

At the same October meeting there was discussed once more the perennial question of American aid. If such support were to be forthcoming the obvious fairy godmother was the Mutual

Weapons Development Programme, and so Wallis had to somersault yet again. In order to emphasise the military potential of *Swallow* he prepared a dossier in which he outlined ideas for a research aircraft which could lead to a 'plane capable of fulfilling strike or reconnaissance roles, adding for good measure and to retain a hint of utility even in civil aviation, the possibility that *Swallow* could become a military transport 'plane. On 8 August 1958 a team of Americans visited Weybridge, and gave their approval in general but enthusiastic terms. But a tiny and multipurpose research aircraft, they argued, would not give the answers required and they urged upon Wallis that instead he should design and Vickers should build a machine with an all-up weight of 40,000 lb. specifically intended for development into a strike aircraft.

There followed a series of meetings at Weybridge, at the Ministry of Supply and at the Paris Headquarters of MWDP, and at none of these gatherings was there given to Wallis the slightest hint that the proceedings were empty and that most of those present had no thought of doing more than suck from him his ideas without ever allowing him to translate those ideas into reality.

It was not until November 1958 when he visited Langley Field, Virginia for the second time, that Wallis caught a glimpse of the true state of affairs, and even then the decisions that were recorded seemed entirely sensible. The Americans, the Royal Aircraft Establishment and Vickers were to pool the results of previous research into variable geometry aircraft and, for the future, would produce a programme of research which, by allotting specific items to each of the participating parties, could hurry the project forward so that by July 1959 there would be available a sufficient body of results to justify an approach to the United States Congress.

Even now Wallis had not lost his faith in the ultimate justification of his theories, nor yet his capacity for obduracy, but he felt himself isolated. He had outlived most of the civil servants and Government advisers who had in the past rejected him, many of those who were still alive were tending their gardens and counting their pennies; the few who were still working had moved into academic life; and yet he was conscious of regret for the past, for the times when, if only in his recollection, he had walked all-knowing through the doors of power and for the days when he had been able to identify friend and enemy. Of this much he was certain: he was no longer dealing with individuals. There was no Masterman to consult, no McLean to act as his advocate, not even a Burney to hate, a Cherwell to despise, a Beaverbrook or a Harris to persuade; now he was alone in the midst of depersonalised entities.

Faced with the possibility, and indeed with the probability that three faceless giants, Vickers, 'the Americans', and Whitehall, were tossing his brain-child one to the other, and that he could do little to stop it from crashing to the floor, there would have been substantial excuse had Wallis stumbled into depression, but for the most part he met with considerable equanimity a succession of blows at the very foundation of the *Swallow* project.

The execution ceremonies began in earnest in June 1959 and Wallis was of the company that gathered to watch the headsman. In that month John Stack of MWDP came to England, ostensibly to report on NASA experiments with swing-wing. At a meeting at Weybridge at which, as well as Wallis, there were present representatives of the Ministry of Supply, the RAE and the new Military Projects office of Vickers, Stack produced his gloomy recital of disappointments with supersonic tests on arrow-wings, notably that the theoretical camber and twist had not given the expected high L/D. He added to the jeremiad the information that subsonic tests on what was basically a *Swallow* without camber or twist, had produced at high incidence undesirable pitching which could not be controlled by the nacelles.

Wallis said very little; work had already begun at Weybridge to cope with just these weaknesses in the subsonic characteristics of *Swallow;* weaknesses which arose not from any inherent fallacy in the principles but from inadequacies in the mathematical treatment of the wing-design and particularly from lack of sophistication in accounting for the magnitude and distribution of wing-thickness and for the growth of the boundary layer on three-dimensional wings. But the alarums sounded for all to hear when John Stack went on to describe the alternative to *Swallow* that the Americans had in mind to produce as an advanced strike aircraft. Wallis saw it as risible: engines within the fuselage and a horizontal tailplane with surfaces having both symmetrical and asymmetrical movement; variable wing-sweep being used as a means of improving the low-speed characteristics of military aircraft.

By Reason of Strength

Timidly, the Royal Aircraft Establishment collapsed before American timidity and insisted on a tail-plane even for a proposed Naval Air Staff requirement. Whatever Wallis's view of its methods and purposes the Military Projects Office at Weybridge did in fact fight, far more fiercely than he would admit, a sturdy rear-guard action for a tailless 'plane, but, in March 1950 it too surrendered and a tailplane was added to the feasibility study for the Naval Air Staff aircraft. And still Wallis did no more than write a token letter of protest.

From that day to this no critic has been able to fault the theories embodied in *Swallow*, but Britain has not built a prototype. The Americans went their own way into disaster with F111, and Britain shared the burden of the fiasco. But Wallis abandoned with such calm the dreams and the work of thirteen years that even those who knew him well thought that at last old age was upon him. There was no spilling of acid and no recrimination; Wallis just bowed out. He had his reasons.

For more than a year before the final collapse of Vickers' efforts for a tailless variable wing-sweep 'plane, the man who had begun it all had been resigned to the end of *Swallow*. It was not the benevolence of old age that kept him calm. Once more Wallis had outstripped his own ideas; for the last two years of the life of the *Swallow* project he had been proving to his own entire satisfaction that *Swallow* and indeed the whole notion of a variable geometry 'plane was obsolescent, and would soon be as obsolete as Concorde, Wellington, the *R.100*—or even the stage-coach and F111.

The theme of airship days still rang through his mind. The lines of communication between Britain and the Commonwealth must be shortened and rendered safe from political, economic or military enmity. He knew how it could be done.

A totally new concept of design was in his thoughts.

He wrote the epitaph for *Swallow* on the last pages of his unposted letters to Molly:

No one, looking at the New Conception could possibly trace its descent back to its Swallow ancestors. But I emphasise here most strongly that, intellectually at least, the new creation derives from the Swallow, by the purest descent; 'by Swallow out of B.N.W.' as a stud record might say. Why do I stress this point so much? Principally, I think, because any stranger reading this queer record in which I attempt to describe some fourteen or fifteen years of hard work, must be left with an impression of failure and frustration; certainly not one of triumphant accomplishment. Yet I go on, always some New Thing springing up, full of promise, meeting or avoiding all the old difficulties, just as it seemed that at last I must admit defeat, and retire, old, discredited and disillusioned . . . but here am I just turned seventy-three years of age, still working all the days of the week and still developing and inventing.[9]

There is a sardonic footnote to the tangled history of political, international and aeronautical decisions that led to the death of the *Swallow* project. Almost a decade later, at a time when Wallis was entirely committed to the revolutionary concept in design that had made him accept so tamely the end of *Swallow*, Denis Healey, the Labour Minister of Defence, announced support for a project which he claimed would be 'a tonic to the aircraft industry'. Britain would provide £250 million to an Anglo-French project for building a variable geometry military aircraft. By 1970 even this archaic programme had died an unnatural death and there was persistent rumour that there would soon be buried with it that other hope for the industry that had stood in the way of *Swallow*, the Anglo-French Concorde. What was by then certain was that among those who were most energetic in digging a grave for Concorde and would dance and drink champagne at her funeral, were members of that very same group that had helped to bury Wallis's swing-wing project: the American aircraft industry lobby. By 1970 they had discovered new and emotive terms of abuse and rallied to their service new allies. Concorde was so noisy and her passage through American airspace would pollute the atmosphere beyond permissible limits; the highly vocal environmental lobby was on the side of the aircraft industry lobby. These objections Wallis had forecast when Concorde was still on the drawing-board; not one of them could have been raised against *Swallow*.

In July 1957, at the time when Wallis was considering coincidentally the imminence of his own end and means for averting the death of swing-wing, he accepted with eagerness and pride a new role which he knew to be sufficiently demanding to fill the days of most ordinary men, and, by accepting, demonstrated the shallowness of his pessimism about his own future. He became Treasurer and Chairman of the Council of Almoners of Christ's Hospital. Memories of the elegant Treasurer's House in Newgate Street made him aware of the great honour that came with the office. But he had been an Almoner for eleven years and from that experience had come to recognise that to be Treasurer of Christ's Hospital is no mere gaudy sinecure. The trappings he enjoyed, insisting, for example, on the privilege of the Treasurer to walk on the right-hand side of the Lord Mayor of London on all occasions when the two are together save only when the Sovereign is also present. Even he added decorations of his own devising to traditions that he inherited, appearing on all public occasions resplendent in the scarlet gown of one of his many honorary doctorates. But, through the Clerk and the Counting House in Great Tower Street, the Christ's Hospital Council of Almoners administers not only two great schools (the Boys' School at Horsham and the Girls' School at Hertford) but also a considerable number of smaller charities, many benefices, vast properties and a necessarily huge portfolio of investments, and for this skein of responsibility the Treasurer is the ultimate arbiter. If he does nothing else he must be present at innumerable meetings, public functions and school occasions, but if he is to be the kind of Treasurer Wallis wished to be he must be at very least aware of the problems that face such a complex organisation, and on occasion must be prepared to direct the manner of their solution. Moreover, at the time when Wallis took office Christ's Hospital, despite its uniquely charitable status, felt itself threatened no less than other public schools by elements in political life and society that were bent upon destroying the independent sector in the British educational system. Add to all this the conviction which Wallis had already proclaimed in *The Christ's Hospital Book* and which he shared with the new Headmaster, C. M. E. Seaman, that if the School was to survive with honour it must adapt itself to the circumstances and *mores* of the second half of the twentieth century, and it will be seen that Wallis had set himself a task that, when added to an energetic professional life, demanded of him almost superhuman energy and resilience.

Barnes Wallis

Wallis was Treasurer for almost thirteen years and in that time spared neither himself nor anyone else in furthering the ends that he thought essential for the future of the institution. His creative ebullience, his fantastic energy and his unmatchable proclivity for detail made him a superbly useful focus and inspiration in a period of change and development, whilst his belief that other men could, and indeed should, give of themselves as unsparingly as did he himself, at once fitted him for leadership in a society that was re-assessing its own role and must also find the means whereby it could fulfil the new or amended tasks that it came to see as essential, and at the same time blindfolded him to all objections that ordinary men might raise against his demands for their collaboration. With some new idea alight in his mind he would summon to Effingham from his home in Sussex and at a moment's notice the Clerk of Christ's Hospital, Alan Allison, rather than leave discussion until their next ordained meeting. Having decided to make it possible for the newly-needy middle-classes to benefit from Christ's Hospital's charity and therefore wishing to present to the Council a case that would convince them to shift upwards in the financial scale the boundaries of need, Wallis announced as his conviction that, were the limits of 1958 translated into the purchasing values of previous centuries most of the notables produced by the School would have been refused entry into the School. To support his case he called upon a fellow-Blue to produce in one week a paper on the subject. Such was Wallis's dynamism that there could be no shirking. Six days later he had on his desk a thirty-page document listing the parental circumstances of every Old Blue in the *Dictionary of National Biography* and, so far as was practicable, converting into contemporary terms the financial implication of those circumstances. Wallis was right. By this significant if inevitably rough-and-ready calculation only one notable, George Dyer (Charles Lamb's *Amicus Redivivus*), could have been certain of a place, only one other, the greatest of them all, Samuel Taylor Coleridge, might have qualified as a member of an inordinately large family— and, incidentally because it was not relevant to the particular argument that Wallis had in mind, only one, Sir Henry Maine, was the child of a broken home. Wallis would descend, without notice, upon West Horsham or Hertford and launch into an inspection of the trees or the fire-precautions. (Perhaps from his

362

experience as an aircraft-designer he had a phobia about fire, and both for the Christ's Hospital schools and for his home designed an elaborate system of fire-precautions and fire-warnings.) When Flecker had left Christ's Hospital Wallis had hoped to replace him with a scientist, and it is some measure of the importance that he attached to the Headmastership that, in private conversation with his eventual biographer, he mentioned as possible candidates two Fellows of the Royal Society, as it is in addition some measure of his naïveté that he was incredulous and even angry when he was told that neither man was likely to quit the comforts of Research Chairs in great universities for the headmastership of a public school, even if that school was Christ's Hospital. But when Seaman was appointed, although like all his predecessors he was a Classic, Wallis found him, if no more amenable than Flecker, in every other respect more to his liking, and the two together set about the tasks of reorganising the Boys' School and of raising the huge sums of money that were needed if reorganisation was to be made physically possible.

His time, his thought, his unceasing care he gave no less to the peripheral charities and to the Girls' School, but it was the Boys' School that had his heart; his obsessive enthusiasm and his well-nigh blatant optimism communicated to others. At a time when almost every independent educational institution in the country was appealing for funds, when, in the adverse economic climate that surrounded them, most were falling far short of their targets, Christ's Hospital asked for £700,000 and raised close to a million. Much of the credit must be given to that devotion to the Foundation that Wallis shared with many Old Blues. (Most of the money came from within the 'family' and much of it in small contributions.) But without Wallis's determination and energy the Appeal would have lacked drive and might well have foundered.

None the less, it was in the spending of the money (even before its availability was assured) that Wallis's skills were most happily exercised. He had said once that, had he been born in some other era than his own he would have enjoyed most the Middle Ages, and had he then been given the choice of calling he would have elected to be a monk living out his life in the seclusion of a monastery, contemplating the magnificent wisdom of the Almighty, and offering to God the service of his hands by chipping out gargoyles for the cloister roof. This claim was a wondrous exaggeration, a superb example of self-deception based either upon a blurred vision of his own nature or upon an interpretation of what he would have liked that nature to be. Wallis was too sensual, even too sexual, for the celibate life; although he seldom sought publicity he enjoyed its glare when it came to him, sought it when it was useful to him and, from the days of his early manhood, was so certain of his own abilities, so close to arrogance, that he could never have suffered with equanimity the oppression of enforced anonymity. True, he loved to work with his hands, and a sculpture in wood that he had made of Molly's head, even if it was engineered in part by an elaborate system of measurement, still stands as memorial to the stone-mason that might have been. True, too, that his religion was simple and unquestioning, but the prime gift that he had offered to his God throughout his life was not acceptance but inventiveness, and he worked most successfully, not at projects on a minute scale, but at the process of deriving order and advance out of a huge mass of variegated detail.

Thus it was that the reconstruction of Christ's Hospital, both in terms of buildings and of social and educational reform, gave to him an opportunity at least as great as that which he had enjoyed in the building of *R.100*. He bustled from theory to idea, from practical problem to practical exposition. Eliminate the Preparatory School (this suggestion, made originally by Seaman, fitted to the precepts already set down by Wallis at the time when he had established the Royal Air Force Foundation), create junior houses, provide for older boys facilities for privacy far more lavish than he himself had known either in Newgate Street or at West Horsham. Add class-rooms, laboratories and playing-fields to meet the needs of the second half of the twentieth century. Every part of the scheme involved measurement, calculation and the preparation of drawings, and so there was little in the scheme to which Wallis could not turn his own skill. He re-designed the central heating system. He calculated the effect upon space requirements of the substantial growth in the average size of boys since the days when the West Horsham Dining Hall had been built. He considered the demands forced upon the School by changes in society at large, and particularly by the prevalence of early marriage; no longer could Christ's Hospital depend for its internal organisation upon a majority of young and bachelor masters; now, even bachelors were no longer prepared to live out their off-duty hours in rooms that were so public that they denied the possibility of there being any such thing as off-duty. So, if it were to be well-staffed, Christ's Hospital must build far more married quarters and better accommodation for its bachelor masters. As had always been his habit as an aircraft-designer so now, when he turned architect, he considered the aesthetic qualities of the buildings he proposed but, because his prime concern was that the new must not clash with what had been built sixty years earlier, he was soon in conflict with the apostles of modernity; Wallis, the man who in aeronautical engineering was always decades ahead of his contemporaries, when he attempted to be an architect, found himself under fire from many distinguished Old Blue architects for his reactionary devotion to the style of the late nineteenth century. But Wallis was adamant and Wallis had his way.

The money for change was found. Wallis prepared drawings in such detail as must have given the architects commissioned to translate them into new buildings little scope for exercising their own creative powers. He supervised the builders like a foreman —or like Wallis at Howden overseeing every detail in the construction of his airship. No sooner were the buildings up than Wallis was once more eagerly in alliance with Seaman. The School needed a new classroom-block, an Olympic-size swimming pool, and a theatre and concert hall. Again Wallis was at his drawing-board. The challenge to his engineering skills implicit in the particular needs of a theatre gave him especial pleasure. He studied the science of acoustics, and with a seriousness that came from long experience of producing aircraft that could be used for many purposes set himself to the task of creating a building that need never stand idle; as always, he looked to the past for new ideas about the future, reading widely in the history of theatre architecture.

But for these new plans again there was no money available and so, towards the end of his term of office but with optimism undiminished even though it came so soon after the earlier Appeal (whose success had surprised everyone except Wallis), he encouraged the Council of Almoners to launch a new appeal for funds.

As Treasurer Wallis's energy was unbounded. He was, without

doubt, the most significant holder of the office in all of its long history, and once when asked to name his memorial he pointed at the new buildings of Christ's Hospital and quoted the words of another Fellow of the Royal Society, Christopher Wren: *Si monumentum requiris, circumspice*. But there was much of gentleness and humility in his attitude to Christ's Hospital— and for the most part a readiness to accept a need to adapt to the modes of times that he did not himself regard as beneficent. Just as he would invade West Horsham unannounced for a tour of inspection so also would he slip unheralded into the day-room of his old house to take Communion with the boys. A stalwart defender of tradition must be capable of amendment. Some of these amendments were to him concessions of considerable sub-stance. For example, he detested but saw as inevitable the relaxa-tion of hierarchical notions, the abolition of the swab-system (in other schools, 'fagging') and the shrugging-off by older boys of responsibility for discipline and organisation. Some concessions were trifling, but no less difficult for a man in his seventies. Again as example, he could not understand why it was that the boys of the 1960s took strong objection to wearing braces, but none the less he set in hand a redesigning of the school uniform that would allow this 'pernicious habit' (his words) to continue without con-tributing outward signs to the inward sloppiness he detected in the young.

For the permissive society he had no patience, and he was deter-mined to keep its evil influence away from Christ's Hospital. The merest hint of homosexuality roused him to fury and a flurry of Biblical quotations, and even the suggestion that Christ's Hos-pital might give some consideration to co-education, although it was put to him by a friend as a topic for lunch-time conversation, and was indeed a suggestion that had been canvassed with some seriousness already in his own school-days, brought blood to his face and angry words to his lips. But, except on what he regarded as immutable moral issues, as his mind was made up, his capacity for driving through the changes that he thought desirable, out-stripped by far the powers of younger and habitually more radical men.

In August 1962 Wallis went into the Middlesex Hospital to undergo an operation for the removal of his prostate gland. It was a self-imposed decision: 'I determined to take the old body in hand before it became necessary'; influenced not a little by his trust in the surgical skill of a fellow Old Blue and fellow Almoner of Christ's Hospital, Sir Eric Riches, whom he described in several of his letters of the time as 'the great urologist'. On his first visit to his patient after the operation Riches said: 'We've added ten years to your life' and next day found Wallis busy with graph paper and pencil working out his chances. The details, together with a lesson in statistics, Wallis set down in a letter to his daughter, Mary; a letter that was never posted, perhaps because he decided that the account with which he prefaced the forecast, a detailed description of the male reproductive organ, though scientific, was too frank even for a young middle-aged woman with a family of her own.

The calculations of life-span are in a charming way reminiscent of those mathematics lessons produced for Molly forty years earlier.

Great-Grandfather d. aged 72 years in 1860
Grandfather d. aged 81 years in 1906
Father d. aged 86 years in 1945
Now it is not really possible to apply mathematical laws to an *individual*, but only to very large numbers of individuals . . . but it is amusing, if no more, to take advantage of the singular regularity of advance shown above, to see how old I should be assuming that mathematical laws *did* apply to an individual. Neglect end effects, as we must do, since historically they are buried in prehistoric times and for the future are unpredictable for a variety of reasons, then we can treat the above sequence as a very small part of a curve that extends virtually to infinity in both directions . . . The simplest form is parabolic and the curve that fits the 3 known points reasonably well is $N = 72x^{0166}$ where N is the age at death and x is the number of generations . . . On this basis I should have lived to just over 90, but now that I have had an op . . . Estimated age at death = 100 years!

Of course it's all nonsense anyway . . . but it has passed a tedious hour in hospital. And who knows but that fractured femur, the motor-bus or the drunken motorist will render it all false anyhow.[10]

Wallis's reputation rests upon his magnificent ingenuity as an innovator. Speak his name, and even the uninformed offer as immediate response 'the dam-buster'. Those who are more sophisticated will add their own count of his achievements: airships, Wellesley, Wellington, variable wing-span; even, if they have access to more intimate affairs, his work for Christ's Hospital. But that there has been a consistent pattern in his efforts for fifty years; a pattern that was broken only by the eccentric necessities of war; is neither generally appreciated nor, were it accepted, would it be regarded with much respect by those who mistake patriotism for chauvinism. Wallis was historian as much as he was prophet. His view of the past might be challenged by many, for it was founded upon the conviction that since the sixteenth century Britain had been the hub of the world. His vision of the future was such that could but seem ludicrous to a nation that from 1918 doubted its own strength and after 1945 seemed to take masochistic pleasure from its own impotence. Britain, he argued, retained many of the advantages of geography, inventiveness and leadership that once had made her the greatest of the powers; it needed only the waving of the wand of genius to excise all contemporary difficulties so that Britain could restore her confidence, revive her strength and return once more to her preeminency. He did not see himself as the unique magician but that the wand had been in his hands on many occasions he could not doubt. Rigid airships, long-range 'planes, variable geometry and, in the last years, the long-range cargo-submarine and the 'square' 'plane—he saw them all as something much more than advances in engineering, for in turn each to him promised a new golden age for Britain. So too, and with no great difference in philosophical texture, did his determination to create at least one educational institution which could provide the reservoir of leadership that must exist if technological advance is to be exploited.

Close to eighty years old, proud of the honours that he had won from his peers but hurt by lack of recognition from the nation that he had served so well, and by his feeling of isolation in the great business corporation which had been the centre of most of his working-life, still he looked forward by looking back, saw what glory had been and planned for its renaissance. The logic of his life was by now clear to him but there were conclusions still to be drawn and dreams as yet unfulfilled. He was not yet finished.

Once more he looked back to consider the factors that had

contributed to Britain's past greatness, not with any intention of writing a threnody but in order to pose for himself and for the nation a question: could those factors be used once more to restore Britain's hegemony and, if so, in the circumstances of the 1960s—so very different from the situation when he had set out upon his career before the First World War—what part could he play in the Second Elizabethan Age?

The answers to both parts of his question were perhaps convenient to his experience: it was *centrality* in terms of sea and air-routes rather than numerical superiority that had created Britain's power; *centrality* is immutable, unaffected by economics or military strength.

To say 2,000 years ago [he wrote in 1965] that 'all roads lead to Rome' was to describe a condition that depended on the continued existence of the Roman Empire; to say now that all *oceans* lead to England is to describe a condition as permanent as the surface of the globe, depending only on our ability to invent, to design and to build merchant submarines that will derive their propulsion power from a machinery installation that is reliable and cheap.[11]

Nuclear submarines would be the cargo-carriers of the future. The power required to drive a submarine at high speed even when submerged deeply is far less than that required for a surface vessel of equal displacement travelling in calm water at equal speed. A submarine is independent of wind and weather and, because it is possible to design an underwater craft that can travel three or four times faster than its surface equivalent, it is not even necessary to contemplate the construction of submarines as large as cargo-liners. Further, if for all sea-faring nations submarines would provide benefits far greater than conventional surface-vessels, for Britain those benefits would be supererogatory for, to a very large extent, the existence of a high-speed submarine cargo-fleet would erase the one factor that throughout her existence as a great maritime power had been an inhibition that accompanied the many advantages of Britain's island situation: her vulnerability to blockade and starvation in time of war.

For years thereafter he accepted his own persuasiveness, and design after design for a nuclear-propelled cargo-submarine appeared on his drawing-board. Each design contained some element of novelty for even had he tried, Wallis would have found it difficult to achieve pastiche, but with the one possible exception that he realised that the grammar of design for all cargo-carriers (even submarines) must be founded upon the newly-developed principle of containerisation, his drawing-board submarines were not radically different from those appearing on drawing-boards in other places, notably in the United States.

However, if the line of argument that urged him forward to the design of submarines was in some senses illusory, because in terms of his own experience it turned him back to his beginnings, most of those same arguments could be used—and were used by Wallis—to establish an unanswerable case for re-thinking Britain's aviation and aeronautical future. Here, though his own past was, as ever, the base on which he intended to build his contribution to the future of Britain, that past was virtually the whole of his adult career and had been enriched by such variety of applicable experience as was available to no other aircraft designer in Britain or, indeed, in the whole world. Because age, which in so many men blunts originality, seemed in Wallis to serve as whetstone, because in this, like many another old man, his energies were increased by the certainty that inexorable time was against him, and because (as must be admitted) his obstinate dislike for most of the men who were creating and managing Britain's aviation policies persuaded him to look suspiciously upon the very premises upon which they founded those policies, he was soon hurling himself into areas of design philosophy that were revolutionary, and in the process hit upon certain entirely novel principles of aeronautics.

At the time when this biography is being written Wallis's 'square' 'plane theories have not been tried even by the most rudimentary testing-processes, so that it is impossible either to deny or to support their validity, but the intellectual history of this, the latest of Wallis's many efforts, which would prove 'the greatest development in aviation since the Wright Brothers', follows a pattern that derives from his heuristic training, that recurs frequently in Wallis's biography, and that set him apart from many (though not from all) discoverers. First came the identification of a need—in this case as so often before—the future of Britain as a great power; secondly, an attempt to design a vehicle that would meet that particular need; and, thirdly and seemingly accidentally, the discovery of a novel theory that was by no means an inevitable concomitant of the first two steps in the pattern; and ultimately, the propagation of the theory in intellectual terms that made it appear at times as if Wallis himself had forgotten his original motives in seeking to identify the need.

The strength of Britain was his text: but—and in this lay the quintessential difference between his thinking about sea-power, both mercantile and strategic, and his new philosophy about the use of air-routes—if Britain was to create a future in the air the British aircraft industry must discard the logic of its own history, deny the seemingly inevitable progress towards larger and ever larger 'planes, and seek out some entirely novel principle which would make it possible for a small, overcrowded island to serve as the greatest mercantile aircraft-carrier in the world.

His conviction that he could and must think in terms that appeared to contradict the tenor of British Aircraft Corporation activity was made even easier for him because he believed that it was through no fault of his own that he had been isolated from the firm's decision-making processes. But, if there is in his whole career any action which can arouse something more than admiration, something akin to adulation, it is the manner in which now, when by all sensible accounting he could be held to be an old man, he was prepared to deny, at least by implication and at times by explicit statement, the validity of his own previous achievement in order to set himself and his countrymen to new modes of thought.

Wallis was confident that what was needed—and was inherently possible—was a short take-off and land aircraft; something that could fly from a runway of no more than 500 yards. Given this, many advantages would follow: a multiplicity of runways within one airport complex close to metropolitan centres so that aircraft could move in and out like trains into a London railway station; runways close to all centres of industry or tourism; frequent economical cargo and passenger service between the continents.

He looked round him and saw a declining situation. In a decade Britain's competitive position had been eroded. Except for the Concorde, which was in any case an Anglo-French project, there was in sight no successor to the Tridents, Comets, Vanguards,

Viscounts and VC10s that were still the mainstay of British airlines. (In the early 1960s the Boeing 707 had been the only American 'plane in regular use by British lines.) Similarly, there was little promise of military heirs to TSR2, P1154 and the Hawker-Siddeley 681. But Britain's aircraft industry must survive and, more important, Britain herself must remain a great power. Both aims could be achieved, not by following blindly in the way others were leading, but by finding instead an entirely new direction for British aeronautical thought. Among Wallis's papers is a note, written it would seem in 1964, which summarises his conclusions:

1. Size of aircraft reverts to something of the size of BAC One-Eleven. Optimum A.U.W. around 100,000 lb.
2. Costs of jigs etc. becomes small fraction of cost of production.
3. Number of aircraft sold even in a market as small as Britain enough to pay development costs.
4. S.T.O.L. less liable to accident. Numbers involved fewer if accidents did occur.
5. Frequency of departures—cargo and passenger—for any given destination greater—a convenience to industry and travellers.
6. Greater possibility of achieving supersonic speed. At least ranges at supersonic speeds of 10,000 miles but equally efficient at subsonic speeds London–Paris.

He had written his own specification for the 'plane of the future. It all seemed so elementary and so obvious that even Wallis felt bound to explain away the blindness of his contemporaries: 'Thus performance,' he wrote in that same paper 'The Strength of England' which had propounded the doctrine of nuclear cargo-submarines,

lies so far outside that of any existing craft that the question will at once be raised as to whether such an aircraft is physically possible, or is merely an idle dream. The answer is that given an adequate amount of invention and research, it should be possible. A second question then arises, as to why this ideal solution has eluded the great experts of the aeronautical world. In this case the answer probably lies in the fact that no other country than England has the same urgent need to build many smaller aircraft rather than a few very large ones, and that hitherto we have been content to follow the lead of the U.S.A.[12]

And, as with his plans for submarines, he soon came to add to his specification one further requirement. His new aircraft must be so designed as to make them amenable to the principles of containerisation. It was this final and seemingly minor addition to his theorising that brought him to a new discovery. Not for the first time, he was made aware of the fact that God is the greatest engineer of them all—and Wallis his disciple. Wallis could do all that he hoped to do because in seeking to do what he wanted, he had hit upon certain aerodynamic principles that had hitherto passed unnoticed. Mathematics was no mere support to his inclinations; instead it enhanced positively the efficiency of his theories. Because a 'square-shaped' aircraft would be more appropriate to containerisation than the streamlined, 'cigar-shaped' form that had become conventional after fifty years of development, Wallis had it in mind to break with the insistent logic of aeronautical history. To achieve this end, he would erase from his thinking a long-held tenet, and with it the memory of the record of which he was so proud: his own consistent ability to demonstrate that what is aesthetically satisfying is, in engineering terms, generally most efficient. With this revolutionary premise as his starting-point he began to consider the possibilities of a 'square-shaped' fuselage, and he discovered to his delight that calculation showed that if he gave to his air-frame two skins, and even though he used not expensive metals such as titanium but the comparatively cheap light-alloys that are commonly employed in aircraft construction, still his 'square-shaped' fuselage was close to eight times as strong as the 'cigar-shaped' aircraft. Next, he discovered that the square-shape had positive aerodynamic advantages. He could reduce to the order of 20–25 per cent the proportion of structural weight to all-up weight at take-off (as compared to $33\frac{1}{3}$ per cent for the VC10) and this of itself implied a reduction in the fuel-load necessary for long-range flight. The strength of his air-frame obviated most of the risks from decompression explosions such as those which had destroyed early *Comets*. Best of all, his investigations proved that the shape he had in mind could survive the heat barrier discarding, with ease far greater than conventional frame-shapes, kinetic heating. All in all he could envisage as a theoretical possibility a hypersonic 'plane flying at five or even six times the speed of sound, and for it a range of at least 10,000 miles. Without refuelling—on the ground or in the air—his 'plane could fly from London to Australia in something like three hours. By adding to his structure small swing-wings it could be made to operate also at subsonic speeds over short routes. On paper he was close to achieving the miracle that he knew to be Britain's necessity. All that remained was for Britain to recognise the wine that flowed from the water-fountains.

A new word had entered into the common vocabulary of critics —'science-fiction'—and they used it avidly when Wallis released to the Press some tiny gobbets of information about his novel theories. Wallis grumbled at them on account of the number of times in the past he had written science-fiction and proved it to be the fact of science; once more he growled that if Britain would not have him the United States could—and went back to his drawing-board to improve upon his plans for the aircraft that would fly Britain first among the nations into a new and glorious age.

There must be some reticence in describing in any detail work that still continues and that is not yet set to paper even in theoretical terms. It would have been simple to omit all reference to Wallis's latest efforts, at least until such time as they could be added with confidence to the list of his achievements. But a biography that is happily incomplete because its subject is still alive and working would be reduced in significance if it did not give some hint of continuing effort, for among the greatest of the many great elements in the life of Wallis is his refusal to accept leisure as the principal benefit of longevity. As with a cricketer the last strokes that bring him to his century are no less arduous of achievement and no less skilful than the first run on the board, so Wallis continues into his mid-eighties the application, the hard work and the originality of thought that he had practised for many decades.

Ten years on from the seventy allowed him by the Psalmist, but still twenty short of the century he had forecast with the aid of Eric Riches and genealogical evidence, for all his protestations of mortality, Wallis behaved as if there could be no terminus to his activities. On every week-day he drove himself from Effingham to Weybridge, his only concession to the years a studied avoidance of rush-hour traffic and dependence upon the services of a chauffeur when he visited London. In his Brooklands office he worked for hours at his drawing-board, served up abstruse mathematical problems to his calculators, with the aid of Pat Lucas maintained an enormous correspondence, but he was seldom in contact with any British Aircraft Corporation colleagues outside his own Research Department. Even professionally their interests were not his and his social isolation he himself emphasised by lunching each day from a tray brought to him in his office. Nor did he entertain often in his own home, where there were few visitors except his children and grand-children. But in London he was by no means unsociable and he had become with the passing of time a familiar figure at the Athenæum, where his sprightly and upright gait, his ruddy complexion and his unruly but still unthinned white hair made him appear by no means the oldest member of a club that is not given to electing young men. He was also, in a sense, a figure familiar to the public at large for the film of *The Dam Busters* continued to tour the cinema circuits, while his own appearances on radio and television, and the perversely likeable explosiveness which he gave to the press-interviews for which he was called upon with ever-increasing frequency, had to some extent eradicated what had hitherto been a commonly-held view: that Barnes Wallis was a fictional or conglomerate character, who had been given reality and uniqueness only by the superb acting of Michael Redgrave. His reiteration, in newspapers, radio and television, of past achievements and long-vanished frustrations had also erased that suspicion, held by some, that there must have been more than one Wallis, for although it was not easy to believe that the same man could have devised *R.80*, *R.100*, Wellesley, Wellington, the war-time bombs, and swing-wing, and almost impossible to accept that the inventor who was still murmuring promises of immediate but inconceivable advance in aeronautics had taken part in the design of Rigid *No.9*, at every public appearance and in every newspaper article, whatever subject Wallis was called upon to discuss he somehow turned into an essay in autobiography.

Even so, Wallis, it seemed, was best-known for being unrecognised. For his part, he did little to remove the confusion or to discourage the conclusion. The wounds would not heal that he had received in a life-time of battling to persuade his countrymen to accept his prescriptions for national health, and there was no balm for the scars earned over almost forty years while he watched other (and, he felt, lesser) men receiving public honours that were unjustly denied to him. He was, it was true, garlanded with distinctions in such number as had been given in his time to few men except successful war leaders. In addition to the Fellowship of the Royal Society, he had six honorary doctorates, was a Royal Designer for Industry, a Fellow of Churchill College, Cambridge, and had won almost every prize appropriate to his profession. But these were all honours granted him by his peers or fellow-practitioners in recognition of scientific superiority, and as such did not compensate entirely for years of deprivation by raising him above his fellows. Seen in the context of British custom his was not an unusual ambition; if it was snobbery that caused him to want to re-create the vanished aristocratic condition of the Wallises it was none the less innocent of snobbery, and justi-fied by his achievements. But, when it seemed inconceivable that the nation could any more redeem the slights of several decades, Wallis (in this no less than in his ambition, typically English) attempted to tease himself out of an attitude that he knew to be regarded by some as a pretentious folly. Questioned by his biographer as to whether he would accept the long-overdue knighthood were it at last offered to him, he replied without hesitation. The Fellowship of the Royal Society was the only distinction that he had coveted; it had come his way and after it many academic honours that he relished. But a knighthood or even a peerage would reduce him to the level of ——, and there followed a catalogue of his private Chamber of Horrors, but with each name in the long list twisted deliciously, and often maliciously, so that the recital sounded like a reading from an edition of Debrett that had been rewritten by Lewis Carroll, and yet with each name so immediately recognisable as the name of one of his many enemies that, had the conversation been over-heard, Wallis would have had no answer save 'justified comment' to several actions for slander.

Then, in 1968, the inconceivable became fact. Wallis was offered a knighthood. He forgot his protestations, turned a somer-sault, and accepted the honour with alacrity, pride and delight. It was inconsistent, perhaps, but those who loved him and admired him—and by now they were many, far more than Wallis would himself credit—paid little attention to consistency, much to his merit, and everything to the removal of a national shame. The congratulatory telegrams and letters poured in, and, close to home and in distant places men, many of them to Wallis unknown, took pleasure in his accolade, and, as he would have wished, privately stole some of the glory for themselves. The few survivors of the Royal Naval Air Service rigid airship projects and of the high adventure of *R.80* and *R.100* felt that the public reward so long refused to them was at last theirs when Wallis's name appeared in the Honours List. Men who had flown in 'Wimpys' remembered that they owed their survival to his ingenuity. Old Blues all over the world read that yet another distinction had come to Christ's Hospital, and knew that justice had been done at last to one of their number, and he *primus inter pares*. Though to close friends Wallis explained away his inconsistency by saying that it was for Molly's sake that he accepted the title, Molly Wallis cared far less than her husband for laurels of this kind, but she was pleased for him and relieved that at long last a major cause for grievance had been taken from him. The scattered remnants of the war-time 617 Squadron saw the knighthood conferred on their Prof. as yet another decoration won by the squadron.

Wallis, whose pleasure in dreaming up heraldic devices had already been shown by the care he had taken in preparing the badge of the RAF Foundation, now decided that he would not revive the old Wallis family crest, but instead would submit to the College of Heralds a coat-of-arms of his own designing. His thoughts turned inevitably to 617 Squadron and the Dams Raids, and through those thoughts there echoed the voice of his brother, John.

Long ago, when Wallis was in the Artists Rifles, a mere lance-corporal whose hope of fame was small and whose chance of surviving the First World War scarcely greater, he had gone for a short furlough to his brother's home at West Horsham. There, one day John had found Barnes digging a ditch in his garden, and had quoted at him a Latin tag, *spernit humum*, adding 'when you get a knighthood you must take that as your motto'. The memory of his brother's words had come back to Wallis when he was designing the RAF Foundationer's badge, and then had seemed wonderfully suitable for his purpose, not merely because the verse that contained the tag was of itself remarkably apt for his purpose, but also because its aptness was strengthened by that other verse from the same Horace ode: the verse that includes the line *dulce et decorum est pro patria mori.* Now that the knighthood had come, he knew that he could have no other motto. For his whole life, Horace's verse—and his brother's quip —took on the awesomeness of prophecy fulfilled.

> Virtus, recludens immeritis mori
> caelum, negata temptat iter via,
> coetusque vulgaris et udam
> spernit humum fugiente penna[13]

It is the inner worth of those who do not deserve death which plots their course, and opens for them a way to heaven that is barred to the ordinary, so that they rise on soaring wings, spurning both the complacent throng and the clogging earth.

Notes

1 Childhood

1 Letter. B.N.W. to Mary Wallis, 20 August 1956.

2 Life as a Scrub

1 B.N.W., 'Science at Christ's Hospital' in *The Christ's Hospital Book*, London, 1953.
2 *ibid.*
3 W. H. Fyfe, 'Looking After and Before' in *The Christ's Hospital Book*, London, 1953.
4 Charles E. Browne, *Henry Edward Armstrong—Educational Work* (privately printed), London, 1954.
5 A. B. Ubbelohde in *Edwardian England* (ed. S. Maxwell-Smith), Oxford, 1964.
6 E. H. Rodd, *Charles E. Browne: an appreciation of his work for the Reform of Education at Christ's Hospital, 1899–1926* (privately printed), London, 1967.
7 *ibid.*
8 Letter. B.N.W. to J.E.M., 15 December 1960.
9 Letter. B.N.W. to J.E.M., 28 December 1960.

3 Christ's Hospital, Horsham

1 H. T. Wickham, *The Transition from London to Horsham* (ed. P. J. Firmin), London, 1961.
2 Reginald Spence, *Reginald Spence Remembers*, Uckfield, n.d.
3 G. A. T. Allan, *Christ's Hospital*, London, 1937.

379

4 Letter. B.N.W. to J.E.M., 7 November 1967.
5 Letter. B.N.W. to W. Donald Douglas, 22 October 1937.
6 Letter. B.N.W. to E. S. Allwright, 29 October 1937.
7 B.N.W. in *The Christ's Hospital Book*, London, 1953.

4 The Thames and Cowes

1 Letter. B.N.W. to Edith Wallis, n.d.
2 Letter. B.N.W. to Edith Wallis, 9 February 1908.
3 Letter. Edith Wallis to B.N.W., 14 January 1907.
4 Letter. Edith Wallis to B.N.W., 20 July 1910.
5 Letter. B.N.W. to E. J. Carnt, 24 March 1912.
6 B.N.W. Notebook, 31 January 1950.

5 Mr Mountain's

1 Letter. H. B. Pratt to B.N.W., 31 July 1913.
2 Letter. V. Caillard to B.N.W. Vickers File Miscellaneous 467, 12 August 1913.
3 Draft Letter. B.N.W. to . . . Fisher. Undated but presumably 1914.
4 58 *H.C. Deb.* 5s. 785, 17 February 1914.
5 Draft Letter to Fisher, *op cit.*
6 *ibid.*
7 Letter. B.N.W. to H.B. Pratt, 20 September 1914.
8 Lord Beaverbrook, *Politicians and the War*, London, 1960.
9 Letter. H. B. Pratt to B.N.W., 20 September 1915.
10 Letter. B.N.W. to J.E.M., 16 January 1964.

6 The First World War

1 Letter. H. B. Pratt to B.N.W., 29 September 1915
2 Letter. Director of Air Services to Messrs Vickers, 6 October 1915.
3 Letter. H. B. Pratt to B.N.W., 22 October 1915.
4 Letter H. B. Pratt to B.N.W., 2 November 1915.
5 Letter. H. B. Pratt to B.N.W., undated but presumably either 20 or 21 November 1915.

6 Letters. E. A. Masterman to B.N.W., 9 November 1918 and 17 March 1919.
7 Robin Higham, *The British Rigid Airship, 1908–1931: A Study in Weapons Policy*, London, 1961.
8 'Metal Aircraft Construction', Vickers File, February 1919.
9 C. H. Gibbs-Smith, *A History of Flying*, London, 1953.
10 Vickers File. PR/6X, November 1915.
11 Robin Higham, *Britain's Imperial Air Routes 1918–1939*, London, 1960.

7 R.80

1 Letter. E. A. Masterman to B.N.W., 9 November 1918.
2 'London–Paris–Rome Airship Service', Vickers File, October 1919.
3 Letter. Victor Goddard to B.N.W., 8 April 1920.
4 Letter. B.N.W. to H. B. Pratt, 28 February 1920.
5 U.S. National Archives. *R.972* Airship History, Box 18.
6 Letter. J. C. Hunaker to B.N.W., 8 February 1921.
7 Letter. Charles Craven to B.N.W., 3 December 1921.

8 Chillon and Courtship

1 J. D. Scott, *Vickers: A History*, London, 1962.
2 Higham, *op. cit.*
3 Letter. B.N.W. to Molly Bloxam, 9 December 1922.
4 Letter. Giles Howard to B.N.W., June 1945.
5 Interview J.E.M. with Lady Wallis, 7 March 1968.
6 Letter. B.N.W. to Molly Bloxam, 6 November 1922.
7 Interview with Lady Wallis, 7 March 1968.
8 167 *H.C. Deb.* 5s. 709–11, 26 July 1923.
9 Letter. B.N.W. to J.E.M., 16 January 1969.
10 Letter. B.N.W. to J.E.M., 17 January 1969.
11 Letter. B.N.W. to Molly Bloxam, undated.
12 Letter. B.N.W. to Molly Bloxam, 26 May 1923.
13 Letter. B.N.W. to Molly Bloxam, 18 May 1923.
14 Letter. B.N.W. to Molly Bloxam, 23 August 1923.
15 Letter. B.N.W. to Molly Bloxam, 19 November 1923.
16 171 *H.C. Deb.* 5s. 886, 21 March 1924.
17 Letter. B.N.W. to Molly Bloxam, 4 March 1924

18 173 *H.C. Deb.* 5s. 1344-9, 14 May 1924.
19 Reported in a letter. B.N.W. to J.E.M., 17 January 1969, from a note recorded in 1924.
20 Letter. B.N.W. to Molly Bloxam, 30 July 1924.

9 *R.100*

1 Nevil Shute, *Slide Rule*, London, 1954.
2 P.R.O. AIR 5/1062, February 1924.
3 Geoffrey Salmond to Secretary of State for Air, P.R.O. AIR 5/1046, 6 August 1925.
4 Letter. B.N.W. to J.E.M., 31 January 1969.
5 F. A. de V. Robertson in *Flight*, 30 August 1928.
6 Letter. B.N.W. to V. C. Richmond, 8 August 1927.
7 Letter. Salmond to Fellowes, P.R.O. AIR 5/1046, 16 October 1925.
8 Letter. Salmond to Fellowes, P.R.O. AIR 5/1046, 10 November 1925.
9 Letter. Fellowes to Salmond, P.R.O. AIR 5/1046, 8 July 1925.
10 Letter. C. Longhurst to L. G. S. Reynolds, P.R.O. AIR 5/1046, 1 May 1924.
11 P.R.O. AIR 5/987. This draft was probably written in 1929 or 1930.
12 A.M.S.R. Letter, P.R.O. AIR 5/1046, 20 September 1926.
13 Letter. B.N.W. to J.M.M., 16 March 1937.
14 Letter. Molly Wallis to Mary, 10 April 1926.
15 *ibid.*
16 Letter. Molly Wallis to Mary, April 1929.
17 Letter. Molly Wallis to Mary, 12 August 1926.
18 Letter. J. Temple to B.N.W., undated but probably 1927.
19 Dennistoun Burney, *The World, The Air and the Future*, London, 1929.
20 Letter. B.N.W. to Molly Wallis, 17 February 1926.
21 Patent No. 22,538/25.
22 Letter. B.N.W. to H. W. S. Outram, 4 March 1927.
23 Memorandum. Burney to B.N.W., 3 October 1928.
24 211 *H.C. Deb* 5s. 491, 30 November 1927.

10 The End of Airships

1 Letter. Molly Wallis to Mary, 27 January 1926.
2 Letter. B.N.W. to Robert McLean, 22 August 1931.
3 Letter. B.N.W. to The Master of Sempill. 8 July 1928.

Notes

4 Letter. E. F. Spanner to The Master of Sempill, 11 May 1928.
5 *ibid.*
6 Letter. A. P. Herbert to the Editor, *The Times*, 16 October 1929.
7 Letter. A. C. Mason to the Editor, *The Times*, 18 October 1929.
8 *The Times*, 21 October 1929.
9 Higham, *op. cit.*
10 Air Ministry Letter 522017/29/D of C/A1386, 6 June 1929.
11 Letter. Molly Wallis to Mary, 11 August 1929.
12 Letter. B.N.W. to Molly Wallis, 26 August 1929.
13 Letter. Molly Wallis to Mary, 13 January 1928.
14 Letter. B.N.W. to Molly Wallis, 26 August 1929.
15 Shute, *op. cit.*
16 Burney, *op. cit.*
17 Higham, *op. cit.*, and James Leasor, *The Millionth Chance*, London, 1957.
18 Quoted in Leasor, *op. cit.*
19 Letter. Molly Wallis to Mary, 18 November 1929.
20 Letter. Molly Wallis to Elaine Barr, 1969.
21 Interview. B.S.W. with J.E.M., 18 November 1969.
22 236 *H.C. Deb. 5s.* 1319, 12 March 1930.
23 Shute, *op. cit.*
24 239 *H.C. Deb, 5s.* 2142–3, 4 June 1930.
25 Letters. B.N.W. to Molly Wallis, 29 April 1930.
26 Leasor, *op. cit.*
27 Letter. B.N.W. to J.E.M., 31 January 1969.
28 Statement of Major Oliver Villiers, P.R.O. AIR 5/911, 24 November 1930.
29 Letter. B.N.W. to J.E.M., 15 February 1969.
30 Letter. B.N.W. to J.E.M., 3 March 1969.
31 *e.g. The Engineer*, 22 May 1931.
32 Letter. B.N.W. to H. Rowley, 20 October 1930.
33 Letter. B.N.W. to Sir Trevor Dawson, 2 April 1931.
34 Letter. B.N.W. to J.E.M., 31 January 1969.
35 *ibid.*
36 Letter. Peter G. Masefield to the Editor, *The Daily Telegraph*, 25 April 1969.
37 Memorandum C.A.S. to A.M.S.R., P.R.O. AIR 2/379, 13 October 1930.
38 Memorandum A.M.S.R. to C.A.S., P.R.O. AIR 2/379, 16 October 1930.
39 249 *H.C. Deb. 5s.* 2135–6, 19 March 1931 and 252 *H.C. Deb. 5s.* 1391–487, 14 May 1931.
40 256 *H.C. Deb. 5s.* 11 September 1931.
41 Letter. P. L. Teed to the Editor, *The Engineer*, 1 May 1931.

11 Wellesley and Wellington

1 *Fortune*, March 1934.
2 Scott, *op. cit.*
3 C. F. Andrews, *Vickers Aircraft Since 1908*, London, 1969.
4 Vickers Report, July 1935.
5 Paper entitled 'Vickers Wellesley Long-Range Medium Bomber (Pegasus Engine)—Vickers–Wallis Geodetic Construction'. Undated but filed with papers for 1937.
6 *The Vickers Wellington I and II*, Profile number 125, n.d.
7 Andrews, *op. cit.*
8 Letter. B.N.W. to J. B. Prior, 18 October 1934.
9 Letter. B.N.W. to H. B. Pratt, 8 October 1934.
10 Monthly report from S. Yamada, Vickers Aviation Representative in Japan, April 1936.
11 Letter. H. B. Pratt to B.N.W., 10 July 1936.
12 Letter. H. B. Pratt to B.N.W., 14 July 1936.
13 Letter. B.N.W. to H. B. Pratt, 26 July 1936.
14 Letter. B.N.W. to Molly Wallis, 14 August 1932.
15 Letter. S. Custance to B.N.W., 18 January 1936.
16 Sir Robert McLean in *The Sunday Times*, 18 August 1957.
17 Andrews, *op. cit.*
18 Letter. B.N.W. to J. E. McCann, 10 November 1938.
19 Letter. B.N.W. to J.E.M., 5 September 1969.
20 Scott, *op. cit.*
21 Interview. B.N.W. with J.E.M., 4 September 1969.
22 Letter. Sir Robert McLean to B.N.W., 21 December 1938.

12 Wallis goes to War

1 Letter. B.N.W. to Nigel Norman, 22 May 1939.
2 Scott, *op. cit.*
3 Letter. B.N.W. to J. S. Pringle of the Admiralty, 21 November 1939.
4 Letter. B.N.W. to N. M. Couch of the Admiralty, 11 December 1939.
5 Vickers Flight Test Report, 21 December 1939.
6 Reported in a note of 8 March 1940 but referring to information received much earlier—probably before Christmas Day 1939.
7 No. 3 Group Report quoted in Denis Richards and others, *Royal Air Force, 1939–1945*, London, 1953–4.
8 *The Aeroplane*, 8 November 1939.

Notes

9 Letter. B.N.W. to N. E. Rowe, 8 March 1940.
10 Note on a visit to Weybridge by Dr Main-Smith of the RAF, 19 January 1940.
11 Letter. B.N.W. to Masterman, 1 August 1940.
12 'Why Not? Why Not?', B.B.C. Television Service, 19 January 1967.
13 Letter. B.N.W. to Alex Dunbar, 21 July 1940.
14 Letter. Beaverbrook to Vickers, 9 January 1941.
15 Constance Babington-Smith, *Evidence in Camera*, London, 1957.
16 F. W. Winterbotham, *Secret and Personal*, London, 1969.
17 Letter. Desmond Morton to F. W. Winterbotham. Winterbotham in his book dates this letter merely 5 July. From the text it seems likely that the year was 1940, though this does not match with Winterbotham's statement that he did not meet Wallis until the Autumn. It seems more likely that the meeting took place in the autumn of 1939.
18 B.N.W. Paper, undated, but presumably written in 1946.
19 Minutes of a Meeting held at the M.A.P., 11 April 1941.
20 Earl of Birkenhead, *The Prof. in Two Worlds*, London, 1961.
21 Letter. F. W. Winterbotham to Director of Scientific Research, 11 April 1941.
22 Letter. H. T. Tizard to B.N.W., 21 May 1941.
23 Road Research Laboratory Report MAP/32/ARC, 1941.
24 David Irving, 'The Night of the Deluge', *Sunday Express*, 8 May 1968.
25 Cranz and Becker, *Exterior Ballistics*, 1921. (The experiments described were carried out by Ramsauer in 1903.)
26 'Spherical Torpedo' (final copy dated 2 April 1942).

13 The Attack on the Dams

1 Sir Arthur Harris, *Bomber Offensive*, London, 1947.
2 B.N.W. Paper. 'Air Attack on Dams' (final version dated 5 February 1943).
3 Winterbotham, *op. cit.*
4 Letter. Lady Merton to B.N.W., 27 October 1969.
5 Conversation. Air Chief Marshal Sir Ralph Cochrane with J.E.M., 5 April 1970.
6 Letter. Norbert Rowe to J.E.M., 1 April 1970.
7 Letter. B.N.W. to Tizard, 16 June 1943.
8 Irving, *op. cit.*
9 Letter. F. W. Winterbotham to J.E.M., 4 April 1970.

10 Richards, *op. cit.*
11 Babington-Smith, *op. cit.*
12 Report on air attack on Möhne and Sorpe Dam. [German] Civil Defence Department, Intelligence Branch. I.O. (J.X.) No 493, 30 September 1943.
13 Interview. B.N.W. with J.E.M., 21 April 1970.
14 German Report headed *Möhnetal—Katastrophe*, 4 June 1943.
15 Letter. Arthur Harris to J.E.M., 28 April 1970.
16 Joseph Goebbels, *The Goebbels Diaries, 1942–1943*. Trs. L.P. Lockner, London, 1948.

14 The Big Bombs

1 Letter. Harris to J.E.M., 28 April 1970.
2 Babington-Smith, *op. cit.*
3 Richards, *op. cit.*
4 Goebbels, *op. cit.*
5 Minutes of a Meeting at the Air Ministry, 8 June 1943.
6 Letter. Bufton to B.N.W., 12 June 1943.
7 Interview. B.N.W. with J.E.M., 18 July 1969.
8 B.N.W. Diary, 13 July 1943.
9 J. E. Morpurgo, *American Excursion*, London, 1949.
10 Letter. B.N.W. to David Pye, 15 November 1943.
11 Quoted in Richards, *op. cit.*
12 Richards, *op. cit.*
13 Paul Brickhill, *The Dam Busters*, London, 1951.
14 Prime Minister to Chiefs of Staff Committee, 25 January 1942.
15 David Woodward, *The Tirpitz*, London, 1953.
16 Brickhill, *op. cit.*
17 Report of Preliminary Investigation into the Sinking of the *Tirpitz*. Dated 5 June 1945 (22 May 1945).
18 B.N.W. Diary 8/'A Visit to Germany in April 1945'.

15 *Wild Goose*

1 Letter. Chief of the Air Staff to B.N.W., 20 August 1945.
2 Quoted in R. W. Clark, *Tizard*, London, 1960.
3 Letter. B.N.W. to Trevor Westbrook, 17 July 1945.
4 Letter. Tizard to B.N.W., 20 June 1944.
5 Scott, *op. cit.*

6 Letter. C. W. Hayes to J.E.M., 29 January 1970.
7 Letter. B.N.W. to Molly Wallis, 17 August 1948.
8 Letter. B.N.W. to Molly Wallis, 23 August 1948.
9 Letter. B.N.W. to Molly Wallis, 24 August 1948.
10 Letter. B.N.W. to Mrs Bloxam-Wallis (sic), 11 October 1948.
11 Interview. B.N.W. with J.E.M., 12 August 1969.
12 Letter. B.N.W. to Molly Wallis, 29 April 1952.
13 Brickhill, *op. cit.*

16 *Swallow* and the Foundation

1 Letter. B.N.W. to Wilfred Freeman, 30 January 1951.
2 Letter. B.N.W. to P. J. C. Prescott, 2 April 1951.
3 Letter. B.N.W. to Molly Wallis, 16 June 1952.
4 British Patent Application No. 29248/1955. 'Improvements in tele-scope mountings'. Vickers–Armstrong (Aircraft) Limited.
5 E. G. Bowen, *Radio Astronomy of Giant Telescopes*, 1963.
6 B.N.W. 'Science at Christ's Hospital', *op. cit.*
7 Letter. B.N.W. to J.E.M., 20 February 1952.
8 Letter. B.N.W. to J.E.M., 28 July 1952.
9 This letter of 17 August was signed by Henry Durrant, Managing Director of the Gallup Poll; Maxwell Martyn, a Director of Hamish Hamilton Ltd, the *Book*'s publisher; the artist, Philip Youngman-Carter, and the authors, Eric Bennett and J. E. Morpurgo. All were Old Blues.

17 By Reason of Strength

1 Letter. B.N.W. to Molly Wallis, 19 March 1954.
2 Letter. B.N.W. to Molly Wallis, 31 March 1955.
3 B.N.W. Diary, 25 September 1955.
4 *ibid.*
5 Letter. B.N.W. to Molly Wallis, 27 October 1955. Unposted.
6 Quoted by B.N.W. in a Television interview, 24 February 1968.
7 *ibid.*
8 A. Wedgwood Benn in BBC Television Programme, 'Late Night Line-up', 19 January 1967.
9 Letters. B.N.W. to Molly Wallis, 11 October 1959 and 7 July 1960. (The two letters though written nine months apart are, in substance, continuous.)

10 Letter. B.N.W. to Mary Stopes-Roe, dated 24 August 1962 but not sent.
11 B.N.W. 'The Strength of England' in *Advancement of Science*, November 1965.
12 *ibid.*
13 Horace, *Odes III*, 2, 21–4.

Index

Abel & Imry, Patent Agents, 88–9
Admiralty: and airship programme, 57, 60–1, 64, 72; and mine threat, 220; Naval Operations Section, 236; new administration 1915, 64–5; recommendations to abandon *No.9*, 61–2; refusal of *No.9*, 74; rivalry with Air Ministry, 85; Special Weapons Section, 239; and Vickers, 54, 61, 76, 78, 85
Aerial Experiment Association, 307
aerodynamic theory: in airships, 77, 127–8, 176–7, 189; in aeroplanes, 198, 307–8, 350, 373
aerodynes, 305, 307–9, 312
Aeronautical Research Committee, 307
aeroplanes, 54; backed by Army, 57; backed by Churchill, 60; developments in First World War, 79–80; first transatlantic flight, 83; tailless, 306–7, 317, 356, 359; use of light alloys in construction, 155–6; without ailerons, 306–7, 328
aeroplanes, design Nos.: SE5a, 71; F7/30, 178; M1/30, 196; G4/31, 196–197; B9/32, 198–9, 212; B1/35, 229; B3/42, 278; F.111 (TFX), 312–13, 317, 359; TSR2, 372; P1154, 372; VC10, 372, 373
aesthetics, 77, 177
Air Council, 85, 100
Air Ministry, 149, 150, 218, 229; Airship Development Section, 122, 141, 150; appointment of Lord Thomson, 119; attitude to Vickers, 210; attitude to Wellingtons, 195–6, 212–13;

Cardington research programme, *see* main entry; and German rockets, 281; opposition to airships, 91; opposition to geodetic construction, 213, 222; opposition to Spitfires, 197, 211–12; Public Relations Section, 287; rivalry with Admiralty, 85, specification for medium day bomber, 198–9; specification for torpedo bomber, 196–7; tender for successor to *R.100*, 164–5
airship construction, experience in, 52–3, 73–4, 188, 307
airship design: information on, 56; Wallis's start on, 55
airship designs: *Nulli Secundus I*, 50–51; *Nulli Secundus II*, 51; *Number I* ('Mayfly'), 52–3, 61, 75, 139, 164; *No.9*, 57, 60–2, 64–5, 68–74, 375; *No.23*, 71, 74; *No.24*, 71; *No.25*, 71; *R.23*, 76, 89; *R.24*, 89; *R.26*, 71; *R.34*, 82, 100; *R.38* disaster, 93, 100, 111, 122, 127; *R.80*, 76–8, 80, 83, 86, 88–91, 132, 310, 375, 377; end of project, 92; *R.81*, 78
  R.100, 77, 121–2, 125, 138, 147–64, 189–91, 196, 244, 310, 359, 363, 375, 377; ballasting operations, 166; construction problems, 152; delays, 171; design problems, 126–30; flight to Canada, 180; full-speed trials, 176–7; gassing operations, 165; geodetic construction, 130–4; maiden flight, 164, 173–4; shed trial problems, 167; Wallis's responsibility, 146, 157;
  R.101, 82, 121–2, 132–3, 138, 147–8, 161–4, 189, 190; alterations and

389

Index

Index

Index

Index

Index

Index

Index

Index

Index

Index

downs, 90, 155, 172; bridge projects, 338; career decision, 37; enlistment, First World War, 58, 62; failure to appreciate aeroplane development, 80–1; first contact with aeroplanes, 108–9; geodetic construction, *see* main entry; growing interest in aeroplanes, 149, 151–2, 155, 166; insularity, 113; interest in flight, 39–40; interest in music, 41, 115, 136; letters to Molly, 111, 114–16, 120, 124, 313–14, 315, 317–18, 337, 348, 359–60, *see also* mathematics correspondence course; letters to his mother, 31–2, 36, 38, 41; life in the army, 63–4; life in Cowes, 41–2, 46–49; London University Matriculation, 35–6, 41; loyalty to Vickers, 89, 108, 303; mathematics correspondence course with Molly, 104–5, 108, 109, 115, 303, 367; Menton holiday, 155; migraines, 27, 79, 90, 107, 146, 155, 171, 227, 245, 297–8, 330, 352; negotiations with Burney, 109–11; O.B.E., offer of, 233; operation in Middlesex Hospital, 366–7; opposition to his projects in Second World War, 225–6, 246–7; patriotism, 58–60, 62, 66, 216–17, 219, 225, 368; persecution mania, 246, 251, 329–31; post at Vickers Contracts Department, 107, 108–9, 110; public recognition, and lack of, 233, 274–5, 279, 301–3, 376; public speaking, 119–20, 153; puritanism, 107, 117–18, 144, 147, 153–4, 200–1, 323–324, 366; quarrels with Burney, 149–151; radio telescopes, 337–8; relationship with mother, 42–3, 45, 46–7; religion, 41–2, 200, 254, 304, 322, 332–3, 364; resignation from Airship Guarantee Company, 160, 174; and 617 Squadron, 259, 300–1; Swallow experiments, *see* main entry; use of light alloys in aeroplanes, 155–6; visit to Sicily, 313–16; visits to America, 316–17, 357; Weymouth holiday 1914, 59; *Wild Goose* experiments, *see* main entry;

work on B9/32 and Wellingtons, *see* Wellington; work on G4/31 and M1/30, 196; work on Wellesley, *see* Wellesley; work with Pierson, 178–179, 198, 218, 223, 225, 228, 278

Wallis, Barnes (son), 37, 208, 236, 303, 350

Wallis, Charles (father), 39, 47, 103, 123; childhood, 1; meeting future wife, 1, 2; engagement, 2–4; study at Oxford, 3; early dissensions, 3–4; marriage, 4; practice in Ripley, 4–5; practice in New Cross Road, London, 5; attack of polio, 5; life at New Cross, 5–9; dealings with Christ's Hospital, 10, 35; death of wife, 45, 46; holiday at Weymouth, 59–60; second marriage, 88, 96; death, 303

Wallis, Charles (brother), 44, 46, 79, 84, 102

Wallis, Christopher (son), 209, 236

Wallis, Elizabeth (daughter), 236

Wallis, John (brother), 4, 10, 33, 43–4, 46, 62, 102, 377

Wallis, Reverend George Winstanley (grandfather), 1, 5

Wallis, Mary (daughter), 148, 207, 236, 367; engagement and marriage, 311–12

Wallis, Molly (wife, née Bloxam), 99, 102, 153, 171–3, 200, 207, 212, 364, 377; courtship, 103–9, 111, 114–16, 123–4; engagement, 124–5; wedding, 134; marriage, 135–7; children, 137, 148, 209; adoption of sister's children, 220; life after war, 304; *Swallow* trials, 349; and Wallis's approaching age, 353

Wallis–Pierson aeroplane B3/42, 247

Walney Island, *see* Royal Naval Air Service

Warneford, Flight Sub-Lieutenant R. A. J., 64

War Office, 281, 286

Warwick bomber, 213, 234, 278

war years (First World War), 58–83

Watson, Jimmy, 174

Wavell, General (later Field Marshal Earl), 198

Index

Webb, A. E., 134

Wellesley bomber, 66, 195, 197–8, 202, 223, 310, 334, 368, 375; formation flight to Australia, 198; long-distance record, 214–15

Wellington bomber, 195–6, 198–9, 211, 212–13, 241, 300, 310, 334, 359, 368, 375; conversion for dam-bombing, 238; first deliveries, 213, 240; in high-altitude flying, 225; improvement of covering, 222–3; mine sweeping, 220–2; new varieties, 263, 278; orders for war, 219; variants, 228–9, 234; Wallis's super-vision of, 224

Westbrook, T. C. L., 206, 212, 213, 219, 302

White's Shipyard, Cowes, 40–1, 46–7, 54, 55

Whitten-Brown, Arthur, 83

Whittle, Frank, 311

Wild Goose, 48, 244, 309, 311, 312, 315–16, 346, 348, 355; trials, 317–28, 337

Willcox prize, 31–2, 36, 37, 44

Willows, E. T., Cardiff, 50

Windsor bomber, 278–9

Winterbotham, Wing Commander F. W., 247, 250; discussion of aerodynes, 313; first meeting with Wallis, 230; support for Dams Raid, 233–4, 240, 244, 246, 248, 261–2

Wolseley-Maybach engines, 78

Woolls, J. 239

Woolwich, 29; The Common, 1, 7–8

Woolwich home, 136

Wren, Sir Christopher, 366

Wright brothers, 39, 306, 327, 370

Wynter-Morgan, Group Captain Wilfred, 239

Zeppelin, Count Ferdinand von, 50, 51, 52, 99, 113

Zeppelin Company, 112–14

Zeppelin design, 56

Zeppelins, 54, 55, 72–3, 80, 81, 85–6, 88, 151; *Bodensee*, 86; *Graf Zeppelin*, 160–1, 162, 164, 167, 187; *Graf Zeppelin II*, 187; *Hindenburg*, 83, 187, 188–9; *L.11, L.24*, 73; *L.33*, 74; *L.45, L.49*, 78; *L.59*, 73; *L.216*, 56; *LZ.37*, 64; *LZ. 126*, 93, 99